Politics at the
Turn of the Century

Politics at the Turn of the Century

Edited by
Arthur M. Melzer, Jerry Weinberger,
and M. Richard Zinman

ROWMAN & LITTLEFIELD PUBLISHERS, INC.
Lanham • Boulder • New York • Oxford

ROWMAN & LITTLEFIELD PUBLISHERS, INC.

Published in the United States of America
by Rowman & Littlefield Publishers, Inc.
4720 Boston Way, Lanham, Maryland 20706
www.rowmanlittlefield.com

12 Hid's Copse Road
Cumnor Hill, Oxford OX2 9JJ, England

British Library Cataloguing in Publication Information Available

Library of Congress Cataloging-in-Publication Data

Politics at the turn of the century / edited by Arthur M. Melzer, Jerry Weinberger, and M.
Richard Zinman.
    p. cm.
    Includes bibliographical references and index.
    ISBN 0-8476-9445-3 (alk. paper) — ISBN 0-8476-9446-1 (pbk. : alk. paper)
    1. United States—Politics and government. 2. World politics. 3. Right and left (Politic
science). I. Melzer, Arthur M. II. Weinberger, J. III. Zinman, M. Richard.

JK271 .P55897 2001
320.9—dc21

                                                                              00-0533

Printed in the United States of America

∞™ The paper used in this publication meets the minimum requirements of
American National Standard for Information Sciences—Permanence of Paper
for Printed Library Materials, ANSI/NISO Z39.48-1992.

Symposium on Science, Reason, and Modern Democracy
Michigan State University

Contents

Part II: The World

Acknowledgments

This is the fifth volume of essays to be published by the Symposium on Science, Reason, and Modern Democracy. Established in 1989 in the Department of Political Science at Michigan State University, the symposium seeks to bridge the gap between the intellectual and political worlds. To this end, it sponsors teaching, research, public lectures, seminars, and conferences on the relationship between liberal democracy and the great issues of contemporary life.

This volume grew from the symposium's fifth and seventh annual programs: "Left, Right, and Center: Party and Ideology after the Cold War," which took place during the 1993–94 academic year, and "The Question of 'Big Government,'" which was held during the 1995–96 academic year. All the essays presented here, with the exception of T. J. Pempel's, were originally written for these programs. Professor Pempel wrote a paper for the 1995–96 program but chose to submit a different essay for this volume.

Seven of the sixteen essays have appeared elsewhere. An earlier version of Seyla Benhabib's essay appeared in *Radical Democracy: Identity, Citizenship, and the State,* ed. David Trend (New York: Routledge, 1996) © 1996; reproduced by permission of Routledge, Inc., part of the Taylor & Francis Group. Alan Brinkley's essay was published in his book *Liberalism and Its Discontents* (Cambridge: Harvard University Press, 1998) © 1998 by the President and Fellows of Harvard College; reprinted by permission of the publisher. Sections of Todd Gitlin's essay appeared in his book *The Twilight of Common Dreams: Why America Is Wracked by Culture Wars* (New York: Henry Holt, 1995) © 1995 by Todd Gitlin; reprinted by permission of Henry Holt and Company LLC. Harvey Mansfield and Delba Winthrop's essay was published as part of a pamphlet, "Tyranny and Liberty: Big Government and the Individual in Tocqueville's Science of Politics" (London: Institute of United States Studies, University of London, 1999). Andrew Nathan and Tianjian Shi's essay appeared in *World Politics* 48, no. 4 (July 1996): 522–50, © Center for International Studies, Princeton University; reprinted by permission of the Johns Hopkins University Press. (The essay was also reprinted in Professor Nathan's book *China's Transition* [New York: Columbia University Press, 1997].) Professor Pempel's essay was published in the *Journal of Japanese Studies* 23 (1997); reprinted by permission. Vladimir Tismaneanu's essay appeared in *East European Politics and Societies* 10, no. 3 (Fall 1996): 504–35, © 1996 by the American Council of Learned Societies; reprinted by permission. We thank these contributors and their publishers for permission to reprint.

The symposium's 1995–96 program culminated in a conference in Prague. This conference, our first collaborative venture, was organized by the symposium and the Center for Theoretical Study, an institute of advanced studies jointly administered by Charles University and the Academy of Sciences of the Czech Republic. In planning the conference, we worked closely with Martin Paloŭs, senior research fellow at the center. We thank Professor Paloŭs for his critical contribution to our joint enterprise. We also thank Ivan Chvatik and Ivan M. Havel, the co-directors of the center, and their colleagues, especially Josef Moural, for their support and hospitality. Finally, we thank Lucie Váchová and Milena Zeithamlová of the Action M Agency, Prague, for their expert handling of conference arrangements.

The symposium's 1993–94 and 1995–96 programs, and indeed all of its activities, were made possible by grants from the Lynde and Harry Bradley Foundation of Milwaukee, Wisconsin; the Carthage Foundation of Pittsburgh, Pennsylvania; the Earhart Foundation of Ann Arbor, Michigan; and the John M. Olin Foundation of New York City. Once again, we are grateful for their support. We are also grateful to the Simons Foundation of Vancouver, British Columbia, which, through a grant to the Center for Theoretical Study, helped make possible the conference in Prague.

Michigan State's Department of Political Science has been home to the symposium for a decade. Throughout that period, the College of Social Science and James Madison College have aided us in many ways. We thank our colleagues in each of these institutions. In particular, we thank Kenneth E. Corey, former dean of the College of Social Science; Brian Silver, former chair of the Department of Political Science; William Allen, former dean of James Madison College; Werner Dannhauser, the symposium's senior research fellow; Alice and Nasser Behnegar, the symposium's postdoctoral fellows for 1993–94; and Michael Grenke, our postdoctoral fellow for 1995–96, for their special contributions during our fifth and seventh years. We also thank Gill-Chin Lim, former dean of Michigan State's international studies and programs; John K. Hudzik, dean of international studies and programs; and Norman Graham, director of Michigan State's Center for European and Russian Studies, for their support of the conference in Prague. As always, we are indebted to Karen Battin, Rhonda Burns, Iris Dunn, and Elaine Eschtruth, the administrative staff of the Department of Political Science. We are especially grateful to Ms. Battin, the symposium's administrative coordinator, for her fine work.

In addition to the authors whose essays are included in this volume, the following individuals took part in the symposium's 1993–94 and 1995–96 programs: Francis Fukuyama, the late François Furet, William Galston, Pierre Hassner, Robert Heilbroner, William Kristol, Kanan Makiya, Josef Moural, Lourie Mylroie, Richard John Neuhaus, Martin Palous, Marc Plattner, Linda Racioppi, Philippe Raynaud, Joel Rogers, Aleksander Smolar, G. M. Tamás, and Nathan Tarcov. We thank them for their important contributions.

Introduction

It is not the calendar alone that makes one feel that a new age has dawned. The close of our century has brought a sudden and remarkable denouement: the collapse of one of the superpowers, the end of the Cold War, the death of Communism, the decline of Socialism, and the movement of Europe toward economic integration. A whole world of urgent challenges and conflicts has suddenly been removed, and we are left to stare giddily at the future with a mixture of hope, dread, and dumb curiosity. As Charles Fairbanks remarks in his essay, "Increasingly, our own moment in the West is named 'postmodernity,' that is, a time of waiting. What are we waiting *for?*"

It is too early to make a serious attempt at answering that question. What would seem to be most useful at the present moment is not far-flung speculation or futurology, but a simple taking of stock. Not everything has changed, not everything remains the same. Where do we actually stand right now? What are the primary issues, ideologies, and parties that structure politics now and for the immediate future? That is the question the present volume attempts to address.

The first part is devoted to the United States, the second to the rest of the world. In the former, we focus primarily on the two major issues or ideologies that have emerged with a vengeance during the last two decades of the century: on the Left, the issue of "identity politics," and on the Right, the problem of "big government."

The rise of identity politics—the topic with which the volume begins—is perhaps the greatest and most unanticipated change on the contemporary political and ideological landscape: Virtually no one writing, say, forty years ago predicted it. And it involves a shocking reversal of many crucial and long-standing tenets of both the liberal and Marxist Left. One way of describing these changes is as follows: The identity politics movement fights on behalf of the marginalized and disadvantaged—and, in that, it is continuous with the past—but it fights with ideological weapons that bear closest resemblance, strange to say, to those of the old romantic and nationalist Right.

Whereas, formerly, leftist thinkers tended to be in the rationalist and universalist camp, they have now largely moved into the antirationalist camp, with its rejection of universal norms and its celebration of uniqueness, diversity, and difference. Similarly, the Left used to place primary emphasis on the uniform rights of all individuals, whereas today the emphasis has shifted to the rights of ethnic and cultural groups, which are viewed as the source of the differing, socially constructed rights and identities of individuals. Finally, the Left, Marxist and otherwise, always inclined to an underlying economism: It tended to define the goods for which it fought, the classes on whose behalf it fought, and indeed the whole conflict system within which it fought in economic terms. But identity politics breaks with "political economy" by defining the goods, the groups, and the sources of conflict and oppression primarily in terms of such noneconomic concepts as ethnicity, identity, recognition, and esteem. What we are suggesting in this brief description, which we hope is not too tendentious, is that identity politics might best be understood as a kind of left-wing nationalism. It is an ingenious effort to transform the concepts, arguments, and passions of nationalism into a force for domestic pluralism and toleration. But can it work?

Todd Gitlin's "The Left's Lost Universalism" is the first of three essays discussing the rise and character of identity politics. Prior to the 1960s, he argues, the Cold War, steadily rising incomes, and expanding opportunities produced a "grand creed," according to which inequality could be overlooked and the leftist ideology of the common man could be absorbed into the mainstream view of universal, equal opportunity. This mainstream universalism broke down as the Vietnam War and the Black Power movement cast doubt on the benevolence and justice of traditional American liberalism. According to Gitlin, the New Left was "a failed attempt to organize new universals." The New Left's universalism was inherently fragile and quickly gave way to the fragmentation of identity politics. As a result, the Left today has little to say about economics, class, and the conditions of work.

Seyla Benhabib continues this theme, with special attention to feminism. In "From Identity Politics to Social Feminism," Benhabib questions the concept of identity construction in recent feminist theory. The doctrine of radical social construction of identities, including both sex and gender, endangers the crucial notions of agency, resistance, and creativity without which no coherent notion of the subject is possible. In a different vein, Benhabib argues that identity politics tends to pit various identity groups against each other as competing clients of the welfare state. Engaged as they are in such competition, identity groups tend to forget their common class and economic interests and problems. But awareness of such common interests and problems, she argues, is essential to clearheaded and effective progressivism.

Finally, in "Identity Politics: The Third Phase of Liberalism?" Alan Wolfe tries to determine whether and how the opposition between identity politics and liberalism might eventually be overcome. Identity politics—with its tendency to find politics in all aspects of life, including those considered private by more old-fashioned liberalism, and with its desire to reform attitudes and proclivities as much as behavior—conflicts in important ways with liberalism. If identity politics is to be a genuine development of liberalism, says Wolfe, then identity groups must allow for exit, group membership must not be allowed to trump common standards of citizenship, and group membership must not be understood to determine how and what an individual thinks.

Our volume now turns to the Right. The movement most directly opposite to identity politics is the Christian coalition, with its emphasis on the need to uphold certain core values and thus to hold the line against multiculturalism, relativism, homosexual rights, radical feminism, and so forth. It remains to be seen, however, whether this movement can broaden its base sufficiently to become a dominating force or ruling party. So far, it seems fair to say, the Christian Right has yet to win a national legislative victory.

By contrast, the movement on the right that has clearly succeeded in this respect is the crusade against Big Government—the Reagan revolution, followed by the Gingrich boomlet and the Clinton capitulation ("The age of Big Government is over."). It has caused a sea change in thinking about Great Society programs and turned "liberal" into a dirty word among a significant proportion of the population. Moreover, beyond our borders, something like the same phenomenon seems to be visible in the retreat from state socialism in Western Europe, in the process of national liberation and disaggregation in Eastern Europe, and in the worldwide movement toward privatization, free trade, and the decline of protectionism. The idea that Big Government is the problem and not the solution would seem to be one of the driving ideas of our time.

Unlike the Left's turn to identity politics, the Right's embrace of the anti–Big Government cause is not a reversal of course but rather a return to its classical liberal roots. The ideal of limited government goes back to Locke; and for more than a century and a half, theorists such as Tocqueville, Mill, Ortega y Gasset, and Hayek have been warning that the inexorable growth of the power and reach of the state is the single greatest danger of modern times.

But the widespread appeal of the anti–Big Government movement and its respectable philosophical pedigree conceal the fact that there is little shared or settled understanding of just what Big Government is and why it is bad. Does it consist in the high level of taxation, or the (now vanished) federal deficit, or the size of the bureaucracy, or the excessive regulation of business, or the comprehensiveness of state goals, or the dangerous intrusion into the private life of the individual? And what exactly is the evil—or the advantage—of Big Government? On the political level, is Big Government needed to secure aid for the needy or justice for the oppressed, or to unite us in genuine community? Or, on the contrary, does it prevent locally tailored policy making, as well as effective administration, while also threatening individual liberty? On the economic level, is Big Government needed to keep big business from monopolizing, polluting, and exploiting; or does it hinder competitiveness, efficiency, and the wisdom of the market? And, on the moral level, is Big Government the indispensable vehicle of progress and moral idealism, or does it demoralize citizens by robbing them of individual responsibility and the energy of self-reliance?

The six essays on the theme of Big Government begin with those of Alan Brinkley and James Ceaser, who provide a historical overview of "Big Government" in America and define the problem. Then the essays by Harvey Mansfield and Delba Winthrop and by Michael Zuckert discuss the more theoretical dimensions of the issue. Finally, Paul Pierson and Richard Epstein discuss in a concrete, but also theoretical, way the contemporary situation.

In "The Two World Wars and the Idea of the State" Brinkley presents a historical picture of the rise of Big Government from the time of World War I. The vast mobilization required by that war demonstrated to Progressives that the state could manage the economy in ways hitherto unimagined. It thus demonstrated the hope that centralized government planning could bring order to society in general. By contrast, the mobilization required for World War II only briefly engendered such hopes. By the end of that war, the dream of a planned economy quickly faded, despite the fact that the two war-fighting mobilizations were similar in many important respects. The difference, according to Brinkley, is that three novel factors prevailed by the end of World War II: fear of totalitarianism was at the center of political thought; the ill-fated National Recovery Act had shown Americans what government could not do; and the principal force in the economy had become consumption, not production. Fiscal policy, not direct planning, became the order of the day. As a result, Big Government in America is neither corporatist nor overly regulatory, but consists rather in the national security state and the compensatory state.

Ceaser argues in "What Kind of Government Do We Have to Fear?" that contemporary defenders of Big Government are wrong to claim provenance in earlier parties of government—the Federalists, the Whigs, and the Republicans. Despite having served the cause of stronger and bigger government, these nineteenth-century parties were primarily concerned with expanding the discretionary power of government for the sake of specific and limited ends as determined by the Constitution. Big Government as we know it today is altogether a twentieth-century development. To the original partisans of Big Government as we know it, the Constitution was an impediment to the development of good government, now understood as the application of social science for the comprehensive transformation of society.

This difference in the ends and means of strong government is decisive, according to Ceaser. From the Progressive era to the New Deal, the combination of an emerging social science with John Dewey's pragmatism led the partisans of Big Government to embrace social engineering. With the advent of the New Deal, social engineering and planning gave way to ensuring security and welfare, justified by a fundamental change in the understanding of rights: What were formerly understood as liberties were henceforth understood as entitlements. With the Great Society came the final steps in the establishment of Big Government: Social engineering returned in the guise of new social programs, the use of federal police power spread from the enforcement of civil rights to other arenas, equality of opportunity gave way to equality of outcomes, the values of the "counterculture" entered the policy mainstream, and government power became a tool for "moral engineering." With Big Government in full bloom, policy considerations now trump constitutional limits, and goods once thought to be private—property, income, children, even the wills of citizens—are taken to be social. Policy now determines the scope of private life, and the private is no longer a fixed limit to the power of government.

Mansfield and Winthrop next examine "Liberalism and Big Government: Tocqueville's Analysis." According to Tocqueville, Big Government is not a departure from pristine liberalism; it is rather a consequence of that liberalism itself. The root of liberalism is the principle of equality, and the principle of equality becomes, in practice, an aggressive egalitarianism that prefers Big Government to limited, democratic self-government. Indeed, the purpose of Tocqueville's *Democracy in America* was to show that Big Government could emerge even from a liberal polity lacking a monarchical heritage and rooted in constitutional limitation of political power.

Tocqueville argues that with the advent of equality the task of judgment becomes a burden for the individual, which burden is relieved ultimately by reliance on public opinion. At the same time, the principle of equality becomes a desire for equality of outcomes: If all are equal in the most important respect, there appears to be no reason that they should not be equal in all others, especially in their material possessions. Finally, equal individuals are moved by compassion, the easy act of feeling others' needy dependence by quick reference to their own. In combination, these aspects of equality incline men in opposite directions. On the one hand, they are freed to associate politically for mutual assistance and independence. But on the other hand, they are tempted to depend on a large, faceless power—the soft despotism of Big Government—to secure those things they are powerless to secure on their own.

As aids to political vigor, Tocqueville praises and recommends the American preference for rights against public power, America's vital Christianity, and the American institutions of local government, juries, a free press, and the widespread existence of democratic associations. Mansfield and Winthrop recommend a Tocquevillian revival of democratic politics as a hedge against Big Government. But the authors warn that such an approach requires accepting some hard facts. Devolution of authority to local powers must be judged by the effect on Big Government and not by expectations of efficiency or even justice. We will have to abandon our addiction to rights understood as entitlements. We will have to resist the

temptations of economic and ethnic determinism, now alive in the theories of globalization and ethnic fragmentation, which denigrates the dignity of politics. And we must appreciate that the separation of church and
state is good not just for toleration but also for enabling religion to work
against the destabilizing effects of materialism and skepticism, and to protect democratic souls from the fact that no democracy can always reward
virtue. For Tocqueville, liberalism is inherently democratic, and democracy inherently tends toward Big Government. Without recognizing and
responding *politically* to this fact, the destiny of democracy will be soft
despotism, not genuine liberty.

In "Big Government and Rights," Zuckert contrasts Rawls, a theorist of
positive rights and Big Government, to Locke, a theorist of negative rights
and limited government. According to Rawls, rights are determined by the
principle of fairness: The distributive rules of society should be derived from
what any rational person, ignorant of how he might fare in that society,
would choose. Such a person would join society only on the condition that
all should bear equal burdens and share equal rewards unless inequality
makes the poorest members of society better off than otherwise would be
the case. Most rights must thus be positive entitlements, setting in motion a
vast redistribution of goods.

For Locke, in contrast, each person has an exclusive claim to his consciousness, his body, his virtues and abilities, and all the things that result
from the exercise of these elements of the self. By natural right, the self *deserves* its qualities and gifts, in the sense that these and their products cannot
be taken or used by others. Justice consists in protecting the right to property in the self, whatever that self might happen to be. Rights are thus negative, since no one has the warrant to take from one person for distribution to
another. As a consequence, government must be no bigger than is required
to preserve each self as it is.

In general, Zuckert prefers Locke to Rawls. But he notes that Locke was
aware of the difference between the goal of securing negative rights and the
means necessary for accomplishing this goal. Thus attention to collective needs
will be a part of political prudence, and the goal of genuine prudence will be
to balance the end—the securing of negative rights—and the means, which
can and will require some intrusion on those rights. For Zuckert, the choice between big and small government can never be as stark as for Rawls, for whom
the person owns none of his natural gifts, or for libertarians, for whom the person is the absolute master of all that nature's lottery has bestowed.

From the foregoing reflections on the theoretical foundations of big and
small government, the volume turns to more concrete reflections on the current situation in America. Assuming that government in America is big, or at
least that it is as big as it has ever been, Pierson asks in "The Prospects for
Democratic Control in an Age of Big Government" if such bigness makes it
more or less difficult for the people to control it. In the face of voter ignorance and apparent inefficacy, political scientists first argued that although

individual citizens may be weak, the groups they form exercise control in modern, mass democracy. But this view—called pluralism—was shaken by Mancur Olson's theoretical critique of collective action, as well as by observations that the means for such action—money, information, and political access—are monopolized by elites. Recently, however, the case for democratic control has regained new vigor. Even though voters have limited knowledge, they use heuristic devices to make efficient use of the relatively limited information they have about specific policy issues. Thus while individual voters may have meager cognitive equipment, as a collective the electorate is capable of impressive social rationality.

Contending with this newfound optimism, however, is an emerging literature maintaining that policy-making elites manipulate and delude public opinion. Despite massive costs and income transfers, for example, the savings and loan debacle went largely unnoticed. Policy makers can, and do, front-load benefits and back-load costs, use indexing mechanisms to hide accountability, and in general take shelter from scrutiny by the sheer complexity of the policy-making and legislative processes in our fragmented, Madisonian constitutional system. In such a system, the policy-making process can be used strategically by and for elites. It follows that the bigger and more complex government gets, the more distant it is from popular control. Even when government programs are trimmed, politicians use their superior command over information to avoid blame for cuts that voters might not like.

So who is right, the optimistic students of mass political behavior or the pessimistic students of policy formation? The truth, says Pierson, lies somewhere in the middle. Even so, Pierson finds formidable opportunities for policy elites to manipulate voter attention, which is very malleable, and thus finds serious limits to mass voter control over public policy. In an age of Big Government, information is the paramount political currency. Thus with Big Government comes the danger that policy will be driven by a "knowledge-rich" minority.

In "From Social to Legal Norms: A Neglected Cause of Big Government," Epstein contends that the rise of Big Government has been a constant of twentieth-century life. One reason for this fact is the temptation to extend the role of government from protection against physical and verbal coercion to protection against supposed "economic coercion." But Epstein investigates another important spur to Big Government: the "relentless effort" to replace social and moral norms with legal rules enforced by the power of the state. The law is of course necessary to enforce the contracts that make social and economic life possible. But it does not follow from this general principle that all contracts require legal enforcement. How much such enforcement is needed should be determined by the contracting parties themselves, and often they would, or at least should, choose social over legal sanctions. Two important such instances, for Epstein, are employment and landlord-tenant contracts.

Quitting or being dismissed from a job can certainly be bad, but it is not the same as physical harm. That it requires legal remedies should depend on whether the contracting parties find such remedies more reliable and efficient than informal sanctions such as goodwill and reputation and the self-interest of employers and employees. It is by no means certain that the legal system is equipped to judge wisely in cases of employment or serve the real interests of employers and employees. Likewise for landlord-tenant contracts. Legal efforts to control the power of eviction have been especially harmful to public housing. Excessive concern for due process guarantees has actually benefited bad tenants and harmed the good ones.

And likewise again for attempts to transform moral obligations to provide rescue and charitable care into legal obligations. A clear example has been the case of hospital emergency rooms when the duty to provide service is mandated in law: Rather than pay the attending costs, emergency rooms have been closed altogether. As admirable as it may seem, the effort to merge morality and law is a mistake that destroys or diminishes the benefits that are supposed to be enhanced, while stimulating the growth of obtrusive Big Government.

The second part of the volume looks beyond America's borders to consider the political situation in a small sampling—inevitably partial and incomplete—of other nations. The first two essays, written from the West European and British perspectives, largely continue the theme of Big Government.

In his "Notes on Markets, Politics, and 'Big Government,'" Claus Offe denies that Big Government is the cause of social malaise and economic underperformance. In Offe's view, the marketization of society, presumably a policy to stop the regulatory intrusiveness of government, is as much a form of political intervention as was its Keynesian and welfare-state predecessors. Neoliberalism of the Thatcher variety, he argues, serves only to disenfranchise citizens and obfuscate the clearly political dimensions of its animus against politics. And when questions of just distribution are stifled, the political scene becomes dominated by concerns about religion, morality, and the various identities.

Offe argues that markets are in fact embedded in socially and politically determined institutions, which are determined in turn by some theory of social justice. In today's Western Europe, the old alliance of liberal, Christian, and socialist normative traditions has been fractured because that alliance's normative elements have disintegrated: Liberals have become libertarians, socialists have nothing to say about production, and Christians have rejected the state and have turned to doctrines of self-help. In this ideological vacuum, market forces permeate every aspect of social life. The causes of this situation are the erosion of strong centers of political agency and the weakening of state sovereignty at the hands of globalization. The only solution, in Offe's view, is the revitalization of civil society and the development of democratic, transnational regimes.

In "The Debate on Big Government: The View from Britain and Western Europe" John Dunn argues that the term "Big Government" was coined by the enemies of government, who argue that government expenditure is economically inefficient and that government protections debilitate individuals. Dunn eschews such loaded terminology, the better to penetrate the real policy issues facing the developed capitalist democracies at the end of the millennium. The real issues concern the trade-off between efficiency, on the one hand, and government action to ease the suffering of the losers in a market economy, on the other. The trade-off problem is all the more pressing since the increasingly powerful global economy is indifferent to the suffering of casualties within successful national economies. In the European democracies, precisely because they are democratic, there is strong pressure to monitor and manage this trade-off. For Dunn, the task of government in general is the prevention of impermissible treatment of its citizens. In Europe and Great Britain, what counts as impermissible has been determined by long-standing political agreements forged among classes. These agreements are extremely resistant to change. Thus if Europe really does need smaller governments to meet the challenges of new global realities, and if such governments require new agreements about what is impermissible, we should not hold our breaths while waiting for such new agreements to appear.

The volume turns at this point to the political landscape in Eastern Europe and Asia, where the issues of Big Government and identity politics are often eclipsed by other problems—although rarely completely absent. In "The Leninist Debris; or, Waiting for Perón," Vladimir Tismaneanu examines the ideological spectrum in the post-Communist world. "Left," "Right," and "Center" are not terms that explain much in the former Soviet Union and east central Europe—indeed they most likely distort. These terms are inadequate to describe the views of an intellectual proletariat that is obsessed with conspiracies and content with empty slogans, or the stew of nationalism, populism, and nostalgia for egalitarianism that inhibit the establishment of liberal norms and institutions. Indeed, in much of the post-Communist world there is little of a civil society and little of an established state to protect or encroach on that civil society. In the face of such near-anarchy, respect for authoritarianism goes hand in hand with reverence for ethnic nationality and impatience with constitutional forms; utopian hopes outstrip political, and especially democratic, reality; and political parties are short-term personal and group affinities. There is little appreciation of constitutionalism and democracy, and old Communist elites reappear in new clothes. In Tismaneanu's view, post-Communist societies have a long way to go before they embrace genuine liberal democracy, if indeed they ever do. We should not be surprised, therefore, by the persistence of ethnic and religious populism, authoritarianism, and dictatorship, or even by the emergence of fundamentalist theocracies.

This dark mood is continued in Charles Fairbanks's "Party, Ideology, and the Public World in the Former Soviet Space." In this long and rich essay, Fairbanks argues that, in the countries of the former Soviet Union, the historical clock has been turned back an entire millennium. The essential elements of political modernity—the political party, ideology, and the state—have all disintegrated in the former Soviet Union. Circles of personal loyalty have replaced the political party. Ideology is weak and diffuse. And the state, quite literally, is being feudalized. The Communist order made a colossus of the formal, public order. And from that colossus the people of the post-Communist order are fleeing toward more intensely personal and voluntaristic forms of loyalty. The free individual has replaced the citizen, and the Communist order has collapsed into the Middle Ages.

Given this bizarre state of affairs, it is hard to predict what the future has in store. There are reasons for hope that capitalism and democracy might prevail. But equally possible—as happened with the Roman principate—is a complete flight from the public world as we know it. Like the "citizens" of crumbling Roman despotism, the peoples of the post-Communist world may just as easily embrace religion and feudal relations. Indeed, powerful forces in the West—postmodernism, multiculturalism, relativism, globalization, and the communications revolution—work to erode the legitimacy of the liberal state and its public institutions. And nationalism, bereft of the state, is a will-o'-the-wisp, however vicious it can be. It is hard to say, concludes Fairbanks, whether the "West" is the fate of the East, or whether what is now happening in the "East" presages our global fate.

When we turn farther east to India, however—as described in Atul Kohli and Pratap B. Mehta's "Ideological Conflicts in Post–Cold War India"—we find a political world which, despite very great differences, rather mirrors and even sheds light upon that of the West. The most obvious difference is that, since modernity is essentially a Western invention, Indian politics, like that of most non-Western nations, is characterized by an ideological cleavage absent from the West: the Westernizers (like Nehru) versus those who seek a more indigenous path (such as Mahatma Ghandi). This great difference notwithstanding, the movement of Indian politics since 1947, as told by Kohli and Mehta, bears a strong resemblance to the changes occurring in the West as described by the essays above. An initial period of patrician socialism under Nehru was followed by a more populist style of rule under Indira Gandhi, yet one still primarily focused on state solutions to the problems of economic distribution and social justice. Beginning around 1980, however, there began a move away from the socialist model—away from Big Government—toward economic liberalization. At the same time there was a marked turn toward identity politics and nationalism—not the anticolonial nationalism that helped to unify India during the earlier period, but an internal nationalism of India's various competing regions, castes, and religions.

Kohli and Mehta describe these changes in all the detail that make them unique to India, but they also make an important observation that is of much wider application. The rise of identity politics, they argue, did not merely accompany the decline of socialism and rise of anti–Big Government sentiment but was in large measure caused by it. The death of the socialist dream (or, in the United States, of the liberal dream) left an ideological vacuum—a need for a new legitimizing and mobilizing creed—and identity politics filled that need. The state, which could no longer mobilize voters through the economic promises of central planning, turned to issues of esteem and identity.

Looking next to China, with Andrew Nathan and Tianjian Shi's "Left and Right with Chinese Characteristics," we find a political world where the phenomena of anti–Big Government sentiment and identity politics are largely absent. Many of the issues of primary concern, such as the Tiananmen reform agenda, are somewhat alien to contemporary Western concerns, as are some of the sociological variables that shape the attitudes of different groups toward those issues—variables such as whether or not one works in a state-owned business or is a member of the Communist Party. But the authors argue that the same two factors that explain ideological alignment in the West nevertheless do so on the Chinese scene as well: socioeconomic interest, and education level or "cognitive sophistication."

Relying upon an opinion survey conducted in 1990, the authors show that the fundamental ideological divide existing (albeit somewhat latently) in the Chinese population is between two camps that can loosely be labeled "liberal" and "conservative." While both groups favor a relatively large role for the government, the former is eager for the government to push ahead with economic and political reform and holds relatively tolerant, pro-democratic political, social, and procedural attitudes. The latter camp wants the government to maintain or restore its central role in managing the individual citizen's economic and social problems; it is thus opposed to reform and holds relatively nondemocratic and nonliberal attitudes. The authors also found that membership in one or the other of these camps had little to do with religion or regional identity, but followed instead from socioeconomic interest and education level. "Liberals" tended to be more highly educated, younger, more urban, male, upper-income, white-collar, employed in state-owned units, and members of the Communist Party. "Conservatives" tended to the opposite of these characteristics. These findings, if correct, do not of course allow one to predict what form of government will rule China in the future. But they do suggest that, whatever the form of government, it will be decisively molded by this fundamental cleavage in the population.

Our volume ends with a consideration of Japan. In "Regime Shift: Japanese Politics in a Changing World Economy," T. J. Pempel argues that since the early 1990s Japan has been undergoing a change of regime almost as fundamental as that taking place in Eastern Europe and the former Soviet Union. As in those countries, however, it is easier to say what things are disappearing than to specify what will replace them. The passing of the *ancien régime* is marked by three changes: on the political level, the end of the unchallenged hegemony of the Liberal Democratic Party, which had enjoyed the longest period of uninterrupted conservative rule among the industrialized nations; on the economic level, the crashing halt to the almost four-decade-long period of very rapid and uninterrupted economic growth; and on the international level, the end to the uniquely close and harmonious relationship with the United States. Although it is difficult to say how the new Japanese regime will be structured, one thing seems certain: It will be characterized by greater economic inequality and greater conflict among different economic sectors.

The causes of all these far-reaching changes are both external and internal, but almost all may be said to derive from Japan's remarkable success. The primary external cause was the international unwillingness—which grew along with Japan's economy—to tolerate the high tariffs and other import barriers and the artificially low valuation of the yen that were the pillars of Japan's export-oriented "embedded mercantilist" economy. Internally, Japan experienced the profound demographic changes that result from successful modernization: rapid decline in farming populations, urbanization, rise in living standards, extension of life spans, and growth of the middle class. If in Eastern Europe instability and change are driven by political and economic failure, in Japan they are driven by a certain kind of success.

It has been our intention in this volume to present a limited survey and not a grand theory of contemporary world politics. Still, by way of conclusion, we might briefly ask whether any large patterns have emerged. It does seem that at many points of the globe there has been a weakening of the nation-state.

The modern nation-state emerged and grew largely on the basis of two promises: modernization and nationalism. The state promised to bring about economic growth and development and to promote national unity, identity, and dignity. Today, on the economic level, the triumph of the free-market understanding of development combined with the globalization of economic institutions and processes is shrinking the role, perhaps even diminishing the legitimacy, of national governments. At the same time, nationalism—while still alive in its older, right-wing form—has to a surprising extent sprung up on the Left: It has been taken up by the minorities and the marginalized, transforming it into identity politics—with complex consequences for the nation. This transformation threatens to turn nationalism from a force for national unity and strength into one for national disintegration and weakness. Even so, identity politics does offer the modern state a new rationale for its power and activism, one that can replace the economic rationale that has increasingly been slipping away. Thus, whereas the forces weakening the state do currently seem to have the upper hand, the complexity of the changes we are undergoing does not allow for any confident predictions about the future.

I

THE UNITED STATES

1

The Left's Lost Universalism

Todd Gitlin

A HISTORIC REVERSAL

The defeat of the Left as a live political and intellectual force is the background to politics today—in the United States as in most of the industrialized world. By defeat, I do not mean only a loss of elections; I mean a fragmentation of vision, a shrinkage of moral scope, a breakdown of confidence. If conservatives have the initiative throughout the West today, this is not so much because they offer practical solutions to urgent problems as because they have succeeded in moving the center of discourse in their direction.

The decline of the Left can be measured by the slackening of its ability to speak in behalf of a common humanity. Between Left and Right there has been a curious reversal. During the nineteenth century, it was the Left that affirmed the universality of the human condition, while the Right declared that human beings were intrinsically different. The main line of the Left stood for the equality of persons, the main line of the Right for distinctions and privileges of birth, position, nation. Here is the royalist Joseph de Maistre writing in 1797: "In the course of my life I have seen Frenchmen, Italians, Russians; I even know, thanks to Montesquieu, that one can be a Persian; but *man* I have never met."[1] It is poignant for the Left—or would be poignant, if this condition were acknowledged—that at the end of the twentieth century it is the Right that affects a language of general rights, while the Left, if it can be addressed with a singular noun, insists on the primacy and irreducibility of difference. Today it is the laissez-faire Right, certifying the rights and powers of capital, that speaks a language of commonalities. Its rhetoric of markets and freedoms has the old universalist ring. To be on the Left, meanwhile, is to doubt that one can speak of humanity at all.

Some of us briefly did think, or hope, during the annus mirabilis of 1989–90, that the collapse of Communism would free the Left of its heaviest twentieth-century burden—free it from a fraudulent universalism. The bogeyman that has haunted the Left since before the Bolshevik Revolution is

3

the all-commanding state, and so, when the states that had been installed by Soviet power fell into rubble, perhaps this was the good news for which the *democratic* Left had long been waiting. Many wondered expectantly whether the classic socialist project might not be renewed, this time stripped of the party-state. Perhaps the time had come for "humanism with a human face." It is no news that such hopes proved to be bubbles. For the most part, the end of Communism has signaled not a new universalism but a revival of nationalist furies. On the Right, there is a coupling of national chauvinism and laissez-faire. On the Left, there is an attempt to defend certain achievements of the welfare state, but little sense that it might be possible to break fresh ground.

We are living through the exhaustion of that core belief shared by all the historic ideals of the Left: a belief in progress through the unfolding of a humanity present at least potentially in every human being.[2] Universalism is in bad odor. On the Left, the very word has an imperial ring. Reason seems frail—or worse, its arrogant claim to progress through understanding is billed as the instrument of white, Western, male domination, hence the pollution and destruction of the common earth. Certainly there remain vigorous ideas and sentiments of a universal humanity, perhaps best expressed in the Universal Declaration of Human Rights, in organizations like Amnesty International and Médécins sans Frontières, in campaigns for the defense of Salman Rushdie and against genital mutilation, in the very words "humanist" and "humanitarian." There remain cosmopolitan spirits, zones where identities mix, multiplicities thrive, and the pleasures of coexistence and the adhesive forces of solidarity outweigh the arrogance of elites, the impositions of millennial religion and imperial power, and the tensions and distentions of difference. There remain, not least, universal predicaments—we live under one ozone layer, in one single greenhouse, though certainly the view from the penthouse looks different than the view from the basement.

But in the secular commons, the sense of prologue is weak. This is most strikingly true on the Left, where the faith in eventual progress was traditionally strong and the affirmation of a common identity (citizen) over particular identities (race, religion, national origin) was central. At the root of the many meanings of what we call the Enlightenment was a conviction that there is a common human condition on the basis of which progress, if not perfection, is at least possible—even imminent. The Enlightenment was a secular version of Christian ideas about human destiny. How fusty these hopes sound today! Marxism, the principal theology of the Left, and socialism, the ideal it professed, are almost everywhere in retreat. The collapse of Communism and the Cold War balance of terror did not clear the slate for a renewed commitment to egalitarian values, but rather revealed social democracy to be in a crisis of its own, unable to rally popular enthusiasm against the pressures of global economic convulsion and declining belief in the public realm. Defenders of some pure, Platonic ideal of the Left have only a tattered flag to wave, and are today, like their counterparts on the

Right, more adept at vituperation against their enemies than at reflection upon, let alone the practice of, human arrangements that would make life more supportable and dignified for humanity at large.

The malaise of the Left does not stop with the Left. In recent decades, a whole family of commonality ideas has lost much of its cogency and power. The Enlightenment belief in progress, in the potential for reason, seems reserved for scientists, or students of society who fancy themselves scientists, or university presidents in need of ceremonial rhetoric; it is not a popular faith. The rational state, in principle the embodiment of reason in Europe for a century, from Bismarck to modern social democracy, steadily loses defenders. The liberalism of individual rights, and the Americanism that mirrored it, is under fire for cultivating systematic irresponsibility and failing to offer a sense of community. Formally free individuals do not seem to cherish their children, or know how to protect them, or form enduring and satisfying social bonds. No wonder people retreat from voting and public participation, seek solidarity among people who resemble themselves, or look for low-risk electronic connections in popular culture or on the Internet, where they may hook up on their own time and cultivate their limited-liability associations. There are pleasures and addictions and evanescent communities galore to be found under the big tent of popular culture, but what there is *not* is a common citizenship. No wonder it will not do to raise the trumpet for a restoration of the grand old unities. An abiding faith in the human future is not summoned up by an act of will.

For two centuries after 1776 and 1789, believers in a common humanity everywhere clustered around the two great progressive ideals: the liberal ideal enshrined in the Declaration of Independence, the Constitution, and the Declaration of the Rights of Man and Citizen; and the radical and socialist ideal which crystallized as Marxism. Even the political metaphor of Left and Right, however much knocked around, survived for two centuries on the strength of an assumption that history is a single story proceeding along a single timeline. The idea of a Left derives, strictly speaking, from the seating arrangements of the French National Assembly,[3] but two-sided political symmetry has another intuitive appeal. Like the Christian division of history into Before and After, the language of Left and Right stems from the idea of a universal history. Revolution, like the story of Christ, splits history down the middle. Past and future are the essential categories. Old regimes want to conserve, new regimes want to change. This melodrama the Left has always been partial to, casting itself as action, thrusting into the future, while the Right represents reaction, the dead hand of the past.

Such legitimacy as the Left enjoyed in the West rested, then, on its claim to a place in the grand story of universal human emancipation. Two hundred years of revolutionary tradition, whether liberal or radical, from the American through the Russian, the Chinese, and the Cuban, along with their Western echoes, were predicated on the ideal of a universal humanity. The Left addressed itself not to particular men and women but to all, in the name of their common standing. If the population at large was incapable, by itself, of seeing the world whole and acting in the general interest, then some enlightened group would take it upon itself to be the collective conscience, the Founding Fathers, the vanguard party. Even Karl Marx, lyricist of the proletariat, ingeniously claimed that his favored class was destined to stand for, or become, all humanity. Whether liberals or socialists, reformers or revolutionaries, the men and women of the Left invited their listeners to see their common interest amply, as citizens of the largest world imaginable. All men were supposed to have been created equal, workingmen of all countries were supposed to unite. The respective founding fathers left at least half the species out of account, yet the logic of their language spelled the eventual defeat of their prejudices.

Even the nationalist revolutions which were the nineteenth century's principal passion understood themselves as tributaries joining a common torrent, a grand surge of self-determination justified in the end by the general need for peoplehood and the equivalent worth of all national expressions. Difference was a universal feature of individuals; only autocrats could deny it. From the quest for personal authenticity, there followed the legitimacy of group associations. As Charles Taylor has argued, the resulting "politics of recognition," building on the writings of Jean-Jacques Rousseau and Johann Gottfried von Herder, was predicated on a *general* human need for the dignity of persons, a dignity inseparable from their right to distinct attachments.[4] This was the basis of the liberal nationalist movement to attach nations to states, on the ground, articulated by Giuseppe Mazzini, that no people were complete without an independent nation.[5] When universalist ideals lined up behind national flags—as they did during most of the nineteenth century—what they paraded was this interesting paradox: nationalism with a universal rationale. Even Mazzini, the guiding spirit of Italian nationalism, told his followers: "You are *men* before you are *citizens*."[6] Even liberal nationalists, in short, understood themselves to be acting in concert, affirming equality in the name of a single human nature. Since they were democrats, republicans, and constitutionalists, theirs was the cause of the Left.

Dissolving the bands that tied them to the British Empire, the American founders felt impelled to justify themselves to the entire world not only by itemizing their grievances against George III but by stating first their conviction that "all men are created equal and that they are endowed by their Creator with certain inalienable rights." Not "all colonists" or "all whites" or even "all North Americans" but "all men"—although it was to take decades of suffering and political clamor to pry open the definition of "men" and include enslaved African Americans and women.

Thirteen years later, with the help of the Marquis de Lafayette and his American-inspired rhetoric,[7] the French revolutionaries produced a Declaration of the Rights of Man and Citizen—not a Declaration of the Rights of Frenchmen—declaring men equal "in respect of their rights" (though again distinctly failing to take women into account). The liberal revolutions leapfrogged, with the French declaration then stirring Thomas Jefferson to urge James Madison to propose a Bill of Rights to the American Constitution.[8]

The membership that counted for political rights was membership in the human race. The member, in the liberal ideal, was the irreducible individual, equal before the law. The power of the discourse of individual rights was such that it could be generalized, perhaps indefinitely, by extrapolation. Within fifty years, women who had been grossly subordinated in the anti-slavery movement were working up a politics based on their constituting half of a human race that had been decreed to share equal rights. Within thirty more years, slavery was abolished. Obviously brutal inequalities were not abolished, but the idea of equal rights remained as a standard against which to measure all injustice, all brutality, all concentrations of illegitimate power. A straight line connects the rights language of the late eighteenth century to the 1948 Universal Declaration of Human Rights, which was couched deliberately as "universal" rather than "international" in order to affirm that the rights of humans supersede the rights of nations.

The United States, in theory, was to be the homeland of an idea: a democracy of free individuals. This new nation was to be more than a new nation—it was to be the homeland of liberty, showing the rest of the world that what it wanted to be was, in fact, America. In its most liberal, least nativist version, America was the truth of the world unveiled. America was what John F. Kennedy was to call "a nation of immigrants," displaying the wholeness and diversity of humanity in common cause. Not only a refuge for the new Adam, America declared itself the dream of perfected humanity, a decisive chapter in the revelation of humanity to itself. By this reckoning, America, alloy of worthy individuals, was the incarnation of embryonic humanity.

From this sense of America as the microcosm of humanity, there also flowed the idea that human beings designated as civilly and legally free were entitled not only to their privileges but to the manifold brutalities of Manifest Destiny—by erasing cultures it deemed lesser, it made the world safe for a fit humanity. In the American idea, when humans reasoned together, what they produced was America—and those who objected, or were judged incapable, forfeited their rights. It was not just by force of arms that the Americans conquered a continent—it was also by force of the idea that America was entitled to be as boundless as it wished.

FROM A THEORY TO END ALL CLASSES
TO A THEOLOGY WITHOUT GOD

The other great political embodiment of Enlightenment faith was socialism, in particular the world view that came to be known as Marxism, combining not simply a critique of capitalism and an affirmation of socialist principles but an idea about how socialism was to come about. The scheme was ingenious, linking the *is* and the *ought*, the material and the philosophical, the empirical and the theological so compellingly as to make history for more than a century.

Leave aside the abundance of colorations under the Marxist flag, many famously renounced by Marx with the cry "I am not a Marxist!" Because ideas have consequences, even when they do not enter the world in conditions of their own making, thinkers do not so readily evade responsibility for the enactment of their errors and silences. Anyway, big intellectual movements are bound to elude the grasp of the founders. Marxism's sacrifices and hypocrites and antagonists alike shared a core idea of what this Marxism was that deserved their sacrifice and hypocrisy and hostility. If the whole of Marxism meant anything, it meant to embody the idea of the Left—the presumption that through a certain type of struggle it was possible to usher in, and speak in the name of, a common humanity. Although it never held sole title to socialism, Marxism with its Hegelian idea of history became the heir of all the other socialisms, the solidarities and *fraternités*, that inhabited France and elsewhere. Marxism was nothing if not audacious.

Marx was philosophically trained, but his pride and joy was to have "brought philosophy down to earth." In the nineteenth century, his thinking gained plausibility and urgency from practical circumstances: the convulsive growth of industrial capitalism in Europe. But had Marxism been nothing more than an economic theory of how capitalism works, he would have accomplished little more than to give capitalists a name and a notion of what they were up to. He would have belonged to the history of economics as a proponent of a oversimple labor theory of value, a questionable "law" of the falling rate of profit, and so on. As founder of sociology, he would be seen as the pioneer in a dynamic theory of classes. As a socialist, he would have been one among many. But Marxism has been an enormous force in the world for neither its economic claims, its sociological insight, nor its values. Marx mattered because he stood for an overarching world view—a vision, to use today's buzzword for something whose absence is as conspicuous as the invocations to it are numerous. Central to the appeal of his intellectual system was its prophetic ambition: to frame the meaning of history and the universal destiny of humankind.

Like the idea of Christ's coming, and the idea of America, the whole intellectual and emotional system was predicated on faith—a good faith to unmask bad faiths. True, in many a tract and letter, Marx dripped scorn for his contemporaries' ideas about the common good.[9] These he saw as nothing more than masks for particular interests—ideologies, not truths. In the *Communist Manifesto*, he sneered at such naïfs as Germany's "true" socialists for claiming to represent "not the interests of the proletariat, but the interests of Human Nature, of Man in general."[10] Generations of Marxists would go on to consider tender-mindedness about universal humanity premature, obscurantist, and (curse of curses!) "idealist." But Marx objected to what he considered shallow universalisms. He proposed, in their place, to offer the real thing, unflinchingly acknowledging the most antagonistic social differences, boldly recognizing the ferocious struggles between them, asserting indeed that these struggles were the engine of history, proclaiming that in the end the war between the different was the prologue to ultimate peace in the commons.

Amid enormous social upheaval, this was a trump. Marx's brilliance was to argue that the imagined future was already in process. All humanity was already represented, if unknowingly, by a class destined to overcome all differences by ending all classes. The Left was to be the marriage of body and soul, muscularity and brains—proletariat and party—prefiguring a world in which the limits imposed by the division of labor have broken down. There exists, Marx asserted in his early writings, a universal identity: the human being as maker, realizing his "species being" in the course of transforming nature.[11] With the audacity of a German idealist primed to think in first principles, Marx adopted from G. W. F. Hegel the idea that there was a "universal class" that, operating with a franchise from the cunning of reason, would give meaning to history. Beginning with people uprooted from the land, his universal class was bound for classlessness. Its universality prefigured the final universality. As capitalism inexorably simplified the class structure, the proletariat would swell into the majority. As the world market spread and "entire sections of the ruling classes [were], by the advance of industry, precipitated into the proletariat," many an astute bourgeois changed sides and "the other classes decay[ed] and finally disappear[ed]," leaving only a shrinking minority of exploiters to be expropriated.[12] The proletariat was not only right—it was destined to be the embodiment of might. No utopian wish, no moralist sermon, it was a dynamo. Like electricity, it was driven by potential. This class-to-end-all-classes pointed to, intimated, was becoming, or rather (and here Marx's grammatical flourish invoked the future as if it were already taking place in the present) *was already* the future in embryo.

An elegant intellectual system! The universal class destined to redeem history would follow in the footsteps of the universal class that had already appropriated and transformed history: the "constantly revolutionizing" bourgeoisie, whose "need of a constantly expanding market for its products chase[d] [it] over the whole surface of the globe . . . nestl[ing] everywhere, settl[ing] everywhere, establish[ing] connections everywhere, . . . giv[ing] a cosmopolitan character to production and consumption in every country," destroying "all old-established national industries," generating "universal interdependence of nations," making "national one-sidedness and narrowmindedness . . . more and more impossible," and in sum, "creat[ing] a world after its own image."[13] The universality of capital was the crucible for the universality of labor.

But not without assistance. To accomplish its transcendent mission, the class-to-end-all-classes required a universal midwife: the revolutionary Communist. No matter where he originated, this agent of universal history overcame his particular class and nation. Taking a cue from the international bourgeoisie, the revolutionary Communists prefigured the workingmen of the future, who "have no country." To every particular circumstance and cause, the universal priesthood of communists was charged with bringing the glad tidings that History was the unfolding of Reason. The Communist Party, like God, had its center everywhere and nowhere. Like the church of Jesus, it was charged with distilling ultimate meaning from the material life. The proletariat was the Communist's nation. Like the émigré Marx, he was at home nowhere and everywhere, this denationalized world citizen,[14] prefigured by Lafayette and Tom Paine, liberated to teach people of all nations that their destinies were intertwined; for all the world was becoming one, "national differences and antagonisms between peoples [were] daily more and more vanishing,"[15] and the proletariat needed to be taught that not a historical event nor a struggle against oppression rose or fell which did not have its part to play in the global transfiguration.

Marx's emissaries discerned the truth that the overwhelming majority of human beings were united by their participation in labor. That position defined them. That was their "identity"—but unlike the race, gender, sexual, and other identities of today, it was *the* identity to overrule all others for the overwhelming majority of mankind. Once the gap between use-value and exchange-value was overcome, all class division and hence all socially created difference would be overcome. So the task of Communists was, in the midst of national and particular struggles, to "point out and bring to the front the common interests of the entire proletariat, independently of all nationality"; they "always and everywhere represent the interests of the movement as a whole."[16] The universalities rang out: *common . . . entire . . . always . . . everywhere . . . the movement as a whole.* However rebuked by local interests, the Communist universalist belonged to the Left, the one true international church, where the Englishman and the German, the Indian and the Chinese, met to prefigure the borderless world to come.

With this lyric did Marxism hope to rescue the universalist hope from the liberationist cause that absorbed most of the energies of idealists during the first half of the nineteenth century—nationalism. Marx's rhetoric, not the particulars of his theoretical framework, imparted to revolutionaries a sense of common cause for a century after the death of the founding father. There were social democratic, syndicalist, and other variants, all claiming to be the true heirs. These were crushed, or crushed themselves, by World War I and their failure to prevent it. Leninism, the universalist technology of revolution and rule later codified by Stalinists, won the war of the heirs—in no small measure because one nation, the German, found Vladimir Ilich Lenin a useful instrument to wield against another nation, the Russian, and transported him across the country in 1917. The leap to the voluntarism of Lenin's Bolsheviks was not inevitable, but Marxism under wartime conditions made its triumph possible. If Bolshevism was not the unshakable shadow of Enlightenment Marxism, it was the scion that succeeded.

Lenin ushered into the twentieth century a fusion of thought and action which brilliantly, and dangerously, updated Marx. Under Lenin, the party, the International, this directive force that sees all and knows all and acts in the ostensibly general interest, presented itself as a perverse incarnation of Enlightenment faith in the knowability of the human situation. The idea was that the will of the Bolshevik party would rescue the working class from its parochial ideas and identities—that is, its attachment to particular proletarians. Without the party's high-minded theorizing and planning, Lenin argued, the working class would bog down in "trade-union consciousness"—the defense of its own particularist interests. Farther down a road already surveyed by Marx, Lenin made intellectuals essential to the revolution, thereby securing the dominion of universalist ideals.

What Lenin developed in theory, the October Revolution of 1917 accomplished in action. The instrument of the party proved infinitely adaptable to circumstances as long as one condition was met—absolute power. What the party did not promise, the State claimed to deliver. When the Russian detonator failed to set off the larger European bomb, Lenin devised a theory for leaping from *a* revolution to *the* Revolution. Just as imperialism was "the highest stage of capitalism," so anti-imperialism would be the highest form of anticapitalism, the passion that united the world proletariat. On a world scale, Lenin argued, it was imperialism that now constituted "radical chains"[17]—*the* form of oppression so fundamental that when the oppressed united against their appointed place in the global system they would bring down the whole structure. The road to Paris, Lenin said, led through Beijing.

Marxism retained the grandeur of a universalist dynamic, and neither Leninism nor Stalinism did much if anything to weaken it. Even in Europe, Marxism took strength from the abundant miseries of capitalism, and Leninism acquired the prestige of an achievement. Nothing secures the longevity of a faith better than institutionalization, even a cynical one. As a faith, Marxism held onto its universalizing spirit partly because of its moral authority as a critique of capitalism, but at least as much because of the peculiar prestige that accrues to existence. Whatever exactly one knew or made of Soviet crimes, the Soviet Union—and from 1949 on, Mao Zedong's China—was an enormous fact. However pointed the criticisms of Trotskyists and anarchists, whatever utopian alternatives were advanced by anti-Soviet socialists, the Soviet Union existed. Existence, the real "propaganda of the deed," apparently clinched the argument. Was not Marxism supposed to be practical? Under the stress of circumstance, it was not difficult for reasonable men and women to persuade themselves that Moscow was the closest approximation to the Jerusalem of the Church Militant—the prerequisite for an eventual triumph of justice and reason.

In the hearts and minds of communists and their fellow travelers, the prestige of existence was yoked to the will to believe. Once one accepted the two-toned logic that excluded all middles, that claimed that the only real choice in the world was between capitalism and socialism and that the command economy of the Soviet Union was as close to socialism as it was possible to get in a harsh world, then Marxism seemed fatally implicated in the fate of Joseph Stalin's machine. Socialists such as George Orwell were superb moral critics of the Stalinists, but the command economy was the only serious economy socialists could offer. While a few "market socialists" did try to imagine combining free pricing with the order and justice that could be organized by limiting the freedoms of capital, they commanded no divisions.

Above all, the command economy gained plausibility because the capitalist economy was devastated. It was the combination of global economic catastrophe in the 1930s and the rise of fascism over much of Europe that prolonged the life of the Marxist framework and its Leninist machinery in the West. Was it not manifest that capitalism manufactured suffering and that ruling groups in the democracies had no compunctions about coming to terms with grotesque police states? In this setting, many an egalitarian was willing to overlook the worst of what he knew, or could have known, about the Soviet Union in the interest of holding the door open to a decent universal future—even if the way lay through a sewer. From 1935 to 1939 and again after the Nazi invasion of the USSR, the Popular Front could even conjure a new commonality—a cobbled-together anti-fascist alliance. And in the end, Marxists asked rhetorically, what was the alternative that promised a universal transformation, universal justice, a single humanity? Partly, then, by default, partly by blindness, partly by sentimentality, partly by despair, from one revision to the next, Marxism hovered over all left-wing thought.

Ideologies end with whimpers, not bangs; with one end after another; over decades, not years, in proportion to the number of years they thrive as an energizing force. (It emerges at this late date that Daniel Bell's main mistake in his much-excoriated 1960 *The End of Ideology* was his title. He was describing the end of *socialism*.) In the history of latter-day Marxism, one disillusion followed another, and yet each time an intellectual generation emerged to reinvent the promise, if not the wheel. Each wrestled with the system's failings, picked up some pieces, and heaped them into a not-so-fresh beginning. But it is clear fifty years on that once the antifascist alliance of World War II was broken, so was the prestige and the universalist promise of Marxism, and correspondingly its appeal in the United States, at least outside university circles.

It was not simply the Cold War and McCarthyism that wrecked the Marxist prospect in America. It was the unignorable evidence that "actually existing" "state socialism" was, to put it mildly, hostile to universalist prospects—except perhaps to the prospect of a Gulag stretching across borders. The Iron Curtain severed not just Europe but the old Mission. The Prague putsch of 1948, the Berlin guns of 1953, and, most of all, the Soviet tanks rolling through Budapest in 1956 made obvious even to not-yet-reconstructed sentimentalists that Soviet Marxism amounted mainly to a *raison d'état.* Each reinvention rallied a smaller number of adepts, confident that they had salvaged the kernel of the faith, only to be set reeling again—by Solzhenitsyn on the Gulag, by many observers on the Khmer Rouge and, eventually, China's Cultural Revolution. It required ever more blindness to miss the pattern. In the face of such crimes, reason wept.

The Marxist cycle of eschatology and disillusion is almost certainly finished now. The collapse of European Communism in 1989–90 wiped out the *état* altogether, leaving Marxist (and indeed non-Marxist) socialists in thin air, whatever their protestations. They point out, accurately, that the breakdown of a theology does not erase the conditions God was supposed to address. Markets generate economic growth, but exacerbate grotesque inequalities. The advocates of unbridled capital also lack a persuasive vision of the unity of the world. (To the contrary: capital's "creative destructions" fuel fundamentalist retrenchments.) Nevertheless, there are more than two possible ideas in the world, and the disturbances of capitalism are unlikely to resurrect Marxism. At this late date in the twentieth century, even the rhetoric of the old prophecy is difficult to repeat with a straight face. Seventy-five years of horrors in the Soviet Union and its offshoots cannot be wished away as a mistake within another otherwise compelling system—as if to say, "Whoops, sorry about that, let's try again."

Marxism after Communism lies in ruins. But even the grander tradition of socialism is reduced to a sketch of an ethical ideal, or a goad to social democracy. As a practical matter, as an idea in the world, the theology is finished. Residual Marxists' hopes of "reinvention" are stretched and feeble. Some of the salvage efforts are ingenious, to be sure. The working class, singular, is redefined in such a way as to obscure "its" evident fissures of working condition, income, culture, gender, race, nationality. Antonio Gramsci's vocabulary is deployed to sanctify a loose assemblage of fragmentary identity movements as a "historic bloc." Watching these efforts at "reconstruction" and "reinvention," one is reminded of Ptolemy's seventeenth-century followers, whose geocentric view of the universe rested on the belief that celestial bodies rotated around the Earth along curves they called "epicycles." As more information was gathered and anomalies piled up, the Ptolemaics spun off a profusion of new epicycles—eventually as many as seventy-nine—as they strained to keep a grip on their antiquated cosmology against the Copernican challenge. Mirabile dictu, the model "worked," actually rendering predictions more efficiently, for decades, than the Copernican paradigm. But it "worked" at the cost of an absurd cumbersomeness. The Ptolemaic paradigm was doomed.

Today, the efforts of Marxist theorists to talk the anomalies away have a forced and anxious tone. Contemporary Marxists are left, for example, with the broken and desiccated "Marxism" of the contemporary Cultural Studies curriculum,[18] as described in this passage from Michael Bérubé, a talented and prominent radical professor of English at the University of Illinois:

> The current Marxism of cultural studies, it turns out, is a Marxism that stopped believing in historical inevitability long before the Wall came down; it is a Marxism that denies the primacy or unity of "class" (and emphasizes the relevance of race, gender, sexuality, subjectivity), no longer believes in an intellectual vanguard, no longer believes in the centrality of Europe, no longer believes that the base "determines" the superstructure, that the ruling class owns the ruling ideas, that class struggle is inevitable, or that ideology is just "false consciousness."[19]

The shapeless mélange that results remains Marxist only in a nostalgic sense. Instead of a brief for unification, it descends to a list of subcultures.

In short, Marxism without a revolutionary proletariat has all the pathos of a theology without God. Failing to take its poetry from the future, as Marx recommended, this gestural Marxism dresses up in a wardrobe from the past. From a history which is either failed or catastrophic, it salvages icons. Perhaps the good father is to be protected from the depredations of bad brothers and bad sons—the real (or early) Marx unblemished by Friedrich Engels; or the one read by Rosa Luxemburg, not Lenin; or by Lenin and Leon Trotsky, not Stalin. Perhaps there is, after all, a global working class in embryo, but it has been unfortunately misled, or its hour has not yet come round—give it time! This shapeless "Marxism" lacking a labor theory of value, lacking the transcendent homogenization of a universal class, lacking a universalizing agency, shrinks into a set of analytic tools with which to grasp the globalization of capital, and a moral critique of exploitation—frequently valuable for analysis, one angle from which to criticize some social arrangements, but hardly a mission or a politics, let alone the invocation of a universal spirit.

THE FATE OF THE COMMON MAN

Leaving aside the idea of the Left as the party of the workers, what of the idea of the Left as the vessel of the common man? What of democratic Americanism?[20]

As in France and Great Britain, the 1930s saw an amalgam of populism, Progressivism, and sentimental leftism. The activist government and the Community Party, unions and popular organizations, were fused into a Popular Front. The enemy consisted of "economic royalists." Song and story celebrated the virtues of little guys who found themselves up against hard-hearted bankers and corrupt politicians. Frank Capra honored John Doe and Mr. Smith; Carl Sandburg sang the praises of *The People, Yes*; Communist Party leader Earl Browder smoothly retailed the slogan Communism Is Twentieth-century Americanism; and Frank Sinatra and Paul Robeson inhabited a "House I Live In" written by two Communists, celebrating "the little bridge at Concord where freedom's fight began."[21] On this view, patriotism amounted to the love of equality. The Working Class melted into the People. "If you like America . . . if you like its Rocky Mountains, its Storm King highway, its low-priced automobiles, the hot and cold running water in your well-tiled bathroom," declared an ad in the Communist *New Masses*, then American Communism was for you.[22] Here was a nationalism that justified assimilation in the name of a higher good: popular well-being. One of the most original of American Marxists, the Trotskyist Leon Samson, went so far as to argue, in 1933, that Americanism was a sort of moral equivalent of socialism, "a substitute for socialism . . . and that is why the socialist argument falls so fruitlessly on the American ear."[23]

Democratic Americanism, a sort of ethnocentrism from below, was an ideology splendidly tailored for the Great Depression. This period of desolation made visible one of the great and decisive American clichés, a cliché so resonant it seems always to have been with us: *the American dream.* The nature of America was to serve as a refuge for minorities, who may have looked or sounded different but were all the same under the skin, willing and even eager to assimilate—but on their own terms: to make themselves at home in an America that would earn their assimilation and not humiliate them. America would honor these outsiders by dissolving outsiders into the mainstream of "ordinary Americans." Of course not all Americans were the descendants of voluntary immigrants. The awkward truth about all celebrants of this American merging was that it was premised, almost exclusively, on the whiteness of all the merging parties. Rhapsodic invocations of fused Americans and new races did not address the problem; they finessed it, for the most part, leaving the descendants of slaves out of consideration. African Americans did not have the luxury of merger fantasies. Their fate was twoness: that famous compound identity named by W. E. B. DuBois. The Popular Front tried to duck this asymmetry. What is remarkable is that, despite segregation and rampant discrimination, it succeeded as long as it did.[24]

The war against fascism gave the Popular Front several years more of vividly evil enemies. Just when the unifying Americanism of the New Deal was slackening, it found a new lease. World War II was the continuation of the Popular Front by other means. It said: Whatever your separateness, transcend your tribe; or rather, fold it into the whole. Popular culture enlisted in the war effort. In books and pamphlets, movies and radio, popular artists and social scientists produced an image of a unified, finally fused America. America embraced an identity that gained coherence from the fact that it was under assault. Many of the propagandists were on the Left. This was, after all, a war against fascism and racial subjugation (even if the Japanese were racially demonized in the process). Ethnicity was inducted into the team.

Popular Front consciousness became virtually obligatory in the multiethnic platoons of World War II movies ("O'Hara! Antonelli! Goldberg! Washington!"), where mutual reliance is the blood bond that distinguishes the good guys from the Nazis.[25] As film historian Jeanine Basinger writes, the clear moral of this movie is: "We are a mongrel nation—ragtail, unprepared, disorganized, quarrelsome among ourselves, and with separate special interests, raised, as we are, to believe in the individual, not the group. At the same time, we bring different skills and abilities together for the common good, and from these separate needs and backgrounds we bring a feisty determination."[26] The formula African American was integrated into Hollywood's army years before he is admitted into the real one—a case of Hollywood's dream factory functioning as a social avant-garde. The dark-skinned members of the platoon often had the good grace to make the ultimate sacrifice for the good of the whole unit, expressing supreme loyalty in the process of expressing their nearly mandatory expendability.[27] The war against fascism became a war of liberation on behalf of what was distinctly American: the diversity of the *demos* fused into a single, solid phalanx.

But victories lead to dissension. The triumph of 1945 might have spurred a round of centrifugal cultural motion—an upsurge of class, race, and political tensions—but for the coupling of two powerful forces: the economic boom and the coming of the Cold War, which between them offered quick and emotionally compelling answers to the perennial predicament of American culture, or at least ways of suppressing lingering doubts. The Cold War told Americans that *we* were what *they* were not, what *they* were trying to crush. *They* were slavery; *we* were freedom. *They* were faceless hordes ruled by faceless bureaucrats and secret police; *we* were middle-class individualists.[28] The time-honored riddle of American identity evidently had a solution: We Americans were all of *us* who lined up against *them*. We were, in fact, the very proof of the commonality of mankind, an *omnium gatherum* of immigrants that had the great gift of absorbing trivial difference into the common crusade—what one could almost call the Popular Front against Communism.

Defined most firmly by what we were not, declaring ourselves to be in our deepest spirit the negation of what we arose so vigorously to fight, America could sustain an appearance, even a conviction, of unity. If any more proof was needed, Henry Wallace's disastrous presidential campaign of 1948 proved that the Cold War consensus represented more than a rapprochement of foreign policy elites; it was a popular cause, *the* popular cause, a rock-bottom conviction that marked the boundary of all legitimate political discourse.

This negative passion moved to the emotional center of America's shared identity. In considerable measure, this unity-through-antagonism continued the fused Americanism of World War II. Propaganda and popular enthusiasm met in extending fused Americanism into the Cold War. Liberal and conservative elites disagreed on whether the enemy was principally without or within, but on one thing they agreed: The necessary condition of anti-Communism was Communism. So flagrantly brutal was its Stalinist incarnation that Communism in the Soviet Union and its satellites mobilized a countertotalist reaction that was as bracing and embracing to its partisans as Communism had been to its own. Still, Communism was not sufficient to explain the paranoid energy of anti-Communism and its assumption that domestic Communists and fellow workers, even liberals, were likely menaces to national security. Communism was a gift to Americans who without it would have lacked a sustaining cause.

With Communism in foul odor, the Americanism of the Popular Front quickly crumbled. The common man had a new cause: to stop the Red Army. No longer were bosses, economic royalists, and Republican skinflints the favored enemies. When President Harry Truman proposed a crusade against the commercial control of medicine, he was beaten back by organized medicine's counterattack against "socialized medicine." The satisfactions of the common man, and woman, acquired a more compelling emotional focus—Communism, imagined as the obstacle impeding twentieth-century Americanism. McCarthyism, a populism of fools, arose out of the Midwest to transform class and regional resentments into a single iron conviction. The common man was now encouraged to express his hostility to striped-pants Eastern Establishment types by sniffing out Communists in the State Department.

Still, for the purpose of shaping popular identity, McCarthyism was of limited value. It was a political crusade—for several years a successful one, but not a source of social location and meaning for most people. Much more than anti-Communism was required to undermine the Popular Front ideology of the progressive common man. The other prerequisite, and a decisive foundation of American political identity during the quarter-century after World War II, was a rising standard of living—rising not just absolutely but in the direction that Americans wanted, namely, toward the improvement of private life. For if the common man was in fact making a good deal of progress, as measured by the sole criterion for progress that was alive in the culture—namely, economic advancement—then Americanism *worked.* It promised a postwar cornucopia of consumer goods and mobilized government policies toward that end.

From the Servicemen's Readjustment Act of 1944, guaranteeing low-interest home loans to the sixteen million servicemen who would return from the war and insuring the builders' investments,[29] to the series of road-building laws culminating in the Federal-Aid Highway Act of 1956, government action created the material base for a culture of affordable acquisition. In the suburban home, the family commanded an array of technical services that in the lifetimes of the previous generation had been available only to the very rich: central heating, indoor plumbing, telephones, automatic stoves, refrigerators, and washing machines.[30] Some *middle* class whose progress was measurable in such things! With such advantages, the sense of having arrived (in the suburbs, in a car) was extraordinary. For the first time in human history, comfort was a material fact for a majority. Who needed a Popular Front? The demobilized troops could disperse to the suburbs, to be middle class with the rest of the lonely crowd.

The salient identity, the one that mattered, was *middle class.* Although there were precedents in American rhetoric, the important thing is that by the mid-twentieth century, "middle-class" had become Americans' catch-all label of choice, beloved of pollsters and politicians and editorial writers, and a brilliantly flexible one it was, enabling office and technical workers to share status with doctors and corporate vice presidents, while enabling corporate lawyers to disguise their privileges by grouping themselves with plumbers rather than the inheritors of wealth. To identify oneself as part of that great blur, the middle class, came to be an affirmation of normality— the averageness that Americans cultivate as an ideal while loudly proclaiming their individualism. To say you were middle class was to say that you were a regular person, an ordinary Joe (or Jane)—and eventually, that you belonged to the majority. For by the 1980s, more Americans identified themselves (to pollsters, at least) as middle class (43.3 percent) than as working class (36.6 percent), and the self-professed middle, supplemented by the self-professed upper-middle (8.2 percent), added up to a majority.[31]

The middle-class ideal took on a special allure in the suburbs. The free-standing home had become integral to American identity. It was the present-day extension of the homestead, the marker of yeoman liberty. Men readily described themselves as *home*owners; the majority of women were *house*wives. The house was not only a shelter, it was the family *home*. To say *home* was to say *family*, and vice versa, and to say either was to say *goodness*—moral goodness as well as a good way of life. The family home was at once the place to make babies and rear children, to display the luster and powers of augmented income, to make the grass grow and the car glow and the television set radiate images of carefree people mowing their grass and burnishing their cars to a fine gloss.

During the first two postwar decades, such were the privileges to which a majority of Americans came to feel entitled. If one's house, one's home, came to appear small, there was a solution to that, too: work harder, earn more money, and trade up. If the ladder upward was real, then opportunity could compensate for envy, which Alexis de Tocqueville rightly considered the democratic sentiment *par excellence*. What did the considerable inequality in income and the far greater inequality in wealth matter, then? Americans were willing to overlook inequality as long as opportunities abounded for improvement. Through the 1960s, enough upward mobility took place among a middle-class person's middle-class friends and relations and neighbors that those who wanted to ascend and failed to do so could only blame themselves or their spouses for not being up to snuff.

Thus did the combination of postwar boom and Cold War make palpable a new basis for national unity. Together they formed a "grand creed." The Popular Front and its ideology of the common man were stirred into the cement of affluence and Cold War. If there remained "pockets of poverty"—the locution of the early 1960s—these could be cleaned up. All the way into the administration of Lyndon B. Johnson, this universalism of the common man was kept alive.

THE NEW LEFT AND THE SEARCH FOR SURROGATE UNIVERSALS

But this national unity broke down in the 1960s under the pressure of Black Power and the Vietnam War. The New Left can be seen in this light as a failed attempt to organize a new universalism.

The intellectual radicalism of the early 1960s was skeptical of Marxism. The failure of even a degraded Marxism in power to live up to its universalist—that is to say, internationalist—prospects was evident to the early New Left. This movement believed in the destiny of neither the working class nor the whole people. It can be seen, in fact, as a search for a substitute universalism—a vital idea of who human beings are and what they have, and need, in common.

In its early years, most of the New Left dismissed Marxism for what C. Wright Mills called its "labor metaphysic." Without quite putting matters in these terms, the New Left project was to compose a surrogate universal. There were two versions. The first, and most absorbing, was the thrust of the civil rights movement. On the surface, the civil rights movement sought an extension of traditional civil and political rights along the lines of the Declaration of Independence, the Constitution, and the Bill of Rights. To oppose racial oppression was to affirm that everyone had the right to sit at the same lunch counter, to vote at the same voting booth, and to ride on the same bus and sit in the same section. But civil rights actions embodied another objective as well: the experience of community. Ostensibly a means to the end of securing equal rights, solidarity was also an end in itself. In the experience of the mass meeting, the organization of the boycott of buses and stores, *fraternité* was manifest alongside *liberté*. This side of the civil rights movement spoke unabashedly of the "beloved community," and dovetailed with the student radicalism of the largely white New Left.

The *Port Huron Statement*, founding document of the Students for a Democratic Society (SDS), was drafted by Tom Hayden in 1962 in an effort to find an intellectual underpinning for this realm of experience in the civil rights movement.[32] This required, at one level, a conventional scheme of liberal reform. The New Left's "agencies of change" were meant to line up in a common direction. "The issues are interrelated" was the New Left's approach to a federation of single-issue groups—so that, for example, the peace, civil rights, and civil liberties movements would unite once they recognized that they had a common enemy, the Southern Democrats, the "Dixiecrats," who were at once warmongers, segregationists, and obstructers of the liberal extension of the New Deal. So much for the practical side of the effort to create a movement of the whole people.

But what was distinctive about the *Port Huron Statement* was neither the document's proposals nor its targets. Rather, it was the rhetoric of total transfiguration. In a revival of the Enlightenment language of Rousseau, SDS spoke self-consciously, with no sense of immodesty, about the entire human condition: "Human brotherhood must be willed . . . as the most appropriate form of social relations." The universal solvent for difference would be the principle that "decision-making of basic social consequence be carried on by public groupings." People Should Make the Decisions That Affect Their Lives: Reduced to a slogan on a button, this was the famous "participatory democracy," an idea about the powers of all human beings. In theory, participatory democracy was a single standard against which to judge all existing social arrangements. To the limited engagements of representative democracy, it opposed the unlimited commitments of direct democracy— enshrined, half-satirically, in the slogan Freedom Is an Endless Meeting. In practice, the principle was tailored to students (elite students at that, "housed

now in universities")—people collected in "knowledge factories" as the industrial proletariat had been collected in mills and mines; young people who
had grown up in relatively democratic families, or who, if not, had been uprooted from their communities of origin and were now being encouraged to
think of themselves as practitioners of reason. They were skilled talkers and
writers and had plenty of time on their hands. They knew how to write
leaflets, to mimeograph and distribute them, to organize meetings. They did
not need authorities to get things done. In effect, the students of the New Left
were syndicalists.[33]

They were syndicalists, that is, in search of a larger movement. And so they
had to argue against the qualifications that were theirs by virtue of middle-
class birth and education. When the early New Left of the Student Nonviolent
Coordinating Committee (SNCC) and SDS set out to find common ground
with a like-minded constituency, it reached out to the impoverished—SNCC
to sharecroppers and SDS to the urban poor, all of whom, by virtue of their
marginality to the world of work, might be imagined as forerunners of a universal democracy to be lived in the world of talk. If students and the poor
were not saddled with "radical chains" in the system of production, at least
they could be imagined with radical needs for political participation. The demand for a direct democracy beyond representation played a vivid part in the
politics of the real world, for it was at work when the Mississippi Freedom Democratic Party refused the official compromise offered at the 1964 Atlantic
City convention. The radical position was immortalized in Fannie Lou
Hamer's famous statement that it would be wrong for the leaders to take seats
because "all of us [in the delegation, which traveled from Mississippi by bus]
are tired."[34]

The student movement tried to generalize itself by extrapolating from the
experience of the civil rights upsurge. The decisive turn came from Berkeley's free speech movement, heavily influenced by students who had tasted
of the spirit and danger of the Mississippi Freedom Summer of 1964 and
wished for a wider and deeper politics. The movement began with a demand
for elementary political rights—the right to recruit on campus, to rally for off-
campus demonstrations, and the like—but the heavy-handed repressiveness
of the University of California administration radicalized the campus, deepened the disaffection, and drove activists to associate craven administrators
with bureaucratic organization. These themes were manifest in radical individualist slogans such as "I am a human being. Do not fold, spindle, or mu-
tilate." The experience of solidarity and endless meetings gave participatory democracy a footing in experience and led to democratizing reforms
within the American university and the cascading antiauthoritarianism of
the counterculture.

It also led to attempts to organize an interracial movement of the poor.
Former House Speaker Newt Gingrich's claim in 1995 that "countercultural
McGoverniks" wanted the poor to suffer the whims of Washington bureau-
crats is exactly wrong. To organize the poor to make their own decisions,

rather than be ordered about by a top-heavy government, was precisely the program of the democratic Left in the 1960s. "Maximum feasible participation of the poor" was the Great Society version enshrined in the War on Poverty law. Universal participation was the byword, to the point of utopian fantasy.

But the student movement's attempts at universalism broke down in both practice and theory. The passion that drove most activists was civil rights for black Americans, not the transformation of everyday life or even of political institutions. Although there were occasional local successes, the interracial movement of the poor failed to materialize. Demands for student power led to ideological absurdities such as a widely distributed pamphlet called "The Student as Nigger." The truth was that participatory democracy was too fragile an objective with which to bind an entire movement, let alone an entire society. Freedom as an endless meeting was only alluring to those with the time and taste to go to meetings endlessly. Eventually, a weaker, though still considerable, tendency developed—a democratization of protest, of movements and assemblies. The spirit of participatory democracy would reverberate throughout the society in the form of a movement for transparency. Citizens would succeed in opening up meetings from faculty councils to government bodies. Outraged stockholders and consumers would mobilize against corporate policies. But the strong form of the idea would crash into the objection attributed to Oscar Wilde: "The trouble with socialism is that it would take too many evenings."

At the level of theory, in the latter half of the 1960s, there were Marxist variations. New Left intellectuals worked up Marxist variants in which universalist students could imagine either that they were entitled to lead a hypothetical proletariat (the Maoist Stalinism of the Progressive Labor group among others) or that they themselves already prefigured a "new working class" (as in the French new-working-class theory imported to SDS in 1966–67). More influential by far was the idea of a global uprising, resurrected from pre-Stalinist Leninism and reemerging in the form of Third World revolution. The New Left had been inspired by the Cuban revolution in the first place. African anticolonialism, especially in the example of Malcolm X and the writing of Frantz Fanon, contributed to the spirit of a seamless world. So did the Chinese Cultural Revolution, along with the Maoist caricature of the Third World as the global "countryside" that would overpower the rich "cities." Most of all, there was the resiliency of Vietnamese Communism, given moral force in contrast to the American expedition. For accessible imagery, there was the ascetic yet romantic, indeed sexy, and finally martyred Argentine-turned-Cuban Che Guevara, the doctor turned professional revolutionary, at home (yet homeless) everywhere, rekindling Marx's ideal of the revolutionary who is no respecter of borders, calling for "two, three, many Vietnams."

This revolutionary impulse subsided, eclipsed by more urgent and palpable general concerns—the war in Vietnam and ecological danger. The crack-up of the universalist New Left was muted for a while by the exigencies of the Vietnam War and the commonalities of youth culture. If there seemed in the late 1960s to be one big movement, it was largely because there was one big war. But beneath the surface, the student movement's universalist impulse was fracturing. Such unity as had been felt by the civil rights movement had started dissolving with the victory over legalized segregation. Blacks began to insist on black leadership, even exclusively black membership. When feminist stirrings were greeted with scorn by unreconstructed men, the principle of separate identities proliferated. If white supremacy was unacceptable, neither could male supremacy be abided. One group after another demanded the recognition of difference and the protection of separate spheres for distinct groupings. This was more than an idea because it was more than strictly intellectual; it was more of a structure of feeling, a whole way of experiencing the world. Difference was now lived and felt more acutely than commonality. The initiative and energy went into the elevation of differences. The very language of commonality came to be perceived by the new movements as a colonialist smothering—an ideology to rationalize white male domination. The time for reunification would come later, so it was said—much later, at some unspecified time.

The entire left-wing tradition was thin in America to begin with. After the bulge of the 1960s, it thinned out again. In retrospect, it is blindingly clear that New Left universalism was fragile from the outset. The vogue of participatory democracy was brief except insofar as the principle could be applied to distinct groups. Its moment came in the early 1960s, and it was passé by 1968. For the most part, the category of citizen, or human being, was a weightless abstraction. It was as members of a specific category—as "a person of color," "a Jew," "a woman," "a lesbian"—that people wished and demanded to be represented in "the decisions that affected their lives." People lived, felt, desired, revolted as members of identity categories, not as citizens, let alone as human beings.

The student movement and the tropical revolutions pumped new life into Marxism, but this proved evanescent, except in university circles, where it choreographed a ghost dance. For the most part, divisions of race, then gender, then sexual orientation, and others, proved far too deep to be overcome by any unification rhetoric. The party of difference looked real; left-wing universalism looked nonexistent, hypothetical, or worse, deceptive—a mask assumed by straight white males as they tried to restore their lost position. Some feminists and all environmentalists would argue that their politics were rightly understood as commonality politics: that is, that their preoccupations deserved to be common preoccupations and that all people, including members of the majority, would benefit from the social transformation led by sectoral groups. But still, attempts at recomposing a sense of a unified bloc on the Left were weak in comparison with centrifugal pressures.

Starting from the early 1970s, the goals of the student movement and the various left-wing insurgencies were largely subsumed under the categories of identity politics. Separatism became automatic. Left-wing politics was "racialized."[35] Every interest organized as a distinct "community." Now one did not imagine oneself belonging to a common enterprise; one did not pour energy into cultivating a sense of general human identity. Instead, one belonged to a caucus, cultivated a separate culture, and scorned the idea of the human condition, or the republic, or the common good, or citizenship— hopelessly pre-postmodernist all.

PROSPECTS

Love and work, Freud wrote, are what human beings need. Toward the provision of love, society is helpless—fortunately, since it is central to modernity that people wish to love one another just as they please. But work is organized by collective action. This social anchorage of Western civilization is where human natures unfold for better and worse. It is where people combine and where knowledge and energy, discipline and love, fuse to transform the world. When work is properly organized, time becomes a friend and ceases to be an enemy. In recent centuries, work for most people has taken the form of jobs where people struggle to make use of their days on earth.

The sum of this human endeavor is only poorly grasped when politicians and pundits speak of "the economy." In the political discourse of Western democracies today, the main thrust of real-world change remains outside the discussion. Everywhere, not least in the most-developed countries, meaningful work is threatened despite apparent successes in economic growth. Worldwide, the annual shortfall of adequately paid jobs is in the tens of millions. Jobs are shipped offshore as capital goes in search of cheaper and more docile labor. Immigrants are pulled abroad by the allure of work and pushed out by the misery of their home countries. Poverty grows, along with inequalities of wealth, and all the pathologies persist to which poverty is heir—drugs, crime, disease. Scarcities of dignified employment are fuel for the ethnic and racial wars which disfigure the so-called advanced world.

In the midst of an upheaval that has become routine, one of the most striking features throughout most of the West is the paltriness of a significant popular Left with economic ideas. Conservatives, overlooking the destabilizations caused by private investment, at least affirm economic policies. In the United States, the main contentions on campuses do not pertain to the problem of funding but to the regulation of speech and the politics of identity groups. The so-called cultural Left features vividly in the national imagery bank, but a Left that is open-eyed about the main currents of change in the world, and aspires to form functioning majorities to address them, can barely be discerned. Everywhere, instead, are signs of displacement and evasion: shadow plays of petty aggression and deafness.

Is a Left conceivable now that Marxism has withered and identity politics smolders? To deplore fragmentation is one thing; to formulate, feel, and act on a common human project, quite another. Many on the Left weary of the fetish of difference and look to ideals of human rights and ecology, but even here, appeals to humanity often unravel into their separate strands. If cultures in much of the world support genital mutilation, does this make Western feminists imperialist? On many matters, the Left's ragtag, residual party of commonality sounds the clarion call and then reluctantly swivels to see that the troops are not following. It speaks for no movement. It brings few of the faithful into the streets. It fails to generate an emotional tide. It does not seem to fathom how the politics of commonality lost its historical momentum.

No fault of ours, but many of the Left's public defenders are white males like myself—easily shrugged off as pale penis people protecting our vulnerable flanks (if not other organs). In the present left-wing culture, such as it is, women and people of color who look askance at identity politics are commonly dismissed as nothing but interested parties, as "male-identified" high achievers or representatives of ethnic groups—East Indians and Afro-Caribbeans, for example—who are not officially sanctioned minorities and hence do not benefit (and may even suffer) from affirmative action. As the split between mind and body, mind and feeling, mind and spirit, comes under attack from radical feminists, the politics of commonality seems to speak from the mere mind, not from the viscera, and insofar as it carries emotion at all, can be accused of resentment, defensiveness, and nostalgia.

At the least, a serious Left would have to appeal to the building of bridges across identity chasms. But if it is to be realistic, this appeal cannot be radiant with the recollections of an innocent world where the parts to be assigned were those of good guys and bad. Those who would make a Left today would have to acknowledge that the old universalisms failed—and not, or not simply, for lack of goodwill. They fell of their own weight; they failed of their flimsiness.

To compose a Left, all the identities of color, sexual preference, gender, and nation would have to devote as much energy to forging common cause as to insisting on differences and protecting their separate prerogatives. Not least among the identities that would have to sacrifice their splendid group narcissism is the majority of white males whose relatively slender privileges, compared to the upper classes, have eroded in recent years with the decline of real wages, and who have been animated by their resentment of the groups thrown into conflict with them for jobs, contracts, admissions, and the rest of the resources distributed by means of affirmative action. The common bond would have to be a measure of social control over capital. Even more difficult, this control would have to be exercised across national boundaries. In the fight to limit the upheavals caused by capital's insatiable and unlimited mobility, people would have to link over borders. They would have to find precedent in environmentalist associations such as Greenpeace and the Rainforest Action Network, the antisweatshop campaigns, and human rights networks such as

Amnesty International and the Watch Committees. Perhaps this assemblage began to appear in the Seattle demonstrations of late 1999. It is too soon to gauge its staying power.

There is no golden past to recover. Neither the good society nor the good political movement is waiting, intact and timeless, for prodigals to return to its welcoming portals. If there is to be any transcendence of its present broken condition, the Left is going to have to be a creation, not a recovery. The Left's only chance is to leave its bunkers and get to work building bridges. Otherwise, it has no future but as a heap of relics.

NOTES

Passages in this chapter appear in the author's book, *The Twilight of Common Dreams: Why America Is Wracked by Culture Wars* (New York: Henry Holt & Co., 1995).

1. Joseph de Maistre, *Considérations sur la France*, 2d ed. (London: Bâle, 1797), 102, trans. K. Anthony Appiah, quoted in K. Anthony Appiah, "Identity, Authenticity, Survival: Multicultural Societies and Social Reproduction," in Charles Taylor et al., *Multiculturalism: Examining the Politics of Recognition*, ed. Amy Gutmann (Princeton: Princeton University Press, 1994), 150.

2. At this writing, Latin America may be the exceptional continent. The decline of military regimes and the recent experience of economic growth have given democratic ideas a tremendous boost. Latin American intellectuals from the moderate Right through the social-democratic Left share an enthusiasm for the future which their North American colleagues can only envy.

3. James H. Billington, *Fire in the Minds of Men: Origins of the Revolutionary Faith* (New York: Basic Books, 1980), 27.

4. Charles Taylor, *Multiculturalism and "The Politics of Recognition"* (Princeton: Princeton University Press, 1992).

5. Billington, *Fire*, 150.

6. Mazzini quoted in Mitchell Cohen, "Rooted Cosmopolitanism," in Nicolaus Mills, ed., *Legacy of Dissent* (New York: Simon and Schuster, 1994), 135.

7. Billington, *Fire*, 21, citing James Thompson, *The French Revolution* (New York: Oxford University Press, 1966), 41–42.

8. Gordon S. Wood, "The Origins of the American Bill of Rights," *Tocqueville Review* 14, no. 1 (1993): 33–48.

9. For this point I am indebted to Marshall Berman.

10. Karl Marx and Friedrich Engels, "Communist Manifesto," in Robert C. Tucker, ed., *The Marx-Engels Reader* (New York: Norton, 1972), 356.

11. Karl Marx, "Economic-Philosophical Manuscripts of 1844: Selections," in Tucker, *Marx-Engels Reader*, 52–103.

12. Marx and Engels, "Communist Manifesto," 343–44.

13. Marx and Engels, "Communist Manifesto," 338–39.

14. The term is James H. Billington's: *Fire*, 275.

15. Marx and Engels, "Communist Manifesto," 350.

16. Marx and Engels, "Communist Manifesto," 346.

17. Karl Marx, "Critique of Hegel's Philosophy of Right: Introduction," in Tucker, *Marx-Engels Reader*, 22.

26 *The Left's Lost Universalism*

18. For a general critique, see Todd Gitlin, "The Anti-Political Populism of Cultural Studies," in Marjorie Ferguson and Peter Golding, eds., *Cultural Studies in Question* (Beverly Hills: Sage, 1996).

19. Michael Bérubé, "Pop Goes the Academy," *Village Voice Literary Supplement*, April 1992, 11.

20. This discussion benefits from my reading of Michael Kazin's *The Populist Persuasion* (New York: Basic Books, 1995).

21. Music by Earl Robinson; lyrics by Lewis Allen [Abel Meeropol], who later adopted the sons of Julius and Ethel Rosenberg. Sinatra's 1945 recording accompanied an Academy Award–winning short film in which Sinatra broke up a fight caused by ethnic scapegoating. (Information courtesy of Richard Flacks.)

22. *New Masses* 29 (Sept. 27, 1938), back cover, as quoted in Paul Buhle, *Marxism in the USA* (London: Verso, 1987), 179.

23. Leon Samson, *Toward a United Front: A Philosophy for American Workers* (New York: Farhat & Rinehart, 1933), 16.

24. Sociologist Robert Blauner, who joined the Communist Party in 1949, writes: "It was not until the 1960s that I began to question my basic love and respect for the United States and its institutions. As a youth I was still influenced by the myths of Washington, Lincoln, the Revolution, and the Civil War. Emerson's 'Concord Bridge,' Whitman's *Leaves of Grass*, and Benét's 'American Names' all inspired an identification with my country's greatness. And Communists during the Popular Front period carried on this nationalist tradition." Robert Blauner, "'But Things Are Much Worse for the Negro People': Race and Radicalism in My Life and Work," in John H. Stanfield II, ed., *A History of Race Relations Research: First-Generation Recollections* (Newbury Park, Calif.: Sage, 1993), 6.

25. Jeanine Basinger, *The World War II Combat Film: Anatomy of a Genre* (New York: Columbia University Press, 1986), 51–53, 56, 61.

26. Basinger, *World War II Combat Film*, 51.

27. Basinger, *World War II Combat Film*, 57–58, 75. Basinger points out: "The minorities almost always die, and die most horribly" (75).

28. I borrow the term from Herbert J. Gans's underappreciated *Middle-Class Individualism* (New York: Free Press, 1988).

29. Kenneth T. Jackson, *Crabgrass Frontier: The Suburbanization of the United States* (New York: Oxford University Press, 1985), 233.

30. Jackson, *Crabgrass Frontier*, 243.

31. Mary R. Jackman and Robert W. Jackman, *Class Awareness in the United States* (Berkeley: University of California Press, 1983), 18; James A. Davis and Tom W. Smith, *General Social Surveys, 1972–1986: Cumulative Codebook* (Storrs, Conn.: NORC-Roper Center, 1986), q. 184, 218, cited in Gans, *Middle-Class Individualism* (New York: Free Press, 1988), 174 n. 13.

32. Students for a Democratic Society, *The Port Huron Statement* (New York: Students for a Democratic Society, 1962).

33. Significantly, one of the first pamphlets defending the radical potential of the student movement was Carl Davidson's "On Student Syndicalism" (Chicago: Students for a Democratic Society, 1966).

34. Todd Gitlin, *The Sixties: Years of Hope, Days of Rage* (New York: Bantam, 1987), 156.

35. Michael Omi and Howard Winant, *Racial Formation in the United States: From the 1960s to the 1980s* (London: Routledge, 1986), 64.

2

From Identity Politics to Social Feminism

Seyla Benhabib

THE PARADIGM WARS OF FEMINIST THEORY

A decade and a half ago a symposium took place at the law school of the State University of New York at Buffalo as part of the James McCormick Mitchell Lecture Series. The participants included Carol J. Gilligan, Catharine A. MacKinnon, Ellen C. DuBois, Carrie J. Menkel-Meadow, among others.[1] This symposium set the stage for the great clash of paradigms which was about to unfold in the coming years within contemporary feminist theory. I will use the term *paradigm* in nontechnical fashion to refer to a coherent set of assumptions, some articulated and some not, that guide, influence, structure, or help "format" a vision of theory and of politics. Let me cite the following exchange which took place between Gilligan and MacKinnon during the symposium.

With reference to Gilligan's work *In a Different Voice*,[2] MacKinnon said:

> I am—it will shock you to hear—ambivalent about it. On the one hand, I feel excited by the strong and elegant sensitivity in the work. There is something deeply feminist here: the impulse to listen to women. . . . On the other hand, what is infuriating about it (which is a very heavy thing to say about a book that is so cool and graceful and gentle in its emotional touch), and this is a political infuriation, is that it neglects the explanatory level. Why do women become these people, more than men, who represent these values? . . . For me, the answer is clear: the answer is the subordination of women. . . . She has also found the voice of the victim—yes, women are a victimized group. . . . What bothers me is identifying women with it. I'm not saying that Carol does this expressly in her book. But I am troubled by the possibility of women identifying with what is a positively valued feminist stereotype. It is the "feminine."[3]

MacKinnon does not altogether reduce Gilligan's "ethics of care and responsibility," which is claimed to characterize women's moral voices, to an ethic of the victim, although subsequent commentators have done so.[4] Yet she is clear that given existing patterns of male domination and female sub-ordination, the values of care, responsiveness to the needs of others, and ability for empathy and for taking the standpoint of the concrete Other—which Gilligan claimed women were more likely to display than men—would hurt rather than help women. MacKinnon's rejection of Gilligan's ethic of care is an instrumentalist one; like many power theorists before her, she argues that the end—that is, ending the subordination of women—justi-fies the means: using an ethic of power instead of being guided by an ethic of care and responsibility.

The exchange continued:

> *Gilligan:* Your definition of power is his definition.
> *MacKinnon:* This is because the society is that way, it operates on his definition, and I am trying to change it.
> *Gilligan:* To have her definition come in?
> *MacKinnon:* That would be a part of it, but more to have a definition that she would articulate that she cannot now, because his foot is on her throat.
> *Gilligan:* She's saying it.
> *MacKinnon:* I know, but she is articulating the feminine. And you are calling it hers. That's what I find infuriating.
> *Gilligan:* No, I am saying she is articulating a set of values which are very posi-tive.
> *MacKinnon:* Right, and I am saying they are feminine. And calling them hers is infuriating to me because we have never had the power to develop what ours really would be.[5]

This dramatic exchange sharply articulated one type of *paradigm* clash within contemporary feminist theory.[6] Name this a paradigm clash between "difference" and "equality" feminism; or name it the clash between "moral-ism" and "realism," or even between "utopianism" and "Realpolitik." The question is whether women, as social and political agents, (1) are the carri-ers of distinctive and new values (not addressing the question how these are acquired, formed, and developed), which they should fight for and promote in the public sphere, or instead (2) should seek power and equality by using to their own advantage the existing structures and institutions of their soci-eties, regardless of whether or not these promote alternative values.

In the years to follow, not only would utopian feminism(s) clash with a militant radical feminism of power, but various "power/gender" theories (built around Michel Foucault's model of "knowledge/power") would enter into shifting alliances, as well as confrontations, with psychoanalytic femi-nisms. As an observer of the Gilligan-MacKinnon exchange, DuBois noted: "There are by this time many feminisms. Women are no longer ignored in the political scene. *Au contraire*, the issues that the women's movement has raised are at the very center of this historical moment."[7] Speaking in 1984, DuBois identified the crucial issues for women in the United States as being abortion and the prospects for electing a female vice president. As the century has come to an end, there are still many feminisms; but it is not at all clear how/where/when/why the "issues that the women's movement has raised are at the very center of this historical moment." After decades of paradigm struggles, we are no longer sure that there is one movement; in fact, we know that there is not a single organization with the agenda of which a majority of women would agree.

More important, we no longer know what "this" historical moment is. As a consequence of postmodernist warnings against grand narratives, we have become skeptical of tales of this or that historical moment, this or that historical sequence or logic of development. In fact, we no longer know who "we" are. Postmodernist theorists tell us that this "we," even if only invoked as a rhetorical gesture of public speech and writing, is politically suspect, in that it tries to create a seeming community of opinion and views where there is none. Relishing in diversity, basking in fragmentation, enjoying the play of differences, and celebrating the opacity, fracturing, and heteronomy of all of this is the dominant mood in much of contemporary feminist theory and practice.

I do not celebrate this mood of reveling in difference and basking in fragmentation; nor am I nostalgic for a sense of lost unity in the women's movement which itself rarely existed. A healthy plurality of visions and strategies about the meaning of women's emancipation has always been an aspect of the various women's movements.[8] From their inception in the eighteenth century, and particularly in the period of their articulation in the mid-nineteenth and early twentieth centuries, feminism and the women's movements have always struggled with dilemmas of equality and difference: equality with men versus being different from them; preserving a women's separate sphere versus becoming full members of existing society by giving up women's traditional spaces. These tensions constitute what the women's struggle is all about; what will change from period to period is the construction of and contestation around these oppositions, but not the fact that women will always be aware of such oppositions, dichotomies, and conflicts.[9]

Nonetheless, all is not well in the contemporary scene of plurality, heterogeneity, and diversity. In particular, I see two major problems.

First, there has been a rapid shift of research paradigms in contemporary feminist theory from what is usually referred to as "standpoint feminism" to various "postmodernist and poststructuralist" feminisms, but neither the presuppositions nor the consequences of this shift have been adequately analyzed. Micro-narratives of class, race, and gender have replaced macronarratives of women's subordination across cultures, societies, and historical periods. While much has been gained in this shift of research paradigms, much has been lost as well: As research paradigms in feminist theory have become more complex and concerned with the varieties of oppression which intersect with one another, concepts of the subject and visions of agency underlying such research have become increasingly simplistic and empty from a normative standpoint. Feminist theory is in danger of losing the forest for the trees and of not being able to develop a voice vis-à-vis the difficult demands of conflicting identity claims.

Second, the politics of identity/difference that have dominated in the last decades have begun to show ugly developments. The clash among multiple identities as well as competing allegiances have come out in the public. The continuous and inevitable fragmentation of identities has made it almost impossible to develop a common vision of radical transformation. These developments in theory and in politics are linked. The theoretical paradigm shift from standpoint feminism to postmodernism is related to political trends in identity/difference politics, insofar as the articulation of certain forms of identity/difference politics was aided by, and in turn influenced, postmodernist critiques of standpoint feminism.

FROM STANDPOINT FEMINISM TO POSTMODERNIST FEMINISMS

I will use the term *standpoint feminism* to designate a type of feminist theory and research that shows the following presuppositions.[10] First is the claim that philosophical as well as social-scientific theories of the past have been cognitively inadequate because they have been "gender blind," that is, because they have failed to take into account the standpoint, the activities, and the experiences of women. Gender blindness, it is claimed, is not an accidental omission or oversight but affects the cognitive plausibility of theories. Second, to correct gender blindness, it is necessary to identify a set of experiences and activities, as well as patterns of thinking and feeling, which can be characterized as "female." Third, such experiences and activities result from women's social position or from their position within the sexual division of labor. Whereas the male of the species has been active in the public spheres of production, politics, war, and science, women's activities by and large and throughout history have been confined to the "domestic/reproductive" and "private" spheres. Fourth, the task of feminist theory is to make this sphere of activity and its consequences for human life at large visible, audible, and present at the level of theory. Feminist theory articulates the implicit, tacit, everyday, and nontheorized experiences and activities of women and allows these to come to the level of consciousness. Fifth, by aiding the articulation of female experience, feminist theory not only engages in a critique of science and theory but also contributes to the process of transforming women's consciousness by giving female activities and experiences public presence and legitimacy. Hence, a number of seminal works, mostly from the late 1970s, had the characteristic titles of *Becoming Visible: Women in European History; In a Different Voice;* and *Public Man, Private Woman.*[11]

To be sure, the paradigm shift to postmodernist feminisms that occurred by the middle of the 1980s was influenced by French thinkers such as Michel

Foucault, Jacques Derrida, Jean-François Lyotard, Luce Irigaray, and Helene Cixous. As the impact of their theories, no matter how diverse and at times contradictory it may have been, was felt upon the core of study of the humanities in the United States, feminist theorists also discovered an attractive ally in these positions for their concerns. What is unique about the American feminist reception of French postmodernist thought is that, rightly or wrongly, the interest in French theory coincided with a set of intense political and cultural struggles within the American women's movement. Linda Nicholson and Nancy Fraser have captured this well in their article "Social Criticism without Philosophy: An Encounter between Feminism and Post-modernism":

> The practice of feminist politics in the 1980s generated a new set of pressures which have worked against metanarratives. In recent years, poor and working-class women, women of color, and lesbians have finally won a wider hearing for their objections to feminist theories which fail to illuminate their lives and address their problems. They have exposed the earlier quasi-metanarratives, with their assumptions of universal female dependence and confinement to the domestic sphere, as false extrapolations from the experience of the white, middle-class, heterosexual women who dominated the beginnings of the second wave. . . . Thus, as the class, sexual, racial and ethnic awareness of the movement has altered, so has the preferred conception of theory. It has become clear that quasi-metanarratives hamper rather than promote sisterhood, since they elide differences among women and among the forms of sexism to which different women are differentially subject.[12]

Fraser and Nicholson have put their finger on some fundamental changes in the theoretical landscape of North American feminism, namely, the collusion of postmodernist sensibilities with the politics of identity/difference. But this collusion is neither obvious nor self-explanatory nor, as I shall argue below, always salutary.

Throughout the 1980s the theoretical message of the French "masters of suspicion" was echoed in the *political critique* voiced by lesbian women, women of color, and Third World women of the hegemony of white, Western European or North American, heterosexual women in the movement.[13] This political critique was accompanied by a *philosophical shift*, away from Marxist and psychoanalytic paradigms to Foucaultian types of discourse analysis and Derridean practices of textual deconstruction. In terms of *social research* models, there was a shift from analyses of women's position in the sexual division of labor and the world of work in general to analyses of identity-constitution and construction, collective self- and Other-representation, and issues of cultural contestation and hegemony.

No concept reveals the nature of this paradigm shift more explicitly than the one that is central to feminist theory, namely, *gender*. Competing theoretical attempts to define "gender" also indicate what has been gained and what has been lost in this theoretical sea change. Historian Joan Kelly Gadol provides a clear statement of the assumptions of early standpoint feminism in her article on "The Social Relations of the Sexes: Methodological Implications of Women's History": "In short, women have to be defined as women. We are the social opposite, not of a class, a caste, or of a majority, since we are a majority, but of a sex: men. We are a sex, and categorization by gender no longer implies a mothering role and subordination to men, except as a social role and relation recognized as such, as socially constructed and socially imposed."[14] Gadol makes a clear distinction between gender and sex; whereas sex is given ("We as a woman are the opposite sex of an equally non-problematic one, namely men"), according to her, gender is socially constructed and contested. Mothering, for example, would be among the socially constructed gender roles for most women, in most periods of history, and in the majority of known human societies.

Postmodernist and/or poststructuralist feminist theory challenges precisely this dichotomy between sex and gender, along with the logic of binary oppositions it creates. Judith Butler's *Gender Trouble* gives a trenchant critique of the epistemic assumptions underlying such previous forms of feminist theory: "Gender is not to culture as sex is to nature; gender is also the discursive/cultural means by which 'sexed nature' or a 'natural sex' is produced and established as 'prediscursive,' prior to culture, a politically neutral surface *on which* culture acts."[15] For Butler, the myth of the already sexed body is the epistemological equivalent of the myth of the given: Just as the "given" can only be identified via a discursive framework which first allows us to name it, so too is it the culturally available codes of gender that "sexualize" a body and that construct the directionality of that body's sexual desire. Writing from within the experiences of lesbian women in the women's movement, Butler's sharp critique of the distinction between sex and gender allows her to focus on how oppressive and debilitating compulsory heterosexual logic has been for some women and men.

The view that not only gender but also sexuality is socially constructed allows one to enter the terrain of political contestation around issues like sexuality and sexual identity which were hitherto considered to lie outside politics. If I may bring this shift in views and sensibilities to a formula: Whereas standpoint feminism was obsessed with the mother and mothering, poststructuralist feminism is obsessed with sexuality and the drag queen. With this shift, however, the theoretical as well as political problems of identity/difference politics gain salience.

DILEMMAS OF IDENTITY/DIFFERENCE
IN THEORY AND POLITICS

The principal consequence of viewing gender as well as sexuality as socially constructed is the fluidity this perspective introduces to categories of identity.[16] Identities, personal as well as collective, are seen as "social constructions" with no basis of givenness in nature, anatomy, or any other anthropological essence. Such social construction, most identity/difference theorists would add, is to be understood as a process of social, cultural, and political struggle for hegemony among social groups vying with one another for the imposition or dominance of certain identity definitions over others. For example, what does "we the people" mean in the celebrated opening of the Constitution? At the time it was written, it meant propertied, white, male citizens. The disenfranchised—women, the African-American slave population who were counted as three-fifths of a person by the Constitution, as well as the Native American Indians—are phantom-like presences lying outside the invocation of the collective "we." The identity of every "we" depends on a power structure; collectivities constitute themselves not only by excluding, but also by oppressing others, over and against whom they define themselves. In this sense, the identity of every "we" contains the results of collective struggles for power among groups, cultures, genders, and social classes. A "we," a collective subject, is formed by the sedimentation of such past struggles for hegemony.[17]

While the perspective opened by this thesis concerning the social construction of collective identities for social and historical studies is extremely fruitful and significant,[18] the difficulties of identity/difference politics, as well as of research paradigms favored by such politics, ultimately derive from what I would like to call "the fungibility of identity."[19] In the contemporary theoretical literature on identity, one term dominates: *construction*. Identities are "constructed" by the clash and conflict of groups, classes, and conflicts. Yet *construction*, sometimes also referred to as *constitution*, is a curious term to designate a process which is supposed to occur behind the back of subjects and without their willful participation and agency. In Foucaultian language, it is supposed to be knowledge/power matrices that "constitute" or "construct" us. Unlike the subject of traditional humanist discourse, in this model the subject does not exist as a locus of agency. According to Butler:

> The question of locating "agency" is usually associated with the viability of the "subject," where the "subject" is understood to have some stable existence prior to the cultural field that it negotiates. Or, if the subject is culturally constructed, it is nevertheless vested with an agency, usually figured as the capacity for reflexive mediation, that remains intact regardless of its cultural imbeddedness. On such a model, "culture" and "discourse" *mire* the subject, but do not constitute that subject.[20]

Against the view that the subject is merely "mired" by discourse, Butler defends the stronger position that the subject is "constituted by discourse although not determined by it." A great deal hides behind this distinction. Contemporary feminist theory is bordering on incoherence if it cannot clarify a consistent and intelligible view of agency and subjectivity.[21] Distinctions between *constitution* and *determination*, between *constituting* and *miring*, do not clarify what views of agency and subjectivity are possible within the framework of a radically constructivist theory. If these agents retain capacities for resistance, resignificiation, or for "subverting gender codes," in Butler's language, whence do these derive? What are the sources of spontaneity, creativity, and resistance in agents? In the transition from standpoint feminism to poststructuralist feminisms, we have lost the female subject. Like a script in search of an author, contemporary feminist theory has nearly effaced its own possibility.[22] *Either the thesis of the radical social construction of identities is too hyperbolic and hides more than it reveals, or another theory of subjectivity, one that can explain the sources of human creativity as well as victimization, agency as well as passivity, is necessary.*

The problematic status of the category of the subject is also evidenced in the way in which "race/gender/class" are strung together as determinants of identity. The question as to what understanding of the self one must presuppose to conceptualize the confluence of these identities is rarely, if ever, raised. Are these identities *additive?* Are they like *layers* of clothing that social actors can wear and remove? How are they experienced by a single individual who is herself a concrete totality uniting all of these into a single life-history? Categories of race, gender, and class are analytical distinctions at the level of theory; in social-historical-cultural research we have to show how they come together as aspects of identities of specific individuals. When we do such research, what kinds of models of life stories or narratives must we adopt?

Within the contemporary theoretical scene of fragmentation and multiplicity, the question of the unity of the self is hardly raised. This issue is not merely of theoretical interest, for very often these identities exist in conflict with one another. The normative demands of race, gender, and class upon the individual, as well as of other self-constitutive dimensions such as sexual preference, may be conflictual—in fact, irreconcilable. Unless feminist theory is able to develop a concept of normative agency robust enough to say something significant vis-à-vis such clashes, and which principles individuals should adopt to choose among them, it loses its theoretical bite and becomes a mindless empiricist celebration of all pluralities. The question of the subject is thus central to contemporary feminist theory and practice.

THE POLITICS OF IDENTITY/DIFFERENCE
WITHIN THE AMERICAN WELFARE STATE

To understand the specificity of "identity/difference" politics, which has characterized political struggles in the United States since the 1970s, it is important to note some of the peculiarities of the relationship of these movements to the welfare state.[23] The American welfare state, more so than its European counterparts, developed within a multinational, multiethnic, and racially divided polity. Throughout the early 1970s, the American polity was faced with the dual challenge of redistributing public goods such as health, education, welfare, housing, and transportation, on the one hand, and of carrying out a civil rights agenda for the elimination of discrimination based on race, gender, ethnic, religious, and linguistic identities, on the other. The most contested issues of the 1970s such as busing, school desegregation, public housing, and an end to discriminatory employment practices, combined issues of redistribution with the realization of the civil rights agenda.

While the new politics of "post-materialist values" (in the words of Roland Inglehart) was a phenomenon observed in most capitalist welfare-states, the coming together of struggles over material redistribution with civil rights issues was uniquely American.[24] The contemporary women's movement in the United States is an heir to this double legacy; in fact, it may be the only social movement in this country which has succeeded in uniting these agendas into a more-or-less coherent platform. North American women, perhaps more so than their counterparts in the rest of the world, used the legal, economic, and social means of struggle and channels of argumentation, created by the combination of redistributionist state policies and the civil rights agenda, to further their goals.[25]

From the struggle for "equal wages for equal work" to the struggle to end sexual harassment and discrimination in the work place, North American women employed both civil rights–type egalitarian arguments and welfare-statist redistributionist conceptions to further their cause.[26] In so doing, the contemporary women's movement entered the arena of politics as a "client" of the welfare state, demanding from the state and its agencies the fair and equitable distribution of certain public goods to women as a group. The logic of such demands and struggles inevitably positioned women against other groups, including African-Americans, Mexicans and other Spanish-speakers, gays, lesbian groups who pursue separatist political strategies and demands, Native Americans, the differently abled, and the elderly, all of whom raised similar demands for special compensation from the state, and very often fought for the same set of goods: jobs, educational opportunities, housing, and health care benefits.

The contemporary politics of identity/difference in the United States emerge out of this multiplicity of trends, movements, organizations, and issues. Perhaps no other incident captured the historical and political difficulties of this situation more than the Clarence Thomas–Anita Hill controversy. The controversy over Judge Thomas's confirmation to the United States Supreme Court pitted race against gender, black men against black women, white feminists against black community activists, in an endless multiplicity of identities and positionings. For the first time, the traumatic aspects of the endless multiplication of identities with their competing allegiances came to the fore. Reneging on their decade of struggle against discrimination in the workplace and sexual harassment, some feminist theorists, Catharine MacKinnon among them, rushed to the defense of race as a more central category of identity and seemed to take to heart Thomas's warning that here was the "lynching of a Black man" by the white media.[27]

Undoubtedly, this remains a complex, multifaceted, and difficult case in recent political memory. However, it was revealing of the incoherence and pitfalls of identity/difference politics.[28] For many women in the movement, it was not news that sexist and misogynistic practices were neither race- nor class-specific; yet faced with the possibility of being seen as opposing the appointment of a black judge to the Supreme Court, many feminists caved in. Instead of addressing the question raised by Anita Hill—that is, what kind of behavior constitutes sexual harassment in the workplace?—it was asked which was more important to her: being a successful black professional feminist? a black diva? or a "soul sister"? The Clarence Thomas–Anita Hill confrontation was a paradigmatic episode which highlighted the problematic fungibility of identity categories: which are you—a black woman professional feminist or a black sister?

It is this peculiar combination of redistributionism with identity/difference politics that colors the contemporary struggles over gays in the military, the recognition of same-sex marriages and homosexual households' domestic partnerships, and the inclusion of partners with AIDS in health insurance and other benefits. The agenda of the politics of identity/difference, welfare-state redistributionism, and the legacy of civil rights and affirmative action policies come together in contemporary political theory and practice in conflicting and difficult ways.[29]

Just as contemporary feminist theory proceeds from a view of the subject as a fungible construct shaped by the clash and conflict of competing identities, the contemporary politics of the redistributionist welfare state encourage competition among divergent groups, some of which share overlapping membership, for the same set of scarce resources. Just as the view of the subject in contemporary feminist theory borders on incoherence, so too does this model of welfare-state redistributionism, coupled with identity/difference politics, result in group particularisms, often with antagonistic consequences. In most major American cities, from New York to Los Angeles, urban blacks have been pitted against Hassidic Jews, or Koreans against blacks and Spanish-speaking residents, in seemingly endless fragmentation. The balkanization of urban America, which started some time ago, is continuing unimpeded. We desperately need a new politics of civility and solidarity, robust enough in its vision to unite those social forces torn apart now by fragmentation and factionalism. In this future task, some of the supposedly discredited and old-fashioned ideals of ethical and utopian feminism have a great role to play.

All participation in the public/political sphere presupposes that there are some common goods, some sense of shared vision, in the name of which we can act. Groups engaged in identity/difference politics are suspicious that behind appeals to commonality lurk the repression and the denial of "difference." But we have to ask: the "difference" of whom from whom, and in the name of what? Creative political action does not mean reciting the injustices and divisions of the past. Creative politics expands the field of political contestation as well as reactivates the principles and values in the name of which such contestation takes place.[30]

The debate around gays in the military is a case in point: despite the unhappy and confused compromise which the Clinton administration had to reach about this issue, what made the chiefs of staff begrudgingly accept this compromise was the logic and power of antidiscrimination claims within the public sphere of the American polity. The military, as one of the last bastions of a closed community of group solidarity, continuously sets up distinction between "them" and "us"; those who are like us and those who are different. Just as black GIs in World War II established the irrelevance of their race as a salient category for determining their suitability to serve in the military, thus challenging the logic of exclusion, so too a person's sexual lifestyle would have to be considered irrelevant to the public performance of his or her task. Now, this compromise is unstable precisely because it turns on distinctions such as those between "private sexual activity" and "public demeanor," which will be extremely difficult to sustain in certain contexts. The motto "Don't ask, don't tell," as applied to gay and lesbian soldiers, basically means, "Erase your identity, who you are, and I will tolerate being with you."

The really difficult political and moral step would be to move from the logic of redistributionism to the ethics of solidarity with those who are different. It is not sufficient to argue that gay people should not be discriminated against in the military, which itself is one of the largest redistributionist agencies in this society, providing opportunity, income, and advancement to certain social classes above others. The question ought to be the very definition of "us" versus "them." Why, in fact, is the military homophobic? Is there a link between a certain form of male sexuality and the virtues considered essential for being in the military? Must military discipline rest on a suppression of erotic behavior? Are eros and militarism incompatible? These are extremely difficult questions, which can only be discussed against the background of mutual respect and solidarity among beings whose fragile identities always need the sustenance and support of a civic polity.

This is my vision of social feminism. Furthering one's capacity for autonomous agency, I believe, is only possible against the background of a community of solidarity which sustains and nurtures one's autonomous identity through mutual recognition. As opposed to the postmodernist vision of the fragmentary subject, I proceed from the assumption that the human being is a fragile, needy, and dependent creature whose capacity to develop a coherent life story out of the competing claims upon its identity must be cherished and protected.[31] And in view of the language of eternal contestation, conflict, and haggling over scarce resources, I would like to recall that the primary virtue in politics is the creation of an "enlarged mentality." To quote Hannah Arendt:

> The power of judgment rests on a potential agreement with others, and the thinking process which is active in judging something is not, like the thought

process of pure reasoning, a dialogue between me and myself, but finds itself always and primarily, even if I am quite alone in making up my mind, in an anticipated communication with others with whom I know I must finally come to some agreement. And this enlarged way of thinking, which as judgment knows how to transcend its individual limitations, cannot function in strict isolation or solitude; it needs the presence of others "in whose place" it must think, whose perspective it must take into consideration, and without whom it never has the opportunity to operate at all.[32]

As we move into the global economic and political uncertainties of the twenty-first century, it will be essential to exercise such an enlarged mentality both in the domestic and the international arena. We must be ready to ask some fundamental questions: Is it clear that the group identity–based system of social and economic redistributionism that indexes racial, gender, and ethnic identity is preferable to a system that indexes income levels as the most relevant criteria for receiving certain kinds of social benefits? Would not a guaranteed annual income for the poor have saved many a welfare mother from the humiliating examination by state officials of her sexual practices and work habits? Could it be more plausible to treat city neighborhoods as fictive collective unities to which one distributes certain benefits, such as health, education, and housing, rather than singling out the various groupings themselves in the cities, thus inadvertently contributing to the antagonism and competition raging in so many of America's cities among these groups? Identity/difference politics, whether in its essentialist or constructivist versions, has not opened up the space for this kind of new questioning: Essentialism in feminist theory fails us by freezing women's identity in the role of the victim; the second paradigm fails by undermining the normative principles around which identity-transcending group solidarities and principles of distributive justice need to be formed. The time has come to move beyond identity politics, in the Hegelian sense of moving beyond—*Aufheben*—that is, by learning its lessons, rejecting its excesses, and moving to a new synthesis of collective solidarities with plurally constituted democratic identities.

NOTES

1. See Catharine A. MacKinnon et al.,"Feminist Discourse, Moral Values, and the Law: A Conversation," *Buffalo Law Review* 34, no. 1 (Winter 1985): 11–87. All page-number references in parentheses below are to this text.

2. Carol Gilligan, *In a Different Voice* (Cambridge: Harvard University Press, 1981).

3. MacKinnon et al., "Feminist Discourse," 74.

4. See Claudia Card, "Women's Voices and Ethical Ideals: Must We Mean What We Say?," *Ethics* 99, no. 1 (October 1988): 125-36.

5. MacKinnon et al., "Feminist Discourse," 74–75.

6. To characterize the different theoretical paradigms underlying Gilligan and MacKinnon's feminisms is more difficult than capturing the differences in their political approaches. At a certain level, MacKinnon's views of gender constitution bear affinity to poststructuralist views that regard gender as a socially and culturally constructed identity in the formation of which power plays a crucial role. MacKinnon claims that when we ask, "What is the gender question a question of?" there are two possible answers (22–23). The first is the approach that says that the gender question is a question of difference; the second is the approach that says that gender difference is a consequence of power and of political hierarchy. She summarizes: "The position that gender is first a political hierarchy of power is, in my opinion, a feminist position" (22).

Gilligan disagrees: "Trying to make gender fit the inequality model is the most traditional way to deal with gender, and it will not work. Gender is not exactly like social class. It is not simply a matter of dominance and subordination. There is no way to envision gender disappearing as one envisions, in utopian visions of society, class disappearing or race becoming a difference that makes no difference" (76). Gilligan does not say why she considers gender difference to be more intractable and basic than racial or class differentials; we can surmise, however, that under the influence of feminist psychoanalytic theory, a society without gender differentiation between the male and the female of the species is inconceivable for her. For MacKinnon, the construction of gender as difference, however, is a matter of power and hierarchy. Who is different from whom? Who defines what is the norm, and who the "normal" person is from whom all others are supposed to differ? While finding Gilligan's position on gender constitution too vague, I would also criticize MacKinnon's views for falling into the same trap regarding identity questions as do the postmodernist constructivists.

7. MacKinnon et al., "Feminist Discourse," 69.

8. For a recent collection that displays these aspects of the movement, see Marianne Hirsch and Evelyn Fox Keller, eds., *Conflicts in Feminism* (New York: Routledge, 1990).

9. See Ann Snitow, "A Gender Diary," in *Conflicts in Feminism*, 9-44.

10. The term, as far as I can tell, was introduced into feminist theory by Nancy Hartsock, who analyzed the possibility of building a feminist theory along the lines suggested by Georg Lukacs in his *History and Class Consciousness* for Marxist theory. See Hartsock, *Money, Sex, and Power: Toward a Feminist Historical Materialism* (New York: Longman, 1983).

11. Renate Bridenthal, Claudia Koonz, and Susan Stuard, eds., *Becoming Visible: Women in European History* (Boston: Houghton Mifflin, 1987); Carol Gilligan, *In a Different Voice*, op. cit.; Jean Bethke Elshtain, *Public Man, Private Woman* (Princeton: Princeton University Press, 1981).

12. Linda Nicholson and Nancy Fraser, "Social Criticism without Philosophy: An Encounter between Feminism and Postmodernism," in Linda Nicholson, ed., *Feminism and Postmodernism* (New York: Routledge, 1990), 33.

13. I thank Barbara Houston and Marilyn Frye for conversations which helped me see that there were also other women who were raising the same kinds of political objections within the women's movement but whose theoretical commitments lay very far from postmodernism. Nonetheless, the tendencies which I depict here also existed, although they may not have been as dominant as I thought at the time.

14. Joan Kelly Gadol, "The Social Relations of the Sexes: Methodological Implications of Women's History," in *Women, History, and Theory* (Chicago: University of Chicago Press, 1986), 6.

15. Judith Butler, *Gender Trouble* (New York: Routledge, 1990), 7.

16. Butler's conclusion to *Gender Trouble*, 142–49, spells out these issues provocatively.

17. For a further elaboration of the political and theoretical implications of questioning identity, see Seyla Benhabib, "Democracy and Difference: The Metapolitics of Lyotard and Derrida," *Journal of Political Philosophy* 2, no. 1 (January 1994): 1–23.

18. For some recent examples of the utilization of these insights in the context of postcolonial studies, cf. Gyan Prakash, "Postcolonial Criticism and Indian Historiography," *Social Text* 10, nos. 31 and 32 (1992): 8–18; Chandra Talpade Mohanty, "Feminist Encounters: Locating the Politics of Experience," in Michèlle Barret and Anne Phillips, eds., *Destabilizing Theory* (Cambridge, England: Polity Press, 1992), 74–92.

19. The *Oxford English Dictionary* (1982 compact edition) defines *fungible* as "taking the place" and "fulfilling the office of." Identity categories are in principle replaceable, substitutable through others.

20. Butler, *Gender Trouble*, 143.

21. In addition to my reflections on this issue in "Feminism and the Question of Postmodernism," see "Subjectivity, Historiography, and Politics: Reflections on the 'Feminism/Postmodernism' Exchange," both in Seyla Benhabib et al., *Feminist Contentions: A Philosophical Exchange* (New York: Routledge, 1995). I have continued to elaborate on these issues most recently in: "Sexual Difference and Collective Identities: The New Global Constellation," *Signs* 24, no. 2 (Winter 1999): 335–61.

22. Linda Alcoff drew attention to some of the difficulties of contemporary feminist theory with her early article, "Cultural Feminism versus Post-Structuralism: The Identity Crisis in Feminist Theory," *Signs* 13, no. 31 (Spring 1988): 405–36.

23. In *The Cultural Contradictions of Capitalism* (New York: Harper and Row, 1977), Daniel Bell already spoke of the "entitlement" revolution and the clash of competing groups as being an inevitable product of welfare-state capitalism. In presenting this development as if it were the consequence of false cultural and moral ideals, however, he neglected to address issues of distributive and compensatory justice which the welfare state also had to resolve when confronted with the claims of hitherto oppressed and socially disadvantaged groups. E. J. Dionne, Jr., in *Why Americans Hate Politics* (New York: Basic Books, 1991), discusses these issues as they affected the fate of the Democratic Party in the last twenty years.

24. See Mary Feinsod Katzenstein and Carol McClurg Mueller, *The Women's Movements in the United States and Western Europe: Consciousness, Political Opportunity, and Public Policy* (Philadelphia: University of Pennsylvania Press, 1987).

25. See Joyce Gelb, *Feminism and Politics: A Comparative Perspective* (Berkeley: University of California Press, 1989). I would like to thank Theda Skocpol for bringing to my attention the sources cited in this and the preceding note.

26. For a critical discussion of how some of these issues affect feminist theory and politics, see Nancy Fraser's "Women, Welfare, and the Politics of Need Interpretation" and "Struggle over Needs: Outline of a Socialist-Feminist Critical Theory of Late Capitalist Political Culture," in *Unruly Practices: Power, Discourse, and Gender in Contemporary Social Theory* (London: Polity Press, 1989).

27. See "Roundtable: Debating Thomas," in *Tikkun* 6, no. 5 (1991), 23–37.

28. For a trenchant analysis of some of the cultural and political "positionings" involved, see Nancy Fraser, "Sex, Lies, and the Public Sphere: Some Reflections on the Confirmation of Clarence Thomas," *Critical Inquiry* 18, no. 3 (Spring 1992): 595–612, and the collection edited by Toni Morrison, *Race-ing Justice, En-gendering Power* (New York: Pantheon Books, 1992).

29. More attention needs to be paid in feminist theory and practice to the way in which the welfare state, while not creating the identities of social groups, definitely encourages their formation along certain kinds of identity-related grievances, while precluding their development along other lines. A brief look at the United States's northern neighbor, Canada, for example, shows that Canadian governments have been more social democratic in the distribution of economic and social benefits; there, cultural identity issues and, in particular, linguistic identity occupy a more prominent position than other forms of identity politics. By contrast, initiatives to make Spanish the official second language of the United States, as placed before the Connecticut state legislature several years ago, were rapidly defeated and did not arouse particular support or even attention from social movement groups and activists except those directly concerned. But is linguistic identity any less fundamental to who one is than gender, race, or sexual orientation? Why are some identities publicly recognized and acknowledged as legitimate markers in being counted as a member of an oppressed group, or a "disadvantaged minority" in the official vocabulary of the welfare state? What is the role of the state in encouraging identity politics? In this process, what other options of social struggle and group solidarities are being precluded? I deal with these questions in my forthcoming book, *Democratic Equality, Cultural Diversity, and Deliberative Practices* (Princeton: Princeton University Press, 2001).

30. See Frank Michelman's concept of "jurisgenerative" politics in his "Law's Republic," *Yale Law Journal* 97, no. 8 (1988), 1493–1537.

31. See Seyla Benhabib, *Situating the Self-Gender Community and Postmodernism in Contemporary Ethics* (New York: Routledge, 1992).

32. Hannah Arendt, "The Crisis in Culture," in *Between Past and Future. Six Exercises in Political Thought* (New York: Routledge, 1992), 220–21.

3

Identity Politics: The Third Phase of Liberalism?

Alan Wolfe

It often seems as if there are as many liberalisms as there are liberals—more, if one takes into account the propensity of political thinkers to change their minds. Rather than a single doctrine, liberalism has changed as circumstances change. Whether or not any particular idea or political movement is liberal depends on which phase of liberalism one is discussing.[1]

The most significant transformation in liberal political theory and practice took place between 1870 and 1920, when "social" or "welfare" liberalism turned the assumptions and policies of classical liberalism upside down.[2] In Great Britain, an identification of liberalism with political economy and utilitarianism was modified by a Hegelian and ethical emphasis on organic unity, producing work such as that of T. H. Green.[3] The development of sociology played an important role in the new liberalism, both in Leonard Hobhouse's England and in the France of Émile Durkheim and Léon Duguit.[4] Pragmatism gave American liberalism its unique coloration, while "in all the history of liberal semantics, no episode was more important than this American shift in meaning" associated with the New Deal.[5] Although social democracy had its origins in socialism, it made its greatest contribution to liberalism, modifying laissez-faire to enable government to insure greater equality, even while liberalism possessed enough resources to make a significant contribution to social democracy.[6]

Because of the emergence of this "new" liberalism, the question of what it meant to be a liberal became contested terrain. Classical liberalism put its faith in the market, welfare liberalism in the state. The former's conception of liberty was negative, the latter's positive. For classical liberals, the private was elevated over the public, while for social liberals, public action could trump private prerogative. Preoccupied with property rights, classical liberals did not speak extensively about civil liberties; outside of more statist societies such as Sweden, welfare liberals would eventually become as protective of civil rights as they were skeptical of property rights. The classical liberal tradition believed in free trade and was suspicious of militarism; social or welfare liberalism was often sympathetic to protectionism and in favor of expenditures on national defense. Welfare liberals were attracted to executive power, while classical liberals, at least in America, looked more to courts. Although there is obvious exaggeration in this statement, classical liberals were liberals first and democrats secondarily, while welfare liberals are democrats first and liberals secondarily.

So great were the differences between classical and welfare liberals that, by some accounts, they could not be described by the same term. As a result, in America at least, classical liberals now call themselves conservatives or libertarians. But America is the exception. Elsewhere classical and welfare liberalism, despite their original differences, are understood to be part of the same pattern of thought. Both, in their time, were reformist. Both, highly rationalistic, were suspicious of revealed truth and noble lies. Both became economistic doctrines, each of which stressed that the possession of material goods helped realize the good life. Although they defined terms such as equality or efficiency differently, each was capable of appealing to equality or efficiency as its major advantage. There were enough similarities between classical and welfare liberalism that one seemed to evolve naturally into the other, which is why a transitional figure such as John Stuart Mill seemed to have his feet in both camps.

In the past decade, the two conditions that made it possible for welfare liberalism to flourish—an expanding welfare state and the persistence of high government expenditures on national security—began to disappear. One result was a pendulum swing back to classical liberalism in the form of Thatcherism and Reaganism. Although both reached their high point before the collapse of Communism, both failed to live up to their laissez-faire rhetoric, and the latter increased military expenditure. But it is also possible that post-Keynesian realities will produce a third phase of liberalism, which resembles neither classical nor social liberalism in its fundamental features.

This third phase could come about as a result of any number of current political developments. In this chapter, I want to focus on one of them: the challenges to liberal theory and practice posed by "identity politics"—defined here as claims by subaltern groups for special recognition as groups. Identity politics asks questions such as these: To achieve equality before the law, must we treat unequal groups unequally? Can we find a way to modify principles of liberal neutrality so as not to exclude those who do not accept the principle of liberal neutrality? Ought we to restrict the speech of those whose words offend people who belong to groups that have experienced discrimination? Should we deliberately create electoral rules designed to allow more effective representation of designated minority groups? Should we replace the notion that once-excluded groups have the right to be included with the notion that all rights are really questions of power?

Just as aspects of welfare liberalism had roots in a socialist tradition which was antithetical to liberalism, those who want to answer questions such as these in the positive often do not think of themselves as liberals.

From a feminist perspective, Catharine MacKinnon argues that "the liberal state coercively and authoritatively constitutes the social order in the interests of men as a gender—through its legitimating norms, forms, relation to society, and substantive policies."[7] In a similar manner, Charles Lawrence, writing in favor of legal restrictions on hate speech, comments that "most Blacks—unlike many white civil libertarians—do not have faith in free speech as the most important vehicle for liberation."[8] Liberalism, for most of those attempting to fashion the key principles of identity politics, is an enemy, not a friend.

It is not difficult to understand the hostility that identity politics demonstrates toward liberalism. While liberalism is a protean concept, it must have some core meaning, and for most liberals, this meaning has to do with the assertion of rights by individuals *against* groups. Because identity politics imagines individuals as constructed by the groups to which they belong—and because those groups tend to be defined by inescapable conditions such as race or gender—the emergence of identity politics appears to have more in common with feudal than modern understandings of the person. "Once gender is grasped as a means of social stratification," MacKinnon writes, "the status categories basic to medieval law, thought to have been superseded by liberal regimes in aspirational nonhierarchical constructs of abstract personhood, are revealed deeply unchanged."[9] Identity politics seems to be part and parcel of what Stephen Holmes calls "anti-liberalism"; indeed one of the writers he discusses, Roberto Unger, is sympathetic to various forms of identity politics.[10]

The issue, however, is more complicated than this picture presents. For one thing, as Will Kymlicka has pointed out, "new" liberals such as Hobhouse discussed group claims extensively; it is only since 1945, Kymlicka continues, that liberals such as John Rawls or Ronald Dworkin concentrated so relentlessly on individuals rather than on collectivities.[11] For another, the questions that are posed by identity politics involve equality, which is a classically liberal concern. Although some writers in the tradition of identity politics are suspicious of "bourgeois" rights, others note that feminism or minority concerns can be added to the historical trajectory provided by T. H. Marshall; the twenty-first century will involve the identity rights of women—and, by implication, other disadvantaged groups—just as the twentieth addressed the social rights of workers, the nineteenth the political rights of citizens, and the eighteenth the property rights of property owners.[12] Finally, new social movements flourish in liberal environments; they have made special inroads into universities, for example, symbolizing the symbiotic relationship between liberal institutions and forms of identity politics which can only succeed under conditions created by other liberal assumptions.

There may, in other words, be no inherent obstacles to a reconciliation between some of the major claims of identity politics and the liberal tradition, as some writers have suggested. Cass Sunstein has shown how feminist concerns with pornography and African-American disquiet with hate speech can be reconciled with liberal ideals of free speech if we develop a New Deal for the First Amendment in a fashion similar to New Deal reinterpretations of economic freedom.[13] Likewise Kymlicka tries to justify special rights for indigenous people on liberal grounds.[14] Although he "acknowledges the possibility of tragic conflict, the possibility that no conception of justice may prove adequate even in principle to eliminate the experience of imposition and injustice in social life," J. Donald Moon nonetheless thinks that political liberalism's "deep commitment to mutuality, and to respect for others" can be inclusive of some of the objectives of identity politics.[15] Efforts such as these raise the possibility that identity politics will ultimately accommodate itself to welfare liberalism just as welfare liberalism adjusted to classical liberalism.

In the short run, however, the prospects of such an accommodation seem dim. In this chapter I examine some of the writings of those urging that we pay more attention to group claims for special recognition. If we contrast what they say with both classical and welfare liberalism along the major schisms that divided liberals in the past, what emerges is a fairly sharp separation between identity politics and both classical and welfare liberalism. This does not mean that an eventual reconciliation between identity politics and liberalism is impossible. But it does mean that identity politics will have to resolve some of its contradictions, and resolve them against the inclinations of some of its more vocal advocates, before that will happen. (Whether or not such advocates want this to happen, of course, is another matter entirely.)

There are numerous ways in which identity politics can be distinguished from both earlier versions of liberalism (see table 3.1), but perhaps the most crucial involves the distinction between the public and the private. For classical liberals not only was the line between these spheres tightly drawn but also there was a preference for one over the other. Contract and property rights clothed private actions with the presumption of legitimacy. The public good could override private freedom in only the rarest of cases; as *Lochner v. New York* made clear, the health of workers was not one of them.

TABLE 3.1 Classical Liberalism, Welfare Liberalism, and Identity Politics Compared

	Classical Liberalism	*Welfare Liberalism*	*Identity Politics*
Privileged space	Private	Quasi-public	Fully public
Distinctions	Natural	Arbitrary	Determined
Locus	Market	State	Society
Theory of liberty	Negative	Positive	Anticipatory
Epistemology	Unknowable	Partially knowable	Knowable
Attitude toward the other	Repressive	Tolerant	Appreciative
Academic justification	Economics	Political science/ sociology	Psychology

The major objective of welfare liberals was to attack the sanctity of laissez-faire, a task in which their success was unquestioned. Yet for all the sympathy toward the public realm and the state associated with the rejection of laissez-faire, welfare liberals never completely repudiated the private sphere. Welfare liberalism stopped far short of socialism; opportunities for economic freedom expanded in some areas even as pure economic freedom contracted in others. But even more important, welfare liberals often expanded the private sector in matters of conscience and thought. The same Justice Louis Brandeis who wrote the brief that led the Supreme Court to modify *Lochner* in *Muller v. Oregon* also wrote the seminal article on the right to privacy which would eventually influence court decisions on contraception and abortion. At the very time that Brandeis argued in favor of government regulation of business, he was establishing limits on government restrictions over speech. The crucial boundary for welfare liberals was not the private versus the public but the economic versus the personal.

As was the case with welfare liberals, the relationship between identity politics and the public/private distinction is uncertain. In some areas associated with feminism or gay rights, the realm of privacy is crucial to the formation of identity. There are feminist writers who think that the Supreme Court was fundamentally on the right track in *Roe v. Wade*, even if they might be critical of one or another aspect of that decision.[16] At least one political theorist seeking to advance a society that would be more tolerant of homosexuality insists that privacy is crucial to such an agenda; H. L. Hirsch would resurrect some aspects of *Lochner* in pursuit of that objective.[17] For those in this tradition, the Court's decision in *Bowers v. Hardwick*—which, in upholding Georgia's sodomy laws, limited the expansion of the right to privacy that began with *Griswold v. Connecticut*—was a disaster.[18]

But this stress on the right to privacy may also turn out to be a minority view among those associated with identity politics. In both feminist and gay theorizing, privacy is generally viewed as a problematic realm to be transcended, not a sanctified realm to be protected. Some gay writers advocate "outing," the deliberate revealing of a person's sexual orientation against that person's wishes.[19] And the dominant trend in feminist theory is strongly critical of any dichotomy that associates the public world with men and the private world with women. In a representative formulation, Chantal Mouffe writes: "The distinction public/private, central as it was for the assertion of individual liberty, acted . . . as a powerful principle of exclusion. Through the identification between the private and the domestic, it played indeed an important role in the subordination of women."[20] Grounding a woman's right to abortion on the concept of privacy is dangerous business, for that concept, as MacKinnon puts it, "has shielded the place of battery, marital rape, and women's exploited domestic labor."[21] Because "men's realm of private freedom is women's realm of collective subordination," it follows that "for women there is no private, either normatively or empirically."[22]

In a similar manner, a suspicion of the private side of the public/private dichotomy informs many advocates of the interests of racial minorities. Such a dichotomy, Lawrence points out, "immunizes private discrimination from constitutional scrutiny."[23] We know, for example, that one of the most pervasive forms that discrimination takes in America is residential segregation.[24] That discrimination is the consequence of millions of private micro-decisions, each of them involving a personal choice on the part of (white) individuals about where they want to live. If we are to create a society in which race plays less of an arbitrary role in determining an individual's outcome in life, government may have to intervene into where people choose to live, as well as where they send their children to school.[25] The very concept of a home—which in *Griswold* defined the boundary of where the private begins—from this perspective can no longer be roped off from public scrutiny.

Even more symbolically expressive of the right to privacy than the home is the sanctity of the voting booth; in drawing the curtain, one closes oneself off into a private world to make choices that have public impact. But precisely because those micro-choices have macro-consequences, they, too, may have to be subject to greater public scrutiny. As Lani Guinier puts it, "the right to vote is a citizenship-status affirming right. But although the [1965 Voting Rights] act protects the right of the voter as an individual, the statute's political inclusiveness value also demands protection throughout the political process for the group to which the individual belongs."[26] If whites will not vote for black candidates, the dignity of blacks suffers such a blow that new voting rules will have to be created which will enable blacks to overcome this insult to their dignity. According to those identified with "critical race theory," private decisions that have deleterious consequences for blacks ought to be regulated by public action.

In the face of some efforts to protect privacy and other efforts to abolish it, is there any one-to-one relationship between identity politics and the public/private distinction? Perceiving what might be a possible contradiction, writers influenced by Foucaultian or postmodern tendencies graft onto the public/private distinction the concept of power. If a group has faced systematic discrimination and powerlessness, its members do have a right to privacy; if a group has been in power, its members do not. Mari Matsuda argues that because speech is understood to be private, civil libertarians ignore the harm hate speech can cause, which they would not do if government caused similar harm.[27] Does it therefore follow that the hateful, but private, speech uttered by members of minorities groups should also be subject to public regulation? Although Matsuda condemns such speech "both personally and politically," she would also "interpret an angry, hateful poem by a person from a historically subjugated group as a victim's struggle for self-identity in response to racism. It is not tied to the structural domination of another group."[28] Hence, "hateful attacks upon dominant group members by victims is permissible."[29] Similarly, Guinier finds a cause for public concern when whites vote privately for other whites, but not when blacks vote privately for other blacks. Just as welfare liberals were more interested in drawing a distinction between the economic and the personal rather than the public and the private, theorists of identity politics subsume the distinction between the private and the public into the distinction between the powerful and the powerless.

In all likelihood the effort to grant privacy to some but not others based on the amount of power they have will prove impossible to sustain. The problems of litigation and constitutional interpretation will be enormous if we presume to judge whether Jews have a right to free speech against Christians but not against blacks, whether Latinos have the right to vote as a block if they choose to vote Republican, or whether black churches can exclude homosexuals. For this reason, identity politics will have to decide whether its primary thrust will be critical or accepting of a fundamental right to privacy. No one can know which of these directions will eventually emerge as the dominant one, but at this moment in time, those who advocate identity politics are more concerned with the dangers of privacy than with the benefits.

One reason advocates of identity politics have a problem with the distinction between the private and the public is that they have a problem with distinctions in general. For classical liberals, distinction-drawing was relatively automatic; the market, because it is natural, drew boundaries around itself, and the task of the judiciary was to reinforce it. Law, like science, was devoted to finding what was already there. And what was there—people divided into classes, sexes, races, and regions—would surely remain there. The prepolitical world was a divided world; the intrusion of politics into what was otherwise "natural" would level distinctions in the name of a false universality.

Such a view was insufficiently modern for welfare liberals, whose objective was to use the state not to abolish distinctions but to make distinctions less arbitrary. Although abstractly committed to principles of universality, the world of welfare liberals contained more distinctions than the world of market liberalism. For one thing, welfare liberals tended to be more sympathetic than classical liberals to national differences; for another, welfare liberals made a very sharp distinction between those who worked, and who therefore contributed to the social product, and those who did not. The key point for welfare liberals was that distinctions required justification. Once subject to rules of justification, distinctions could no longer be regarded as natural or inevitable. Rather, they were functional, necessary for the workings of a society in which people did not share what Durkheim called the feature of "likeness."[30] Theodore Lowi's "interest group liberalism" was the defining feature of the new liberalism in practice.[31] The ideal world of a welfare liberal would be one in which boundaries between groups still existed, but the factors that determined those boundaries would have more to do with merit or occupation than with birth.

The trouble with this way of thinking, at least according to advocates of identity politics influenced by deconstruction and postmodernism, is that there is no such thing as a nonarbitrary distinction. Attempts to differentiate one thing from another are exercises in naming, not descriptions of an actual world. Even the most apparently natural distinctions—say, the one between men and women—are arbitrary. "The category of sex," Judith Butler writes, "imposes a duality and a uniformity on bodies in order to maintain reproductive sexuality as a compulsory order." Such distinctions are therefore "violent" and "forceful" because they establish "what will and will not signify, what will and will not be included within the intelligible."[32] We should, from this perspective, be wary of all distinctions. Visual languages are just as complex as spoken ones, if not—because of their ability to represent space—more so.[33] Schools and hospitals should not establish separate wards for the disabled or the dying.[34] Humans are no different from any other species.[35] The postmodern world is a polymorphous one in which boundaries, rather than distinguishing one thing from another, are playfully established here only to be ignored or mocked there.

The withering away of distinctions is an odd stance for a style of politics which, by its very definition, is an effort to give distinct groups distinct rights. As ideals about nondiscrimination and color blindness give way to affirmative action and concerns about the "dilution" of minority voting, distinction-making becomes an essential ingredient of real-world identity politics. Rather than universal ideals of citizenship, what we need, in Iris Marion Young's words, is "the articulation of special rights that attend to group disadvantage in order to undermine oppression and disadvantage."[36]

But if special rights are to be granted on the basis of disadvantage, and if these rights are valuable, one can expect a multiplication of identities, which means a multiplication of distinctions. Even with a relatively rigorous definition of oppression, Young singles out as eligible for special rights thirteen or fourteen groups, constituting, by my rough estimation, about three-quarters of the American population: "women, blacks, Native Americans, Chicanos, Puerto Ricans and other Spanish-speaking Americans, Asian Americans, gay men, lesbians, working-class people, poor people, old people, and mentally and physically disabled people."[37] And there are, no doubt, experts in these matters more qualified than I who will note the significant groups Young neglected to mention (transvestites, children, illegal aliens, the homeless, prisoners, and victims of childhood sexual abuse, to name a few; it is even possible, as Stephen Macedo argues, that conservative fundamentalist Christians can quality as an oppressed group by Young's criteria, justifying their demands for special rights in schooling).[38] If one wing of identity politics questions the idea of difference, the other has a vested interest in pointing out as many differences as imaginable. Determined to make an escape from it, we seem to be back in the world of interest group liberalism.[39]

Advocates of identity politics are often split by what Martha Minow has called "the dilemma of difference."[40] In order to gain a foothold in power, disadvantaged groups have to call attention to what makes them different, but their objective in wanting power is to abolish the differences they find invidious. One response to the dilemma is to claim that distinction-making is temporary. Reinforcing difference, from this point of view, is strategic, not principled. Indeed the principle is often asserted to be the exact opposite of the strategy. Bernard Grofman and Chandler Davidson insist that they are "committed integrationists," invoke Martin Luther King's words about a color-blind society, find race-conscious remedies "inherently undesirable," and express the hope that "one day race and ethnicity will not be important factors in electoral choices"—all the while justifying special voting rights for minorities. For, as they put it, "ours is still a race-conscious world in which there remains a need for race-conscious remedies."[41]

If distinction-making is what Grofman calls the "realistic politics of the second best,"[42] then, in the long run, advocates of special rights for minorities can return to the task of exposing differences as artificial. But there are at least two reasons to question whether the distinction-making that is at the heart of public policies such as affirmative action will ever disappear. One is that advocates of this point of view give no reason why it should disappear. Since it is white resistance that causes blacks to call attention to their race, only a sharp reduction in white racism can relax the pressure toward distinction-making. Yet writers in the tradition of critical race theory usually find no evidence of any progress in white attitudes toward blacks, despite increases in black voting, the growth of a black middle class, or the legal end to segregation.[43]

Second, there are differences in difference. Welfare liberals, as I argued above, accepted difference as a fact of modernity. Their insistence that difference required justification, however, assumed fluid boundaries between groups. The liberal ideal of freedom of association, Nancy Rosenblum has pointed out, "encourages both access to groups in which one has a 'voice' and the possibility of 'exit' from them."[44] Is there "exit" from the categories of race, gender, sexual preference, or physical disability? Some argue that there is; Young, for example, bases her concept of group status on self-identity, not definition by others. As we have seen, moreover, there are frequent efforts made to argue that sexual preference or ethnicity are socially constructed categories.[45] But if these claims are true, there is little reason to argue on behalf of special rights, for they could be then claimed by anyone who self-identified into the protected categories. Hence, whatever the theory, in practice identity politics insists that exit is not a valid option. This conclusion is illustrated by the experience of gays, who argue now that their sexual preference is not a "choice" but is determined biologically, an argument rejected by many gay activists just a decade ago, when, it was believed, biological determinism was viewed as a conservative idea.[46] The groups that are identified by identity politics are distinct from those identified by interest group liberalism because they are permanent groups.

Either way this issue is resolved, identity politics thinks about difference differently than welfare liberalism. If we abolish distinctions, the pluralistic bargaining that constitutes welfare liberalism will be transcended. But if, as is more likely, we need to reinforce distinctions, the brokering of welfare liberalism will intensify, since each group, being fixed, can only negotiate from its own standpoint. If anything, the distinction-making of identity politics resembles classical liberalism more than it does the welfare liberalism it replaced. For we are once again living with distinctions that are biologically determined, from which no escape is possible. Hierarchies of preference may be reversed, but hierarchies of preference still exist. In identity politics, the world has been turned upside down, but it is still a world recognizable to eighteenth-century eyes.

Accompanying the transformation from classical liberalism to welfare liberalism to identity politics has been a gradual expansion of the political. Each phase in this history involves an effort first to narrow, and then to expand, the line between what is considered political and what is not. For classical liberals the market was important precisely because it was not the state. Since market activity was the very definition of capitalism, the scope of the nonpolitical was large and the corresponding scope of the political small. Jurisprudence under the regime of classical liberalism usually involved ingenious ways of not finding politics where state legislators found it.

The attraction of the term *political economy* for welfare liberals was the assumption inherent in the term that economic activity was by its very nature political; in regulating business, the state was not intruding where it did not belong but simply recognizing that business was already involved in making authoritative decisions for society. It was not only business that the new liberals incorporated into the way they defined the political: Hobhouse's sociological approach involved the recognition that private associations sometimes exercised public powers and therefore could be subject to government regulation.[47] Interest group liberalism is defined by the proposition that "quasi" public authority can be exercised by powerful private groups.[48] By the time the welfare state reached its limit, the conception of what was political had been expanded considerably. Welfare liberalism was committed to the proposition that the market, or at least large parts of the market, *was* the state.

But if, for welfare liberals, the market was political, *society*—by which I mean the intimate world of family, community, and friendship—was not. Welfare liberals did not generally imagine that the family was a political unit. Concepts of civil liberty and privacy protected intimate relations from government intrusion. Even some associations, especially if they were local, small, and voluntary, could still be considered private, and it was widely believed that universities should not be politicized. In theory the realm of the nonpolitical might be small, but it still existed. (In practice, however, especially in countries such as Sweden with a history of state activism, the world of civil society could shrink.)[49]

At least in some of the forms in which it is expressed, identity politics has a difficult time imagining that *anything* can be nonpolitical. Just as Chicago School economists find markets everywhere, postmodern theorists find politics everywhere. New social movements, according to Ernesto Laclau and Chantal Mouffe, "begin to displace the line of demarcation between the public and the private and to politicize social relations," thereby exploding "the idea and the reality itself of a unique space of constitution for the political."[50] In a similar vein, MacKinnon writes: "The private sphere, which confines and separates women, is therefore a political sphere, a common ground of women's inequality. Rather than transcending the private as a predicate to politics, feminism politicizes it."[51] When "the personal is the political," a number of consequences follow that are relevant to whether identity will eventually become a third phase of liberalism.

One such consequence involves how much we can know and predict the world around us. Classical liberals celebrated the market because it embodied freedom, but, as Friedrich Hayek often pointed out, the realm of freedom does not require perfect knowledge.[52] The business of organizing a society is so vast, the imponderables so numerous, that the best defense against the pride of believing one can determine outcomes is to leave things alone. Ignorance, in short, can be rational; the fact that there are always things we do not and cannot know, which might seem a vice, is actually a virtue. One of the reasons that economics is the preferred way of knowing for classical liberals is the tendency of economists always to argue that what we think we know really is not true.

The new liberalism reacted strenuously against the notion of rational ignorance. The idea that we could not make men or society better was impossible to accept; it not only violated the ethical postulates of certain strains of evangelical Christianity but also was incompatible with the can-do spirit of an emerging social science. In the new liberalism that developed at the end of the nineteenth century, the state was both an ethical and a sociological agent. What Karl Mannheim called "the age of reconstruction" would be characterized by rational knowledge, not rational ignorance.[53]

Yet even though state intervention was predicated on the assumption that the social world was knowable, there would always be limits to how much could be known. Keynesianism sought to predict macro-outcomes, not micro-decisions. The need to accommodate the political interest groups spawned by the modern state tempered planning initiatives by making it impossible to ignore parochial and local concerns. Social science proved to be far less able to predict events than its early practitioners hoped. Although welfare liberalism therefore began with a firm belief that state action could make the world far more knowable, political realism eventually forced accommodation to principles of uncertainty.

Identity politics looks past both the market and the state to society, and in so doing, it extends the reach of what is, or ought to be, knowable. The market is preoccupied with the *results* of exchange and inquires not at all into the *motives* for exchange. Although the state would like to know more about motives, it usually is satisfied to know more about behavior: If we can achieve the objective of obedience to law, we need not be concerned with why people obey the law. But identity politics by its very nature is concerned with motive: Right outcomes are insufficient if produced by wrong reasons. People should not think like racists or homophobes, and, if they do, their motives ought to be open for examination by others.

Rather than accept unknowability, identity politics peers into the mind. Its corresponding social science is psychology, for, just as welfare liberals like Brandeis turned to social science as an ally in the writing of legal briefs, advocates of identity politics are convinced that there is hard evidence that pornography "makes normal men more closely resemble convicted rapists psychologically,"[54] that "psychologists and sociologists have done much to document the effects of racist messages on both victims and dominant-group members,"[55] or that even the achievement of economic and political success by members of racially disadvantaged groups "does not diminish the psychological harm caused by prejudice."[56] Despite frequent bows to postmodern epistemological skepticism, identity politics, at least in practice, is an unabashed advocate of social science positivism in the sense that it believes it can know what people are really thinking.

Because we can know, we can also act. Negative liberty and rational ignorance are linked: If the world is unknowable, we make fewer mistakes by not acting than by acting wrongly. Positive liberty, by contrast, involved what Isaiah Berlin called "liberation by reason."[57] "A just order," he writes critically, "must in principle be discoverable—an order of which the rules make possible correct solutions to all possible problems that could arise in it."[58] But because most conceptions of positive liberty did not imagine the politicization of civil society and an inquiry into motives, methods of discovery would eventually be directed toward secondary rather than primary causes. The quintessential example of this indirect link was the theory, advanced by sociologists, that delinquency was caused by blocked opportunities.[59] If we could open more opportunities, we could reduce crime. Whether the theory was true or false is not the point. The importance of the theory was that we need never inquire into criminal, or for that matter, normal, behavior. Manipulate the macro-levers of social structure, and micro-behaviors will fall into place.

Beyond negative and positive liberty lies what can only be called "proactive" liberty. Under earlier forms of liberalism, illegal behavior was accepted as inevitable, but public policy could moderate its severity by raising its cost. There were even occasions when illegality would be welcome, if the amounts paid by offenders back to society were high enough. Proactive liberty, by contrast is anticipatory; if I am going to rape you, then it makes far more sense to stop me before I do it than to punish me after I do it. Every social system requires that some people's liberty be curtailed so that others will have more. Because "victims are restricted in their personal freedom,"[60] the liberty of potential victims of hate crimes is dependent on restricting the liberty of those who are likely to commit them. What makes the regime of identity politics different is that such restrictions take place *before* the acts that justify placing restrictions on liberty take place.

Such anticipatory measures require a new way of thinking about how majorities should treat minorities. Classical liberals, to the degree that they concerned themselves with this issue, treated minority others with disdain or even outright intolerance; sympathy with laissez-faire in the economic realm coexisted with an active state in matters of cultural repression. Against this, welfare liberals promoted the notion that the state should be neutral with respect to conceptions of the good life. But tolerant neutrality, from the perspective of anticipatory liberty, can turn into repression by other means. If, for example, the state, in the name of tolerance, allows all forms of hate speech, black as well as white, its silence "is public action" since "the strength of the new racist groups derives from their offering legitimation and justification for otherwise socially unacceptable emotions of hate, fear, and aggression."[61]

What lies beyond tolerance? There seem to be two answers, neither of which seems easily compatible with liberal principles. "When individuals are unaware of their prejudice," Charles Lawrence writes, "neither reason nor moral persuasion will likely succeed."[62] To the degree that advocates of identity politics view racism as "culturally ingrained" and "unconscious,"[63] the only stage beyond tolerance would seem to be separate subcommunities— ones more equal in terms of power but not necessarily more understanding in terms of respect. Such a world is testimony to the breakdown of liberal pluralism, not its success.

In contrast, advocates for identity politics could become pedagogical optimists, convinced that we can point out the error of their ways to those who hate and change them in the process. But even under this more hopeful scenario, the potential for antiliberalism is still there if such advocates remain convinced that a person's opposition to a *political* position is in reality opposition to the racial or sexual identity of the person articulating that position.

In a recent book, political scientists Paul Sniderman and Thomas Piazza argue that it is the policies advanced in the name of minorities, and not the rights of minorities themselves, which most whites find problematic.[64] But this, according to some theorists of identity politics, is untenable; blacks, Lani Guinier argues, have a "default" position in favor of active government and income redistribution.[65] Districts designed to elect blacks are insufficient because they do not encourage black voters to "monitor" their representatives to ensure that they are faithful to that default position.[66] It is not the geographic proximity of blacks that defines their groupness. Nor is it even necessarily their race. Voting rules have to be designed not just to elect more blacks, but to elect more blacks committed to one particular approach to public policy. Guinier is agnostic on the question of human nature; her concern is not how to get whites to accept blacks, but how to enable blacks to represent themselves. Yet her attempt to conflate race with a specific policy program does seem to worsen the "scar of race" identified by Sniderman and Piazza.

It is a long way from a theory of rational ignorance which posits that we not try to set the world right to a theory of irrational ignorance which suggests or implies that those who do not like affirmative action as a remedy for past discrimination suffer from a lack of knowledge. There is no other area in which the assumptions of identity politics seem farther removed from earlier forms of liberalism than this one.

In trying to answer the question of whether identity politics is a challenge or a continuation of liberalism, it is insufficient to conclude that because liberalism is about individuals and identity politics is about groups, they are bound to be incompatible. The opposition between the individual and the group is absurd, given that individuals cannot exist apart from groups and that groups cannot exist without individuals. The more appropriate criteria are two: what kinds of groups? and what kinds of individuals?

In this chapter, I have suggested a number of principles that the groups identified by identity politics would have to possess in order for identity politics to constitute a third phase in the history of liberalism. By way of summary, let me just list some of the more important of them. First, such groups must allow exit. This does not mean that blacks can become white or whites black. Nor is it meant to answer the question of whether homosexuality is biologically determined. It is rather to suggest that race, gender, or sexual orientation have to be viewed as important *but not essential* categories in determining one's political identity. Second, group membership cannot be used to override common standards of citizenship that apply to everyone who is defined as having formal legal equality. If informal legal inequalities persist in spite of formal rules, the objective must be to bring the exceptions within the rules, not to change the rules to accommodate group demands. Third, group membership states a sociological, not a psychological, truth. Groupness means that a number of people have defined themselves, or have been defined by others, as sharing common characteristics. Aspects of mind can be shaped by group membership; it is not surprising, except perhaps to psychologists, that psychology has a cultural component.[67] But while groups influence how people think, they do not determine how people think. People can be black—or female or gay—and still have different patterns of moral development, cognitive style, clinical disposition, or memories.

We also need to pay attention to how we conceptualize individuals if liberalism and identity politics are ever to be reconciled. First, individuals must be understood as plastic in nature, able to change as the circumstances they face change. An individual is not inherently racist because he is white (or, for that matter, because he is black). Second, individuals whose political views run counter to the "default" positions of the groups to which they belong ought to be appreciated, for, in defying the categories we tend to impose on people, they enliven the meaning of pluralism. Third, if individuals are to change, they ought to change through a process of self-reflection. This can certainly come about because others try to persuade them that they are insufficiently appreciative of the pain of people different from themselves. But such recognition cannot be coercively obtained, even if the form of coercion is group pressure. In trying to live together, we should appeal, as much as possible, to each other's minds, not to each other's feelings.

As a result of the rise of identity politics, liberalism will never again be the same. Universal utilitarianism and public neutrality have not been the most attractive aspects of liberal theory. While the dangers of irrational nationalism are as apparent to liberals now as they were in the early nineteenth century, there is also much that is positive about the rediscovery of culture and identity. In the rhetorical form it often takes, identity politics positions itself as antiliberal in tone and consequence. From a longer term perspective, however, it may turn out to be less critical of welfare liberalism than welfare liberalism was of classical liberalism. The final chapter in the story I have been discussing here will obviously not be written for some time to come.

NOTES

1. Richard Bellamy, *Liberalism and Modern Society: A Historical Argument* (University Park: Pennsylvania State University Press, 1992); John A. Hall, *Liberalism: Politics, Ideology, and the Market* (Chapel Hill: University of North Carolina Press, 1988).

2. This story has been told many times. See, for example, Michael Freeden, *The New Liberalism: An Ideology of Social Reform* (Oxford: Clarendon, 1978). A recent exemplary account is J. G. Merquior, *Liberalism Old and New* (Boston: Twayne, 1991).

3. Melvin Richter, *The Politics of Conscience: T. H. Green and His Age* (London: Weidenfeld and Nicolson, 1964).

4. Stephen Collini, *Liberalism and Sociology: L. T. Hobhouse and Political Argument in England, 1880–1912* (Cambridge: Cambridge University Press, 1979); Stephen Seidman, *Liberalism and the Origins of European Social Theory* (Berkeley: University of California Press, 1983).

5. Merquior, *Liberalism Old and New*, 5.

6. James Kloppenberg, *Uncertain Victory: Social Democracy and Progressivism in European and American Thought, 1870–1920* (New York: Oxford University Press, 1986).

7. Catharine A. MacKinnon, *Toward a Feminist Theory of the State* (Cambridge: Harvard University Press, 1989), 162.

8. Charles R. Lawrence III, "If He Hollers Let Him Go: Regulating Racist Speech on Campus," in Mari J. Matsuda et al., eds., *Words That Wound: Critical Race Theory, Assaultive Speech, and the First Amendment* (Boulder, Colo.: Westview, 1993), 76.

9. MacKinnon, *Feminist Theory of the State*, 163.

10. Stephen Holmes, *The Anatomy of Antiliberalism* (Cambridge: Harvard University Press, 1993), 141–75.

11. Will Kymlicka, *Liberalism, Community, and Culture* (Oxford: Clarendon Press, 1991), 206–10.

12. Helga Maria Herness, *Welfare State and Women Power: Essays in State Feminism* (Oslo: Norwegian University Press, 1987). I am indebted to Jytte Klausen's "T. H. Marshall in the Hands of Social Reformers," *World Politics* 42, no. 2 (January 1995): 244–67.

13. Cass R. Sunstein, *Democracy and the Problem of Free Speech* (New York: Free Press, 1993). For a spirited rejoinder, not to Sunstein per se but to what he is trying to do, see Jonathan Rausch, *Deadly Inquisitors* (Chicago: University of Chicago Press, 1993).

14. Kymlicka, *Liberalism, Community, and Culture*, 182–205.

15. J. Donald Moon, *Constructing Community: Moral Pluralism and Tragic Conflicts* (Princeton: Princeton University Press, 1993), 220.

16. Jean L. Cohen, "Rethinking Privacy: Autonomy, Identity, and the Abortion Controversy," in Jeff Weintraub and Krishan Kumar, eds., *Public and Private in Theory and Practice* (Chicago: University of Chicago Press, 1997), 133–65.

17. H. L. Hirsch, *A Theory of Liberty: The Constitution and Minorities* (New York: Routledge, 1992), 72–76.

18. Hirsch, *A Theory of Liberty*, 134–46.

19. Larry Gross, ed., *Contested Closet: The Politics and Ethics of Outing* (Minneapolis: University of Minnesota Press, 1993); Richard D. Mohr, *Gay Ideas: Outing and Other Controversies* (Boston: Beacon, 1992); Michelangelo Signorile, *Queer in America: Sex, the Media, and the Closets of Power* (New York: Random House, 1993).

20. Chantal Mouffe, "Feminism, Citizenship, and Radical Democratic Politics," in Judith Butler and Joan W. Scott, eds., *Feminists Theorize the Political* (New York: Routledge, 1992), 377.

21. MacKinnon, *Feminist Theory of the State*, 193.

22. MacKinnon, *Feminist Theory of the State*, 168, 191.

23. Lawrence, "If He Hollers," 63.

24. Douglas A. Massey and Nancy Denton, *American Apartheid* (Cambridge: Harvard University Press, 1992).

25. Lawrence, "If He Hollers," 63.

26. Lani Guinier, "No Two Seats: The Elusive Quest for Political Equality," *Virginia Law Review* 77 (November 1991): 1430.

27. Mari Matsuda, "Public Responses to Racist Speech: Considering the Victim's Story," in Matsuda et al., *Words That Wound*, 49.

28. Matsuda, "Racist Speech," 39.

29. Matsuda, "Racist Speech," 36.

30. Émile Durkheim, *The Division of Labor in Society*, trans. George Simpson (New York: Free Press, 1964), 70–110.

31. Theodore Lowi, *The End of Liberalism: Ideology, Policy, and the Crisis of Public Authority* (New York: Norton, 1969).

32. Judith Butler, "Contingent Foundations," in Butler and Scott, *Feminists Theorize the Political*, 17–18.

33. Harlan Lane, *The Mask of Benevolence: Disabling the Deaf Community* (New York: Knopf, 1992), 122–23.

34. Martha Minow, *Making All the Difference: Inclusion, Exclusion, and American Law* (Ithaca, N.Y.: Cornell University Press, 1990), 26–31.

35. Donna Haraway, *Primate Visions: Gender, Race, and Nature in the World of Modern Science* (New York: Routledge, 1989).

36. Iris Marion Young, "Polity and Group Difference: A Critique of the Ideal of Universal Citizenship," *Ethics* 99 (January 1989): 251.

37. Young, "Polity and Group Difference," 261.

38. Stephen Macedo, "Liberal Civic Education and Religious Fundamentalism: The Case of *God v. John Rawls*," *Ethics* 105 (April 1995).

39. This is Mouffe's critique of Young. See Mouffe, "Feminism, Citizenship, and Politics," 380.

40. Minow, *Making All the Difference*, 19-48.

41. Bernard Grofman and Chandler Davidson, "Postscript: What Is the Best Route to a Color-Blind Society?" in Bernard Grofman and Chandler Davidson, eds., *Controversies in Minority Voting: The Voting Rights Act in Perspective* (Washington: Brookings Institution, 1992), 300–17.

42. Grofman and Davidson, "Color-Blind Society," 316.

43. Derrick Bell, *Faces at the Bottom of the Well: The Permanence of Racism* (New York: Basic Books, 1992).

44. Nancy Rosenblum, *Another Liberalism: Romanticism and the Reconstruction of Liberal Thought* (Cambridge: Harvard University Press, 1987), 60.

45. For examples, see David Greenberg, *The Construction of Homosexuality* (Chicago: University of Chicago Press, 1988); Mary Waters, *Ethnic Questions: Choosing Identities in America* (Berkeley: University of California Press, 1990); and Celia Kitzinger, *The Social Construction of Lesbianism* (Newbury Park, Calif.: Sage, 1987).

46. See Mohr, *Gay Ideas*, 221–42, for a critique of constructionist theories of homosexuality. Mohr does not take a position on the biological origins of homosexuality.

47. Rosenblum, *Another Liberalism*, 64.

48. Grant McConnell, *Private Power and American Democracy* (New York: Knopf, 1966).

49. I make this point in Alan Wolfe, *Whose Keeper?: Social Science and Moral Obligation* (Berkeley: University of California Press, 1989).

50. Ernesto Laclau and Chantal Mouffe, *Hegemony and Socialist Strategy: Towards a Radical Democratic Politics* (London: Verso, 1985), 81.

51. MacKinnon, *Feminist Theory of the State*, 192.

52. Friedrich A. Hayek, *The Political Order of a Free People*, volume 3 of *Law, Legislation, and Liberty* (Chicago: University of Chicago Press, 1979), 65–70.

53. Karl Mannheim, *Man and Society in an Age of Reconstruction: Studies in Modern Social Structure* (Glencoe, Ill.: Free Press, 1940).

54. MacKinnon, *Feminist Theory of the State*, 304.

55. Matsuda, "Racist Speech," 26.

56. Richard Delgado, "Words That Wound: A Tort Action for Racial Insults, Epithets, and Name Calling," in Matsuda et al., *Words That Wound*, 91.

57. Isaiah Berlin, "Two Concepts of Liberty," in Isaiah Berlin, *Four Essays on Liberty* (Oxford: Oxford University Press, 1969), 144.

58. Berlin, "Two Concepts of Liberty," 145–46.

59. Robert K. Merton, "Social Structure and Anomie," *American Sociological Review* 3 (1938): 672–82; Richard A. Cloward and Lloyd Ohlin, *Delinquency and Opportunity: A Theory of Delinquent Gangs* (Glencoe, Ill.: Free Press, 1960).

60. Matsuda, "Racist Speech," 24.

61. Matsuda, "Racist Speech," 49.

62. Lawrence, "If He Hollers," 78.

63. Matsuda et al., *Words That Wound*, 14.

64. Paul M. Sniderman and Thomas Piazza, *The Scar of Race* (Cambridge: Harvard University Press, 1993).

65. Guinier, "No Two Seats," 1470.

66. Guinier, "No Two Seats," 1456.

67. Richard Shweder, *Thinking through Cultures: Explorations in Cultural Psychology* (Cambridge: Harvard University Press, 1991).

4

The Two World Wars and the Idea of the State

Alan Brinkley

In the spring of 1917, as the United States prepared finally to enter World War I, Walter Lippmann published an article in which he expressed something of the excitement that many Americans felt when they thought about what joining the conflict might do for the nation. "I do not wish to underestimate the forces of reaction in our country," he wrote. But, he added:

> We shall know how to deal with them. Forces have been let loose which they can no longer control, and out of this immense horror ideas have arisen to possess men's souls. There are times . . . when new sources of energy are tapped, when the impossible becomes possible, when events outrun our calculations. This may be such a time. . . . We can dare to hope for things we never dared to hope for in the past.[1]

Like other liberals, Lippmann hoped for many things from the war: a new international order, or as he put it "a Federation of the World"; moral regeneration at home; and (committed pragmatist that he was) an assault on old orthodoxies and outmoded institutions. But Lippmann had another hope for the war as well, a hope he had first expressed a few years earlier in his precocious second book, *Drift and Mastery*, published when he was only twenty-five: a hope for a new kind of political economy.

The characteristic ailment of modern, industrial society, Lippmann believed, both in individual lives and in the public world, was "drift," the tendency to move aimlessly through life buffeted about by great, impersonal forces. "We drift into our work," he wrote. "We fall in love, and our lives seem like the intermittent flicker of an obstinate lamp. . . . Men go to war not knowing why, hurl themselves at cannon as if they were bags of flour, seek impossible goals, submit to senseless wrongs, for mankind lives today only in the intervals of a fitful sleep. There is indeed a dreaming quality in life."[2]

But there was, he argued, no need for society to drift. The scale of modern life had grown enormously, it was true, and it was now much more difficult for individuals, or nations, to control their fates. But the scale of human thought had grown enormously too. And so it *was* possible for society to seize control of its destiny, to master the great forces that industrialization had unleashed, if only it had the will to do so. "That is what mastery means," he wrote: "the substitution of conscious intention for unconscious striving. Civilization, it seems to me, is just this constant effort to introduce plan where there has been clash, and purpose into the jungles of disordered growth."[3]

In most respects, the American experience in World War I did very little to reinforce the liberal hopes Lippmann and others had expressed. The dream of a new international order foundered at Versailles and in the bitter political battles at home; the expectations of moral regeneration fell victim to the nativist and antiradical hysteria that gripped the nation both during and after the war; the hopes for a challenge to old orthodoxies collided with a growing popular conservatism, which culminated in the election in 1920 of Warren G. Harding. But there was one respect in which the war *did* reinforce liberal hopes: It produced a brief experiment in state management of the economy that many progressives, and many others, came to consider a model for the future. Harmony and order, they believed, had, even if briefly, replaced the conflict and disorder of modern industrial life; government, capital, and labor had learned to cooperate with one another on behalf of a great national mission. The war provided an example of what an enlightened state could do to introduce Lippmann's "plan" and "purpose."[4]

The end of the war brought a chorus of tributes, from many sources, to the success of the mobilization effort and to the lessons that could be learned from it. Bernard Baruch, who had served as chairman of the War Industries Board, the chief agency of economic management, argued that "the experience of the War Industries Board points to the desirability of investing some Government agency . . . with constructive as well as inquisitorial powers—an agency whose duty it should be to encourage, under strict Government supervision, such cooperation and coordination in industry as should tend to increase production, eliminate waste, conserve natural resources, improve the quality of products, promote efficiency in operation, and thus reduce costs to the ultimate consumer."[5] The national Chamber of Commerce proclaimed: "War is the stern teacher that is driving home the lessons of cooperative effort." And former secretary of war Elihu Root predicted: "There will be no withdrawal from these experiments. We shall go on; we shall expand them."[6]

Grosvenor B. Clarkson, who had directed the Council of National Defense during the war and had developed a great admiration for Baruch and his works in the process, incorporated such "lessons" into a massive semiofficial history of war mobilization published in 1923:

> If we had a Government business manager with a free hand to run the business
> side of Government, as free as Baruch had in the War Industries Board, we

should have a successful Government of business. . . . It is little wonder that the men who dealt with the industries of a nation, binned and labeled, replenished and drawn on at will for the purposes of war, and its train of consequences, meditated with a sort of intellectual contempt on the huge hit-and-miss confusion of peace-time industry, with its perpetual cycle of surfeit and dearth and its eternal attempt at adjustment after the event. From their meditations arose dreams of an ordered economic world.[7]

The war, in other words, had shown Americans what they could do if they had the will to do it. It had proved that it was, indeed, possible to create order in the economy, to make it harmonious and efficient, to achieve mastery. And for more than a generation, the war remained an inspiration to those progressives who hoped to achieve in peacetime what they liked to think they had achieved in war: "an ordered economic world." The war helped inspire efforts throughout the 1920s to harmonize the business world through the creation of associational arrangements. It supported even larger visions of a "planned economy," in which the government would play a much more intrusive role. It served as a model in 1933 for the creation of the New Deal's National Recovery Administration (NRA). And for some, it continued throughout the 1930s, even after the failure and collapse of the NRA, to drive hopes for an economic system in which business, government, and labor would build a working partnership on behalf of the common good.[8]

The outbreak of World War II in 1939, and the American entry into the war two years later, seemed at first to encourage some of the same hopes that World War I had inspired twenty years before—including the hopes for a new political economy. "We have learned," the New Deal administrator, Clifford Durr, wrote in 1943, "that we cannot obtain the production we need for waging the war as an undirected by-product of what we commonly refer to as 'sound business principles.' Neither can we expect such by-product to furnish us after the war with the standard of living which we shall be warranted in expecting. . . . There must be some over-all source of direction more concerned with [these] objectives than with the profits or losses of individual business concerns."[9] Or as Herbert Emmerich, another New Deal official, wrote in 1941: "With a farewell to normalcy and an appreciation of the greater opportunities that the war crisis presents, public administrators today have an opportunity to enhance and permanently to establish the prestige of their calling in the United States."[10] The rhetoric was more muted perhaps, but the hopes seemed much the same: The war would legitimize an expanded state role in economic life and would show the way to new, more cooperative and harmonious economic arrangements; it would help produce "an ordered economic world."

But the end of the Second World War, unlike the end of the First, brought very few public tributes—from liberals or from anyone else—to the achievements of wartime economic mobilization in bringing order and harmony to the economy. There was, to be sure, substantial satisfaction with the way the economy had performed: with the "miracles" of production that had over-whelmed the Germans and the Japanese and with the new prosperity that had finally ended the Great Depression. But little of the credit for those achievements redounded to the government, to the mobilization agencies, or to the concept of a new, harmonious economic order. Baruch had emerged from World War I a national hero, a symbol of the nation's hopes for a new political economy; he remained even forty years later a celebrated sage and adviser to presidents. Donald Nelson, Baruch's World War II counterpart, emerged from that war discredited and largely forgotten. Nelson spent his last years serving as a public relations flak for a minor Hollywood trade association and pursuing obscure and unsuccessful business schemes. When he published his memoirs in 1946, many reviewers took the occasion to compare him unfavorably to Baruch.[11]

All this raises an obvious question. Why did these two experiences, in many ways very similar, produce such different political legacies? Why did World War I come to serve as a model to many progressives and liberals of what an enlightened state could do to bring order and harmony to American economic life, while World War II did not?

There were, of course, differences between the two experiments in mobilization, and they account for some of the differences between their legacies. The biggest and most obvious difference was that the United States spent only about two years mobilizing for World War I (and only a little over a year fighting in it), while the World War II mobilization spanned more than five years (and the fighting nearly four). There was much more time during World War II for the problems and shortcomings of the mobilization effort to become evident, more time for things to go wrong, more time for grievances to accumulate. There were other differences as well: differences in the way power was delegated among the war agencies, differences in the quality of leadership, and differences in the size and complexity of the economies the war agencies set out to manage.

But in most respects, the way the federal government mobilized and managed the economy during the two world wars was strikingly similar. Both Woodrow Wilson and Franklin Roosevelt looked beyond the existing federal bureaucracies and created special new agencies to handle the task of war mobilization. (This was not entirely a matter of choice: Neither in 1917 nor in 1941—despite the New Deal—did the federal government possess anything approaching sufficient institutional capacity to manage a wartime economy from within the existing bureaucracy.)

In both wars, these new agencies staffed themselves almost entirely from the private sector, relying largely on businessmen and financiers (many of them drawn directly from the industries they were then called upon to regulate, and many still officially in the employ of their prewar firms and paid only a token sum by the government—hence the term, common in both wars, "dollar-a-year men"). At the same time, in both 1917 and 1942 there were efforts to balance the presence of businessmen in the war agencies with representation from other groups, especially labor: efforts to create a tripartite partnership of business, labor, and government capable of cooperating to increase production and promote the common good.

In both wars, the government stumbled through a period of unsuccessful experimentation with various decentralized or divided administrative structures before settling in the end on (to use a phrase popular in 1941, when critics were clamoring for change) "a single responsible agency with a single responsible head": the War Industries Board, which Wilson created in 1918, headed by Baruch; the War Production Board, which Roosevelt created in 1942, headed by Nelson.

And in both wars, the war agencies, in the end, did on the whole what they were supposed to do. They oversaw impressive feats of production, which tipped the military balance decisively in favor of the United States and its allies, and they avoided major disruptions of civilian life at the same time. If anything, the War Production Board performed rather more impressively than the War Industries Board, if only because World War II was so much larger and (for the United States) so much longer than World War I and hence demanded far greater productive achievements.[12]

The two war mobilization efforts experienced similar failures as well. In neither war did labor ever achieve anything like equal standing in the supposed partnership the government was attempting to create. In neither war did business very often subordinate its own interests to a larger public good, as in theory the wartime arrangements required. Complaints about war profiteering were rampant in 1918, and for decades thereafter, just as complaints about corporate greed were rampant in World War II. Some progressives criticized the War Industries Board in 1918 for creating too many millionaires and for discriminating against small business. Twenty-five years later, liberals were criticizing the War Production Board, and the mobilization effort in general, for the same things: for failing to protect small business and for giving too much power to conservative corporate figures more interested in their own profits than in the interests of the nation. I. F. Stone wrote caustically of the War Production Board in 1942, in a statement typical of liberal complaints: "The arsenal of democracy . . . is still being operated with one eye on the war and the other on the convenience of big business. . . . The men running the program are not willing to fight business interests on behalf of good will and good intentions."[13]

But despite the substantial similarities in both their achievements and failures, even though a strong case could be made that the mobilization experiments of World War II were considerably more successful than those of World War I, the two experiences came to have very different retrospective images. World War I became an inspiration. World War II did not; indeed, to many liberals, it became a warning of what efforts by the government to coordinate the economy could become: a mechanism by which members of the corporate world could take over (or "capture") the regulatory process and turn it to their own advantage.

What explains that change is less the differences between the ways the United States mobilized for the two wars than the contexts in which those mobilizations occurred—the assumptions and expectations Americans brought to the two experiences. The context changed in many ways between 1918 and 1941. But three changes are particularly useful to an understanding of why Americans in 1945 thought so differently about the state, and its role in economic life, from the way they had a generation before.

One of those changes involved the way Americans viewed the two world wars themselves, the way they explained what the nation was fighting for—and, perhaps more important, against. World War I was, in the American imagination, essentially a war against German culture, which in the hysterical anti-German atmosphere of 1917 and 1918 seemed savage, barbaric, and innately belligerent—a culture (as the California Board of Education noted in banning the teaching of the German language in public schools) steeped in "the ideals of autocracy, brutality, and hatred." Wartime propaganda was filled with personifications of the enemy as the "Prussian cur" and "the German beast," a hostility to the German people and their society that quickly spilled over into a hostility toward German-Americans as well. G. Stanley Hall, the eminent American psychologist (and the man who had first brought Sigmund Freud to America), expressed a widespread assumption when he said in 1917: "There is something fundamentally wrong with the Teutonic soul."[14]

World War II evoked a different image: less of a barbaric people than of a tyrannical regime; less of a flawed culture than of a flawed political system and a menacing state. Wartime propaganda in World War II did not personify the European enemy, at least, as an evil people (although the same cannot be said, of course, about the Japanese). It focused instead on the German and Italian states.[15]

The war, in short, pushed a fear of totalitarianism (and hence a generalized wariness about excessive state power) to the center of American political thought. In particular, it forced a reassessment of the kinds of associational and corporatist arrangements that many had found so attractive in the aftermath of World War I. Those, after all, were the kinds of arrangements Germany and Italy had claimed to be creating. "The rise of totalitarianism," Reinhold Niebuhr noted somberly in 1945, "has prompted the democratic world to view all collectivist answers to our social problems with increased apprehension." Virtually all experiments in state supervision of private institutions, he warned, contained "some peril of compounding economic and political power." Hence "a wise community will walk warily and test the effect of each new adventure before further adventures."[16]

To others, the lesson was even starker. *Any* steps in the direction of state control of economic institutions were (to use the title of Friedrich A. Hayek's celebrated anti-statist book of 1944) steps along "the road to serfdom."[17] One of those who had by then come to share that fear was Lippmann, whose earlier dreams of an enlightened government creating "mastery" over great social forces had been replaced by a fearful opposition to the growing power of the state. Lippmann spent the war years denouncing the New Deal and corresponding with Hayek, discussing ways to mobilize what he and Hayek called the "real" liberals around the world to rescue liberalism, the liberalism of individual freedom and economic liberty, from its statist traducers.[18]

But Americans in the 1940s did not have to look to Europe for examples of state efforts to solve economic problems. They could look to their own experiences of the preceding two decades. And that, of course, suggests a second important difference between the two world wars. Americans in World War I had very few previous efforts at state management of the economy against which to measure their wartime experiments. Americans in World War II had the New Deal.

We are accustomed to thinking of the New Deal as a phenomenon that created and legitimized much of the modern American state, which in many ways it did. But the New Deal is also important for the options it foreclosed, for the way it tried to take certain paths and failed in the trying, for the ways in which it delegitimized certain concepts of the state even as it was legitimizing others. One of those concepts was the vaguely corporatist vision of economic harmony that had emerged from World War I and that culminated in the ill-fated National Recovery Administration of 1933–35.

The sorry history of the NRA is already the subject of a considerable scholarly literature. But it is worth noting how powerfully the memory of the NRA continued to influence the way New Dealers and others thought about what the state could and should do even after the agency itself met its demise in 1935. There were, to be sure, some (including, at times, Franklin Roosevelt) who continued to defend what came to be known as the "NRA approach." But there were many more who talked instead of the "NRA disaster" or the "NRA of evil memory," who saw in it a sobering lesson in what *not* to do, who considered it a disastrous mistake never to be repeated.[19]

Chief among the complaints was that the NRA had, in the name of promoting the common good, become a license for big corporations to collude and hence to threaten the interests of small producers and consumers. The NRA, according to the *New Republic*, "gave employers the opportunity to raise prices and restrict production . . . and so encouraged monopolistic practices that interfered with the very object sought—more abundance."[20] It had, according to the *Nation*, "hindered recovery instead of helping it."[21] It had proved that "whenever business men are allowed to come together to 'cooperate,' the result is almost inevitably an effort to get more profits by some form of price-raising."[22] It was "merely the trust sugar-coated," which had "pinned a policeman's badge" on monopolies.[23]

But the case against the NRA was not just a case against big business; it was also a case against certain kinds of government intervention in the economy, a case against the feasibility of imposing effective public control over the behavior of private institutions, a case against certain notions of planning, regulation, and state management. The NRA had collapsed, Thurman Arnold argued in the late 1930s, for the same reason that all economic "master plans" must collapse—because it could have succeeded only through a "vast extension of state control," an extension that Americans would not (and should not) contemplate.[24] Henry Wallace said of it that "there is something wooden and inhuman about the government interfering in a definite, precise way with the details of our private and business lives. It suggests a time of war with generals and captains telling every individual what he must do each day and hour."[25]

The New Deal, in short, had helped teach liberals not only what the state could do, but what it could not do. And one of the things it could not do, they had come to believe, was reorder the corporate world. Such efforts would lead either to domination by private monopoly or domination by an excessively powerful state. Or it would lead, as many believed the NRA had led, to both. And thus when the United States began, for the second time in a generation, to mobilize the economy for war, liberals brought to that mobilization a much greater sensitivity than had their counterparts two decades earlier to the problems inherent in creating partnerships between the corporate world and the state, and a sensitivity to the problems inherent in giving the state responsibility for managing the affairs of private institutions. Hopes for this second wartime experiment were, as a result, much lower from the beginning; disillusionment set in much more quickly.

But there is a third, and in my view more fundamental, reason for the difference between the way American liberals conceived the role of their state in 1918 and the way they had come to conceive it by 1945. We cannot understand the way liberals defined the state without understanding how they defined the economic problems they were asking the state to resolve. They defined those problems very differently in 1945 from the way they had in 1918.

At the end of World War I, as for several decades before and for many years after, those who tried to prescribe a more active role for the state tended to think largely in terms of somehow changing the way private economic institutions behaved: curbing monopoly power, promoting industrial cooperation, regulating corporate activities. The problem was institutional. The function of the state was to stabilize, or regulate, or even to restructure capitalist institutions.

That belief rested not only on uneasiness about the size and power of the new corporate institutions in America but also on an assumption about the way all economies worked, an assumption rooted in classical economic doctrine and in centuries of social experience. The great economic challenge, most American liberals believed in 1917, was to expand society's productive capacities and create enough goods to satisfy everyone's needs. The great economic danger was scarcity. What drove the economy, therefore, was production. The task of economic life (and, to those who believed that the state had a role to play in the economy, the task of public life) was to promote investment and production, to ensure that new factories were built, new crops were harvested, new energy sources were exploited. Economic life also required consumption, of course, but if production could be sustained and enhanced, then consumption would automatically follow.[26]

By the beginning of the 1940s, many Americans—and in particular many of those most interested in defining a role for government in the economy—had begun to embrace new assumptions. No longer did the problems of production dominate their thinking about public policy; those problems, they believed, had been largely solved. There was now no real danger of scarcity; the danger now was inadequate consumption. Consumption, not production, was now the principal force in the modern economy. Consumption drove production, not the other way around.[27] This was a significant redefinition of the nation's fundamental economic goals and, by implication, of its political goals. And the question naturally arises of why it occurred.

Anyone familiar with recent scholarship in twentieth-century American history will be aware that these new economic assumptions reflect parallel changes in popular culture—changes that have been the subject of an important literature in the last two decades exploring advertising, public education, family behavior, and other social and cultural issues. That literature has made a powerful case for the ways in which the ideas of abundance and consumption were defining the concepts of the "American dream" and the "American way of life" in the first half of the twentieth century. It is reasonable to assume, although such things are hard to demonstrate in decisive ways, that these cultural shifts were penetrating economic and political thought as well.[28]

But it was not just cultural phenomena that were changing political assumptions. Among other things, it was the economy itself, which had come to rely much more heavily on the production and sale of consumer goods than it had in the past. It was also the economic boom of the 1920s, which had been driven largely by consumer spending on automobiles, appliances, and housing and which had suggested that the traditional problems of scarcity and the traditional preoccupation with production might have become obsolete. And most of all, it was the Great Depression, which (whether or not correctly) was widely interpreted not as a problem of inadequate production but as a crisis of underconsumption and which thus reinforced the idea that the principal mission of economic life should now be to raise purchasing power and stimulate aggregate demand.[29]

The specific implications of these ideas for policy were not, at first, entirely clear through most of the 1930s. Even those who agreed that raising purchasing power and stimulating consumption were the proper aims of policy (which was far from everyone, even within the New Deal) disagreed over the best way to accomplish those goals. To some of these "under consumptionists" (as they came to be known), the most important goal was organizing consumers as a coherent interest group, able to act in much the same way as organized business and labor interests. To others, the best course was the passage of legislation to protect consumers from misrepresentation and fraud; there were even calls for the creation of a new, cabinet-level Department of the Consumer. There were campaigns to promote "consumer education," modest efforts to create "consumer co-operatives," and generally unsuccessful attempts to organize consumer strikes and boycotts. Indeed, the rhetoric of consumption became at times an almost universal political language—used to support antitrust crusades, planning initiatives, regulatory mechanisms, and many other models for policy; it was used in fact by supporters of almost every position to justify (or at least rationalize) their efforts.[30]

Slowly, however, one set of ideas began to emerge from this welter of approaches, a set of ideas that gradually became central to the liberal concept of the state. Government could stimulate consumption quickly and easily by using its fiscal powers. It could spend money on public works and on jobs programs. It could fund relief and welfare mechanisms. It could accumulate deliberate deficits. Public spending was the best vehicle for attacking deflation and stabilizing the economy. It need no longer be considered a necessary evil, used sparingly to achieve particular ends; it could become a positive good, to be used lavishly to promote the health of the economy as a whole.

These are ideas now associated principally with John Maynard Keynes, who by the end of World War II had developed a substantial following in the American economics profession and in broader liberal circles. But long before Keynes had found any significant audience in America, ideas that are now considered "Keynesian" were receiving independent expression from many sources: from popular economists William Trufant Foster and Waddill Catchings, who published a series of books in the 1920s and 1930s promoting public spending as the cure for underconsumption;[31] from academic economists such as John M. Clark, Arthur Gayer, and James Harvey Rogers, who promoted the concept of "counter-cyclical" public works spending throughout the 1930s;[32] and from Marriner Eccles, the chairman of the Federal Reserve Board beginning in 1934, who had read Foster and Catchings and admired them, and who (though he was, as head of the Fed, charged with overseeing monetary policy) was principally interested in fiscal matters. Eccles, who never read Keynes, was the principal Keynesian in the New Deal's inner circle in the mid- and late 1930s—a tireless and ultimately effective advocate of using public spending to increase purchasing power.[33]

The spending argument received an important (if indirect) boost in 1937, when the administration made substantial cuts in public funding of relief and public works in order to balance the budget and almost immediately precipitated a severe recession. It received another (more positive) boost in 1938, when, partly in response to Eccles, Roosevelt reversed himself and launched a massive new spending program, justifying it for the first time not in terms of the particular, targeted problems the spending might solve but in terms of the way it would contribute to the health of the economy as a whole.[34]

But to most liberals, the clearest confirmation of the value of public spending was World War II itself. Liberals may have derived little comfort from the performance of the War Production Board and the other war agencies, but they could not fail to be impressed with the way in which massive public spending helped end almost overnight a depression that had proved resistant to institutional reforms for more than a decade. Suddenly an economy that many Americans had feared was irretrievably stagnant was expanding more rapidly and dramatically than almost anyone had believed possible. The lessons for the future seemed obvious: The government's role in supervising the behavior of institutions was less important than its role in seeing to the health of the economy as a whole.

Alvin Hansen, the principal American advocate of Keynesian ideas in the 1940s and a major figure in the New Deal, expressed the new faith toward the end of the war. "Clearly fiscal policy is now and will continue to be [the principal] factor in the functioning of the modern economy."[35] Its purpose, he said, was "to develop a high-consumption economy so that we can achieve full employment. . . . A higher propensity to consume can . . . be achieved by a progressive tax structure combined with social security, social welfare, and community consumption expenditures."[36] If World War I's legacy to American political economy was the dream of an "ordered economic world"—a more rational distribution and exercise of corporate power—World War II's was the dream of full employment and economic growth.[37]

By 1945, therefore, many American liberals were rallying to a new concept of the state, substantially different from those ideas they had embraced at the end of World War I. It was now possible, they believed, to achieve economic growth without constant involvement in the internal affairs of corporations, which was both endlessly complex and politically difficult. It was now possible for the state to manage the economy without managing the *institutions* of the economy. The state had already succeeded in curbing the most egregious abuses of corporate behavior through the regulatory initiatives and labor legislation of the 1930s. The task now was to find a way for government to compensate for capitalism's remaining flaws through aggressive fiscal policies and through expanded welfare and social insurance mechanisms. The task was to build not a corporate state or a regulatory state, but a compensatory state.

All this is not to say that the liberals of the 1940s had consciously repudiated the dreams of their forebears a generation before. They still used much of the same language. They still spoke of planning. They still hoped for economic harmony and order. They still dreamed of what Lippmann, thirty years earlier, had called "mastery." But those words did not mean the same things in 1945 as they had in 1918. They referred, for example, to the principal liberal initiative of 1945: the so-called Full Employment bill, which would commit the federal government to aggressive fiscal policies to sustain purchasing power at high levels at all times. And they referred to the raft of legislative initiatives that Harry Truman promoted throughout his eight years as president: the expansion of social security, the creation of national health insurance, the construction of public housing, the protection of the consumer. The older, more institutional dreams—of partnerships between government and business, of planning production and investment (or what we now call "industrial policy"), of extensive state regulation of corporate behavior—had come, in the view of many Americans, to seem politically unrealistic, bureaucratically impossible, and socially dangerous. But most of all, to many liberals at least, they had come to seem irrelevant.

And yet when one looks back from the perspective of a later era at the bright liberal hopes of 1945, it is hard not to sense that the confidence of that time was to some degree misplaced. Liberals in the postwar decades did follow, and to some degree still follow, the path they devised for themselves in the 1940s. But the weak and embattled liberal state that has emerged from their efforts has fallen far short of their hopes—its cumbersome and inadequate welfare mechanisms battling constantly for legitimacy, with uncertain results; its primitive fiscal mechanisms never coming close to fulfilling the liberal dreams of the 1940s and ultimately, in the 1980s, becoming a grotesque inversion of the Keynesian model; its claim on popular loyalties consistently frail.

Nor is it at all clear that the model of state development liberals rejected in the 1940s—the model of war mobilization, of the War Industries Board and the War Production Board—was as irrelevant to the nation's future as they believed it to be. For in the postwar era there emerged—alongside this frail and struggling liberal state—what became, in a sense, a second government: a national security state, powerful, entrenched, constantly expanding, and largely invulnerable to political attacks; a state that forged intimate partnerships with the corporate world, constantly blurring the distinctions between public and private; and a state that produced some of the very things—strengthened private monopolies and expanded state power to sustain them—that the liberal vision was supposed to prevent.[38]

Sometime in the early 1930s, it is not clear exactly when, Franklin Roosevelt read a book by Foster and Catchings, the proto-Keynesian popular economists who helped draw public attention to the idea of dealing with economic problems through public spending. The book was called *The Road to Plenty*, and its distinctly utopian overtones made it reminiscent of William Harvey's free-silver tract of thirty years earlier, *Coin's Financial School*. *The Road to Plenty* outlined what Foster and Catchings considered a safe, painless, and certain route to prosperity and social justice: a redirection of government's efforts away from the profitless (and, in their view, dangerous) effort to manage economic institutions and toward the safer and more promising effort to manage the aggregate economy through taxation and

72   *The Two World Wars and the Idea of the State*

public spending, through attention to consumption instead of to investment. Roosevelt's copy of the book is in the Franklin D. Roosevelt Library in Hyde Park, New York. It contains his marginal commentary, of the sort one sometimes finds scrawled in books in undergraduate libraries. Toward the end, he recorded a general reaction: "Too good to be true—You can't get something for nothing."[39]

Later, of course, Roosevelt seemed to change his mind, if not about Foster and Catchings themselves then about the general constellation of ideas they expressed. But there is, I think, room to wonder whether, had Roosevelt lived to see where this new concept of the liberal state would eventually lead, he might have concluded that he had it right the first time.

NOTES

1. Walter Lippmann, "The World Conflict in Its Relation to American Democracy," *The Annals* 72 (July 1917): 7–8.

2. Walter Lippmann, *Drift and Mastery: An Attempt to Diagnose the Current Unrest* (New York: Mitchell Kennerley, 1914), 147–48.

3. Lippmann, *Drift and Mastery*, 148.

4. David Kennedy, *Over Here: The First World War and American Society* (New York: Oxford University Press, 1980), chaps. 1, 2, and 6; Alan Dawley, *Struggles for Justice: Social Responsibility and the Liberal State* (Cambridge: Harvard University Press, 1991), 254–94.

5. Bernard M. Baruch, *American Industry in the War* (New York: Prentice-Hall, 1941), 105–6.

6. Root and the Chamber of Commerce quoted in Paul A. C. Koistinen, "The 'Industrial-Military Complex' in Historical Perspective: World War I," *Business History Review* 41 (1967): 393.

7. Grosvenor B. Clarkson, *Industrial America in the World War: The Strategy behind the Line, 1917–1918* (Boston: Houghton Mifflin, 1923), 312, 475–88.

8. Ellis W. Hawley, "Herbert Hoover and Economic Stabilization, 1921–1922," in Ellis W. Hawley, ed., *Herbert Hoover as Secretary of Commerce* (Iowa City: University of Iowa Press, 1981), 43–77; Robert F. Himmelberg, *The Origins of the National Recovery Administration: Business, Government, and the Trade Association Issue, 1921–1933* (New York: Fordham University Press, 1976), 43–74; Louis Galambos, *Competition and Cooperation: The Emergence of a National Trade Association* (Baltimore: Johns Hopkins University Press, 1966), 89–138; Rexford G. Tugwell, *The Industrial Discipline and the Governmental Arts* (New York: Columbia University Press, 1933), 4–6, 189–219; Rexford G. Tugwell, *The Democratic Roosevelt* (Garden City, N.Y.: Doubleday, 1957), 229–30, 284–86, 308–11; Adolf A. Berle, Jr., and Gardiner C. Means, *The Modern Corporation and Private Property* (New York: Macmillan, 1932), 124–25, 352, 356, and passim; Charles R. Van Hise, *Concentration and Control: A Solution of the Trust Problem in the United States* (New York: Macmillan, 1912), esp. 8–20, 277–78. For a discussion of the roots of New Deal corporatism in the decades preceding the Great Depression, see (in addition to the works cited above) Donald Brand, *Corporatism and the Rule of Law: A Study of the National Recovery Administration* (Ithaca, N.Y.: Cornell University Press, 1988), part 1.

9. Clifford Durr, "The Postwar Relationship between Government and Business," *American Economic Review* 33 (1943): 47. See also George Soule, "The War in Washington," *New Republic*, September 27, 1939, 205–6; "New Deal Plans Industry Council," *Business Week*, March 20, 1943, 15.

10. Quoted in Robert D. Cuff, "American Mobilization for War, 1917–1945: Political Culture vs. Bureaucratic Administration," in N. F. Dreisziger, ed., *Mobilization for Total War: The Canadian, American, and British Experience, 1914–1918, 1937–1945* (Waterloo, Ont.: Wilfred Laurier University Press, 1981), 80.

11. *New York Times*, September 21, 1948; *New York World Telegram and Sun*, March 10, 1950; letter, W. M. Jeffers to Ferdinand Eberstadt, March 20, 1950, Ferdinand Eberstadt Papers, Box 116, Princeton University Library; Eliot Janeway, "Where Was Mr. Nelson?" *Saturday Review*, September 7, 1946, 11; letter, Eberstadt to multiple correspondents, August 23, 1946, Eberstadt Papers, Box 116.

12. The best account of economic mobilization during World War I is Robert D. Cuff, *The War Industries Board: Business-Government Relations during World War I* (Baltimore: Johns Hopkins University Press, 1973). For World War II, see Richard Polenberg, *War and Society: The United States, 1941–1945* (Philadelphia: J. B. Lippincott, 1972), chaps. 1 and 6; and Alan Brinkley, *The End of Reform: New Deal Liberalism in Recession and War* (New York: Alfred A. Knopf, 1995), chap. 8.

13. I. F. Stone, "Donald Nelson Has Chosen," *Nation*, March 21, 1942, 332. See also I. F. Stone, "Nelson and Guthrie," *Nation*, June 27, 1942, 731; Michael Straight, "Dollar-a-Year Sabotage," *New Republic*, March 30, 1942, 418; "Don Nelson's Men," *Business Week*, July 4, 1942, 50–52; "The Pain and the Necessity," *Time*, June 29, 1942, 18; *Kiplinger Washington Letter*, August 15, 1942; letter, Bruce Bliven to Max Lerner, August 24, 1942, Max Lerner Papers, Box 1, Yale University Library.

14. Kennedy, *Over Here*, 55–56, 62–69; John Higham, *Strangers in the Land* (New Brunswick, N.J.: Rutgers University Press, 1963), 201–2; Paul L. Murphy, *World War I and the Origin of Civil Liberties in the United States* (New York: W. W. Norton, 1979), chaps. 4 and 5.

15. See Allan M. Winkler, *The Politics of Propaganda: The Office of War Information, 1942–1945* (New Haven: Yale University Press, 1978), 38–72; John M. Blum, *V Was for Victory* (New York: Harcourt, Brace, Jovanovich, 1976), 45–52; Clayton R. Koppes and Gregory D. Black, *Hollywood Goes to War: How Politics, Profits, and Propaganda Shaped World War II Movies* (Berkeley: University of California Press, 1987), 82–112, 278–316.

16. Reinhold Niebuhr, *The Children of Light and the Children of Darkness* (New York: Charles Scribner's Sons, 1945), 117. See also Reinhold Niebuhr, "The Collectivist Bogy," *Nation*, October 21, 1944, 478–80.

17. Friedrich A. Hayek, *The Road to Serfdom* (Chicago: University of Chicago Press, 1944).

18. Letter, Friedrich Hayek to Walter Lippmann, April 6, 1937, Walter Lippmann Papers, Series III, Box 77, Yale University Library. See also Theodore Rosenof, *Patterns of Political Economy: The Failure to Develop a Democratic Left Synthesis in America, 1933–1950* (New York: Garland, 1983), 228–32; and Theodore Rosenof, "Freedom, Planning, and Totalitarianism: The Reception of F. A. Hayek's *Road to Serfdom*," *Canadian Review of American Studies* 5 (Fall 1974): 150–60.

19. James T. Flynn, "Other People's Money," *New Republic*, January 26, 1938, 337; Walter Millis, "Cross Purposes in the New Deal," *Virginia Quarterly Review* 14 (Summer 1938): 357–67. The best account of the NRA is Ellis W. Hawley, *The New Deal*

and the Problem of Monopoly (Princeton: Princeton University Press, 1966), chaps. 1–7. See also Donald R. Brand, *Corporatism and the Rule of Law* (Ithaca, N.Y.: Cornell University Press, 1988).

20. "National Minima for Labor," *New Republic*, December 1, 1937, 88; "Again— The Trust Problem," *New Republic*, January 19, 1938, 295.

21. "A New NRA," *Nation*, March 25, 1939, 337; "Liberals Never Learn," *Nation*, March 18, 1939, 309.

22. George Soule, "This Recovery: What Brought It? Will It Last?" *Harper's*, March 1937, 342.

23. Robert Jackson, "Business Confidence and Government Policy" [speech], December 26, 1937, Raymond Clapper Papers, Box 200, Manuscripts Division, Library of Congress.

24. Thurman Arnold, *The Folklore of Capitalism* (New Haven: Yale University Press, 1937), 221, 268; Thurman Arnold, "Feathers and Prices," *Common Sense*, July 1939, 6.

25. Quoted in William E. Leuchtenburg, "The New Deal and the Analogue of War," in John Braeman et al., eds., *Change and Continuity in Twentieth-Century America* (Columbus: Ohio State University Press, 1964), 135.

26. Alan Brinkley, "Origins of the 'Fiscal Revolution,'" *Storia NordAmericana* 6 (1989): 37–39.

27. Brinkley, "Origins of the 'Fiscal Revolution,'" 37–42.

28. On the role of the advertising industry in encouraging and legitimizing consumption, see Roland Marchand, *Advertising the American Dream, 1920–1940* (Berkeley: University of California Press, 1985), 25–43, 120–63, and passim; Stuart Ewen, *Captains of Consciousness: Advertising and the Social Roots of the Consumer Culture* (New York: McGraw-Hill, 1976), 81–109 and passim; T. J. Jackson Lears, "From Salvation to Self-Realization: Advertising and the Therapeutic Roots of the Consumer Culture, 1880–1930," in T. J. Jackson Lears and Richard Wightman Fox, eds., *The Culture of Consumption: Critical Essays in American History, 1880–1890* (New York: Pantheon, 1983), 1–38.

29. Michael Bernstein, *The Great Depression: Delayed Recovery and Economic Change in America, 1929–1939* (New York: Cambridge University Press, 1987), 21–40; Stanley Lebergott, *Pursuing Happiness: American Consumers in the Twentieth Century* (Princeton: Princeton University Press, 1993), 69–72, 148.

30. On the rise of consumer activism, see Horace M. Kallen, *The Decline and Rise of the Consumer* (New York: D. Appleton-Century, 1936), 153–200; Helen Sorenson, *The Consumer Movement: What It Is and What It Means* (New York: Harper & Brothers, 1941), 3–30 and passim. The growing importance of consumer activism was not lost on the Roosevelt administration. Tugwell, among others, courted consumer groups and told one of them in 1934: "The organization of consumers' leagues in the United States has been a recognition of the inherent power of organized consumer action. Historically your organizations have endeavored to use this latent power . . . in support of numerous attempts by various groups to raise living standards for working people." Tugwell speech draft, May 1, 1934, Thomas Blaisdell Papers, Box 40, National Resources Planning Board Archives, RG 187, National Archives.

31. William Trufant Foster and Waddill Catchings, *Money* (Boston: Houghton Mifflin, 1923), 351–56 and passim; idem, *Profits* (Boston: Houghton Mifflin, 1925), v–vi, 223–46, 398–418; idem, *Business without a Buyer* (Boston: Houghton Mifflin, 1927), v–vii; idem, *The Road to Plenty* (Boston: Houghton Mifflin, 1928), 3–10 and passim.

32. Arthur D. Gayer, *Public Works in Prosperity and Depression* (New York: National Bureau of Economic Research, 1935), 366–401; John M. Clark, *Economics of*

Planning Public Works (Washington: National Planning Board, 1935), 155–59; Alan Sweezy, "The Keynesians and Government Policy, 1933–1939," *American Economic Review* 62 (May 1972): 118–19; letters, James Harvey Rogers to Marvin McIntyre, October 28, 1937, James Roosevelt to Rogers, November 8, 1937, Rogers to Robert S. Shriver, December 9, 1937, all in James Harvey Rogers Papers, Box 21, Yale University Library; Byrd L. Jones, "James Harvey Rogers: An Intellectual Biography," Ph.D. diss., Yale University, 1966, 146, 175, 210–11, 297, 506–7.

33. Brinkley, "Origins of the 'Fiscal Revolution,'" 48–56.

34. Herbert Stein, *The Fiscal Revolution in America* (Chicago: University of Chicago Press, 1969), chaps. 6 and 7; Dean L. May, *From New Deal to New Economics: The American Liberal Response to the Recession of 1937* (New York: Garland, 1981).

35. Alvin Hansen, "Planning Full Employment," *Nation*, October 21, 1941, 492.

36. Letter, Alvin Hansen to Marriner Eccles, August 18, 1944, enclosing a copy of "Postwar Employment Program," dated August 17, 1944, Marriner Eccles Papers, Box 7, Folder 12, University of Utah Library.

37. "Is There a New Frontier?" *New Republic*, November 27, 1944, 708–10; "A New Bill of Rights," *Nation*, March 20, 1943, 402; Stein, *Fiscal Revolution*, 175–77.

38. The literature describing the origins and character of what has come to be known as the "military-industrial complex" is vast. C. Wright Mills was among the first scholars to describe its characteristics in *The Power Elite* (New York: Oxford University Press, 1956), 171–224. William Appleman Williams, similarly, cited the military-industrial complex as part of "an imperial complex" that dominated American foreign policy and political economy; see his *Americans in a Changing World: A History of the United States in the Twentieth Century* (New York: Harper & Row, 1978), 375. Daniel Yergin describes the complex as a central element of the "national-security state" in his *Shattered Peace: The Origins of the Cold War and the National Security State* (Boston: Houghton Mifflin, 1977). See also Paul A. C. Koistinen's *The Military-Industrial Complex: A Historical Perspective* (New York: Praeger, 1980) and "Mobilizing the World War II Economy: Labor and the Industrial-Military Alliance," *Pacific Historical Review* 42 (November 1973): 443–78; Bruce G. Brunton's "The Origins and Early Development of the American Military-Industrial Complex," Ph.D. diss., University of Utah, 1989, and "An Historical Perspective on the Future of the Military-Industrial Complex," *Social Science Journal* 28 (1991): 45–62; Charles A. Cannon, "The Military-Industrial Complex in American Politics, 1953–1970," Ph.D. diss., Stanford University, 1975; Gregory Hooks, *Forging the Military-Industrial Complex: World War II's Battle of the Potomac* (Urbana: University of Illinois Press, 1991); Steve Fraser, *Labor Will Rule: Sidney Hillman and the Rise of American Labor* (New York: Free Press, 1991), 481–83; Gerald D. Nash, "The West and the Military-Industrial Complex," *Montana* 40 (1990): 72–75; Ben Baack and Edward Ray, "The Political Economy of the Origins of the Military-Industrial Complex in the United States," *Journal of Economic History* 45 (1985): 369–75; Roger W. Lotchin, "The Political Culture of the Metropolitan-Military Complex," *Social Science History* 16 (1992): 275–99; Samuel P. Huntington, *The Soldier and the State* (Cambridge: Harvard University Press, 1957), chaps. 12 and 13; Gautam Sen, "The Economics of U.S. Defense: The Military-Industrial Complex and Neo-Marxist Economic Theories Reconsidered," *Millennium* 15 (1986): 179–95.

39. Foster and Catchings, *The Road to Plenty*, 3–10 and passim; Arthur M. Schlesinger, *The Crisis of the Old Order* (Boston: Houghton Mifflin, 1957), 134–36.

5

What Kind of Government Do We Have to Fear?

James W. Ceaser

The main struggles in American domestic politics over the last two decades have focused on the theme of "Big Government." Republicans waged four successful presidential campaigns by running against Big Government (in 1980, 1984, 1988, and 2000), and they made it the centerpiece of their huge victory in the congressional elections of 1994. Yielding tactically to the message of that election, President Bill Clinton retreated and famously declared that "the era of Big Government is over."[1] But many of Clinton's subsequent proposals, as well as the central themes advanced by Al Gore in his presidential bid in 2000, show clearly the Democrats' continuing commitment to what Republicans call Big Government. The first decade of the new century opened with no clear victor in this struggle and both sides fighting to establish their governing philosophy.

The combination of words "big government" has of course been used for many years. But Big Government, written with a capital *B* and a capital *G* as if it were some kind of great German metaphysical concept, is a partisan expression of recent origin. Just as the Progressives at the turn of the century popularized the term *individualism* (often with a capital *I*) to identify the late-nineteenth-century public philosophy they opposed, so conservatives have made Big Government a symbol of the supposed excesses and flaws of modern liberalism.

But apart from their common opposition to expanded domestic social welfare programs and extensive economic regulations, conservatives have not been entirely clear or consistent in what they mean by Big Government. For some it refers primarily to the size of the government, while for others it designates the failure to pay for the level of government in existence. For some it means programs enacted only by the federal government, while for others it can identify the actions of state and local level government as well. Finally, for some, Big Government has always been less a matter of size or level than of direction: it refers to an egalitarian and secularist project that has been promoted largely, but not exclusively, with the backing of public authorities.

Conservatives have been successful in making Big Government an expression of general opprobrium. Although liberals might defend against the attack on government, they never champion Big Government. When they have not avoided the term altogether (which has been their usual approach), they have tried to turn the tables and connect it to certain conservative policies such as interference with a woman's "right to choose" or federal rules designed to enforce certain ideas of morality.

From a conservative viewpoint, much was achieved—tactically at any rate—by introducing the term "Big Government" into contemporary politics. As a general rule in politics, it is always better to control the major symbols and to frame the debate on one's own terms. But conservatives have paid a price for this victory. Too many have treated Big Government as if it provided a full political theory supplying all one knows and all one needs to know. This inflation of a slogan has led to confusions and errors.

In a search to discover the origins of Big Government, conservatives have tried to trace the views of "the party of government" in the twentieth century (chiefly the Democratic Party since the New Deal) back to the ideas of the earlier parties of government (the Republicans of the Civil War period, the Whigs, and the Federalists). The assumption has been that because all of these parties argued for more authority for the national government than their opponents, they share something essential. By the same token, the various parties that have opposed the federal government all along are praised for representing the wise viewpoint. Conservatives have thus moved away from the reasoning of the Federalists and have grown more enamored of the thinking of Anti-Federalists and Jeffersonians, including their "populist" and isolationist positions. Conservatives have looked for instruction more from the likes of John Randolph than from Alexander Hamilton or Abraham Lincoln. Under the influence of an overwrought concept of Big Government, conservatives are now often apt to believe that because they are against Big Government they must be for Little Government. They have forgotten that there is a difference between little government and *limited* government.[2]

This chapter is intended to clarify what conservatives actually oppose when they refer to Big Government, not what they now often *think* they oppose after entrapping themselves in a web of confusions. To accomplish this purpose, it is essential to distinguish between the case for bigger government before and after the twentieth century. These two are quite different things. They obey a different logic, follow a different legal standard, and seek different ends. Under the elementary rules of common sense the same term should not be used to refer to both. Either the term "Big Government" should be abandoned altogether, or else it should be reserved—as I shall do here—for the modern variant only.

The nineteenth-century parties favoring bigger government—bigger, mind you, in relation to the parties that sought to stringently limit the federal government—argued for the need for broad discretion to handle the tasks assigned to a limited government. They promoted their position on the basis of an understanding of the Constitution and relied as much as the opposing parties did on the text of the document and the intentions of the founding generation. The ends they sought included liberty and national development. By contrast, the original proponents of the theory of Big Government in the twentieth century rejected the idea of a government of limited ends, favoring instead a national government that could enter any realm and that should be "experimental" in its projects of "social engineering." These theorists, led by John Dewey and Herbert Croly, had reservations not just about the Constitution but also about the idea of constitutionalism itself. Finally, Big Government theorists sought ends that went well beyond what the nineteenth century contemplated; they sought objectives that only a large and active national government could achieve: a benevolent and egalitarian order (a welfare state with "social justice") and the promotion of the vague ideal of true "individuality."

For those seeking continuities between these two positions, some can obviously be found. But then it is rare that continuities cannot be discovered where one is earnestly looking for them. It has been argued, for example, that Federalist and Whig interpretations of the national government's constitutional powers anticipated the expansive constitutional interpretations of Big Government advocates. In this view, Hamilton's economic program prepared the way for Lyndon Johnson's War on Poverty, and John Marshall's jurisprudential nationalism was the inspiration for William Brennan's judicial activism. Yet from anything but the narrowest legal perspective—and perhaps even then—it is clear that Big Government enthusiasts have thought in entirely different terms about not only the purposes but also the functions and scope of government. And they said as much initially, before they discovered that the idea of "continuities" provided rhetorical cover for the break that they had in mind.

The first contest between the parties of bigger and smaller government occurred in the struggle over the Constitution. Proponents of the Constitution—the Federalists—argued that there were certain tasks Americans wanted government to handle that could only be achieved with a new and much stronger national government. These tasks included providing a capable foreign policy and a credible national defense, promoting the flow of commerce and economic development, and protecting the security of rights (especially property rights from the effects of inflationary policies). The most distinctive aspect of the Federalist position, however, was not the purposes it assigned to the national government, but the discretion it gave to the government in carrying out those purposes. "A government ought to contain in itself," Hamilton wrote in *The Federalist Papers*, "every power requisite to the full accomplishment of the objects committed to its care, and to complete execution of the trusts for which it is responsible."[3] It was this logic of discretion that most disturbed the opponents of the Constitution—the Anti-Federalists.

Limited government, in the view of the Federalists, can become quite extensive in order to meet the demands of particular situations or deal with the grave problems the nation may confront. Government must have great leeway in determining what means to employ because it is never possible to foresee what measures may be needed to cope with a problem. For example, preparing for or waging war can require high taxes, a national mobilization of manpower, and extensive government economic planning. Granting to government discretion of this magnitude obviously means that it has enough authority to practice abuses. This is a risk that cannot be avoided. To protect against abuses, *The Federalist Papers* offered the "composition and structure of the government," the prudence of those in office, and the vigilance of the people.[4]

Anti-Federalists contended that the Constitution promoted a "consolidated government"—the eighteenth-century term of opprobrium for a "Big Government"—that would absorb virtually all of the power of the state governments into the national government. "Although the government reported by the [Constitutional] convention does not go to a perfect and entire consolidation," wrote the Anti-Federalist "Brutus," "yet it approaches so near to it that it must, if executed, certainly and infallibly terminate in it."[5] This charge relied not just on an analysis of the powers that were actually granted to the national government—though these were enough to make the case—but also on whispers about what some of its principal advocates of the Constitution had really wanted. At the Constitutional Convention in Philadelphia, Hamilton suggested abolishing existing state boundaries, James Madison argued for a national veto over all state legislation, and both men expressed doubts about the wisdom of trying to enumerate specific grants of power to the federal government.

These "extreme" consolidationist positions were rejected by the convention, and both Hamilton and Madison went on to plead the case for the Constitution as it was written. But even their reasons for favoring their initial positions show them to have been thinking more in "defensive" than "offensive" terms. In their estimation, the power of the states was so great and the people's attachments to them so strong that an effective national government required at least as much authority as they were suggesting in order to be established and to survive. *The Federalist Papers* is surely a nationalist work, but it expressed little interest in using federal power "creatively" to control local matters: "The administration of private justice between citizens of the same state . . . [and] all those things which are proper to be provided for by local legislation can never be desirable cares of a general jurisdiction."[6] For Hamilton it was inconceivable that national politicians, whose horizons he expected to be fixed on the higher concerns of "finance, negotiation and war," would want to interfere in state and local concerns and play the role of mayors and aldermen.

The first partisan conflict under the Constitution had both parties—the Federalists and the Jeffersonian Republicans—claiming fidelity to the

Constitution. The party of bigger government was the Federalist Party, whose core ideas were developed by Hamilton during the Washington administration. Hamilton's bold legislative program, which included the funding plan for the national debt, the establishment of a national bank, and the imposition of higher tariffs, became the focal point of opposition of the Republicans, who criticized it not only for promoting consolidation but also for trying to implant a system of centralized "monarchy."

Yet, nationalist as Hamilton's program may have been, it is important again to recall its "defensive" character. The reasoning behind a program of this sort—if not exactly this program—had already been articulated in *The Federalist Papers* and was shared by Madison. In this view, merely ratifying the Constitution was insufficient to establish the new government. An early demonstration of "good administration," in Madison's words, was needed to prove the new government's strength and to form bonds of interest and emotion between the central government and a large number of citizens.[7] Otherwise the new structure might disintegrate under the centripetal force of preexisting attachment to the states. Hamilton viewed his program not as an ordinary act of government, but as an essential part of the founding itself: a full display in real policy of the power and capacity of the new government.

Those trying to establish the connection between modern Big Government and the Federalists sometimes like to point out that Hamilton's program, especially the plan to protect manufacturing, contained a "regime" (or character-forming) objective of promoting "the spirit of enterprise" among the American people. (In his "Report on Manufacturing," Hamilton argues that his proposed program will "stimulate the activity of the human mind," "provoke exertion," and generate wealth.)[8] This kind of character-forming goal, it is said, takes us well beyond any purpose outlined in the Constitution. But it is important to point out that this goal was being pursued indirectly through the general effects of a legislative program that served a direct constitutional purpose. Surely everyone understood that national policies might have such consequences. In this respect Hamilton's program was no different from Jefferson's, which had a character-forming objective of its own: creating an independent-minded yeoman by promoting agriculture and discouraging manufacturing.[9]

The next party of government was the National Republicans, later called the Whigs, which never really held the full reins of power in Washington. As Croly remarked, "they were on the defensive throughout, and they accomplished nothing at all in the way of permanent constructive legislation."[10] The party's program in its support for a national bank and for federally funded internal improvements—the so-called American plan—hardly went beyond anything that the Jeffersonians had at one time endorsed. The founder of the opposition Democratic Party, Martin Van Buren, never ceased ridiculing John Quincy Adams's first message to Congress, which made a high-minded appeal for "a civilizing mission" for the federal government that would include support for "light houses in the sky" and fund "*an* astronomer." This was not exactly Big Government in the model of the Great Society, and in any case federal support for scientific research had previously existed and would continue thereafter.[11] Van Buren's attack, one suspects, was less an expression of genuine indignation than a calculated tactic to rekindle partisan sentiments in his efforts to revive partisan competition.

The final pre-twentieth-century party of government was the Republican Party. Republicans continued to support elements of national development in the tradition of the Federalists and Whigs, including the Homestead Act, a land-grant college act, and acts designed to promote railroad development. But it was the Republicans' opposition to slavery that made them, from the Democrats' viewpoint, a consolidationist party. In a strict legal sense, the Republicans' initial position represented not an expansion but merely the reassertion of a rightful federal legal jurisdiction to ban slavery from certain federal territories. The claim to this jurisdiction, which had undergirded the Missouri Compromise, was abandoned by the federal government in the Kansas-Nebraska Act and then declared unconstitutional in the *Dred Scott* decision. Of course, the Republican Party's principled opposition to slavery and the statement of Abraham Lincoln that "a House divided against itself cannot stand" led the slaveholders in the South to conclude that their own aim of protecting and expanding slavery could not be maintained inside the Union. In any case the Civil War and its aftermath changed everything, bringing into the arena of national politics the problems of slavery and race relations. Dealing with these issues went well beyond any of the legal powers originally granted to the federal government under the Constitution, although many knew at the time of the founding that a resolution of this issue would eventually require the exercise of national power.

The federal government now assumed new ends or objects, which were added to the Constitution in the Civil War amendments. First was the elimination of slavery by the Thirteenth Amendment, which abrogated an entire realm of previous state power and "consolidated" national authority on this question. But fundamental as this change was, once it occurred it turned out that its enforcement in the strict sense did not require a huge or permanent new presence of the federal government. Matters were different with the second objective of assuring an equality of treatment for the former slaves. Around this question emerged the great constitutional debate of the period.

Many Republicans understood that the purpose of the three Civil War amendments taken as a whole—the Thirteenth, Fourteenth, and Fifteenth Amendments—was to give the federal government broad power to deal with the "badges" or aftermath of slavery. This view, for example, lay behind the enactment of the Civil Rights Act of 1875, which outlawed discrimination in inns, public conveyances, and places of public amusement. They envisaged that the federal government had been invested, under something like the logic of Hamilton's argument in *The Federalist Papers*, with "every power requisite to the full accomplishment of the objects committed to its care." What had been committed to its care was the question of race relations as they flowed from the aftermath of the institution of slavery. How far the national government should go, how much it should legislate directly in the area of municipal affairs in order to accomplish this purpose, was a question left to the discretion of Congress and the president. This new national authority clearly did not fit into the previous system of federal-state relations. But that was the very purpose of the amendments. The old federalism had to yield to new national requirements.

There was a very different view of the Fourteenth and Fifteenth Amendments which held that they were intended only to *prevent* state action that was taken to deny certain rights. No new plenary authority was given to the federal government directly to legislate on local affairs. This interpretation was endorsed by the Supreme Court in *The Civil Rights Cases* (1883), which declared unconstitutional the Civil Rights Act of 1875. Speaking for the Court, Justice Joseph P. Bradley concluded that the Fourteenth Amendment did not "invest Congress with the power to legislate upon subjects which are within the domain of state legislation . . . or create a code of municipal law for the regulation of private rights," but only "provided modes of redress against the operation of state laws, and the action of state officers . . . when they are subversive of the fundamental rights specified in the amendment."[12] On the basis of this reasoning—although surely not legally sanctioned by this ruling—many southern states soon took the step of constructing segregation regimes based on whites-only political participation. By the time this occurred, there was no will left in Congress or the nation to defend the blacks' civil rights.

Legal scholars are still debating today how much power the Civil War amendments sought to entrust to the federal government. Behind this debate lies the substantive question of whether any viable federal policy existed at that time for resolving the race problem in the South. It may be, as some argue, that short of a half-century military occupation and military rule—something there was not enough political will to sustain—no national government solution was then feasible. Not every problem in politics has an immediate solution. Yet even if one accepts this rather fatalistic view, the course of history suggests that in the end the race issue could not have been handled without the exercise of broad federal power. When the dismantling of segregation finally began in the 1960s and 1970s, it was the federal government that took the lead, and it did so by measures that went well beyond those permitted under *The Civil Rights Cases*. (That these were claimed under the Commerce Clause rather than as a plenary power under the Fourteenth Amendment does not change the point.) The use of federal power in this case confirms the logic of the Federalist position. A government has to have authority commensurate to what is required to solve the problem.

The parties of bigger government in the nineteenth century operated largely within the context of *The Federalist Papers'* logic that argued for broad government discretion in the performance of certain limited ends. The Civil War clearly changed the scope of the ends, but it did not really change the basic logic of the argument. This understanding was opposed by the Democratic Party, which, in theory at any rate, looked much more closely for an explicit grant of constitutional authority for any action.

What existed, then, were two parties with two different interpretations of the Constitution—one "looser," the other "stricter," yet both conceiving of themselves as constitutional parties. Neither view triumphed unequivocally. The Federalists at the outset established some important precedents for a broad construction of the Constitution. But they were rejected decisively in 1800, and the Jeffersonians became the predominant party for the next sixty years. Yet in power the Jeffersonians were not as stingy with federal authority as their doctrines would have suggested. In 1860 the Republican Party brought back a looser-construction view and presided over the expansion of federal authority under the Civil War amendments. By the end of the century, however, Republicans had all but abandoned their civil rights agenda, and with business classes often favoring a laissez-faire position, they were less disposed to speak as favorably of national power.

Big Government is a creation of the twentieth century. It was supported initially by a philosophy mixing Darwinism and pragmatism that rejects any fixed idea of human nature and thus any permanent limit on government. The scope of government, including even the practical objects it pursues, cannot be determined in advance, but—to cite Dewey's formulation—is "something to be critically and experimentally determined."[13] Proponents of Big Government reject the idea of limited government, but they also bring a new attitude or spirit to the use of government. It is not a need for discretion that they emphasize so much as an experimental or creative use of government power under the direction of social science. Big Government cannot really begin to be understood without appreciating the excitement engendered among elites at the prospect of applying social science to transform society. Society is the canvass on which these new artists paint—and repaint—their masterworks. Their medium is the government program.

Not any end, of course, is consistent with the idea of Big Government. The objectives are to create a society that achieves social justice—meaning greater equality and uniformity of treatment—and that produces a better (or today perhaps a healthier) individual. Proponents of Big Government are so convinced that these goals represent the deepest and truest aspirations of modern democracy that they never doubt that the good citizen is the policy analyst devoted to the use of government (which is never in fact admitted to be an object of private ambition or pleasure). Some of the new uses of government go well beyond any that were intended for the federal government under the Constitution. This fact was widely understood at the beginning of the twentieth century not only by the opponents of the new logic but also by its proponents. Advocates of Big Government regarded the Constitution—not just in its late-nineteenth-century interpretation by the courts, but in its conception—as an impediment to the development of a positive state.

According to J. Allen Smith, the "framers of the Constitution wished to bring about the limitation of governmental functions because they feared the consequences of majority rule . . . and [sought to] perpetuate the ascendancy of the property-holding class in a society leavened with democratic ideas."[14]

Today, of course, no one speaks of a tension between the Constitution and Big Government. Everything has been hidden or denied. This change in discourse results from the success Big Government has had in grafting new powers and responsibilities onto the federal government without any formal changes in the Constitution. Once this success began to be enjoyed, it was not very difficult to decide that is far better to run with the Founders than against them.

To prepare for and legitimize this pro-Constitution position, Big Government advocates adopted a two-part strategy. They offered a new theory of interpreting the Constitution that effectively eliminates the idea of any permanent limits or restrictions—reading it in light of "present-day" needs—and they began to emphasize the continuities between their understanding of federal power and that of the pre-Progressive parties of government. Herbert Croly pioneered this last part of the strategy in his famous plea in *The Promise of American Life* to adopt "Hamiltonian means to Jeffersonian ends," even though a fair reading of his book shows that, even in his own thinking, the "Hamiltonian means" went well beyond anything Hamilton ever had in mind. Conservatives today have been induced to accept this view, and the more they have done so, the more they have been obliged to distance themselves from *The Federalist Papers* and from all of the nineteenth-century parties of government and to adopt the constitutional views of their opponents.

To stress the anticonstitutional character of Big Government thinking is not, of course, to claim that every expansion of federal power called for by the twentieth-century parties of government was contrary to the logic of *The Federalist Papers*. The advent of the case for Big Government did not abrogate the previous justification of broad discretion in the pursuit of the limited ends of government. On the basis of the previous thinking of the nineteenth-century parties of government, there would clearly have been grounds for an expansion of federal power to handle some of the new problems posed by the conditions of the twentieth century. The huge new demands connected with providing national security for a world power, the wider range of problems associated with a far more interdependent economy among the states, and the whole range of unfinished business relating to race relations in the South—any and all of these, by an understanding of the Constitution akin to that of the parties of bigger government of the nineteenth century, would have allowed for a much wider use of federal power. A large part of the Progressive movement thought this way, as illustrated by steps that were taken during the administrations of Theodore Roosevelt, William Howard Taft, and Herbert Hoover.

The fact that an older justification for the use of federal power in many areas continued to operate complicates any analysis of Big Government, because not all of the expansion of government in the twentieth century can be attributed to Big Government thinking. In addition, some of the major programs for the government expansion occurred during the economic collapse of the Depression, and Big Government proponents could easily have blurred in their own minds—indeed often had an interest in blurring—the distinction between the previous justification for government action and the new one. Despite these difficulties, however, it is important to keep the theoretical distinction between these two views in mind, even if it cannot be calculated with mathematical precision. As a general matter, one can say that the amount of government attributable to Big Government represents the amount we have actually gotten, less the amount that a discretionary view would have yielded. And that difference by any reckoning is huge.

Big Government made its greatest advances during the Progressive era, the New Deal, and the Great Society. In each of these periods, its advance was promoted by a key presidential election (1912, 1936, and 1964, respectively) in which the party of government won a landslide victory over the Republicans, who in turn received three of their lowest vote totals of the century.[15] In the election of 1912, the party of government was represented not by one but two candidates: Woodrow Wilson, the nominee of the Democratic Party, who ran on the program known as the New Freedom, and Teddy Roosevelt, the nominee of the newly formed Progressive Party, who offered the more statist vision of the New Nationalism. (Roosevelt's new position marked a dramatic change, to the point of being almost a repudiation, of his earlier position while president.) These two parties of government finished first and second, with the Republican Party under Taft, which by default became the party opposing government, winning just 23 percent of the popular vote.

There were important problems facing the nation in 1912 relating to the operation of trusts and the banking system, and these no doubt would have led to new (or renewed) exercises of federal power under a previous understanding of the role of government. (The Federal Reserve system, for example, only reintroduced a type of authority that the federal government had already exercised in chartering the national banks.) Yet one of the Progressive candidates—Roosevelt—went well beyond previous understandings and became a spokesman for the new view of Big Government. The other Progressive, Wilson, was more cautious during the campaign, having begun to wonder whether Roosevelt's brand of Progressivism, which was inspired by Croly, did not go too far in undermining constitutional government.

But whatever hesitations Wilson himself expressed during the 1912 campaign, he had earlier gone quite far in questioning the Constitution, regretting its outmoded "Newtonian" foundation in an era that demanded a "Darwinian" perspective. The spirit of this enterprise was captured in two of Wilson's favorite words, "state" and "administration," which together conveyed a preference for securing results by collective public action guided by "scientific" knowledge rather than by the spontaneous coordination of individual behavior. "The idea of the state is the conscience of administration. Seeing everyday new things which the state ought to do, the next thing is to see clearly how it ought to do them."[16]

The Progressive period, and later the New Deal, occurred at a time when the dominant philosophical school in the nation was pragmatism. It has sometimes been wondered why this school and its leading proponent, John Dewey, showed so decided a preference for the "state" and "administration" when the case in favor of collective public solutions had never been proven on the "pragmatic" grounds of actual performance. But this mystery dissolves once one distinguishes the vernacular use of pragmatic today (a common-sense view of what works) from the actual philosophy of pragmatism as it was espoused by Dewey. Rexford Tugwell, who would later become a leader of Franklin Delano Roosevelt's brain trust, offered the best explanation of what Deweyian pragmatism was really all about. What Tugwell learned from Dewey, he said, was that pragmatism in the social sphere "meant something more than judging things or institutions by working tests. It meant the future could be brought into focus; judged in advance as a working hypothesis, and altered before it was reached. This was and is the essence of planning."[17] In this view not only was the old presumption in favor of restraint in the use of governmental power eliminated, but a new presumption in favor of experimentation and social engineering was instituted.[18]

The philosophy of pragmatism that supplied much of the foundation for Big Government rested on the idea that there were no fixed natures, but rather matter in motion. A Constitution based on a static idea of natural rights was thus an impediment to progress. To move forward, the human species must employ what Dewey called "social intelligence" and the "technique of social and moral engineering" in order to control and master social processes.[19] Dewey extended his idea of no fixed natures to human nature, arguing that there is no self-subsisting or "ready-made" individual; instead, there is an entity that is wholly moved, shaped, and formed by something outside of itself. Social institutions "are means of *creating* individuals," who are endlessly malleable and subject to alteration through social control.[20] Social engineering was hampered by the arbitrary limits imposed by constitutional government, even under a discretionary view of the exercise of that power.

The Progressive impulse to organize and administer was by no means limited to the federal government. It extended to other levels of government, and Progressives in addition pressed a full-scale strategy for altering the institutions of civil society, from educational to religious institutions. State and local governments had, of course, always exercised wide discretion—under their traditional "police powers"—over controlling individual behavior and shaping human character.[21] Yet nineteenth-century constitutionalism never came close in its principles to sanctioning the scope of social intervention permitted under the pragmatic view, in part because it held to a view of fixed human nature that placed a conceptual limit on what institutions could aspire to produce. Not so for the pragmatists for whom the individual is a "social construction, and discursive practices go all the way down."[22] What Progressives also brought to the table was the new idea of efficiency through central bureaucratic institutions. And the most ardent Progressives generally tried to introduce national support for their programs, as planning at the national level offered the greatest scope for exercising "social control." At whatever level or in whatever form it operated, Progressivism was not the least hesitant in prescribing and molding certain forms of behavior. It did not operate under a "do-as-you-like" ethic. In welfare policy, for example, Progressives often took rather stern measures to compel clients to be industrious, or, when dealing with immigrants, to moralize and "Americanize" their charges.

Big Government thinking in its first phase was a discourse that emphasized not rights but power and authority. Rights were understood as limitations on the power of government that protected a form of "individualism" devoted to egoism and money making. The aim of Big Government was to free people from this low system of rights and, in Croly's phrase, to "raise human nature" by promoting a genuine "individuality."[23] As Dewey wrote, "the problem of constructing a new individuality consonant with the objective conditions under which we live is the deepest problem of our times."[24] The new individuality had a vague and airy quality to it, but its construction depended on a new form of education and on the secularization of society. Government could not do this by itself, but it was clearly conceived as the instrument that would take the lead in promoting this transformation and in leveraging other parts of civil society.

The second period in the advance of Big Government occurred with the New Deal. Big Government now underwent a name change, from progressivism to liberalism. Because Franklin Roosevelt's actual party, the Democratic Party, had not traditionally been a party of government, he concluded that some other label would be necessary to designate and distinguish his governing program. Henceforth, liberalism, which was the name that Croly and Dewey employed in their writings in the *New Republic*, became the label for the expansion of government—especially the federal government—to protect the "many" from the "few."

Roosevelt's approach was endorsed in the election of 1936, in which the Republican Party, whose platform warned that "the preservation of political liberty was for the first time threatened by Government itself," was soundly defeated, winning only eight electoral votes. Big Government was triumphant. Indeed, some argue that this election provided a de facto ratification of a constitutional amendment that gave the federal government the power to take whatever measures it wanted in the economic realm.[25] The Supreme Court, it is true, continued for a brief moment to defy this "amendment," prompting Roosevelt to respond with his Court-packing plan, and while Roosevelt suffered a technical rebuke in his unsuccessful battle for that plan, he nonetheless won the war when the Court acceded to his views. And even his partial setback later turned into a huge victory for liberalism, as the Court proceeded to use its independence in the next generation to become the foremost instrument of Big Government, pushing its agenda farther than either the legislature or the executive.[26]

The New Deal program—actually, there were two or three different variants of the program over this period—was enacted during the most severe economic crisis in American history. Previous discretionary constitutional thinking would surely have provided in this situation for using national powers to their fullest—and perhaps even asking for more. But it is noteworthy that the radical judgments that capitalism was a dead letter and that further economic growth was impossible were espoused mostly by those who, before the crisis, had *already* championed Big Government. Big Government thinking—and not merely a discretionary response about how to meet the crisis—lay behind the first New Deal program of corporatist economic planning.

For many, the Depression represented a kind of vindication, proving that limited government had failed and that only planning and collective solutions could now succeed. Markets, many of the New Deal planners thought, were obsolete and destructive. As Tugwell wrote, "when industry is government and government is industry, the dual conflict deepest in our modern institutions will be abated."[27] Reflecting for a time this current of thought, Roosevelt stated: "The day of enlightened administration has come."[28]

The corporatist model of planning was eventually abandoned, having been blocked in part by certain decisions taken by the Supreme Court. The core of New Deal thinking shifted thereafter to federal programs to ensure welfare and security. To build support for these programs, Roosevelt eventually turned to the language of "rights," which Big Government theorists had previously scorned for being the source of our problems. Roosevelt called for a "Second Bill of Rights" that included "the right to earn enough to provide adequate food and clothing and recreation," "the right of every family to a decent home," "the right to a good education," "the right to adequate protection from the economic fears of old age, sickness, accident and unemployment," and "the right to adequate medical care."[29]

In one deft stroke Roosevelt thus turned the language of limited government on its head, using it to support Big Government. Indeed, he used the most restrictive variant of that language—the emphasis on rights found in Jeffersonian discourse—rather than language of discretion often relied on in the Federalist tradition. The result was a complete revision: Big Government was now pursued under a discourse of rights rather than under an assertion of government authority and social control. "Individualism" was likewise given a new meaning that favored Big Government. As Dewey remarked in *Individualism Old and New*: "Fear of loss of work, dread of the oncoming of old age, create an anxiety and eat into self-respect in a way that impairs personal dignity. Where fears abound, courageous and robust individuality is undermined."[30] This formulation became the foundation of Roosevelt's famous declarations of "freedom from want, freedom from fear."[31]

The third and final moment in the development of Big Government came with the Great Society. Running appropriately on the longest party platform in American history, the party of government in 1964 offered a cornucopia of new federal governmental programs. Republicans in that year nominated Barry Goldwater and launched a frontal attack in their platform on Big Government: "Year after year in the name of benevolence, [the Democrats] have sought the enlargement of the Federal power. Year after year, in the guise of concern for others, they have lavishly expended the resources of their fellow citizens." Goldwater suffered a defeat comparable in magnitude to Alf Landon's in 1936, which opened the door to a still more rapid expansion of the federal government. So many new programs were created during this time that there are still disputes about the exact number.

The Great Society, which commanded policy thinking from the mid-1960s through much of the 1970s, brought together a number of different and sometimes partially conflicting elements. At the same time that Big Government philosophy was expanded to its outer limits, certain of its traditional underpinnings—chiefly, a faith in social science and a belief in progress—were beginning to come under attack from within the Big Government party itself. These attacks grew more pronounced as disenchantment with the Vietnam War increased.

Five elements of Great Society thinking can be identified. First, in the tradition of social engineering, the Great Society was accompanied by an unparalleled confidence in the federal government and in the expertise of public policy analysts. Professors of social science armed with proposed government programs in their briefcases were shuttled in and out of Washington at a rate that has never been equaled. This aspect of the Great Society, representing the undistilled essence of Big Government thought, is best captured in a passage by Harry McPherson, President Johnson's speech writer and chief advisor. It summarizes the aspirations of the Great Society and the faith that its adherents had in governmental programs:

> People were suffering from a sense of alienation from one another, of anomie, of powerlessness. This affected the well to do as much as it did the poor. Middle-class women, bored and friendless in the suburban afternoons; fathers, working at "meaningless" jobs, or slumped before the television sets; sons and daughters desperate for relevance—all were in need of community, beauty, purpose. . . . What would change all of this was a creative public effort: for the middle class new parks, conservation, the removal of billboards and junk, . . . better television, aid to the arts; for the poor job training, Head Start, decent housing, medical care, civil rights; for both, and for bridging the gap between them, VISTA, the teacher corps, the community action agencies, mass transportation, model cities.[32]

Second, the Great Society created what amounted to a national police power for assuring civil rights for black Americans, especially in the South. The term "national police power" was not, of course, used, because the federal government was held to possess no such general power. It was carried out under other grants of federal authority, most notably under the authority to regulate interstate commerce.[33] The Supreme Court now admitted a power through the back door that it had kept out through the front door. This part of the Great Society had its roots in the Republican program of a century earlier and operated initially from the same logic: that if a government was to be assigned an objective—handling the problem of race relations and ensuring equality of treatment—it must be given adequate power to achieve that objective. But this logic was quickly distorted or lost because the objective or end was not specified in the Constitution. The justification for the expansion of federal power to achieve civil rights allowed for federal power to be used for any end or objective, not just civil rights on racial questions. A breach was opened in the Constitution through which Big Government advocates pushed an entire transformation in the relation of the national to the state and local governments. If legislating on civil rights in the matter of race relations was to be permitted under a package of general federal powers, then legislating on any other matter became no less permissible.

Third, the Great Society took a step beyond the traditional objective of trying to guarantee an equality before the law. The new objective for federal policy was to ensure that all people start the race for the goods and benefits of society on more equal terms. This objective went under the name of "equality of opportunity," and it led to new federal programs that entered deeply into the institutions of civil society. The purpose of these programs was to help people to get ready for this race. As Lyndon Johnson remarked in his famous 1965 commencement address at Howard University:

> You do not take a person who, for years, has been hobbled by chains and liberate him, bring him up to the starting line of a race and then say, "you are free to compete with all others," and still justly believe that you have been completely fair. . . . We seek not just freedom but opportunity. We seek . . . not just equality as a right and a theory but equality as a fact and equality as a result.[34]

The scope of federal intervention was subsequently expanded still further when "equality of opportunity" was transformed in its meaning to include, under the rubric of "affirmative action," the achievement of certain results for designated minority groups. Promoting equality of opportunity and then requiring equality of results followed so quickly upon the goal of trying to guarantee civil rights in the original sense of equality before the law that all three were thought of as parts of the same thing: "civil rights" in a general sense. This conflation was a deliberate rhetorical strategy of Big Government proponents that allowed a broad array of programs to be justified by an idea that supported a more limited kind of intervention.

Fourth, the Great Society came to include a "countercultural" element that accepted and in some ways embraced a distrust of traditional social norms and of all existing authority, including government authority. As the Vietnam War continued, opposition grew within the Big Government coalition to the whole "system" of liberal democracy and liberal capitalism. Pressures came for both more government and less enforcement of anything that could smack of "bourgeois" values. The ethic of doing one's own thing—or the group doing its own thing—became a neutral way of claiming a right not to do what the general society or system wanted. The Great Society incorporated programs of "community control" and endorsed norms of "self-cultivation" or "self-direction," at least where these norms came from groups that were critical of American society. Many apparently held the view that the government should be financing a revolution against itself. The peculiar combination of a widening of the scope of government and a weakening of a resolve to move it in any particular direction became one of the most re-marked-upon features of the Great Society period.[35]

Finally—and in what looks like a partial contradiction of what was just said—the Great Society period was characterized by a quite strong, if usually unavowed, movement by the federal government to impose a new morality on many communities. The endorsement of the norm of "self-direction" may have meant giving up on a vigorous and positive national program of social control, but the norm clearly contained within itself a secularist, liberationist, and multiculturalist agenda. It was antitraditional, often aggressively so. Included as examples of this agenda were policies banning the acknowledgment of religion in the schools, a full right to abortion, and promotion of multilingual schooling. Liberals often depict this agenda as a freeing of individuals from the dictates of local communities (and therefore as a reduction of the scope of government). But many in these communities saw these actions as the interferences of Big Government that overrode the legitimate community prerogatives and sought to dictate national "avant-garde" standards. It was the nonelective branches of the national government—the bureaucratic agencies and especially the courts—that took the lead in promoting this program, which created a new alliance between Big Government supporters and defenders of judicial and bureaucratic activism. In reaction to this connection, conservatives naturally identified Big Government with these institutions and began to embrace, perhaps too hastily, a populist Jeffersonian philosophy of local government and antijudicialism.

It is a notable general feature of the Great Society that almost all aspects of its agenda were advanced under a banner of promoting rights. Many who write on this period today refer to it as an age of "rights talk" in which policies were justified by reference to what the "demanding" individual wanted rather than to what the individual owed to others by way of restraint or duty.[36] While this characterization correctly identifies a great deal of the rhetoric of this period, there is a need here to avoid being taken in completely by what has often been, after all, no more than a rhetorical strategy. The putative rights involved are so indiscriminate as to drain the term of any special meaning. Some are the traditional rights of individuals, such as speech (but rarely property), or the traditional civil rights of the type proclaimed as early as the Civil Rights Acts of the 1860s and 1870s. But other rights were claims to programmatic benefits, from long-established benefits (education) to new programs that were being advanced (medical care, day care, extensions of welfare, and so forth), while others still were broad demands for cultural recognition of various groups. Rights talk has thus often become a reflection of Big Government discourse, which has led certain conservatives to turn too quickly against rights and against individualism. The consequence has been to compromise the protection of what are real rights and to forget their underpinning in Nature and the Constitution.

Big Government is more than a legal doctrine. It is a general posture or orientation toward governing and the role of government that is supported by certain mental habits and modes of thinking. The more its modes of thinking are accepted as normal or neutral, the more the nation has fallen under the sway of Big Government, regardless of any setbacks on particular issues. All orientations toward government, of course, rest on certain modes of thinking. Seen in this way, the major intellectual and political battles since 1912 have reflected confrontations between modes that support limited constitutional government, in which governmental action is an intervention and thus something to be justified, and modes that support Big Government, in which governmental action is taken as the norm or rule in need of no special justification.

A primary mode of thought associated with Big Government is the substitution of policy thinking for constitutional thinking. Policy thinking conceives that for every major arena of society there must in principle be a public policy to govern it. Society is blocked out into its different domains, and the full task of governing involves developing a national policy for each one: an education policy, an arts policy, a family policy, an "industrial" policy, and so forth. This disposition, it must be said, does not dictate any particular kind of government action, or even necessarily that any government action be taken. But as a mode of thought, policy thinking endorses the notion that if no action is taken, it is the result of a policy determination that there should be none, not the result of a constitutional limitation. Under this view, the mental default option about government changes. Nonintervention is put on the same plane as intervention, and the absence of government action has no more presumption in its favor than the presence of government action. Nothing, except perhaps the protection of certain rights, is placed in a special constitutional zone in which action is proscribed. Policy thinking thus dismisses or negates the whole logic of constitutional thinking. According to constitutional thinking, federal government action in certain areas is off-limits—not for reasons of efficiency or of a better immediate outcome, but because of a solemn legal pact entered into on the basis of calculations about the effects over time of the exercise of government power in a certain arena.

A perfect illustration of policy thinking may be seen in the work of Professor Robert Reich, who served as secretary of labor during the first Clinton administration. In his book *Tales of a New America*, which collected his thoughts from the 1980s, Reich called for what was then the central new agenda item of proponents of Big Government, namely, a full-scale "industrial policy." Under this kind of policy, the United States would review its specific, piecemeal laws and policies in the fields of taxation, patents, and research and proceed to adopt a comprehensive strategy for economic modernization and development relying on an extensive new role for the federal government. In doing so, the United States would be following the examples of other countries, such as Japan and Germany, which were taken at that time to be the models of economic development. But recognizing the resistance, partly on constitutional grounds, to the adoption of such a policy of large-scale and systematic governmental intervention into the economy, Reich shifts grounds. He claims that we already have an "industrial policy," albeit unconsciously, because a decision *not to* intervene is as much a decision as a decision *to* intervene: "A decision not to decide simply forces private parties to rely on a priori decisions." He continues: "The doubt over whether government should enter upon a centralized 'industrial policy' has tended broadly to miss the point. Our government and every government is continuously engaged in devising industrial policies."[37]

Reich's point is that if a "non-policy" is already as much a policy as is a policy, then all policies ought to be laid out side by side to determine which one is most advantageous. The distinction between a positive legal intervention and a nonintervention is purely formal. The merits of one or the other are to be based strictly on the grounds of policy analysis. The way of thinking associated with limited constitutional government, for which the formal distinction between intervention and nonintervention is central, is defined out of existence to make way for the thinking that characterizes Big Government, where policy analysis alone will decide the merits of intervention.

A second mode of thinking connected with Big Government is the "socialization" of all aspects of society. "Socialize" has generally been a term connected with socialism, where it refers to the specific programs under which government assumes legal title to ownership of the major means of production or redistributes income and property. But there is a more fundamental meaning of "socialize" that must precede the enactment of any such program; this meaning refers to the way of thinking in which, theoretically, the goods and property in society are conceived as being in the first instance socially or collectively, rather than privately, owned. Government then has the rightful jurisdiction to decide on their legal title of ownership and their distribution. Socializing in this meaning need not require an actual program of socialization, but it allows such a program to take place as a normal decision of government.

The project of Big Government in America, while it has rejected most of the specific nostrums of socialism, has promoted a socializing way of thinking. This way of thinking is, in a sense, the opposite of individualism. As Dewey wrote, "the only form of enduring social organization that is now possible is one in which the new forces of productivity are cooperatively controlled and used in the interest of the effective liberty and the cultural development of the individuals that constitute society."[38] The socializing way of thinking is most often associated with economic questions of wealth and income redistribution. At the outset Herbert Croly declared that "if wealth, particularly when accumulated in large amounts, has a public function, and if its possession imposes a public duty, . . . [that duty] should be assumed and should be efficiently performed by the state."[39] Ever since, Big Government thinking has regarded national income as a nationally owned resource subject to being divided up according to good policy that may take into account policy considerations of efficiency and justice.

Socializing thinking extended well beyond wealth and included other objects, such as property in our children. The extensive policy of forced busing of school children was a primary example. This was an experiment in which, under the most expansive conceptions, children were socialized and viewed as resources "owned" by government during certain hours of the day, to be distributed to achieve a benevolent social result. Indirectly, the same way of thinking lies behind government affirmative action policies. Here jobs or positions are conceptually socialized and regarded as a publicly owned resource, which are then distributed by government in accord with some criterion of equity.

A more subtle and far-reaching instance of a socializing thinking is found in the notion of the collectivity owning people's volition or will. People's volition here is conceptualized as something government has a right to control in order to break down resistance to Big Government. People are deliberately put in a position where they become so dependent on government that they cannot easily exercise a choice against it. Under the carrot variant of this strategy, as expounded by (among others) sociologist Theda Skocpol, the party of government should seek universal, as distinct from limited or means-tested, social programs. Means-tests programs are to be avoided because all "measures that start out small and are narrowly focused must wither and lose support or . . . fail to receive the resources they need to meet crying social needs."[40] To deal with this problem—the "problem" being that middle-class citizens do not willingly consent to Big Government—a way must be found to alter the character of middle-class people and eliminate their will to resist. Universal programs are the means, and Skocpol recommends, regardless of the recipient's income, "child support for all single custodial parents, parental leave and child-care assistance for all working families, and universal health benefits." Programs of this kind are more important for their effect on people's volition than on the services they deliver; they create a mass clientele and transform people into partisans of Big Government.

Under the stick variant of this strategy, government asserts its control over people's volition by passing a threshold at which it becomes so big and costly—and thus taxes become so high—that average families lack the means to purchase certain basic things on their own in the market, such as daycare or education. Families must therefore turn to government to receive these essential services. This strategy is best followed in an era of limited economic growth and of high taxes, where a squeeze is placed on families that can force them to seek still more services from the government, which in turn requires still higher taxes. Something of this sort occurred in France and Germany in the late 1980s, and many advocates of Big Government envisaged putting a similar strategy into effect during the low-growth periods of the late 1970s and early 1980s, and then again in the early 1990s.

A third mode of thinking associated with Big Government alters people's mental picture of the social world so that the distinction between the realm of government and the realm of civil society begins to lose intuitive sense. This change may take place when the sheer size of government attains a level at which people begin to consider the reciprocal effect of government programs on one another as greater than the impact of government programs on society. To select an example almost at random, when it is government's responsibility to pay for the medical costs of poor children, then a proposed program to supply prenatal care for mothers may be presented, not as a further intervention of government into society but as an effective administrative step to save money. Big Government is invoked as a cause for yet-bigger government. Whatever the actual economic logic of such cases, the effect of people thinking about the world in this way represents an enormous boost to Big Government. Government policies are no longer conceived as interventions into a private sphere, but as adjustments in a vast national accounting system in which everything is already on the public books and in which costs are merely being shifted from one area to another.

A fourth mode of thinking that has promoted Big Government is an understanding of public finance that substitutes a moralistic reasoning based on "justice" for an economic reasoning of scarcity. Under this way of thinking, public spending is not governed so much by considerations of what we can afford as by a notion of what we "deserve." Escaping the logic of economic scarcity was one of the most important mental habits that favored the growth of Big Government during the long period of budget deficits from the late 1960s through the mid-1990s. It represented a remarkable transformation of the traditional view based on people's "natural" approach that issues of public finance bear some relation to people's own life experiences: One can spend what one can afford, and if one comes up short, something must be sacrificed, however much one would like to keep it.

The reversal of the traditional way of thinking about public finance has been promoted by a series of economic ideas that began with Keynesianism and continued through some of the extreme versions of "supply-side" economics. Each of these undermined in its own way the analogy between private and public finance and was used in the end to justify dismissing economic reasoning that emphasized scarcity and restraint. This reversal has also been promoted by the shift in the locus of programs and spending from the state and local to the national level. An economic mode of thinking in government still tends to prevail at the state and especially the local level, where public authorities must balance budgets and where additional spending programs are known to show up noticeably in higher taxes. But when decisions take place in a government so far from home and so large that each individual program hardly affects one's own tax rate, and when the government in question does not have to pay now for current expenditures but borrows or makes a promise on the basis of what someone else at some future time will pay, then the constraint of scarcity may begin to diminish in the public's conception of public finance. Although many may mention the issue of limits—Washington politics for a whole decade paid lip service to the crisis of deficits—it functioned more as an abstract proposition than a real constraint. When it came down to it, spending for the party of government tended to be set by what people were said to deserve or to be entitled to. A budget cannot be cut, because it would be "unfair."

Economic reasoning in moral terms was the characteristic rhetorical mode of Big Government thinking, and under its sway a whole set of concepts was to shield people from a genuine encounter with the economic principle of scarcity. In the 1960s and 1970s the Brookings Institution published a whole series of books on the national budget in which their leading economists called for balancing the budget on the basis of calculations of "full employment." But America never had "full employment" during this period, and thus balancing the budget at full employment never balanced the real budget. The concept was nothing more than an elaborate linguistic device to justify Big Government. Behind it lay the idea that it would be "unfair" to balance the *real* budget because too many new social programs would have to be forgone. Later, in the 1980s, the same Brookings economists introduced a new concept that had a similar effect: the "non-defense budget." The idea here was that if there was to be an increase in spending on defense, it should not "count" against anyone. The non-defense side should not be cut to pay for the defense side because this would not be "fair" to those whose benefits might be reduced or to those who might benefit from some new programs.

In more recent times such linguistic transformations have been elevated to the status of a refined art. President Clinton called the sums needed for his 1993 program of government expansion not "spending" but "investments," as if these programs did not cost anything. The Progressive Policy Institute, along with a number of prestigious newspapers, began speaking of corporate "tax subsidies" instead of corporate "tax breaks." A tax break carries the connotation that a corporation has avoided paying what it should have paid and leads to the conclusion that the "break" should be eliminated and everyone's taxes reduced proportionately. By contrast, a tax subsidy carries the connotation that the government has unjustly given money away which properly belongs to the government; the subsidy should be ended so that the government can then keep *its* rightful revenue, which it will then presumably invest. A simple change of words alters the whole presumption from the idea that the wealth of society is privately owned (in which case taxation is regarded as a taking in need of justification) to the idea that wealth is publicly owned (in which case what private entities keep is a gift or concession of government).

An early discussion of the problem of public finance is found in *The Prince*, wherein Niccolò Machiavelli poses the question of how "liberal" a prince should be in his spending (*liberal* here refers to being generous in the spending of money). The first answer he gives is that a prudent prince cannot afford to be too liberal, because in order to secure the requisite funds he will have to take money from his subjects by confiscation, murder, or higher taxes. These measures will make his position more precarious. But Machiavelli then offers a second answer. A prince *can* be liberal—and will serve his interest in being so—if he can acquire his money by plundering it from someone else: "And you may indeed be very generous with what is not the property of yourself or your subjects . . . for spending the wealth of others will not diminish your reputation."[41]

Modern democratic leaders often follow this course of action, albeit in a novel way. They are liberal with their present citizens by plundering the citizens of future generations. This is known as deficit spending. It is also the foundation of modern public pensions systems. These originally were sold to the public on the basis of the fiction that they were "insurance" schemes. As an "insurance" program, people had the right to think that they were paying the full weight of their own benefits, which could then properly be called entitlements.

This policy represents a socialization of wealth across generations. The present generation has assumed the power to make decisions not only for those who are now here, but for those yet to come. If this generation owns the wealth of future generations, the agency best suited to impose the future tax and collect this debt is the government. So baldly stated, a "taking" of wealth of this kind might seem immoral. But if a mass distribution of wealth across generations has already happened and has become, so to speak, the standard way of doing business, then nothing immoral has occurred.

Finally, Big Government is promoted by a way of thinking that views the current size of government, if not its continued growth, as an inevitability beyond human control. Government is thought to be so enormous that no one could reasonably think that he or she could do anything to curtail it. Likewise, the enormity—and hence the abstractness—of the sums involved eliminates the possibility of feeling shame at demanding more or of taking pride at making a sacrifice. Anyone who would agree to a sacrifice would not be admirable, but a chump. One's own piece of the crime is so small that it cannot make a difference in the final result. Big Government is now almost a thing apart from us—an entity that moves on its own and that is subject to no one's control. It is bigger than all of us. It has become a force of its own that no one really believes can any longer be controlled or mastered. As

Jonathan Rauch has said, "the public and political activists are growing gradually, if grudgingly, more accepting of the natural limits on government's ability to change society. Now they need to begin accepting the limits on society's ability to change government."[42]

The success of Big Government appeals from 1912 through 1964 led many to conceive that the twentieth century would ratify an inexorable march toward an expanding federal government. Yet history has not proven so kind to this cause. Although the federal government has grown in many respects since the Great Society period, public support for the general idea of Big Government (or for liberalism) has fallen. The election of Ronald Reagan in 1980 and the Republican congressional election victory of 1994 demonstrated the political force of the suspicions against Big Government. The twenty-first century begins with the question of the scope of government still very much a live political issue.

Modern conservatism has made its stand by opposing Big Government. Conservatives have taken their case to the nation, and they have had at least some success in awakening people to what they regard as the danger of Big Government. But if conservatives have a fairly good idea of what they are against, they are unsure about what they would put in its place. In their sincere opposition to Big Government, they have—understandably perhaps—gravitated to its opposite. They have increasingly embraced "Little Government," a set of ideas that is populist, often hostile to necessary government authority, and sometimes isolationist. This approach represents a tacit admission that conservatism has lost the ability to define for itself its own view of government and has adopted as its own guiding principle the mirror image of what it opposes.

Some conservatives might say that raising this kind of objection is both unfair and imprudent. The great object today, they will argue, is to defeat Big Government. To do so, one should follow the simplest and clearest method, which is to make the case for Little Government. Practical politics is not a place for the overly scrupulous or fastidious. There is, one must concede, some force to this argument. But the loss of direction I have charged to modern conservatism is not without practical implications of its own. Is it really possible to imagine a viable conservative movement today that governs by the principles of Little Government? It would be the cruelest of ironies if conservatives were to win the battle against Big Government only to lose the war for establishing effective constitutional government.

NOTES

1. William Jefferson Clinton, State of the Union Address, January 23, 1996; <http://www.law.ou.edu/hist/state96.html>.
2. This does not mean, of course, that conservatism is obliged to accept every Federalist premise and reject every element of Anti-Federalism. Some of the best

expressions of conservative thought have drawn on both of these traditions and have sought to devise constructive syntheses between them.

3. Alexander Hamilton, James Madison, and John Jay, *The Federalist Papers*, ed. Clinton Rossiter (New York: Mentor Books, 1961), essay 31, 194.

4. *The Federalist Papers*, essay 31, 196. For a classic explanation of the Founders' understanding of the role of government, see Herbert Storing, "The Problem of Big Government," in *Toward a More Perfect Union*, ed. Joseph Bessette (Washington: AEI Press, 1995), 287–306.

5. Ralph Ketcham, *The Antifederalist Papers and the Constitutional Convention Debates* (New York: Mentor Books, 1996), 271.

6. *The Federalist Papers*, essay 17, 118.

7. *The Federalist Papers*, essay 46, 295. See also essay 27.

8. Morton J. Frisch, ed., *Selected Writings and Speeches of Alexander Hamilton* (Washington: AEI Press, 1985), 292.

9. Some argue that whatever the different ends of the two parties, Hamilton's program required positive intervention by government, while the Jeffersonian end was promoted by a policy of laissez-faire, or no federal government action. But it should be recalled that the Jeffersonians embraced their own schemes of nationally funded internal improvements and that they purchased the Louisiana Territory—despite doubts about the government's constitutional authority—in large part in order to try to promote an agricultural-based economy.

10. Herbert Croly, *The Promise of American Life* (New York: Dutton, 1963), 67. The only time the Whigs had control of both branches of the government was after the election of William Henry Harrison in 1840. But Harrison died almost immediately and was replaced by John Tyler, who was a Whig in name only. Tyler vetoed almost all of the Whigs' program—indeed, many congressional Whigs wanted him impeached—and the Democrats recaptured a majority in the House in the election of 1842.

11. Despite their lack of practical success, the Whigs did at least in theory pioneer some of the methods later used to expand the reach of the federal government. For example, Henry Clay was among the first to hit upon the idea of "revenue sharing" in which the federal government would distribute funds to the states to be spent for specified purposes. Daniel Walker Howe, *The Political Culture of the American Whigs* (Chicago: University of Chicago Press, 1979), 137. And Whigs occasionally tried to use these methods for purposes that seem reminiscent of modern programs, once helping to pass a bill disbursing federal aid to insane asylums that was ultimately vetoed by the Democratic president of the time, Franklin Pierce. Still, the broad tenor of their policies at the national level was consistent with that of their Federalist and National Republican predecessors.

12. *The Civil Rights Cases*, 109 U.S. 3 (1883).

13. John Dewey, *The Public and Its Problems* (New York: Henry Holt, 1927), 73–74.

14. J. Allen Smith, *The Spirit of American Government* (New York: Macmillan, 1907), 295, 298.

15. Taft won 23.2 percent in 1912; Alf Landon, 36.5 percent in 1936; and Barry Goldwater, 38.5 percent in 1964. George Bush received 37.7 percent of the vote in 1992, which was less than Goldwater, but Bush's score came in a three-way race.

16. Woodrow Wilson, "The Study of Administration," *Political Science Quarterly* 2 (June 1887): 201.

17. Rexford Tugwell, *To Lesser Heights of Morningside* (Philadelphia: University of Pennsylvania Press, 1982), 157.

18. See Dewey, *The Public and Its Problems*, 34.

19. John Dewey, *Reconstruction in Philosophy* (Boston: Beacon Press, 1957), 173. "Social control" was one of Dewey's favorite terms to express the potential influence of social science in modern society.

20. Dewey, *Reconstruction in Philosophy*, 194.

21. See William Novak, *The People's Welfare: Law and Regulation in Nineteenth-Century America* (Chicago: University of Chicago Press, 1996).

22. This is the characterization of Richard Rorty, who is describing Dewey's view (and his own) of the subject. Richard Rorty, *Achieving Our Country* (Cambridge: Harvard University Press, 1998), 35.

23. Croly, *Promise of American Life*, 399, 410.

24. John Dewey, *Individualism Old and New* (New York: Minton, Balch and Co., 1930), 32.

25. See Bruce Ackerman, *We the People* (Cambridge, Mass.: Belknap Press of Harvard University, 1991).

26. Much of this judicial promotion of Big Government occurred through statutory interpretation of welfare laws and antidiscrimination statutes. See Shep Melnick, *Between the Lines: Interpreting Welfare Rights* (Washington: Brookings Institution, 1994).

27. Rexford Tugwell, "The Principles of Planning and the Institution of Laissez-Faire," *American Economic Review* 22 (1932): 85–86. The New Deal position on planning is discussed in Donald Brand's "Competition and the New Deal Regulatory State," a paper presented at a conference on the New Deal at Brandeis University, Spring 1998.

28. Franklin Roosevelt, *Public Papers and Addresses* (New York: Macmillan, 1941), 1:7551–52.

29. Franklin Roosevelt, State of the Union Address of 1944 and campaign address of October 28, 1944, cited in Roosevelt, *Public Papers and Addresses*.

30. John Dewey, *Individualism Old and New* (New York: Capricorn Books, 1962), 68.

31. These rhetorical revisions, particularly the adoption of the language of rights, have had certain consequences for the Big Government project. In *Democracy's Discontents* (Cambridge: Harvard University Press, 1996), Michael Sandel contends that the change entailed an abandonment of the "soul-forming" part of the project that had sought to define the good human being and citizen (the "raising of human nature" of which Croly spoke). Big Government now had to content itself with the goal of achieving social justice. Sandel goes farther and argues that this change represents the fundamental turning point in American history. Before this change, the American regime was "republican," meaning it was concerned with an idea of the good of the citizen; afterward it became "liberal," meaning it was concerned only with rights and distributive justice. Although Sandel is quite right to point out the change of rhetoric, one wonders whether he was not too much taken in by what was, after all, mostly just a change of rhetoric. Sandel's position loses sight of the common links that bind the Big Government project together from one period to the next.

32. Harry McPherson, *A Political Education* (Boston: Little, Brown, 1972), 301–2. Much of the same rhetoric, in a slightly more subdued form, can be found in Lyndon Johnson's Great Society speech given at the University of Michigan, May 22, 1964.

33. See, for example, Title II of the Civil Rights Act of 1964, which assures access of all persons without regard to race in any place that "serves the public" or is a place of "public accommodation," "if its operations affect commerce." Commercial operations are defined very broadly to include almost any inn or restaurant. This law was upheld in *Heart of Atlanta Motel, Inc. v. United States* (1964) and *Katzenbach v. McClung* (1964).

34. Lyndon B. Johnson, Commencement Address at Howard University, June 4, 1965; <http://www.lbjlib.utexas.edu/archives.hom/speeches.hom>.

35. See Aaron Wildavsky, "A World of Difference," in Anthony King, ed., *The New American Political System*, 2d ed. (Washington: AEI Press, 1990), 263–87. Certain conservatives went along as well, on principled libertarian grounds: Enforcing morality meant bureaucracy and social workers and someone from the state looking over your shoulder, which was a kind of state paternalism. So the view of some conservatives was, just give people the money and get out of their lives. Such ideas as the negative income tax as a replacement for welfare also enjoyed support among some conservative thinkers.

36. See Mary Ann Glendon, *Rights Talk* (New York: Free Press, 1991), and Sandel, *Democracy's Discontents*.

37. Robert Reich, *Tales of a New America* (New York: Times Books, 1987), 228–31.

38. John Dewey, *Liberalism and Social Action*, cited in Deborah Morris and Ian Shapiro, eds., *John Dewey: The Political Writings* (Indianapolis: Hackett Publishing, 1993), 154.

39. Croly, *Promise of American Life*, 382.

40. Theda Skocpol, *Social Policy in the United States* (Princeton: Princeton University Press, 1995), 267.

41. Niccolò Machiavelli, *The Prince*, ed. and trans. Mark Musa (New York: St. Martin's, 1964), 134.

42. Jonathan Rauch, "Demosclerosis Returns," *Wall Street Journal*, April 14, 1998, A22.

6

Liberalism and Big Government: Tocqueville's Analysis

Harvey C. Mansfield and Delba Winthrop

In our time and in America, liberalism has become identified with Big Government, and neither term is in good repute. Liberalism became the "L-word" of the 1988 presidential campaign, used as a label to belittle and dismiss; more recently it has been associated, unflatteringly, with "the nanny state." In response many liberals now call themselves "progressives" and try to find their roots in populism or republicanism understood as distinct from liberalism. Most impressive is the fact that the president of the party of Big Government, Bill Clinton, said in his 1996 State of the Union speech: "The era of Big Government is over."

How did liberalism get into this predicament? Predicament it is, because liberalism began in the thought of John Locke in the seventeenth century as a philosophy of limited government. It was, of course, also a doctrine of sovereignty (even more so for the proto-liberal Thomas Hobbes), and thus no enemy to the authority of government. But sovereignty was an instrument, not the end, of liberalism; it provided the means by which government could act decisively and definitively. Sovereignty in a definite place would put a stop, it was thought, to argument and quarrel over jurisdiction, especially between the temporal and spiritual powers. But the end was to liberate men from higher powers over themselves, particularly the Church, and thus to release human powers for the preservation and enhancement of human life. In Locke's thought, government is unlimited in authority—there is no place it cannot go—and where it goes it is vigorous and energetic. But it is limited in scope by the natural rights on which it is based, and consequently by the policy of toleration and the concern for private property to which those rights give rise, and the limitation is enforced by a constitution that requires elections and maintains a separation of powers.

Big Government, however, is intrusive and not liberating. It does not forsake the goal of liberation; it does not tell you directly how to live. But after promising liberation, it constrains your choices so severely that you feel powerless to follow your own way. Big Government constrains you for the sake of equality so that your freedom is no greater than anyone else's. It also constrains you for your own comfort and security. Its constant tendency to control and equalize the conditions of life leads it to attempt to diminish the risks of life by which inequalities of fortune, and even of merit, occur. In diminishing your risks Big Government diminishes your virtue, because it assumes responsibility for making things come out well for you despite your errors or, as is more and more likely, your inaction. Big Government gathers up and exercises on your behalf the human powers that liberalism was supposed to release. Just as, before liberalism, divine power was engrossed by the clergy, so under liberalism human power becomes the government's.

TOCQUEVILLE'S PREDICTION

To learn how Big Government came to America in stages from the Progressives to the New Deal to the Great Society, and then to compare this history to the actions and experience of other liberal democracies, would be very useful. But in its essentials and in many details, our history has been anticipated by the foresight of Alexis de Tocqueville. Tocqueville made a point of his foresight. The gradual development of equality of conditions, he said, was a "providential fact."[1] Whether because of his ability to see what was providential or because he could infer the direction of things from knowing their nature, he offered predictions, sometimes identifying them as such. Tocqueville is famous for his predictions, but this is partly because he actually made them—by contrast to the more formal political science of liberalism, which laid emphasis on, if it did not confine itself to, the statement of principles without saying how they were expected to be applied. Perhaps the formal liberals were more confident than Tocqueville that their principles would be applicable as intended.

What Tocqueville saw, and foresaw, was the democratic revolution and its consequences: individualism and despotism. Democracy in America, in the New World, in the modern world, is not a settled regime but essentially a revolution; democracy is constantly in the process of democratizing itself.[2] It has led, and will lead, to "individualism," Tocqueville's concept of the individual isolating himself alone, or at most in a small society of his familiars within the mass.[3] There in his weakness he submits to a new "mild despotism" of a democratic government that oppresses the people without cruelty or violence, behaving like a schoolmaster rather than a tyrant.

Tocqueville goes so far as to call such a people a "herd of timid and industrious animals,"[4] thus anticipating Friedrich Nietzsche's denunciations of democratic herd morality.[5] Since we get the same diagnosis of liberalism from a friend of liberalism, what need was there for the instruction of an enemy? And what need for Nietzsche to have become an enemy, when he could have read Tocqueville? Tocqueville the liberal speaks on liberalism as from a distance.

Tocqueville shows his distance from liberalism by presenting Big Government as a consequence of liberalism, not as a development that has occurred despite liberalism. What we now speak of as "Big Government" was for Tocqueville in a sense what every government desires to be, for every government desires to decide every question.[6] Still, there is now a new menace in the world, something "nameless" which the old terms tyranny and despotism do not quite fit.[7] While Tocqueville refuses to equate this novelty with liberal government, he shows that such a government would have been impossible, indeed almost inconceivable, without the philosophic principles underlying liberal politics.[8]

To the extent that Big Government is possible and conceivable, it is because the liberal principle of equality becomes egalitarian in practice.[9] First, that principle vitiates the "secondary powers" that serve as natural obstacles to the unlimited expansion of governmental authority; then it makes not only sovereigns but also citizens see themselves in a way that vastly simplifies the use of a centralized and enlarged governmental authority. Last, having made Big Government not only possible and conceivable, liberal egalitarianism makes it seem desirable and all but inevitable. Let us now examine these stages of degeneration.

UNDER THE OLD REGIME

Tocqueville's nameless phenomenon occurs not only, and not first, in democracy in America, the subject of Tocqueville's first book; it is also described in his last book on the Old Regime in France. In *Democracy in America* Tocqueville uses the terms "administrative despotism" and "mild despotism," as well as "democratic despotism," to describe it and sketches its character in the concluding section of that book.[10] But he also speaks of "democratic despotism" in *The Old Regime*,[11] and there gives the chilling details in his description of the eighteenth-century French monarchy. Here is a sobering reminder that Big Government, though democratic in nature, is as compatible with the form of monarchy as with that of democracy, when substantial political freedom is lacking.[12]

Thus we see Big Government arising from the attack of liberalism on the Old Regime long before it begins to transform democracy. It is characteristic of Tocqueville's political science to show democracy in contrast to aristocracy rather than to show liberal government as it is derived theoretically from the state of nature. He substitutes liberalism as historical fact for liberalism as abstract principle, and the result is to bring to view the actual consequences of liberalism that are obscured by the arguments and rhetoric offered on its behalf.

As Tocqueville presents it, democratic despotism is characterized from the first by its apparent rationality and good intentions. It concentrates intelligence and resources in one central, sovereign power so as to provide uniform, yet detailed, rules applicable to all equally.[13] Thus it appears to be at the farthest extreme from the arbitrary government of traditional, harsh despotism. With such rationality and uniformity, democratic despotism must apparently mean well to its subjects. The people are not exploited for the use and pleasure of a tyrant, but on the contrary they are made safer, healthier, and in regard to safety and health, wiser. For while governing rationally, the government teaches rationality. The consequence ought to be justice made comprehensive and effective.

Yet justice so described—even as "democratic"—does not require the *form* of democracy.[14] It is democratic in a social sense because rationality in administration requires that uniform rules be applied equally, without regard to individual or group variation. But it is not necessarily democratic in the political sense of self-government. In Tocqueville's view, therefore, Big Government is far from being a recent or even a postrevolutionary phenomenon. It was easy to predict for the future because one could see it far in the past. The change in the old order throughout Europe, which culminated in France in the revolution of 1789, was, in part, the work of kings. Looking back over the course of seven centuries, one could see that self-aggrandizing French kings had innovated at first to weaken the nobility, and later also to meet their need for more revenue.[15] At the beginning of the sixteenth century, however, other more deliberate reformers conceived the idea of replacing feudal institutions as a whole with "a more uniform and simpler social and political order that had equality of conditions as its basis."[16]

Thus the nobility were gradually deprived of their political authority while retaining their ancient privileges and even acquiring new ones in the form of exemptions from ever more burdensome taxes. Local governments lost their autonomy or were required to purchase it, and then repurchase it, at intervals. The Church was the last to lose its power, but it too succumbed to the monarchy's indirect attacks. Its property, like all property, was subject to increasingly minute regulation, while its very reason for being was called into question by public discussions about the nature and existence of God which the government saw no necessity to suppress. Eventually the "secondary powers"—nobility, local officials, and clergy—that had characterized feudal aristocracy were deprived not only of their independence, but of their functions. They lost justification for their very existence, not merely for their privileges. In the end they were impotent for good and capable only of arousing hatred and envy in others.

While in England the governing class chose to forgo its privileges in order to deliberate with the other classes about common interests, France suffered under the "abstract literary politics" of intellectuals, superimposed on seething, unarticulated political passions that the intellectuals stirred up but were unable to control.[17] The notion of an entirely new "rational" order of politics and law captured the imaginations of all Frenchmen and prevailed in their minds untempered and unchallenged by tradition. For the traditional and now apparently arbitrary complex of custom and law was to be substituted a single, central government issuing and administering simple, uniform laws. In principle, the whole nation of equal and similar individual citizens would have the king as an agent to do their will; in fact, it would have a master.[18]

Thus, already in the Old Regime one sees the translation of liberal principle to illiberal fact.[19] By the time the monarchy fell at the end of the eighteenth century, it had acquired not only new powers but, more important, an altogether new spirit closer to nineteenth-century socialism than to feudalism.[20] Imbued with a new faith in reason and in progress made probable or necessary by the application of reason, the monarchy sought to bring the benefits of rational progress to the people in all things. It attempted, for example, to improve agricultural production by having bureaucrats distribute instructional pamphlets to farmers. Agriculture was not in fact much improved by such measures, but from then on people knew just whom to blame when something went wrong. Just as today, government even took on responsibility for unseasonable weather.[21]

In wishing to cover every risk to which the people might be subjected, the central government tried to do more than any political power is capable of.[22] Thus it often did more harm than good by raising unreasonable expectations that were easily disappointed. In the meantime, while people were waiting impatiently for progress in rational control, the existing rigid rules, coupled with lax enforcement, made it seem to all that government and law were little more than obstacles in their way; and these were obstacles one could get around.[23] So, as the monarchy eliminated its rivals and habituated virtually everyone to depend on nothing but itself, it won no enthusiasm and little support, while earning contempt for its weakness. Only the imaginary rational polity of the intellectuals generated enthusiasm, but that was the source of the difficulty.[24]

SOVEREIGNTY OF THE PEOPLE AND INDIVIDUALISM

In *The Old Regime* Tocqueville shows how Big Government grew up under the French monarchy, how it prepared the demise of that monarchy, and how it made the establishment of liberal politics very difficult after the Revolution. But in *Democracy in America* he shows how Big Government can emerge from a liberal polity that began with a constitution of limited government and with an animus against monarchy.

The foundation of American politics, indeed of American life as a whole, is the principle of the sovereignty of the people. In Tocqueville's formulation, the principle says: "Providence has given each individual, whoever he may be, the degree of reason necessary for him to be able to direct himself in things that interest him exclusively." This is the great maxim on which all of American society rests.[25] The sovereignty of the people presupposes the capability of the people. Yet this same principle grounds, or amounts to, "individualism," an "erroneous judgment" that produces weakness in the people.[26] Individuals who are supposed to be able to figure out how to live their lives well cannot look to their contemporaries for advice or to tradition as embodying a collective wisdom. For to consult either source of help would be bowing to an authority, thus admitting that one is not capable on one's own. At the same time, since most people spend most of their time worrying about personal everyday problems that usually can be solved, they easily come to believe that reason can solve every problem.

With no help yet with infinite responsibility, judgment becomes an immense burden for each individual. The burden is relieved in part by simplification. By making broad generalizations, one can bring oneself to believe that similar facts and beings are actually identical or equal. This makes thinking a little easier. Even more effective relief can be found by seeking refuge in public opinion. An individual looks around and sees many other people holding more or less similar opinions, and their similarity makes them more credible. What everyone thinks must be so! Yet no particular person claims responsibility for public opinions, so one's pride is not at risk in adopting them. When conforming, one does not seem to submit to a superior authority.

Tocqueville shows that democratic public opinion holds to two other dogmas besides individualism: egalitarianism, and a sort of "honest materialism."[27] The three dogmas combine and nourish one another.[28] First, democratic equality is the presupposition of individualism, because everyone, regardless of social status or group identity, is held to reason well enough about his own affairs. Equality individualizes and then, as we have seen, tends to create a conforming mass. But equality also becomes an end in itself. After all, if individuals are equal in the most important respect, why should they not have equal results to show for equal exertions or even from the mere fact of equal existence? "Equality of result" is not a recent idea; it was not the invention of President Lyndon Johnson (who in 1965 contrasted it to "equality of opportunity").[29]

The kind of equal result that most recommends itself is equal well-being or comfort. Enjoyment of well-being is individual, and we are all more or less equally capable of it. So honest materialism becomes the content of equality and the end of democratic life. In America, Tocqueville observes, "care of satisfying the least needs of the body and of providing the smallest comforts of life preoccupies minds universally."[30] In this preoccupation Americans are not happy, but "grave and almost sad."[31] Because they come to think that the happiness they seek consists in experiencing pleasures of the mortal body, they fret under the awareness that they have a limited time for such experiences.[32] So while they methodically pursue desire after desire, they are ever saddened by the thought of still another new pleasure they cannot attain.

Two consequences of the three dogmas push Americans into the arms of Big Government. One is the doctrine they hold of "self-interest well understood." Tocqueville is not as admiring of that doctrine as is often supposed.[33]

He contends that in "marvelously accommodating to the weaknesses of men," the doctrine is "of all philosophic theories the most appropriate to the needs of men in our time."[34] That is qualified praise. Nonetheless, the doctrine does more or less successfully persuade citizens to sacrifice some of their private interests for the sake of preserving other private interests. It is avowedly not a doctrine of public spiritedness.

Although the Americans Tocqueville describes are selfish and preoccupied with themselves, they are still quite capable of compassion. Compassion is literally an ability to feel what another human being is feeling, and so it requires an act of imagination to put oneself in the place of another. This act is made easy, indeed effortless, by the equality and similarity that democracy brings, or more precisely by the dogmatic belief in equality on which it rests and the customs and conventions of equality that it produces and maintains.[35] Tocqueville says of Americans: "Each of them can judge the sensations of all the others in a moment: he casts a rapid glance at himself; that is enough for him. There is therefore no misery he does not conceive without trouble."[36]

Such easy compassion again reveals the difference between the principle of equality—which is strength—and the actual sense of weakness when men are equal. In principle the equality that Tocqueville's Americans recognize is an equality of ability, an equal amount of reason to look after their own affairs. In fact, they are in the habit of acting on the neediness they feel. Since each is all too aware of his own "misery"—of his needs and unsatisfied desires—"a sort of tacit and almost involuntary accord is made between them according to which each owes the others a momentary support which he himself will be able to call for in his turn."[37] Compassion is part of self-interest, hence not far from selfishness.[38] Even the explicit and intentional agreements that articulate a democratic sense of justice tend to be constituted with a view to "the permanent and general needs" of mankind.[39] Democratic justice has the same reference to needs as democratic compassion.

Both the doctrine of self-interest well understood and the sympathetic awareness of neediness and unfulfilled desire ought to make Americans determined to associate voluntarily to overcome their individual weakness. And in truth Tocqueville was surprised, he said, at the facility with which Americans formed associations of all sorts.[40] But self-interest and compassion may also have the contrary consequence of undermining the determination to associate. Individuals need to associate for common ends because they are weak, and they will associate when they can anticipate that it will be in their self-interest to have assisted each other. But how reliable for sustaining association will this calculation prove to be? And will a collection of self-consciously weak individuals overcome their weakness or merely confirm it? Consequently, Tocqueville says:

> The citizen of democracies [has] very contrary instincts. His independence fills him with confidence and pride among his equals, and his debility makes him

feel, from time to time, the need of the outside help that he cannot expect from any of them, since they are all impotent and cold. In this extremity, he naturally turns his regard to the immense being that rises alone in the midst of universal debasement. His needs and above all his desires constantly lead him back toward it, and in the end he views it as the unique and necessary support for individual weakness.[41]

The doctrine of the sovereignty of the people, or individualism, is intended to establish and justify self-government in the broadest sense through association. But it is precisely that doctrine which makes Big Government— the Immense Being!—so desirable. The liberal notion of a government of limited ends will not prevent Big Government.[42] A government that limits its ends to securing an equal right to "life, liberty, and the pursuit of happiness" for all citizens will not necessarily be a small one because achieving the ends of equality and material well-being are limitless tasks. Even Tocqueville's Americans willingly grant that "the social power" constituted by the people "has the right to do everything."[43] This government will care, as we say; it will be ever attentive to the obvious needs of all citizens and responsive to pressures to satisfy unfulfilled desires. Yet certain "interests" will not be well served by the Immense Being — the independence, freedom, and dignity of individuals.[44] Big Government tends to smother the liberty of the individuals whose needs it aims to satisfy.

LIMITING BIG GOVERNMENT

Is Big Government therefore inevitable? Tocqueville himself concedes that government will and should be bigger in the modern democratic era. He even worries that the central government will not be strong enough in the United States.[45] Yet for the very reason that democratic government must and will be big, the first object of the legislator then becomes to fix "visible and immovable limits" to it.[46] Tocqueville's description of the dangers of mild despotism is intended as a warning to democrats; he encourages them to resist their natural inclinations, which endanger their democratic freedom.[47]

To arm this resistance, Tocqueville recalls to us some of the most typical and still-cherished American mores, institutions, and laws. Although most of them are usually thought of as liberal in origin and character, he strikingly refers to them as "aristocratic."[48]

The first of these is rights. Tocqueville insists that a democratic people must be given rights, together with a certain "political spirit that suggests to each citizen some of the interests that make nobles in aristocracies act."[49] The essence or animus of aristocratic politics is, in a notion taken from Montesquieu, the determination to resist an indefinite extension of public power, whether monarchical or popular;[50] in effect, rights exercised against democratic despotism have an aristocratic spirit. Moreover, America's still-vital

Christianity is its "most precious inheritance from aristocratic centuries."[51] Its taste for local self-government, its jury system, its free press, its idea of individual rights—all are said to have been brought from aristocratic England.[52] Democratic associations are comparable to "aristocratic persons."[53] Even the Constitution was essentially the work of the Federalists, a party inspired by "aristocratic passions."[54]

To the American reader of today, many of Tocqueville's recommendations for limiting Big Government might appear ineffectual. One might even say that the remedies he relies on are parts of the problem rather than the solution. Lawyers, judges, and juries, for example, are said by Tocqueville to "temper" a government that acts in the name of a tyrannical majority.[55] In recent years, however, America has experienced a judicial activism in which its lawyers and judges have sought—like the eighteenth-century French intellectuals and jurists whom Tocqueville deplored—to thwart not merely majority tyranny, but also majority rule.[56] They have been more progressive and more democratic than the democratic people, enlarging the scope of the judiciary in order to enlarge the rest of the government. Juries, too, overcome by democratic compassion, have shown contempt for legal niceties, not to mention the law and common sense. The free press, and the media generally, have, until the recent advent of populist and conservative talk radio, been predominantly countermajoritarian and favorable to Big Government.[57]

The very notion of rights has for the most part been reinterpreted to mean "entitlements"—no longer rights to be exercised in an aristocratic spirit, but rights to receive benefits from government not requiring any attitude other than listless acceptance.[58] Entitlements do, however, require a big—and wealthy—government. They are expensive because they guarantee a definite result to beneficiaries as opposed to establishing a formal right that would enable them to gain and protect on their own and at their own risk. In our day, attention to legal and constitutional formalities, much recommended by Tocqueville, has been fading.[59] Either formalities are overlooked when they get in the way or they are multiplied when obstruction is desired; in either case, formalities are seen as conveniences to be used or ignored and are not respected as such. They have been made into *instruments* of democracy and Big Government instead of *checks* on them. In sum, either Tocqueville's predictions have gone awry, or they have been all too accurate and the democratic revolution is proving inexorable. But perhaps his thought would still offer useful counsel.

What effective limits on Big Government remain at the end of the twentieth century? If the era of Big Government really were over, as President Clinton has asserted, government would do less and would do it differently, even if it never again became small. Some of the powers of the national government would be "devolved," as has been proposed. That would be a return toward the "administrative decentralization" Tocqueville admired when he came to America.[60] Other responsibilities would be "privatized." What would these shifts mean? They would, in effect, constitute anew the secondary powers so natural to aristocracy and so foreign to democracy.[61]

Such secondary powers do not rely mainly on reason and do not necessarily produce better results than government from the center. When America's founders established a federal rather than a national government, they treated the states as "power[s] that had to be managed."[62] But manage them they did. Devolving government to localities and states today may result in policies that meet local needs more effectively—but not necessarily.[63] In fact, Tocqueville expects that administrative decentralization probably will not be all that efficient or economical.[64] The ornery "intractability" on which democracy rests, and to which it gives rise, can be worrisome, even though Tocqueville praises the untaught instinct for political freedom it reflects.[65] It is also true that the American people, animated by intractable "decentralizing passions," have been known to oppose reasonable policies.[66] And as Tocqueville himself reminds us, local and state governments can act unjustly, even tyrannically.[67] From our standpoint, it could be said that nothing in America's history did more to undermine popular confidence in the states and to increase expectations from the national government than the failure of the states to right the wrongs created by slavery and racial discrimination.

Tocqueville has other hopes, however, more reliant on reason. Today's conservatives who say that they want to end the dependency exacerbated, if not created, by government programs fall into a rhetoric that reflects the characteristic "misguided judgment" of Americans that individual independence is or ever was a real possibility. Such rhetoric is also found in empty talk of autonomy by today's liberals. Human beings are dependent on one another. But the manner of our dependence, and consequently the extent of our dependence on Big Government, is worth reexamining and debating. *Democracy in America* is, in effect, Tocqueville's correction of his mentor Jean-Jacques Rousseau[68] and of Rousseau's followers in his own Europe and in our America, including among others today's self-styled "Kantian" intellectuals and many feminists.

Rousseau argued that the only way dependence could be made compatible with freedom and dignity was to make it wholly impartial: Each citizen was to be made wholly dependent on the whole society of which he was a part, not partly dependent on any particular, identifiable persons. The latter form of dependence is unacceptable, Rousseau thought, because it gives opportunities to self-interest, hence to injustice, and because it challenges human dignity by requiring individuals to recognize the inequalities inevitably found in their lives. Universal, anonymous dependence on an entity constituted by a "general will," in whose formulation everyone takes an equal part, is as close as we can come to dependence on ourselves alone. In Tocqueville's judgment, as we have seen, this form of dependence effectively vitiates each person's awareness of his or her particular interests and abilities and thus increases the extent of everyone's dependence and degradation. As an alternative to total dependence, he proposes mutual but partial dependence, in the form of private contracts and of voluntary participation in associations.

Contracts, Tocqueville shows, allow us to confront our necessary dependence with a semblance of dignity because they maintain both real and illusory freedom and equality. As an example, consider American women, who, especially in Tocqueville's time, more or less had to marry. But with whom they contracted to marry was, to an unprecedented degree, a matter of informed choice. Women could make the best of this situation by choosing well.[69] American men, for their part, were expected to work, however fortunate their economic and social position might be.[70] Thus, even the wealthiest entrepreneur would be in need of hiring workers, *almost* as the poorest laborer was in need of a daily wage to survive. Maintaining the pretense that an employment contract was *as* necessary to one party as to the other would in fact embolden workers to demand more equal terms and possibly more freedom of contract.[71] Democratic contracts may not create partners that care about each other, as did aristocratic lords and vassals and as Big Government claims to do about everyone, but they can require partners to respect each other as beings equally capable of exercising will and reason.

Similarly, Tocqueville applauds American political institutions and mores not primarily because they are just or efficient but because they sustain an attachment to free institutions, a propensity to form voluntary associations, and a level of political activity which, he says, must be seen to be believed.[72] He praises these things not only as bulwarks against tyranny, but even more as democracy's means of nurturing civilized human beings.[73] Local governments, he says, are the "primary schools" of freedom, and political associations such as parties are its "great schools, free of charge."[74] These are better instructors than the schoolmaster (*tuteur*) of Big Government.

By participating in local government, citizens acquire a taste for freedom and learn its habits. They meet frequently to discuss public business and serve short terms in numerous minor elective offices. Their ambitions are aroused, while at the same time they are tempered by affection for their neighbors and disciplined to respect the formalities of political order. The link between self-interest and a stable general good is made visible, as when citizens vote to tax themselves to pay for a school that benefits the children of all, or most. Political associations, because they appeal to ambition and aim at common benefits, do not require a sacrifice of one's self-interest. Nor do they seek a sympathetic identification of self-interest with the interests of all. Instead of sacrificing themselves for the common good, citizens join parties that unite similarly interested selves to advance their common interest. The self-interested ambition of individuals is enlarged to partisanship, which is no longer narrow self-interest. At the same time, self-interest is recognized as partisan, that is, partial, and not assumed to be in harmony with the whole. That is why political associations are *free schools*: The demands they make are not onerous, and the advantages they promise are not in principle unreasonable.

The exercise of political rights as distinguished from the enjoyment of what we now call entitlements, Tocqueville thinks, ultimately makes possible a rational, if not disinterested, patriotism. "A man understands the influence that the well-being of the country has on his own . . . and he interests himself in the prosperity of his country at first as a thing that is useful to him, and afterwards as his own work."[75] We might then have citizens who could take pride in themselves as well as their government. They would be neither excessively dependent nor alienated. Their sentiment would not accord with the superior reason of the modern intellectual, which is cosmopolitan and unwilling to compromise with interestedness, partisanship, or instinct. But such patriotism would accord with the "human reason" of Tocqueville's political science.[76]

Tocqueville wrote at a time when he could expect patriotism to be local, regional, and at most national. Of course, national patriotism could be imperialistic, but in the mid-nineteenth century, neither political nor economic powers, nor the interests and ambitions that attach people to them, were global. Has the possibility of smaller and closer government at the end of the twentieth century been vitiated by this new development?

Tocqueville, to repeat, recommends smaller and closer government not for the sake of efficiency, but for the sake of freedom. That luxury, he conceded, might have to be forgone in a world where war between nation-states is a possibility that must be anticipated.[77] Even a federal republic as well constructed as the United States could not sustain the relative independence of jealous secondary powers like the states and still carry on an active foreign and military policy. Now, surely, war remains a possibility for America today, as it was for the nations of nineteenth-century Europe about which Tocqueville worried. What is less sure is that the highly technological wars we are now more likely to fight will require the massive marshaling of men and resources that Tocqueville himself thought characteristic of democratic warfare.[78] Will technology now permit the luxury of federalism and defensible nations?[79]

Big Government, some argue, will be needed to confront Big Business.[80] In fact, Tocqueville did appreciate much of the complexity and importance of modern industry.[81] His concern, however, was that Big Business would be just one more excuse for an all-too-willing Big Government to extend the sphere of dependence on it and to transform rights, including property rights, into government entitlements.[82] At the same time, he could caution even in the 1830s that the concentration of capital and the division of labor characteristic of modern industry must be matters of great concern to democratic legislators.[83] His description of what Karl Marx was to call "alienation" caused by the division of labor is memorable enough so that we could wonder whether we need either Marx or Nietzsche when we have Tocqueville. Tocqueville feared that the degradation of workers' abilities resulting from the need for capital and the division of labor would lead to the first true or just aristocracy, a meritocracy, against which democrats would be hard-pressed to argue.

Today's legislators, or even national governments, may be incapable of regulating supranational corporations—an "industrial aristocracy" of CEOs, financiers, and stockholders. They may, however, be all-too-capable of dampening the entrepreneurial spirit that combats monopolies through competition.[84] And if the command economies of socialism failed economically as well as politically on a national scale, regulation by supranational political entities should hardly inspire greater confidence.

Moreover, economic globalization at the end of the twentieth century is accompanied by a tendency toward ethnic fragmentation, which is in turn facilitated by this globalization. Together, these contrary forces endanger the very notion of political life itself, for each makes it seem that neither individuals nor communities are constituted by the choices they make. To convince democrats that they need not surrender their choices to economic or ethnic determinism any more than to any other sort of "insurmountable and unintelligent force" in whose existence men come to believe is a central purpose of Tocqueville's political science.[85] In smaller and closer governments, the effects of individual and collective choices, not to mention rights and injustices, are more visible than in Big Government. They make the case for the necessity and dignity of politics more convincingly than Big Government, which looks on politics as an instrument for the delivery of benefits. Big Government paradoxically takes a low view of politics.

This thought reminds of the final secondary power between the individual and the state in Tocqueville's design. In contrast to the formal liberal theorists, Tocqueville is an outspoken advocate of religion, of Christianity.[86] Liberal theorists argue at most for reasonable accommodation of religion; he wants reasonable respect for it. We may grant that the Christianity Tocqueville admired in America had been made reasonable enough to please even John Locke. It was a Christianity that modern democrats could tolerate because it in turn tolerated much in modern life of which premodern Christians would have been intolerant, for example, its dislike of ritual.[87] Nonetheless, this democratized religion served as a restraint on democracy, and it might still be a corrective for democratic dependency. Tocqueville thought it necessary that the human power released by modern political philosophy impose a sense of limitation on itself going beyond liberal constitutional limits, but expressing their spirit. The intent should be to ease the burden of individual judgment and to curb the excessive taste for well-being that characterizes democracy. At its best, religion could do this for the sake of keeping democratic political power vigorous within its proper sphere.[88] Tocqueville drew this hopeful lesson from the Americans' insistence on the separation of church and state, which restrains the state but prevents citizens from giving themselves over to materialism, on the way to dependency. Religion, he thought, should be deployed as a secondary power.

If the American religion Tocqueville observed in the 1830s had come to a beneficial accommodation with democracy, he was not oblivious to the threats posed to Christianity by further democratization.[89] On the one hand, individualism, in the form of a desire for individual self-affirmation, might lead to a continuous redefinition of traditional religious forms, eventually depriving them of all authority.[90] On the other hand, egalitarianism might weaken the sense of personal responsibility that makes Christianity an ally of democratic self-government, generating in its place the kind of sympathetic, pantheistic identification with all of creation that we find in environmentalism now.[91]

Tocqueville nonetheless remains hopeful that religion and democratic political freedom can aid one another. Democratic eras and ages of religious skepticism both suffer from an instability of condition and desire that tends to confine those who live in them to immediate goals requiring only brief exertions. Once again, liberal principle is at odds with its actual life. The modern principle of skepticism is not intended to justify passive contemplation but to produce greater human power and better control of events. In effect, however, democracy's instability gives greater scope to chance than has been seen in polities *not* believing themselves to be in their own control but rather at the mercy of higher powers.

What is necessary, Tocqueville insists, is that democratic governments set distant goals for peoples, goals to be achieved by moderate, yet steadfast efforts. Appropriately, Tocqueville does not propose any grand project—no war on poverty, no closing of the ozone hole. Rather, he suggests the seemingly limited task of seeing to it that political office comes only as a reward for skill and effort, for moderate ambition, and not for pleasing the people.[92] That is in truth not a small task because it is unending. There will always be elections that can be won by pleasing the people or by feeling their pain, and winning the favor of the people, especially of a democratic people with unstable desires, will depend in large part on chance. It is beyond the capacity of a democracy to reward virtue regularly. Partial success is within reach to the extent that political institutions and mores can be wisely shaped; but without the support of a greater power, the goal will remain elusive. Insofar as men can act confidently in the hope that virtue will always be rewarded—accomplishing much along the way—they will, in effect, have returned to religious faith.

In this way, religion rightly understood and political freedom rightly exercised come to the aid of one another, giving democracy the possibility and the sense of accomplishment.

TOCQUEVILLE'S POLITICAL SCIENCE

We may conclude with some remarks on Tocqueville's new political science. In contrast to what we have called formal liberalism, his political science is concerned with the society actually inspired by liberal principles. But Tocqueville does not make the criticism Marx was to set forth: that liberalism is merely formal, untrue to its universal principles because it offers rights only to the bourgeoisie. That criticism has been repeated by many who are not Marxists and who consider themselves liberals. For Tocqueville, liberal society is actually democracy and not a sham. In a way it is more democratic than liberal principles, because they are *designed* to be formal in order to protect and foster human inequalities. For liberalism of course asserts that all men are created equal, but they are equal only in the state of nature before they have consented to civil society and its inevitable inequalities.

Tocqueville shows, however, that equality in the state of nature tends to become equality in society too. He does not speak of the state of nature, but he makes clear that the formal principle of equality has a constant democratizing effect. The fact that equality is not perfect, that all citizens are not equally secure, does not mean that equality does not exist; on the contrary, it creates pressure to perfect equality.[93] Democracy, or modern democracy, is a democratic revolution. One could call it an institutionalized revolution if it were not apparent that the revolution operates against every institution so as to make it more democratic. The consequences of that revolutionary pressure are "individualism" and government by the "Immense Being."

Individualism, in Tocqueville's sense, addresses a topic left undiscussed, for the most part, in formal liberalism: the actual capacity of individuals to exercise their rights and stand up in their defense. Liberalism assumes that by relying on the desire for self-preservation, supposed to be active in everyone, one need not enter into the question of capacity (though Kant considers the capacity for independence in deciding who should vote).[94] Marxists, and others who demand more democracy, make the same assumption that everyone's capacity for exercising rights is or can be made adequate. But Tocqueville does not. He argues that modern democracy makes its people increasingly incapable as citizens as they become more isolated and weak. For formal liberalism, individualism is good; for him, it is bad.

Formal liberalism relies on institutions instead of virtue; in the manner stated most extremely by Kant, a republic can be maintained for a nation of devils if only they are intelligent (not a slight condition, by the way).[95] Tocqueville believes that the working of institutions requires virtue—not lofty virtue but the virtue available in democracy, ranging from raw intractability to active self-interest to moderate ambition. Formal liberalism does not appreciate that formal practices and institutions in a democracy have to be defended against the laziness and impatience of a democratic people. That liberalism was conceived, not for "a world quite new" like Tocqueville's new political science,[96] but to attack the privileges and prejudices of the Old Regime. It does not see that the principle used to attack the customary forms of the Old Regime will also be applied to undermine the artificially constructed forms of democracy. It does not see that the Big Government of monarchy reappears, or continues, in democracy.

Thus, for Tocqueville's political science the problem becomes the reconstruction of the secondary powers between the central government and individual citizens that once were held by aristocrats. Democratic versions of such institutions must be found, and they must be manned by democratic aristocrats, or by democrats behaving as aristocrats, and justified in democratic terms. His purpose is to repoliticize liberalism, for which he must recapture its original critical spirit and put it to work, moderately and constructively, on a daily basis, in the business of self-government. The business of America is self-government, and it must be attended to. The private sphere, economic or spiritual, must be understood politically: It is both apart from government and part of self-government.

To gain his purpose, Tocqueville stays within liberalism. He does not criticize it as a theory; he does not even describe it as a theory. In our day he offers an alternative to the school of civic republicanism deriving from Hannah Arendt, which also wants to revive democratic politics. But civic republicanism attacks the liberal tradition, though not very successfully because it remains devoted to liberal equality and security. It worries more about the acquisitiveness of the few than the dependency of the many, and so it presents itself as the recovery of democracy together with politics. Thus it wastes itself in struggling against self-interest, as if stable democracy could be grounded on self-sacrifice rather than self-interest well understood. Thus, too, it fails to see the ills of democracy that come from democracy and fails to consider the problem of defending democracy's forms and formalities. Seeing democracy as it is, and not in principle, Tocqueville looks for democracy's strengths to remedy democracy's weaknesses.[97] Although he lives in a democratic era and therefore rejects the notion of a mixed regime, he recognizes, without endorsing the privileges of the past, that the strengths of democracy are aristocratic in origin and function. He repoliticizes liberalism by bringing aristocracy to the support of democracy.

NOTES

1. Alexis de Tocqueville, *Democracy in America*, trans. Harvey C. Mansfield and Delba Winthrop (Chicago: University of Chicago Press, 2000), I.Introduction: 6.

2. On this point, see Pierre Manent, *Tocqueville and the Nature of Democracy*, trans. John Waggoner (Lanham, Md.: Rowman & Littlefield, 1996), esp. 27–28, 65, 80–81.

3. See Jean-Claude Lamberti, *Tocqueville and the Two Democracies*, trans. A. Goldhammer (Cambridge: Harvard University Press, 1989), 168–78; Karl-Heinz Volkmann-Schluck, *Politische Philosophie: Thukydides, Kant, Tocqueville* (Frankfurt: Klostermann, 1974), 163–66; and, for the connection between individualism and Big Government, Seymour Drescher, *Dilemmas of Democracy: Tocqueville and Modernization* (Pittsburgh: University of Pittsburgh Press, 1968), 268–69.

4. Tocqueville, *Democracy in America*, II.4.6: 663.

5. For many intelligent, though unsystematic, comparisons of Tocqueville and Nietzsche, see Joshua Mitchell, *The Fragility of Freedom: Tocqueville on Religion, Democracy, and the American Future* (Chicago: University of Chicago Press, 1995).

6. Alexis de Tocqueville, *The Old Regime and the Revolution*, ed. François Furet and Françoise Mélonio, trans. Alan S. Kahan (Chicago: University of Chicago Press, 1998), II.5: 136; Tocqueville, *Democracy in America*, II.4.3: 645.

7. Tocqueville, *Democracy in America*, II.4.6: 662.

8. Tocqueville, *Democracy in America*, II.4.5: 640, 661, 665; Tocqueville, *Old Regime*, I.2: 96.

9. See Drescher, *Dilemmas of Democracy*, 48.

10. Tocqueville, *Democracy in America*, II.4.6: 662–64.

11. Tocqueville, *Old Regime*, III.3: 212.

12. See Tocqueville, *Democracy in America*, II.4.6: 664; and Lamberti, *Tocqueville and the Two Democracies*, 186–87.

13. As François Furet and Françoise Mélonio put it: "It was not . . . arbitrary authority that Tocqueville saw as typifying the French old regime. On the contrary, it was this daily, organized, rational desire to be involved in everything and to have everything under control" (Tocqueville, *Old Regime*, I.Introduction: 25–26).

14. Hence the importance of the notion of *social state* (*état social*) in Tocqueville's political science. But as Furet notes, a form of government is required for political liberty, hence for democracy proper, according to Tocqueville; see François Furet, *Penser la Révolution française*, rev. ed. (Paris: Gallimard, 1983), 191–92.

15. Tocqueville, *Democracy in America*, I.Introduction: 4–5.

16. Tocqueville, *Old Regime*, I.5: 106; Tocqueville, *Democracy in America*, II.1.1: 404.

17. Tocqueville, *Old Regime*, III.1: 195–97; III.8: 243. James W. Ceaser argues that Tocqueville's political science as a whole is an attempt to preserve the original Cartesian core of rationalism, as distinguished from its late-eighteenth-century "distortion." At the same time, he contends that even this original rationalism would be inadequate were it not infused with the "values," though not the antirational animus, of traditionalism. James W. Ceaser, "Political Science, Political Culture, and the Role of the Intellectual," *American Political Science Review* 79 (September 1985): 656, 662–63, 667–69.

18. Tocqueville, *Old Regime*, III.3: 213. Michael Hereth, in his *Alexis de Tocqueville: Threats to Freedom in Democracy*, trans. George Bogardus (Durham, N.C.: Duke University Press, 1986), offers a similar presentation of Tocqueville's analysis of the two roots of the transformation of Europe's political order and of its consequences. He, however, finds its intellectual root specifically in the doctrines of sovereignty of Bodin and Hobbes; see pp. 26, 42.

19. As Manent argues, the fundamental distinction for Tocqueville is between aristocratic politics—a politics that has always been characterized by unequal individuals influencing one another—and modern, or liberal, or democratic politics, which begins with the dogma that human beings are equal and radically independent individuals. Manent, *Tocqueville*, 111.

20. Tocqueville, *Old Regime*, I.5: 104–5; III.3: 213. For discussion of Tocqueville's understanding of the link between eighteenth-century rationalism and nineteenth-century socialism, see Peter Augustine Lawler, *The Restless Mind: Alexis de Tocqueville on the Origin and Perpetuation of Human Liberty* (Lanham, Md.: Rowman and Littlefield, 1993), esp. 11–31; and Daniel J. Mahoney, "Tocqueville and Socialism," in Peter Augustine Lawler and Joseph Alulis, eds., *Tocqueville's Defense of Human Liberty: Current Essays* (New York: Garland, 1993), esp. 180 84.

21. Tocqueville, *Old Regime*, II.2: 124; II.7: 145.

22. Tocqueville, *Old Regime*, II.6: 141.

23. Tocqueville, *Old Regime*, II.6: 142. Furet emphasizes the importance of administration in Tocqueville's understanding of the Old Regime; Furet, *Penser la Révolution française*, 29–31, 186–89. See also Harvey Mitchell, *Individual Choice and the Structures of History: Alexis de Tocqueville as Historian Reappraised* (Cambridge: Cambridge University Press, 1996), chap. 8, which discusses centralization without considering its connection to rational control.

24. Tocqueville, *Old Regime*, II.1: 201. For an account of Tocqueville's understanding of the extremes of materialism and idealism, characteristically combined in modern thought, see Ralph C. Hancock, "The Uses and Hazards of Christianity in Tocqueville's Attempt to Save Democratic Souls," in Ken Masugi, ed., *Interpreting Tocqueville's* Democracy in America (Savage, Md.: Rowman and Littlefield, 1991), 355–66.

25. Tocqueville, *Democracy in America*, I.2.10: 381.

26. Tocqueville, *Democracy in America*, II.2.2: 482.

27. Tocqueville, *Democracy in America*, II.2.1: 479; II.2.13: 512; II.2.11: 509.

28. See Jack Lively, *The Social and Political Thought of Alexis de Tocqueville* (Oxford: Clarendon Press, 1962), 72, 85–87.

29. The contrast was first made in a speech at Howard University. See *Public Papers of the Presidents: Lyndon B. Johnson* (Washington: GPO, 1966), 635–40.

30. Tocqueville, *Democracy in America*, II.2.10: 506.

31. Tocqueville, *Democracy in America*, II.2.13: 511.

32. This chapter of *Democracy in America* figures importantly in Lawler's argument that Tocqueville's Americans exhibit a fundamentally Pascalian understanding of the world, while lacking Blaise Pascal's faith. See Lawler, *The Restless Mind*, 125–39.

33. For a more nuanced treatment of the doctrine, see Peter A. Lawler, "Tocqueville on the Doctrine of Interest," *Government and Opposition* 30, no. 2 (Spring 1995): 221.

34. Tocqueville, *Democracy in America*, II.2.8: 502–3.

35. See Manent, *Tocqueville*, 48–50, on the democratic phenomenon of the "semblable."

36. Tocqueville, *Democracy in America*, II.3.1: 538.

37. Tocqueville, *Democracy in America*, II.3.4: 545.

38. As Zetterbaum says, "in effect, the spirit of compassion reinforces domesticity, and thus reinforces the atomism of democratic society." Marvin Zetterbaum, *Tocqueville and the Problem of Democracy* (Stanford: Stanford University Press, 1967), 68–69.

39. Tocqueville, *Democracy in America*, II.3.18: 589.

40. Tocqueville, *Democracy in America*, II.2.5: 492.

41. Tocqueville, *Democracy in America*, II.4.3: 644. Rousseau's Savoyard Vicar refers to God as the *Être immense*; *Émile*, in Jean-Jacques Rousseau, *Oeuvres Complètes*, Pléiade ed. (Paris: Gallimard, 1959–95), 4:592. See also René Descartes's description of God as "immense, incomprehensible and infinite" in his *Meditations*, vol. 4. Our thanks to Terrence Marshall for these references. Tocqueville himself also uses the term in describing the pantheistic conception of the whole, which incorporates all of creation and the Creator himself; Tocqueville, *Democracy in America*, II.1.7: 426.

42. Manent suggests that in fact the notion of the sovereignty of the people, or individualism, all but requires a power external to society to exercise the power of individuals. Manent, *Tocqueville*, 35.

43. Tocqueville, *Democracy in America*, II.4.2: 641.

44. Tocqueville, *Democracy in America*, II.4.7: 666–67, 670.

45. Tocqueville, *Democracy in America*, I.2.10: 371–72.

46. Tocqueville, *Democracy in America*, II.4.7: 672.

47. Tocqueville, *Democracy in America*, II.4.2: 642–43.

48. See Delba Winthrop, "Rights, Interest, and Honor," in Lawler and Alulis, *Tocqueville's Defense of Human Liberty*, 215–19; and Lawler, *The Restless Mind*, 173.

49. Tocqueville, *Democracy in America*, II.3.26: 634.

50. Tocqueville, *Old Regime*, II.11: 172–73; Tocqueville, *Democracy in America*, I.2.2: 167, 170. Cf. Montesquieu, *The Spirit of the Laws*, II: 4; III: 10; IV: 2; V: 11, 14; VIII: 7. What Montesquieu wants aristocracy to do for monarchy, Tocqueville wants for democracy. On Tocqueville as a classical umpire, see Robert Eden, "Tocqueville and the Problem of Natural Right," *Interpretation* 17 (1990): 379–87.

51. Tocqueville, *Democracy in America*, II.2.15: 519.

52. Tocqueville, *Democracy in America*, II.4.4: 646.

53. Tocqueville, *Democracy in America*, II.4.7: 667.

54. Tocqueville, *Democracy in America*, I.2.2: 167, 170. Sanford Lakoff remarks: "Even the ever-insightful Tocqueville failed to appreciate the degree to which the dogma of popular sovereignty had been vitiated in its implementation." Sanford Lakoff, *Democracy; History, Theory, Practice* (Boulder, Colo.: Westview, 1996), 227. But Tocqueville's insight was that the Constitution had been democratized in its implementation; Tocqueville, *Democracy in America*, I.2.7.

55. Tocqueville, *Democracy in America*, I.2.8. As Harold L. Levy correctly notes, whatever benefits might accrue to democracy from the influence of lawyers and judges and the experience of jury duty are, as Tocqueville himself concedes, likely to be of no more than secondary importance. See Harold L. Levy, "Lawyers' Spirit and Democratic Liberty: Tocqueville on Lawyers, Jurors, and the Whole People," in Lawler and Alulis, *Tocqueville's Defense of Human Liberty*, 243–63.

56. Tocqueville, *Democracy in America*, I.2.8: 254–55. Thomas G. West contends, not implausibly, that "if America today stands on the edge of despotism," the fault lies not with a populace passionate for equality but with political leaders "imbibing the doctrines of intellectuals." Thomas G. West, "Misunderstanding the American Founding," in Masugi, *Interpreting Tocqueville's* Democracy, 169. He criticizes Tocqueville for failing to predict this, but the point is essential to Tocqueville's analysis.

57. James W. Ceaser applies Tocquevillean political science to the media in his *Liberal Democracy and Political Science* (Baltimore: Johns Hopkins University Press, 1990), 158–59, 169–72.

58. See R. Shep Melnick's account of the transformation of our understanding of rights in his "The Courts, Congress, and Programmatic Rights," in Richard A. Harris and Sidney M. Milkis, eds., *Remaking American Politics* (Boulder, Colo.: Westview, 1989), 188–212.

59. Tocqueville, *Democracy in America*, II.4.7: 669. For an elaboration of this point, see Harvey C. Mansfield, Jr., "The Forms and Formalities of Liberty," in Harvey C. Mansfield, Jr., *America's Constitutional Soul* (Baltimore: Johns Hopkins University Press, 1991), 193–208.

60. Tocqueville, *Democracy in America*, I.1.5: 82–93. For the clearest statement of what Tocqueville meant by "administrative decentralization," see Martin Diamond, "The Ends of Federalism," in Peter Augustine Lawler, ed., *Tocqueville's Political Science: Classic Essays* (New York: Garland, 1992), 116–29.
61. Tocqueville, *Democracy in America*, II.4.2: 640.
62. Tocqueville, *Democracy in America*, I.1.8: 113.
63. Tocqueville, *Old Regime*, Appendix: 253.
64. Tocqueville, *Democracy in America*, I.1.5: 85–88; I.2.5: 199–202.
65. Tocqueville, *Democracy in America*, II.4.1: 639.
66. Tocqueville, *Democracy in America*, I.2.10: 377. For the tension between the passion for liberty and reason in Tocqueville's understanding, see Lawler's *The Restless Mind*, especially 89–108, 119, 162–63.
67. Tocqueville, *Democracy in America*, I.1.5: 65; I.1.10: 320–23.
68. However profoundly indebted Tocqueville may have been to Rousseau for his understanding of the predicament of modern man, his remedies are not quite the same as Rousseau's. For an informative comparison that somewhat overstates the particulars of Tocqueville's debt, see Wilhelm Hennis, "Tocqueville's Perspective: *Democracy in America*: In Search of the 'New Science of Politics,'" in Lawler, *Tocqueville's Political Science*, 66–84. Lawler, in his *The Restless Mind*, treats Tocqueville's intellectual debts thematically and argues that it was Pascal who first defined the problem with which both Tocqueville and Rousseau are concerned and which each then redefines in his own way. See also Manent, *Tocqueville*, 60–65; and J. Mitchell, *The Fragility of Freedom*, throughout.
69. Tocqueville, *Democracy in America*, II.3.9–11: 563–70. For an attempt to apply this insight to contemporary America, see William Kristol, "Women's Liberation: The Relevance of Tocqueville," in Masugi, *Interpreting Tocqueville's* Democracy, esp. 490–93.
70. Tocqueville, *Democracy in America*, II.2.18: 525; II.3.18: 595.
71. Tocqueville, *Democracy in America*, II.3.7: 555–57.
72. Tocqueville, *Democracy in America*, I.2.6: 232. As Darcy Wudel correctly notes, Tocqueville's use of the term "association" in *Democracy in America* is "almost perversely wider" than ours is. His term encompasses all the "healthy political activity" that liberal individualism fails to encourage. Darcy Wudel, "Tocqueville on Associations and Association," in Lawler and Alulis, *Tocqueville's Defense of Human Liberty*, 341–42.
73. Tocqueville, *Democracy in America*, II.2.5: 492. For discussion of the benefits Tocqueville seeks from civil and political associations, see Diamond, "The Ends of Federalism," 120–29; Ralph C. Hancock, "Tocqueville on the Good of American Federalism," in Lawler, *Tocqueville's Political Science*, 133–55; J. Mitchell, *The Fragility of Freedom*, 115–26, 240–44; Bruce James Smith, "A Liberal of a New Kind," in Masugi, *Interpreting Tocqueville's* Democracy, 63–95; and Wudel, "Tocqueville on Associations," 341–57. For a brief insightful treatment in the context of a critique of Robert Bellah's interpretation of Tocqueville, see Bruce Frohnen, "Materialism and Self-Deification: Bellah's Misuse of Tocqueville," in Lawler and Alulis, *Tocqueville's Defense of Human Liberty*, 140–45.
74. Tocqueville, *Democracy in America*, I.1.5: 57; II.2.7: 497.
75. Tocqueville, *Democracy in America*, I.2.6: 225; cf. I.1.5: 90.
76. Tocqueville, *Old Regime*, 299–300 n. 53. For the necessity of such compromises see Manent, *Tocqueville*, 126.

77. Tocqueville, *Democracy in America*, I.1.8: 159–61.

78. Tocqueville, *Democracy in America*, II.3.26: 632–33.

79. For an evaluation of other difficulties Tocqueville foresees in democratic warfare, see Eliot A. Cohen, "Tocqueville on War," in Lawler, *Tocqueville's Political Science*, 313–33. See also Manent, *Tocqueville*, 57–60.

80. See John Adams Wettergreen, "Modern Commerce," in Masugi, *Interpreting Tocqueville's* Democracy, 221–33, for an argument that, in Tocqueville's understanding, attempts at bureaucratic management of the economy would only exacerbate the pernicious effects of modern commerce on the character of democratic citizens. See also Wudel, "Tocqueville on Associations," 350.

81. Tocqueville, *Democracy in America*, II.2.19: 526–29; II.4.5: 656–60.

82. Tocqueville, *Democracy in America*, II.4.5: 657–58.

83. Tocqueville, *Democracy in America*, I.2.10: 387; II.2.10: 438–39; II.3.7: 557.

84. Tocqueville, *Democracy in America*, I.2.10: 385–86; II.2.19: 526–29.

85. Tocqueville, *Democracy in America*, II.4.8: 675–76.

86. For two different, but not contradictory, discussions of the place of religion in Tocqueville's analysis of and recommendations for American democracy see Lawler, *The Restless Mind*, 141–58; and Manent, *Tocqueville*, 83–107, 126–27. For still another account, as well as a criticism of Manent, see Hancock, "Uses and Hazards of Christianity," 348–93. And last, for an account that features St. Augustine rather than Pascal, see J. Mitchell, *The Fragility of Freedom*.

87. Tocqueville, *Democracy in America*, I.2.9: 275–77; II.1.5: 420–31.

88. Tocqueville, *Democracy in America*, I.2.9: 278–82.

89. See Sanford Kessler, *Tocqueville's Civil Religion* (Albany: State University of New York Press, 1994), chap. 7. John C. Koritansky puts Tocqueville closer to Rousseau in the matter of religion in his "Civil Religion in Tocqueville's *Democracy in America*," *Interpretation* 17 (1990): 391–92, 399.

90. Tocqueville, *Democracy in America*, II.1.5: 423–24. In *Habits of the Heart: Individualism and Commitment in American Life* (New York: Harper and Row, 1986), 221, 235, Robert N. Bellah, Richard Madsen, William M. Sullivan, Ann Swidler, and Steven M. Tipton describe "Sheilaism," the personal faith of a woman named Sheila Larson, which they contend is a "significantly representative" form of American self-deification. Bellah et al. distinguish Sheilaism from pantheism, while Frohnen, "Materialism and Self-Deification," 146–62, links them.

91. Tocqueville, *Democracy in America*, II.1.7: 425–27. See also Peter Augustine Lawler's "Democracy and Pantheism," in Masugi, *Interpreting Tocqueville's* Democracy, 96–120.

92. Tocqueville, *Democracy in America*, II.2.17: 523–24.

93. Tocqueville, *Democracy in America*, II.4.3: 644–45.

94. Immanuel Kant, "On the Proverb: That May Be True in Theory, but Is of No Practical Use," in Immanuel Kant, *Perpetual Peace and Other Essays*, trans. Ted Humphrey (Indianapolis: Hackett, 1983), 76–77.

95. Kant, "Perpetual Peace," in Kant, *Perpetual Peace*, 124.

96. Tocqueville, *Democracy in America*, I.Introduction: 7.

97. See Philippe Raynaud, "Tocqueville," in Philippe Raynaud and Stéphane Rials, eds., *Dictionnaire de Philosophie Politique* (Paris: Presses Universitaires de France, 1997), 693–94.

7

Big Government and Rights

Michael Zuckert

The topic "Big Government and Rights" announces itself as part of the larger discourse of liberalism, broadly conceived, for it is the liberal tradition that highlights both rights and the size of government, particularly in relation to each other. Prior to the emergence of liberalism, the issue was not framed in terms of the size of government, but in terms of the goodness or the justness of government. I wish to take my stance within this liberal discourse by setting forth at the very outset two texts—proof texts if you like. My two texts derive from thinkers who stand at the two ends of the liberal tradition: The first is by the man usually considered the greatest political thinker in the liberal tradition of our day, John Rawls. The second is by the man usually seen as the founder and perhaps greatest representative of the liberal tradition altogether, John Locke. The two statements, fully spun out and explicated, contain in a nutshell what each of these two understands the core of liberalism to be:

> *Rawls:* "Each person possesses an inviolability founded on justice that even the welfare of society as a whole cannot override."[1]
> *Locke:* "Every man has a Property in his own person. This no body has any Right to but himself. . . . And where there is . . . property, there [can be] justice [and injustice]."[2]

These two statements are statements about justice, about what justice requires, and ultimately about its source. As such, they present the theme of greatest dignity in political philosophy, the theme central to political reflection, much as the divine is to theology or the beautiful to aesthetics. The statements are variants of the liberal answer to the two leading questions of political philosophy: Is justice by nature, and if so, what is it?

Both men would answer yes to the first question, and to that degree stand within the tradition of political philosophy extending back to Socrates but denied by many of our more recent or postmodern political thinkers. Locke and Rawls differ from the founders of that tradition, Socrates and Plato, however, in that they would answer the second question in terms of rights, or in terms that can easily be translated into rights. Furthermore, both could more or less accept the formula contained in the Declaration of Independence: that the *just* powers of government derive from the rational consent of the governed, and the governed consent to governmental powers in order to secure rights. Just government is for the sake of rights, therefore, or to put it another way, justice is rights-securing.

Where Locke and Rawls part company, however, is in their understanding of the nature and source of rights. Locke understands rights (and therefore, justice) to be or to derive from *property*—although, I hasten to add, not in the vulgar sense this formula might evoke in a late-twentieth-century mind. Rawls, on the contrary, understands justice and thereby rights to be or to derive from *fairness.* These two formulas register the course of liberalism over the roughly three hundred years separating Locke from Rawls—from property to fairness.

My topic, however, is Big Government and Rights, and I must now step back in order to bring out the connections between my two proof texts and this topic. Events in Washington and all around the nation since the Ronald Reagan years testify unquestionably to the fact that Big Government has been on the table, so to speak, in a way it has not been since the New Deal more or less successfully overcame the traditional American antipathy to it. I say "on the table" advisedly, for Big Government lies there both as a subject for discussion and debate as in the academy, and as patient (or victim) for curative surgery, amputation, or vivisection as in Washington and elsewhere.

The debate about Big Government, like its subject matter, is itself big. A range of important issues is implicated in the debate—federalism, the administrative or bureaucratic state, dependency, cultural breakdown and fragmentation, and policy efficiency and effectiveness are among these important issues. None is more important, however, than the issue of justice, for the current debate is in large part a debate about justice, about the warrant government has—or does not have—to do the things that have made government big.

In America, the debate about justice occurs largely, although not entirely, in terms of rights. To some degree, the debate about Big Government is a debate over whether a proper understanding of rights mandates large government and active public policy, or whether it mandates considerable downsizing and a far smaller role for government in society. As an example, let me dredge up an issue from the early years of the Clinton administration: health care reform. The discussion of health care turned in part on the question of whether health care is or is not a basic right that government and society ought to secure. Partisans on both sides frequently spoke in the language of rights. Just as there is a debate over Big Government, there is a debate over rights. One reason there *is* a debate over Big Government is because there is a debate over rights.

The terms of the latter debate become clearer if we return to the beginning and attempt to define rights. A right, I suggest, is a justified claim to do or to have something, or as it used to be called, a moral power. Both parts of the definition are important. That a right is a claim or a power helps to distinguish rights from the broader and overlapping category, "the right." *Rights* inhere in claimants—that is to say, in persons who may opt to assert them or not; they are subjective, in the sense of belonging to subjects, agents who can assert them or not, as they wish. *The right*, in contrast, can just as well apply to a description of a state of affairs; the right is thus in this sense objective, the "right thing itself," as some have put it.

To take an example: We widely concede that persons in the United States have a right to freedom of speech, a right which includes the right to speak critically, harshly, even falsely of public figures, so long as we do not do so in "reckless disregard of the truth." Although there is, in effect, a right to speak falsely (within certain broad limits)—that is, a morally protected power or liberty to do so—nonetheless we would also admit that false statement is bad, an evil of some sort, not the "right thing itself"; the right situation would be better realized if all persons exercised their rights in such a manner that false claims about public figures were not made at all. Yet, within limits we have the subjective right to do what is objectively wrong.

Rights are claims, and thus active options for the rights holders; yet not every claim is a right—only justified claims. For example, some persons claim a right to prevent others from speaking if they do not agree with what the others have to say. By itself this is not a justified claim, and therefore normally we deny that it amounts to a right.

The two dimensions of debate about rights relate to the two parts of the definition of rights. One dimension has to do with the kinds of claim persons can raise. The other has to do with the issue of justifiability—what makes a claim justifiable, or alternatively put, what is the source of rights? An easy way to think about the first issue is to consider some concrete examples of two kinds of rights people lay claim to. Take the alleged right to health care, for example. Although we do not normally make much of it, there is a certain ambiguity in this claim. Consider a nation that strongly disvalues its elderly. It is thought in this nation to be a waste of resources to lavish medical care on the elderly, a thought embodied in its very legal code: It is forbidden for any qualified medical personnel or medical facilities to supply any kind of health care to persons over sixty years of age except assistance in committing suicide. Let us suppose that Dr. Keats comes upon his elderly friend, Mr. Wordsworth, while the latter is having a heart attack and injects Mr. Wordsworth with adrenaline and administers CPR. Unfortunately for Dr. Keats, this all occurs in the village square, and the public-spirited Mrs. Coleridge, who happens to be walking by, turns Dr. Keats in to the authorities. At his trial the kindly and good Dr. Keats attempts to defend himself by arguing the law is unconstitutional and immoral, in that it denies Mr. Wordsworth and all other older people their right to health care.

Let us consider another kind of claim. Mr. Shelley has a rare tongue ailment, the chief symptom of which is that he can never keep still. His health insurance has run out, and he does not wish to spend all his savings for the tongue transplant the doctor assures him is his only hope. Mr. Shelley claims he should not be forced to bankrupt himself and his family in order to receive a potentially life-saving medical procedure. He claims that the government should supply or pay for the medical procedure he requires. He claims, in other words, a right to health care.

Now the right claimed on behalf of Mr. Wordsworth and that claimed on behalf of Mr. Shelley, although each is called a right to health care, are in fact quite different claims in at least one very important respect: In each case, at the other end of the claim is an imputation of a duty or an obligation. In the case of Mr. Wordsworth the duty that correlates with his rights claim is the duty of the state not to interfere with him in his effort to procure, or the efforts of others to offer, that to which he claims a right. His right is violated, he says, because the government has prevented him and others from supplying him with medical care. The duty at the other end of his right is a duty in the government to *forbear* from this interference.

At the other end of Mr. Shelley's rights claim lies something quite different. The government's duty here is not mere forbearance from interfering with his attempt to exercise his right, but rather the actual provision of that to which he claims a right—health care itself. Mr. Shelley is claiming a positive right, or as it is sometimes called, a welfare right. Mr. Wordsworth is claiming a narrower thing: a negative right, or, as it is sometimes called, a liberty. The key to the distinction lies in the duties correlated to the rights claim in question: If the duty is merely the duty to forbear—to not do something—then we have a negative right or liberty. If the duty is the duty to supply that very thing to which the rights claimant has a right, then it is a positive or welfare right.

This distinction between positive and negative rights is, as should be obvious, central to the debate about Big Government. Indeed it is perhaps not too much to say that, so far as the debate concerns justice, it is hardly anything *but* a debate about positive and negative rights—the pro–Big Government side arguing, in effect, that individuals possess positive rights which society, via government, is obliged to provide for (e.g., rights to health care, rights to education, and so forth), and the anti–Big Government side arguing that our rights are mainly negative rights and that not only has government no obligation to supply all the goods and services the pro–Big Government side would wish but in the very effort to supply them it violates the real, that is, negative, rights of people. Of course, this is too stark a contrast—one is not necessarily committed to a pure positive or negative rights stance. Most of us indeed are committed to some mix of the two, but the relation between this distinction and the recent debate should nonetheless be clear enough, even with that complication.

This distinction between positive and negative rights also helps make clear the difference between our two philosophers. Locke, for the most part, is a negative or liberty rights man. Indeed, he does not seem to possess a clear concept of positive rights. In his most systematic discussion of the matter, Locke endorses a distinction first made by his predecessors Thomas Hobbes and Samuel von Pufendorf, a distinction between law and right. A law binds, obliges, or limits one's options; in contrast, a right is a liberty.[3] The rights Locke recognizes as "natural" rights—the rights to life, to liberty, to property, to liberty of conscience—are negative rights. This is not to say that Locke recognizes no positive rights, but only that the natural rights, strictly speaking, are negative rights. The very fundamental civil right established when government is instituted—the right to legal protection in one's rights—is a positive right (the government has the duty to supply the protection), but it is not strictly natural. Likewise, many positive rights may vest due to legal enactments, such as the right to one's health care benefits under the Medicare legislation. These are not natural rights, however, and while it is a part of natural justice that one's legal rights be honored (under most conditions, at least), there is no natural right in Locke's account to health care in the positive right sense.

Rawls's position is more complex, for he recognizes as natural rights both negative rights, such as the right to free speech, and positive rights, such as the right to social support, that is, to economic resources, at a certain level. He does not endorse an ipso facto positive right to health care; his famous Difference Principle establishes a right in everybody to a share of the wealth of the community, equal to that of all others, with the only allowable inequalities being those that benefit the least well off in society by producing more wealth for them.[4] Assuming that the society can afford health care, Rawls's Difference Principle implies a right to a share of the national wealth at such a level that could procure for all at least a basic level of health care; alternatively, publicly provided or funded health care would surely count under Rawls's scheme of justice as a way of satisfying the rights claims citizens possess under the Difference Principle. Rawls is thus much friendlier to Big Government than is Locke.

RAWLS

We come now to the overwhelming question, the second question posed by the definition of rights: What justifies claims, or what is the source of rights? This question brings us finally to our two proof texts. Although both Locke and Rawls affirm individual inviolability and therewith rights, their views on the source of rights are almost the complete reverse of each other's. According to Rawls, individual inviolability, that is to say, rights, derives from justice; according to Locke, justice derives from inviolability, that is, from rights. For Rawls, justice first, then rights; for Locke, rights first, then justice. In that reversal lies the chief difference between the two, and the chief source of their disagreement over the nature of rights, the source on the one hand of

Rawls's affirmation of positive rights and therefore Bigger Government, and on the other of Locke's affirmation of negative rights and therefore Smaller Government.

From here we need to ask three questions of our philosophers: (1) What do they mean by their respective formulas on rights and justice; (2) Which, if either, is philosophically sound, or at least sounder; and (3) What kind of practical guidance can we derive from these rights theorists on the question of Big Government?

Rawls's formula has come to be familiar-sounding through frequent repetition, yet we need to recover a sense of how much it jars our intuitive or commonsense notion of justice. As Rawls has it, our rights derive from justice. The more natural thought is the reverse—that justice as the rendering or respecting of what rightly belongs to each is respecting our rights, or inviolability, or what is our own. Justice, we tend to think, follows from and does not ground or serve as source of rights. The uniqueness and great interest of Rawls's political philosophy derives precisely from his reversal of this normal feature of our thinking about justice.

This turn in Rawls's thought derives from another important claim he raises: that the core or source of justice is fairness.[5] Despite the great attention Rawls has received during the past thirty years, this derivation of justice from fairness, and rights from justice, remains an insufficiently explored theme in his work.

Examination of Rawls's pre–*Theory of Justice* writings reveals a somewhat surprising fact: He came to his great discovery about justice and rights more or less accidentally, in the course of investigating a quite different question. Indeed, many things about Rawls's theory become much clearer if we place his chief insight back into the context from which it emerged. That context—ironical, given his later reputation as a fervent opponent of utilitarianism—was an effort to resolve certain inconsistencies that appeared to exist between utilitarianism as a moral theory and the moral judgments that people ordinarily make, and thereby to save utilitarianism from its critics.[6] Rawls was committed from his very earliest efforts in moral philosophy to the view that the existence of serious conflict between ordinary moral judgments and a given moral theory is an insuperable objection to the theory in question.[7]

It was widely known that utilitarianism frequently led to such conflicts. For example, in an essay that he published in the 1950s, Rawls discussed well-known inconsistencies involving punishment, on the one hand, and promise-keeping, on the other. If the moral justification for punishment (and other social institutions) is social utility, as utilitarians say, then it might turn out to be morally justifiable to punish innocent persons under certain conditions, for example, when it is necessary to produce a deterrent effect with regard to a type of crime the actual perpetrators of which cannot be caught and when the innocence of the parties punished is not known publicly. Although the utilitarian calculus might support punishment of the innocent in this case, Rawls points out that this result would conflict with the moral judgment ordinary persons would make about this case, that it is an instance of injustice.[8]

Rawls also takes up the case of a son who, in the privacy of his dying father's hospital room, makes his father a promise, but then later chooses to break the promise on the ground that the action he now wishes to undertake will produce more social utility than the action he promised his dead father. He wishes, let us say, to help the homeless, rather than to build a network of shelters for injured skunks, as his father wished him to do. Again, a utilitarian moralist would appear to support the son's action, but Rawls thinks ordinary persons would condemn it.[9]

In his later work, Rawls would take the existence of conflicts of this sort as evidence of the untenability of utilitarianism, but the young Rawls does not take that tack. He attempts instead to save utilitarianism by making it more complex.[10] Our moral judgments, he argues, trace out a slightly more complicated pattern than simple utilitarianism allows for. Certain parts of our moral life are governed by practices—large patterns or institutions formed by sets of rules that define and shape behavior within the practice. Practices themselves, Rawls maintains, find their justification in the utilitarian calculus, but individual actions within practices do not. They claim their validity, their very logical meaning by reference to the practice itself.[11]

In the case of these actions we are disbarred from appealing directly to the utilitarian calculus to weigh the moral quality of any given action. Within the practice, the rules of practice have moral authority per se. It is the practice itself that has (or does not have) utility. In our two examples this means that the son does not have the moral right to calculate the utilitarian social benefits accruing to his various possibilities of action, but, being a participant in the practice of promising, has a prima facie moral obligation to keep his promises. Similarly with punishment: Officials within the practice of punishment are precisely part of that broad practice which contains rules providing against the punishment of the innocent for utilitarian purposes. Only a practice that protects the innocent could satisfy the utilitarian test for practices; a practice that contained rules allowing officials at their discretion to punish the innocent could not do so.[12]

Rawls believed he had thus saved utilitarianism from some of the most potent criticisms raised against it by restricting the domain of application of the utilitarian principle itself. He believed utilitarianism could thus be the ultimate ground of morality as the justification for practices and rules, which by a kind of principle of transitivity transferred moral obligations to actions proscribed or prescribed by the rules of practices.

Rawls soon came to think otherwise, but the distinction between practices and actions remained determinative for his later thinking and was instrumental in his almost accidental discovery of "justice as fairness." He came to see, however, that utilitarianism was more hopeless than he had first thought, because he came to see that his distinction between practices/rules and actions did not suffice to save utilitarianism from serious conflict with our normal moral judgments.

He came to see that the utilitarian way of thinking about practices was just as inadequate as the standard utilitarian way of thinking about specific actions within practices. There are some practices that utilitarianism just cannot deal with: Rawls fixed on the example of slavery—even though utilitarians might condemn the practice of slavery, they would not do so in a way that tracked normal moral judgment (at least not the normal moral judgment of mid-twentieth-century Americans). If utilitarians condemn slavery, they will judge it to be wrong contingently: As a matter of fact, as a practice it does not (normally) produce a net balance of positive utility. Yet a utilitarian must admit that in principle, the judgment could go the other way under some circumstances.

Rawls believed this was incorrect, in that we do not condemn slavery merely as a contingent matter—we condemn it in principle. We would not accept as a moral justification of slavery a utilitarian calculus that showed that the practice produced, on balance, positive social benefit.

Rawls stood by his first discovery, that the moral character of individual actions and outcomes was a result of the playing out of rules of a practice, but he was forced to look for something other than the utilitarian account of the moral legitimacy of practices themselves. In the course of this inquiry Rawls stumbled across the discovery that was to shape all his later work.

The most obvious candidates for answers to his question were that either participation per se or consent was the source of the moral force of practices. But, he argued, neither could be so. People frequently find themselves participants in a practice in which neither they nor outside observers identify them as incurring obligations to the practice.[13] Take again the institution of slavery. Even slave owners normally recognize that slaves have no moral obligations to their slave status. Perhaps participation in some practices binds but certainly not all; at best, participation is a necessary but insufficient condition of obligation to the practice.

Since slavery is an involuntary condition, the thought next naturally arises that it is voluntary participation or consent that generates the moral ties of practices. The son, for example, willingly made that promise to his dying father and thus stepped voluntarily into the set of rules defining the practice of promising. But just as mere participation seems to be overinclusive as a standard, so voluntariness seems underinclusive.[14] We participate in many practices to which we have not given our consent in any realistic sense. Rawls thinks, for example, of the political system itself. We have no real choice whether to participate or not, and yet we recognize prima facie duties within it. Rawls thus rejects the classic doctrine of the social contract theorists, like Hobbes, Locke, and Jean-Jacques Rousseau, on the ground that their contractarianism, according to which consent generates obligation, is too fictitious and does too little of the work a theory of moral obligation must do.[15]

The most obvious candidates for accounting for the moral bite of rules of practices fail, then, but Rawls found the clue to an answer from a particular type of practice which, he believed, was especially revealing of the nature of practices as such. This was the game. Baseball and other such games display the character of practices especially well, for the actions taken within them have meaning, one might say, have existence even, only within the game as defined by the rules. One can, Rawls points out, strike out only within the game of baseball. A strikeout has no existence apart from the rules of baseball.[16]

Although games are typically voluntary activities, there is quite another standard in terms of which they are assessed: their fairness. The rules of the game must be fair whether it is voluntarily entered on or not.[17] Moreover, one who fails to play by the rules, or who greatly benefits from rules themselves unfair, is denounced as unfair. Those who are disadvantaged by unfair action or practices are not seen to have the same obligation to the practices as those who participate in a fair game; the outcomes of unfair games lack the legitimacy of the outcomes of fair games.

With the discovery of fairness, Rawls believes he has discovered a whole new universe of moral ties, or rather that he has clarified the character of a whole realm of previously misunderstood moral ties.[18] Yet the discovery of fairness merely pushes the inquiry back a step farther: What makes a game or practice fair? A practice, Rawls concludes, "will strike the parties as fair if no one feels that, by participating in it, they or any of the others are taken advantage of, or forced to give in to claims which they do not regard as legitimate."[19] If they are participants in a practice they can or should regard as fair, whether they have voluntarily participated or not, "there arises," says Rawls, "a prima facie duty (and a corresponding prima facie right) of the parties to each other to act in accordance with the practice when it falls to them to comply."[20] Rawls's notion of the fairness of practice thus circumvents the difficult issues posed by under- and overinclusiveness of the two candidate principles of participation per se and consent. It recognizes that we are not obliged to all practices (and the legitimacy of their outcomes) in which we are somehow engaged, but it also recognizes that we can be obliged to practices (and their outcomes) to which we have not actually consented.

Rawls's trajectory of thought then is from the anomalies of utilitarianism to practices to fairness. Fairness, and thus the obligation inhering in practices, depends on the terms of participation in the practice, in the way the burdens and benefits of the practice are distributed to the participants. Here is Rawls's Eureka moment, for this kind of distribution of burdens and benefits is nothing but distributive justice. That is, Rawls has stumbled onto justice via his investigation of the rules of practices. It reminds a bit of that moment in Plato's *Republic* when Socrates, momentarily at a loss as to where to find justice in the city he and the others have constructed, suddenly discovers it has been rolling around at their feet all along.[21]

The curious priority for Rawls of justice over inviolability and rights derives from the structure of thought just uncovered. Because the moral legitimacy of practices depends on the ability of each and every participant to say that he or she is not taken advantage of, is fairly and personally benefited by the practice, then indeed it follows that the rights of each derive from justice rather than vice versa. One's rights, Rawls insists, are one's "legitimate expectations" under valid principles of justice.[22] This follows necessarily for Rawls because the realm of justice is a realm of practices and a resultant of the character of practices rather than of something inhering in individuals or in the world per se. It is as impossible for there to be justice outside of practices as it is to strike out outside of baseball. As Rawls says, justice inheres in "the basic structure" of society (the rules of the biggest practice of all) and not in individuals or actions, except derivatively.[23]

The just result is the one produced by fair practices. Thus Rawls jettisons almost from the outset the very terms in which justice had been conceived in earlier theory and practice: Justice is "receiving what one is due," what one merits, or what is one's own. One has no claims other than to what the rules (or principles of justice) allocate to one.

It is at this point in his thinking that the well-known features of Rawls's scheme kick in—the original position, the veil of ignorance, the two principles of justice, and all that. These features of Rawls's scheme are required because he is not, after all, asking whether people actually do accept as fair the practices in which they find themselves. Rather, he must construct a purely hypothetical situation, itself characterized by fair conditions, in which he can ask hypothetical participants what rules of participation they would consider fair. It must be hypothetical because participants in actual ongoing practices could not be expected to agree to a rule of fair distribution that would in effect disadvantage them relative to their current situation. Ongoing practices are just to the degree they conform to principles that would be selected in this truly fair but purely hypothetical base situation, the so-called original position. Thus the well-known abstractness of Rawls's system is justified and even required by his approach to justice as fairness.

Since justice is fairness in practices, Rawls concludes, justice is in the first instance equality in the distribution of burdens and benefits of the practice, for it would seem that all could accept that as a fair distribution. Yet, he observes, all participants in a practice could accept an addendum to the equality rule: Inequalities from which each and every one of them benefits would also be acceptable. If unequal distribution of benefits (and burdens) means that everyone gets more than they would under conditions of simple equality, then it is rational for all of them to accept the rule of unequal distribution. Thus Rawls derives his most general "conception of justice" as the rules all would consider fair for their participation in the big games called society and economy: "All social values—liberty and opportunity, income and wealth, and the bases of self-respect—are to be distributed equally unless an unequal distribution of any, or all, of these values is to everyone's advantage."[24]

The basic rights of the individual are derivative from the principle of distribution that makes the practice fair or just. That principle requires that society recognize and honor the claims of all the participants to their fair share of the benefits produced and distributed within it. It follows from Rawls's scheme, in other words, that at least some of the important rights individuals possess are positive rights. Rawls's state must be a redistributive or strong welfare state unless fortuitously the "natural" (that is, market) distribution corresponds to his principles of justice. Neither Rawls nor anybody else believes that will happen, so the Rawlsean state perforce must possess Big Government in order to secure to citizens their positive rights.

LOCKE

Locke's derivation of justice from rights sounds more familiar on its face than Rawls's reversal of that formula, yet Locke's saying on justice has its own puzzles. Let us first recall Locke's parallel statement. "Every man has a Property in his own Person. This no body has any Right to but himself. . . . And where there is property, there can be justice and injustice." The structure of Locke's thought seems to be that property in the self is the source of rights, and rights are the basis for justice and injustice. The puzzling element within this chain of ideas is property. To the point is another saying of his. By property, Locke tells us, he means life, liberty, and estate; that is, the kind of rights or objects of rights that he claims human beings possess by nature are themselves property.[25] Locke adopts the language of property to describe what we would be more inclined to delineate as the domain of rights in part to clarify where he stands relative to an ambiguity in the concept of rights that was much discussed in the seventeenth century.

Thomas Hobbes, who was responsible for much of the conceptual innovation at the time, treated rights, at least natural right, as a pure liberty, as a moral faculty, or power, or liberty with no correlative duty attached to it of any kind. Thus Hobbes affirmed that under the right of nature, every person has a right to everything, including one another's bodies, to say nothing of one another's possessions.[26] "Hugo has a right to his own life," by which Hobbes meant, Hugo by nature has the right, the moral liberty, to do whatever it takes to preserve himself. This includes a right to harm, even kill, Samuel, for he may be a threat to Hugo's life. Of course, the reverse is true also: Samuel may, with right, also kill Hugo, or take all his stockpiled nuts, berries, and filet mignons. Hobbes concludes from this situation that there is no justice by nature, for justice is rendering to each his own, but in nature there is nothing that is, properly speaking, one's own.[27] Hugo's life is not juridically his own, all others—Samuel, Thomas, Francisco—have a right to Hugo's life just as much as he does himself. Hobbes sees an analytic connection between property and justice—where there is no property, there is no injustice. And in nature there is no property. All justice for Hobbes, then, is conventional.

Objections to Hobbes's analysis arose almost immediately, the most cogent being that Hobbes is misusing the term *right* when he describes it as a pure liberty with no correlative duty of any sort. A right, it was countered, implies a duty in others of some sort. During the late seventeenth century there was a controversy as to the meaning of the word "right," Hobbes's meaning and this other meaning, argued most forcefully by Samuel von Pufendorf.[28] Locke means to clarify which meaning he is adopting by using the language of property to define the language of rights. Property, as even Hobbes concedes, implies an exclusivity: To say Hugo has property in his life is to say Samuel does not have a right to it. Property is a rights claim with a correlative duty of forbearance.

By using the term *property* to refer to the realm of natural rights Locke is very concisely saying at least these three things: first, that he means by a right the sort of moral claim that carries along with it claims to exclusivity; second, that he means there is such property in or by nature—that is, human beings possess natural rights of the sort that imply natural duties; and third, that justice is, therefore, by nature. This last claim can be readily understood in terms of the point Hobbes made: If justice is rendering to each his or her own and if human beings have an "own" by nature, then—reversing Hobbes's conclusion—there is justice by nature.

The foundation or ground of rights, and therefore of inviolability ("this no body has a right to but himself") is, according to Locke, self-ownership.[29] Note that Locke here appears to claim the allegedly impossible— the derivation of an "ought" from an "is." He concludes from an "is," the fact of self-ownership, the "ought" of moral inviolability. However, this derivation of "ought" from "is" is not so mysterious or even problematical as the notorious difficulty of the problem would imply. Locke's point is that if it is indeed a fact that human beings are self-owners, then they are inviolable, for inviolability—exclusive right—is precisely what ownership means or implies. If Samuel has a simple right to appropriate what Hugo possesses, then Hugo does not have property. So, to have property is to have moral inviolability.

On the rock of self-ownership Locke builds his doctrines of natural rights, justice, and limited government. But what can this claim mean, and how can it be supported? The prerequisite for the understanding of self-ownership, for Locke, is the understanding of the self. When Locke investigates personal identity he comes to see that the identity of the person is nothing like the identity of inanimate objects, or of nonhuman animals. Human beings uniquely find their identity in self-consciousness, that is, in the consciousness of self, of the "I" persisting over time that stands as the basis for the unity of experience, intention, and action of the person. Indeed, the "I" not only persists over time but is the very basis for constituting the temporality of the human being; the human self is a temporal entity as no other is.[30] The "I" is not, Locke argues, anything given in nature. Other animals have no "I" center, and human beings themselves develop the "I" consciousness only over time.

Most significant for the questions we are interested in here is Locke's picture of the structure of the self as self-owner. The self in its very nature is posited as self-owning—a fact witnessed in our most elementary locutions: I, me, me, mine, to quote an old Beatles' song. The center of the self is the "I," the pure abstract and empty ego, possessor of its own data of consciousness (*my* feelings, *my* ideas, *my* experiences), always found in these experiences (that is, what makes them mine) yet never lost in them (that is, how the "I" can stand above and possess them). The self is the compound of the "I" and the "me," the abstract and empty ego and the contents of consciousness understood as mine, and thus as me.

Moreover, Locke argues, if the human person were not a body with pleasures and pains, the self would never come into existence, as he shows via a mechanism too complex to summarize here.[31] At the same time, the self is most intimately concerned with—attached with care to—its pleasures and pains, and ultimately its happiness and misery. Human beings are unique in that, as selves, they can seize on their entire lives as wholes, seeing them as unities, or potential unities spread over the dimensions of time and aiming toward happiness or misery as such. The self can give or attempt to give some shape to this life as a whole that comes to view for it; life has "meaning" for a human person in a way it has not for any other mortal being. The self possesses not only its data of consciousness but also its body, which is the source of most of these data of consciousness. The self appropriates the body and makes it its own—that is to say, makes it the instrument of its intentional actions in relation to its broader purposes in life. Action becomes in the full sense intentional, and the body, itself inseparable from the happiness and the misery of the "I" and thoroughly involved with intentionality, becomes the self's own.

Self-ownership procures ownership of body and action. The possession by the self of itself is of the nature of an exclusive claim, of the nature of a property right. My self, my happiness and misery, my body and its action, are mine in such a way that my sovereignty over them necessarily and ipso facto excludes similar claims to them by others. In the first instance, this ownership is a fact of the structure of self-consciousness. Yet it has deep moral implications. The "I" necessarily is concerned with its own happiness and misery. So far as it accurately understands its situation, it necessarily raises rights claims over its body, actions, and road to happiness. The self posits itself as possessor of rights to life, liberty, and pursuit of happiness. Its very claim for itself as a self contains a claim of exclusivity vis-à-vis others.

Each self claims a right that others forbear from interfering with what is the self's own, and logic (although not the practical conditions of existence) requires that each self raising such a claim recognize that every other self raises ipso facto the very same claim on the very same ground. Each self cannot help but raise the claim and logically must recognize the claim of all others. It demands for itself and must recognize correlative duties. This is a very imperfect duty, however, in that there is very little to require that it actually be honored. In nature, human beings are apt to overlook claims of others. The result is war; the solution, of course, is government and law, which, if properly made, recognize each person as a self with rights and take their bearings from the natural standards of justice—to respect what is each one's own, that is, to respect their "property," or their rights—to life, liberty, and pursuit of happiness.

Given the nature of rights as property, and of the concomitant duties that are co-constituted with rights, it is clear that Lockean rights are and must be negative rights. Government exists to secure these negative rights, and thus Locke is rightly known as a friend to limited—that is, smaller rather than larger—government. This in brief is the trajectory of Locke's thought—from consciousness to self-consciousness to self-ownership to natural rights to the need for liberal (limited) government "to secure these rights."

CONCLUSION

In conclusion we must now ask two further questions: Which of these two important liberal rights theories is sounder? and what kind of guidance can we derive from this discussion about rights with regard to the issue on the table before us, Big Government?

As to the first question, I think more must be said and done before any kind of decisive answer can be given, but I suspect that the Lockean theory is sounder than Rawls's, and let me just mention four reasons why I believe so. First, Locke conforms much more closely to our natural insights into justice than Rawls does. Locke is able to articulate, in what I believe is a plausible manner, the ground of the claim individuals raise in a way that resonates with the way individuals do raise rights claims. Second, Rawls's derivation of rights from fairness in practices leads to an extraordinarily anomolous result—that there are no rights claims between persons not engaged in common practices.[32] The implication would seem to be, to take a classic example, that Hugo would be perfectly in the right to gratuitously kill Samuel if they met on a desert island and had no ongoing relation with each other. This surely runs counter to our ordinary understanding of rights as holding between human beings as such, whether friends and fellow countrymen or not. Locke can account for this while Rawls cannot.

Third, Rawls's fairness argument is itself parasitic on something like a Lockean claim for individuals, in that there is some antecedent claim individuals have that gives them, in effect, a right to fairness within practices. But Rawls hardly explores this prior claim and instead attempts to derive rights from the practice.[33] He needs to step back a bit and consider more carefully the preconditions for his own edifice of fairness. In his more recent work Rawls is attempting something like this, reconceiving the nature of the argument for fairness and attempting to discover principles of international justice, in response to the desert island problem I mentioned just before.[34] I obviously have no time to follow out Rawls's more recent efforts, but I do not believe they succeed any better than his *Theory of Justice*.[35]

Finally, Rawls's notion of fairness is greatly deficient. While it is true that games are measured against a standard of fairness, that does not correspond to Rawls's "basic conception of justice" as equality tempered by inequalities from which everyone benefits. Equal benefit (outcomes) is not at all the baseline for assessing the fairness of games; indeed rules of games are structured so as to differentially reward those who perform the game's actions at higher levels of skill. That is what makes a *good game*. Games thus track much more closely the kind of equal opportunity principles of justice Rawls dismisses. A good game is one structured so that the "best man" or woman or team wins.

What guidance, then, does Locke give on the problem of Big Government? He is the classic thinker of limited government but is not for all that a partisan of Little Government. Locke is not a libertarian, that is, one who argues that government's mandate extends to protecting negative rights and only that. Locke does not argue this position, made famous in recent years by Robert Nozick, because he has a richer and more supple understanding of the requirements of politics.

The purpose of government, Locke does insist, is the securing of (negative) rights, but he sees with perfect clarity that the conditions for the existence of rights—the self in its self-ownership—and the conditions for the effectual securing of rights are not the same. The ground of rights is indeed individualistic in Locke, but rights can be secured only under social conditions. Government must be concerned directly with the securing of negative rights and indirectly with the conditions for the securing of rights. An effective rights-securing society requires institutions of education and training in personal qualities that fit individuals to be part of a rights-respecting community. This means that a Lockean society would be one that does pay attention, for example, to "family values," as Locke himself did, for families have historically been the institutions best suited to this kind of "socialization."[36]

Locke does not supply us with so clear-cut a formula about the optimal or legitimate size of government as does either Rawls or the libertarians, for both of whom a doctrine of rights more or less adequately lays out the legitimate or morally required sphere of public action. For Locke, rights define only part of the task, although admittedly a most important part. But a large sphere of proper governmental action escapes the strict rule of principle and rests in the realm of prudence. Locke tells us that this sphere of prudential policy must be guided by the task of rights-securing, but there is no blueprint Locke can offer for this sphere. Locke does argue, though, that negative rights serve as limits that must be respected in the sphere of prudence, and thus he always remains a voice for limited government. He also gives us grounds to see that the legitimate claims beyond negative rights-securing are not positive rights, but the broad conditions for negative rights-securing.

It might appear that Locke's inability to supply clear and determinate answers to the questions of Big versus Little Government is a great disadvantage. In some sense perhaps it is, but in a broader sense it surely is not. The political sphere is, after all, part of the empirical world, subject to all the variety of circumstance, uncertainty, and change to which the empirical world is subject. If Locke argued, as do Rawls and the libertarians, that some set of theoretical principles completely governs the sphere of practice, we would have reason to wonder whether he had given us a theory truly adequate to the world it is to govern. The very inadequacies of the Lockean approach indicate a deeper adequacy to the fundamental contingency of existence. Locke does not leave us, as do so many who question principle in the name of practice or prudence, with a sphere ungoverned by normative principle, or a sphere related to normative principle only in the extremely attenuated form of an ideal or a standard of a "best regime," realizable nowhere and at no time and thus of completely uncertain application at any particular place or time. Locke's rights theory is thus a very Goldilocks-like thing—he supports neither Big Government nor Little Government but government that is just right.

NOTES

1. John Rawls, *A Theory of Justice* (Cambridge: Harvard University Press, 1971), 3.

2. John Locke, *Two Treatises of Government*, ed. P. Laskett (Cambridge: Cambridge University Press, 1970), II.27; John Locke, *An Essay Concerning Human Understanding*, ed. P. Nidditch (Oxford: Oxford University Press, 1975), IV.3.18. I have changed Locke's formulation of the principle about justice to make his version more clearly parallel to Rawls's. Locke's original reads: "Where there is no property, there is no justice."

3. John Locke, *Questions Concerning the Law of Nature*, ed. Robert Horwitz, Jenny Strauss Clay, and Diskin Clay (Ithaca, N.Y.: Cornell University Press, 1990), 11.

4. Rawls, *Theory of Justice*, sect. 13.

5. Rawls, *Theory of Justice*, sect. 3.

6. John Rawls, "Two Concepts of Rules," *Philosophical Review* 64 (1955): 3–4, 18.

7. See John Rawls, "Outline of Decision Procedure for Ethics," *Philosophical Review* 60 (1951); John Rawls, "Justice as Fairness," *Philosophical Review* 67 (1958): 334. Consider Rawls's comments on the continuing presence of this principle in his thought at least through *Theory of Justice*, sect. 9.

8. Rawls, "Two Concepts of Rules," 9–10.

9. Rawls, "Two Concepts of Rules," 13–15.

10. Rawls, "Two Concepts of Rules," 3–4.

11. Rawls, "Two Concepts of Rules," 24–26.

12. Rawls, "Two Concepts of Rules," 12.

13. Rawls, "Two Concepts of Rules," 26, 32.

14. Rawls, "Justice as Fairness," 325–26.

15. Rawls, "Justice as Fairness," 324.

16. Rawls, "Two Concepts of Rules," 25–26.

17. Rawls, "Justice as Fairness," 325–26.

18. Rawls, "Justice as Fairness," 326–27, 334.

19. Rawls, "Justice as Fairness," 324–25.

20. Rawls, "Justice as Fairness," 325, 328.

21. Plato, *Republic*, ed. Allan Bloom (New York: Basic Books, 1965), 432d.

22. Rawls, *Theory of Justice*, sect. 48.

23. Rawls, *Theory of Justice*, sect. 2.

24. Rawls, *Theory of Justice*, sect. 11.

25. Locke, *Two Treatises*, II.87.

26. Thomas Hobbes, *Leviathan*, ed. Richard Tuck (Cambridge: Cambridge University Press, 1991), chap. 14.

27. Hobbes, *Leviathan*, chap. 14.

28. For a more complete discussion of this debate, see Michael P. Zuckert, *Natural Rights and the New Republicanism* (Princeton, N.J.: Princeton University Press, 1994), 275–78.

29. Locke, *Two Treatises*, II.27.

30. Locke, *Essay Concerning Human Understanding*, II.27.

31. For further discussion, see Zuckert, *Natural Rights*, 283–85.

32. Rawls, "Justice as Fairness," 328.

33. Rawls, "Justice as Fairness," 327–29, 333; Rawls, *Theory of Justice*, sect. 77.

34. See John Rawls, *Political Liberalism* (New York: Columbia University Press, 1991).

35. For a critique of the new Rawlsean position, see Michael Zuckert, "Is Egalitarian Liberalism Compatible with Limited Government?: The Case of Rawls," in R. George, ed., *Natural Law and Modern Liberalism* (Oxford: Oxford University Press, 1996), 49–85.

36. See John Locke, *Some Thoughts Concerning Education* (Indianapolis, Ind.: Hackett, 1996).

8

The Prospects for Democratic Control in an Age of Big Government

Paul Pierson

Robert Dahl asked the central question thirty-five years ago: "In a political system where nearly every adult may vote but where knowledge, wealth, social position, access to officials, and other resources are unequally distributed, who actually governs?"[1] Although Dahl's famous study focused on the distribution of influence in a single city, his work on democratic theory and practice emphasized that confronting the question of who governs in the twentieth century means addressing social organizations of massive scale. Societies of tens or hundreds of millions, facing tasks of enormous complexity, could not operate like city-states. For those with a commitment to democracy, the question was how, if at all, popular control over government could be exerted in such a context.

This enduring question is the subject of this chapter. Dahl's own answer, which came to be called pluralism, emphasized the crucial role of interest groups in promoting a wide dispersion of political influence. While this argument retains some force, it has taken a beating in the past two decades—not least from Dahl himself. In its place, a New Pluralism has slowly asserted itself, based on the rather surprising claim that voters are pretty capable of taking care of themselves.

I wish to raise suspicions—the evidence is not fully persuasive yet, even to me—that this New Pluralism also rests on shaky foundations. Voters lack many important resources needed to exercise effective control over the development of public policy. The resource I emphasize is knowledge: knowledge of what politicians do, and knowledge of what those actions mean for citizens' welfare. Moreover, I stress that the scarcity of knowledge has become more of a problem as the scale of government has grown, as policy initiatives have become more complex, and as the necessity of imposing pain on voters has become a more prominent part of contemporary politics.

THE VIEW FROM MAIN STREET:
FROM THE OLD PLURALISM TO THE NEW PLURALISM

Efforts to establish empirical support for the normative goal of citizen control over government have come full circle over the past four decades. At the end of World War II, voters were often viewed as the foundation for democratic practices. During the 1950s and 1960s, however, political scientists largely abandoned this idea. Proponents of the "behavioral revolution" gradually accumulated evidence that real voters generally failed to live up to the standards suggested in high school civics classes. Disillusioned, analysts then sought a new theoretical and empirical basis for democratic governance. In Dahl's pluralism, they found the answer in interest groups. Individual voters could not enforce popular control over government, but collectivities of voters, organized in groups, could. This powerful line of argument quickly became the new orthodoxy, but in the fifteen years from 1965 to 1980 it too came under serious attack. Ultimately faced with decisive criticisms (including virtual repudiations from leading pluralists such as Dahl and Charles Lindblom), the focus on groups as the basis of citizen control largely evaporated by the 1980s. Haltingly, in the past fifteen years a new (old?) solution to the problem has emerged based on a renewed faith in that much-maligned political actor, the voter. It is this curious journey that I wish to retrace briefly before I critically examine the latest solution to the old puzzle.

Analysts seeking an intellectual foundation for democratic politics have long had to contend with the argument that voters seem poorly cast for their central parts in the drama. Skepticism about the competence of ordinary citizens is as old as political theory, but in the past century one should at least mention the writings of the elite theorists Robert Michels, Gaetano Mosca, and Vilfredo Pareto and the famously scathing writings on public opinion of Walter Lippmann. In the period after World War II, these views were given more systematic foundation in the work on public opinion of Philip Converse and others in what came to be called the Michigan School. Voters on the whole were woefully ill-informed; survey research showed that, for most voters, there was little or no connection between views on issues, little capacity to link views on issues to broader concepts such as liberalism and conservatism, and little consistency over time in the views that voters expressed.[2] Opinion polls continue to reveal disturbing findings. For most citizens, the simple equation relating expenditures, revenues, and deficits remains elusive. In a recent survey, less than one-third of those polled could identify their own congressperson, and a similarly small number were able to name both of their senators. As three careful observers recently concluded, "the evidence is compelling that citizens, even well-educated citizens, tend to pay only intermittent attention to politics and to possess a fund of information about politics conspicuous for its thinness."[3]

These unsettling results contrast sharply with our mythical images of democratic citizens, but they actually conform to a growing body of evidence and theory about the nature of social cognition. The ground-breaking work of Herbert Simon, James March, and others was driving home the implications of a massive imbalance between the overwhelming complexity of the social world and the very modest capacities of the human brain.[4] The possibilities for human rationality were, at best, severely "bounded." Fields from decision science to organization theory were revolutionized by these findings, and they had a considerable impact on political science as well.

The dismal evidence about voters created a gaping hole in the efforts of social scientists to make a convincing empirical case for the possibility of democratic governance. Dahl's famous solution focused on groups: Power was decentralized in democratic polities not because of the activities of isolated voters but because an enormous number of groups could organize and effectively fight for their interests. The genius of Madisonian democracy, Dahl argued, was to create many points of entry into the political system. This institutional fragmentation encouraged a proliferation of political cleavages, which in turn generated a multitude of political organizations. Because cleavages were numerous and overlapping, political coalitions were likely to be transient, shifting fluidly from issue to issue. Minorities on one issue would be majorities on the next, and vice versa. Fragmentation also meant that different kinds of political resources would be useful in different venues, which further counteracted the possibility of concentrated power.

The pluralists were not utopian, and they were not blind to the existence of resource inequalities in modern societies. They never claimed that democratic institutions imply political equality. They did, however, hold that these institutions severely limit concentrations of power and give significant voice to all major groups in society. While not a perfect solution, the emphasis on groups nonetheless suggested the possibility of real popular control over the broad direction of government. For two decades, pluralism provided the leading interpretation of American politics. And while few scholars would today adopt the label as a self-description, pluralist assumptions and impulses still provide a foundation for much analysis of American political life.

That the label itself has gone out of fashion reflects the success of two quite different critiques. Both attacked the pluralist premise that the nature of group organization in democratic societies is relatively egalitarian. The first critique stressed the acute difficulties involved in organizing precisely the kinds of groups that would represent the broadest interests and concerns of ordinary citizens. The second developed new and more powerful arguments about the unequal distribution of political resources in democratic polities. Together, these analyses did much to undermine the claim that a plurality of groups creates the foundation for democratic politics.

The catalyst for the first critique was Mancur Olson's *The Logic of Collective Action*, which represents the single most important contribution of economists to our understanding of politics.[5] Olson challenged a core pluralist argument: that significant political grievances "naturally" give rise to political mobilization. When political goals represent a "public good"—by which economists mean goods that are necessarily available to an entire group if they are made available at all—the "logic of collective action" is activated. Individuals have strong incentives to "free ride" on the actions of others, hoping to obtain benefits without incurring the costs of producing them. Unless certain highly restrictive conditions are met, public goods of this sort are unlikely to be supplied.

Olson's work shattered the conventional understanding of interest groups and reoriented the efforts of political scientists. Students of interest groups turned to the investigation of collective action problems. In the process, many of the original, dramatic claims of *The Logic of Collective Action* were modified. Collective action turns out to be less difficult than Olson supposed, in part because social actors participate in group activities for reasons other than the rational, instrumental pursuit of private benefits.[6] Still, Olson's core insight remains profound. There is nothing natural or automatic about the process through which citizens organize to pursue political ends. Many grievances are unlikely to translate into commensurate efforts at mobilization.

Crucially, Olson showed that the problem is especially severe for the broadest and most diffuse concerns of citizens. Achieving clean air, safe consumer products, or a healthy economy are classic examples of public goods. It is not that such concerns will be totally unrepresented in politics—there are, after all, many environmental and consumer groups in Washington. But there is good reason to believe that they will be vastly underrepresented in comparison with narrow, particularistic groups that find collective action problems easier to overcome. Olson thus cast serious doubts on the pluralist claim that the world of interest groups roughly reflects the concerns and preferences of ordinary citizens.

The second critique of pluralism also focused on the distribution of political resources, but highlighted the role of economic inequality and particularly the powerful role of business in American politics. The arguments took different forms and occurred both in neo-Marxist debates and in more mainstream discussions in political science. Some stressed the inequality of financial and organizational resources. In E. E. Schattschneider's famous phrase, "the flaw in the pluralist heaven is that the heavenly chorus sings with a strong upper-class accent."[7] Pluralists had claimed that political resources are widely dispersed and tend to be off-setting; those rich in one kind of resource are poor in others. On the contrary, these critics argued, political resources are generally rather concentrated, and resource inequalities tend to be highly correlated and reinforcing rather than off-setting. Those with more money, better information, and greater political access tend to be not three distinct groups but rather the same people.

Other analysts emphasized the structural position of private firms in a market-based economy. Because investment—and ultimately jobs and income—depends on inducements (that is, profits) for business, politicians face overwhelming incentives to respond to market signals in shaping government activity. The need for business confidence confers tremendous political power on employers, even if they do not engage in vigorous lobbying of public officials. In the famous phrase of one disenchanted pluralist, Lindblom, business occupied a "privileged position" in democratic polities. The market, he added, is a prison, in which government officials are confined to a restricted range of activities.[8]

Political scientists have paid surprisingly little attention to the fact that Dahl, the dean of American pluralism, joined in this critique.[9] Accepting the main tenets of Lindblom's analysis, Dahl came to believe that the distribution of political resources is far more unequal than he had originally maintained. Indeed, he suggested that movement toward a decentralized socialism, based on democratic political institutions and worker-owned enterprises, is a precondition for true pluralism. In contrast to the attention lavished on his earlier analysis, which had implied a largely favorable view of the American polity, this much more critical judgment was met largely with silence. Yet it undoubtedly reinforced the spreading disillusionment with pluralist interpretations of American politics. Facing the combined weight of Olson's and Lindblom's critiques, analysts have largely backed away from the proposition that interest groups provide a strong foundation for effective citizen control over government.

In the past decade, however, propositions about the possibilities for citizen control have been reoriented and revitalized.[10] So far, there has been little effort to synthesize these new analyses into a coherent view of American politics, but the core of such a synthesis seems straightforward. I choose to term this body of work the New Pluralism, because it points toward the same conclusion reached by the original pluralists: that a rough version of citizen control over politicians and policy exists, even though political resources are distributed rather unequally. The extraordinary thing about the New Pluralism is that it reverses the intellectual moves made by the old pluralism. Dahl and others, who had lost confidence in the capacities of voters, put their faith in interest groups. The New Pluralists, skeptical about interest groups, have a renewed optimism about the capacities of voters to protect their own interests.

This new optimism has not been based on any revision of the traditional view that voters know relatively little about politics. Students of public opinion remain struck by how minimally informed most voters are about issues, how inconsistent their views seem to be over time, and how difficult it is for most voters to aggregate their perspectives on particular issues into any coherent orientation toward political life. The changed evaluation of voters, and consequently of the prospects for popular control, is based instead on new arguments about the relatively efficient manner in which voters employ the limited information available to them. In this new perspective, voters exhibit bounded rationality. Effectively managing limited information and cognitive skills, they can nonetheless produce outcomes not radically different from those that would emerge if they could somehow be fully informed about politics.

The New Pluralism is based on two main lines of argument. The first focuses on the ability of *individual* voters to overcome information problems and is organized around a series of claims about *heuristics*—cognitive shortcuts that allow individuals to simplify an overwhelmingly complex political reality.[11] As Paul Sniderman, Richard Brody, and Philip Tetlock have summarized the argument:

> Citizens frequently can compensate for their limited information about politics by taking advantage of judgmental heuristics. Heuristics are judgmental shortcuts, efficient ways to organize and simplify political choices, efficient in the double sense of requiring relatively little information to execute, yet yielding dependable answers even to complex problems of choice. . . . Insofar as they can be brought into play, people can be knowledgeable in their reasoning about political choices without necessarily possessing a large body of knowledge about politics.[12]

In short, for voters to act effectively they do not need a tremendous amount of information, nor do they need sophisticated analytical skills to interpret the information they have. Using simple and widely available information and tools, voters can produce a rough approximation of clear thinking, enabling them to use the vote to protect their interests.

This is a sophisticated and multifaceted literature, and I can only give the flavor of the arguments here. Central to it is the concept of "cues"—the idea that voters receive signals from other social actors, such as prominent politicians, political parties, or interest groups—or, in many cases, from social acquaintances who pay more attention to politics and whose views are respected.[13] So without knowing anything about the stealth bomber, voters can get a sense of where they stand by simply observing where, say, Ted Kennedy or Jesse Helms stands on the issue. I might feel little need to read the text of a gun control bill up for a vote in Congress; knowing how the NRA feels about it could be sufficient. Alternatively, I might turn to a friend, family member, or colleague who I think knows more about the matter and who shares my general outlook on politics.

Other tools help as well. Sniderman and his colleagues have emphasized what they term the "likability heuristic." Rather than relying on cold cognition to develop a clear understanding of a complicated issue, voters can turn to their feelings, particularly about those carrying out a policy or those the policy is meant to address. As Sniderman and his colleagues conclude, "reasoning about political choices is rooted in people's feelings as well as their beliefs—in fact, it is both fueled and facilitated by knowing whom one likes and whom one detests."[14]

Other analysts have pointed to the techniques through which individuals choose which aspects of a complicated world to consider and which to tune out. On the whole, these investigators argue, the techniques employed work pretty well. Individuals exercise *selective attention:* They pay the most attention to the issues that they care about the most. Voters also possess an *accessibility bias*: They retrieve the information that is the easiest to retrieve. Frequently, Shanto Iyengar has suggested, voters "invoke a built-in accessibility heuristic by which they consult categories or subject-matters about which they are relatively expert when making their political choices."[15] To the extent that these cognitive techniques direct voters to what they care most about and know most about, decisions are likely to be based on a relatively high level of knowledge, albeit in a restricted domain.

Thus while acknowledging that voters' rationality is bounded, these analysts nonetheless emphasize its fundamental rationality. Voters, the New Pluralists argue, can do a lot with very little. Of course, there may be important limitations in these various cognitive shortcuts. The overwhelming theme of the recent research, however, is that voters would end up in more or less the same place if they could somehow be perfectly informed about the social world.

The second line of argument within the New Pluralism focuses not on the cognitive capabilities of individual voters but on the collective properties of the electorate. As Ben Page and Robert Shapiro have argued forcefully in *The Rational Public*, apathy, limited information, and weak cognitive skills may cause problems for each of us, but collectively we are likely to do much better. The magic of aggregation produces a level of social rationality far in excess of that which each of us can attain alone. As the Marquis de Condorcet demonstrated two hundred years ago, given certain assumptions, if individuals have a reasonably good chance of producing the correct answer to some problem, the probability of a collectivity (for example, a jury) of these individuals doing so is vastly greater. Random elements in individual views will tend to offset each other and cancel out; aggregation acts as a filter for "noise," allowing the enduring and reasoned elements in public attitudes and beliefs to emerge. In this view, the electorate functions something like the stock market. Individual investors (voters) may have quite limited information and may be prone to error or eccentricity. Collectively, however, random elements drop out, and the market as a whole embodies the range of available information relevant to judging the value of stocks.

Page and Shapiro maintain that the erratic patterns detected by individual-level analyses of American voters are much less evident at the aggregate level:

> The collective policy preferences of the American public are predominantly *rational*, in the sense that they are *real*—not meaningless, random "nonattitudes"; that they are generally *stable*, seldom changing by large amounts and rarely fluctuating back and forth; that they form *coherent* and mutually consistent (not self-contradictory) patterns, involving meaningful distinctions; that these patterns *make sense* in terms of underlying values and available information; that, when collective policy preferences change, they almost always do so in *understandable* and, indeed, *predictable* ways, reacting in consistent fashion to international events and social and economic changes as reported by the mass media; and, finally, that opinion changes generally constitute *sensible* adjust-

ments to the new conditions and new information that are communicated to the public.[16]

This is a striking conclusion, and it is backed up by a careful examination of decades of polling results. Page and Shapiro do indeed uncover considerable evidence that polls show general stability of policy preferences over time. Furthermore, when the numbers move, they generally do so gradually or in response to clearly visible changes in the real world. At the macro-level, a reasonable and informed electorate seems to replace the micro-level view of voter ignorance.

Thus, in reaction against the conventional wisdom regarding the profound shortcomings of mass publics, the New Pluralism points to reasons for optimism, echoing V. O. Key's assertion of thirty years ago that "voters are not fools."[17] Although most citizens have limited interest and information about politics, they appear to have good techniques for managing reasonably well. Furthermore, even if each voter remains somewhat overwhelmed, the movement from the individual to the collective level serves to filter out elements of cognitive weakness while magnifying areas of strength. Thus, New Pluralism boldly stakes its case for democratic control on that object of pluralist skepticism, the average voter.

One must be careful in moving from these disparate investigations of political psychology, public opinion, and voting to overall judgments about the character of American democracy. After all, the "New Pluralism" is my phrase, and it imposes a somewhat artificial suggestion of coherence and scope onto work which often has had narrower goals. Much of this research has been an effort to "bend the stick" the other way in reaction to a widely held view that voters are incapable of playing a real part in political life. There has been relatively little effort to systematically explore the broader implications of these new claims about voters, in part because the hyperspecialization of political science has meant the virtual demise of synthetic, system-level analyses of American politics.[18]

Nonetheless, many of these analysts have not been shy about making big claims. James Stimson, for example, in an essay emphasizing the role of cues, concludes that his analysis "suggests that study after study demonstrating the ignorance of the individual citizen will have no consequence for the phenomenon central to applied democracy, whether electorates make policy-conscious decisions at the polls. It suggests that electoral mandates are real."[19] Iyengar maintains that, "contrary to much conventional wisdom, the average citizen is far from overwhelmed by the issues, events, and personae that enter and leave the political stage. By resorting to various simplifying strategies, people wrestle the 'booming, buzzing confusion' of politics into meaningful information, and, in so doing, provide themselves with the 'intelligence' to formulate their political preferences and decisions."[20] This new portrait of a collectively informed electorate possessing the power of the vote suggests that popular control remains viable even in a huge—and hugely complex—polity.

THE VIEW FROM WASHINGTON:
POLITICAL ELITES AND THE LIMITS OF POPULAR CONTROL

In a pattern now common in American political science, a wholly separate—and possibly incompatible—stream of thought regarding the national policy-making process has been developing just as the New Pluralism began to take shape.[21] This body of work focuses on the politics of policy formation and reformation, and it centers on the swirl of activity in Washington involving politicians, bureaucrats, and interest groups. Voters are not seen as irrelevant to this process. On the contrary, winning elections is viewed as *a*—if not *the*—major goal of central political actors. The potential role of the electorate in guiding and constraining the actions of political elites is a crucial building block of these arguments about policy making. Yet in contrast with the hopeful view of voters presented in the New Pluralism, these scholars have stressed just how hard it is for voters to act effectively. Ironically, they emphasize precisely the impact of the impoverished knowledge base of average Americans—and the asymmetries between the knowledge-poor and the knowledge-rich—which the New Pluralists have sought to discount.

The central claim of these studies of policy making is that while voters might not be fools, it is often possible to fool them. At least, the actions of political elites strongly suggest that *they* see considerable opportunities for manipulation. Examination of political struggles over major policy issues indicates that policy makers invest tremendous energy in efforts to direct the attention of voters in particular ways. Namely, political elites seek to attract voter attention to those activities for which they expect to receive credit, while distracting attention from those actions for which they anticipate the possibility of incurring significant political blame.

The distinguishing characteristic of democratic polities is the central role of elections in determining who wields political authority. Voting gives average citizens a crude instrument of control, providing the foundation for the New Pluralist claim that voters can protect their interests. Yet recent studies of policy making argue that it is likely to be effective only if voters can become aware of the relevant activities of policy makers.[22] The role of "visibility" in politics is often mentioned casually but little understood. All political actors possess imperfect information about issues relevant to their interests. Furthermore, the distribution of information is highly unequal. In particular, mass publics often have limited information about the impact of changes in public policy. In this context, it may be possible for policy makers to manipulate information flows to voters in ways that highlight their positive actions while obscuring their negative ones.

As Douglas Arnold has argued, electoral retribution against incumbents for unpopular policies requires three things.[23] First, the undesirable effects must be *discernible*: Voters must be cognizant that they have experienced particular negative outcomes. Second, these outcomes must be *traceable*: Voters must be able to determine that those outcomes are connected to government policies. Third, there must be *accountability*: Voters must be able to determine who should be held responsible for the undesired policies. As Arnold and others have found, these are not easy conditions to fulfill. Under some circumstances, of course, the connections are obvious. When the president declares that he is sending troops to the Persian Gulf, many of the consequences will be apparent to voters, most of whom will be able to determine who is responsible for the decision.

Yet while some decisions are marked by clarity, these represent one end of a very long continuum. Given the enormous complexity of the social world, in most cases one or more of Arnold's three stages will present formidable cognitive hurdles. These difficulties become a critical aspect of politics because policy makers and other political elites possess tools to lower or heighten the prominence of their actions in each respect, and the structure of the electoral system gives them every incentive to do so. Discernibility, traceability, and accountability can vary independently of a policy's actual impact and in ways that are subject to political manipulation. Both the manner in which policies are introduced and the design of the policies adopted may have a tremendous impact on the likelihood that voters will be able to exercise effective control. Specific features of a policy help determine its informational content, influencing discernibility, traceability, and accountability.

Given the complexity of social life, it will often be difficult for voters to recognize the impact of government policies at all. Policies that distribute benefits widely and intermittently are less likely to be visible than policies that distribute benefits to a concentrated group and in a single package. Whether those affected are part of a network (e.g., geographical or occupational) allowing communication with others affected (what Arnold calls *proximity*) is another important factor. Homeowners living near a toxic waste dump and dairy farmers sharing a common occupation generally participate in social networks that facilitate communication and therefore improve the chances that they will become aware of outcomes that affect them; recipients of disability payments who have their benefits cut and consumers purchasing potentially unsafe products are not. These examples echo the conclusion of Olson's critique of pluralism—relatively concentrated groups are much more likely to get the information they need to protect their interests.

The recent savings and loan debacle illustrates the problem well. The cost of restoring the system to solvency was enormous, but it was spread over all taxpayers. It was difficult for individual taxpayers to determine the size of the burden imposed directly on them. Most voters have little idea where their taxes are going, and in this case the "cost" was buried in a complex mix of higher budget deficits and reductions in available funding for other programs. The bailout was spread over a number of years, making it even more difficult for voters to develop a roughly accurate estimate of the burdens imposed. In retrospect, it is not surprising that despite the massive costs and transfers of income involved, the savings and loan scandal caused barely a ripple in American politics.

The traceability of policy initiatives varies as well. A crucial factor in linking outcomes to policy, as Arnold notes, is the "length of the causal chain." The more stages and uncertainties that lie between a policy's enactment and a perceived outcome, the less likely it is that those affected will respond politically. Farmers, who see a direct link between price supports and their own profitability, are much more likely to mobilize than are consumers, for whom the causal chain is longer. Consumers may not like the prices they pay in the supermarket, but they are unlikely to attribute those prices to government farm policies. In general, the more difficult it is to sort out causal arguments—the more complex the policy—the less likely it is that voters will trace even major problems to specific government decisions.[24]

Policy makers have a significant degree of control over the traceability of policies. There are usually multiple ways of tackling social problems, so they may choose policy interventions that create causal chains of varying lengths. Ideally, they hope to design initiatives for which the benefits involve short causal chains and the costs involve long ones. Time lags, for example, add greatly to the length and complexity of causal chains, so policy makers favor programmatic designs that front-load benefits and back-load costs.

Accountability—the ability to link government action to specific elected officials so that the vote can be used as an effective means of control—is also subject to manipulation. Policies can either illuminate or obscure the role of decision makers. As R. Kent Weaver has argued, indexation mechanisms, which put particular policies on "automatic," have proven attractive precisely because they lower the accountability of particular decision makers for policy outcomes.[25] To return to the savings and loan case, the intricate legislative and regulatory history surrounding the government bailout made it practically impossible for even the most incensed taxpayer to know which politicians to hold accountable for the massive costs imposed on the Treasury.

It is worth emphasizing that this problem of accountability is probably worse in the United States than it is in most democratic polities. Our system of checks and balances, designed to fragment political authority, fragments accountability as well.[26] In parliamentary systems, especially when a single party governs, it is generally simple to determine who is responsible for government actions and inactions. If a new policy is wildly unpopular, voters will be in a strong position to signal their displeasure at the next election. The fall of Margaret Thatcher, whose stubbornness in pursuing the widely loathed poll tax led her terrified Tory colleagues to mutiny, illustrates the relatively clear lines of accountability in a highly centralized polity.

In the American system, determining who to hold accountable may be very difficult, and political actors will often try to make that determination as tough as possible. The fragmentation of a Madisonian system, with its range of decision-making centers and veto points, can make it very hard to figure out who is responsible for policy action or inaction. National, state, and local authorities, courts, executive agencies, and legislatures, all share partial responsibility for policy. Unsurprisingly, the result for voters is often confusion. This is especially true in the era of divided government, when the game of finger-pointing has become a full-time activity. A single party has controlled both White House and Congress for only six years since 1968, meaning that voters generally confront a chaos of claims and counterclaims concerning who deserves credit (or more often, blame) for what happens in Washington.

Thus each of the three cognitive steps needed to exercise control is subject to potential manipulation. The recent debate in Washington over devolution—the distribution of responsibility for social policy between national and state governments—provides a good example of all these processes at work. Discernibility, traceability, and accountability are all at stake in the formulation of major new policies affecting the most vulnerable and politically powerless American citizens. As the new Republican congressional majority began to focus on deficit reduction as its central initiative after 1994, it incorporated a series of new proposals calling for a radical shift of authority over poverty policy to the states. The major federal programs of Aid for Families with Dependent Children (AFDC) and Medicaid, as well as a range of smaller initiatives, were to be transformed into block grants and transferred to the states. Ultimately the AFDC part of these proposals was a key component of the welfare "reform" legislation passed in 1996.

One should note that these proposals were quite new; prior to the election, Republican welfare proposals had called for increased spending and new federal controls. Devolution became a tremendously appealing alternative, however, once the Republican leadership determined that their deficit reduction plans would require dramatic, painful cuts in social spending.[27]

Advocates of devolution stress a desire to bring government "closer to the people," but it is easy to see why the issue appeared on the policy agenda only after spending cuts became imperative. Although the matter remains politically controversial, there is a reasonably strong consensus among economists that a shift in redistributive policies to the states is likely to produce considerable pressures for lower spending.[28] States compete with one another through tax rates and fear attracting poor citizens through generous benefits. With a sharp reduction in federal standards, pressures to curtail spending would be severe, and a "race to the bottom" scenario is plausible.[29]

These changes are unlikely to be highly visible. Rather, state-level programs are likely to suffer a "death of a thousand cuts." Changes will be highly fragmented, incremental, and spread unevenly over fifty states, but they will move in a consistent direction. Discernibility, traceability, and accountability will be limited. If the number of homeless on the streets of Akron increases eight years from now, how many voters will think to blame the 1994 Republican Congress?

The cumulative picture emerging from a range of recent studies about policy making is one of an enormously complex environment where control

over flows of information is politically crucial. Whether particular social actors are mobilized or not, and who and what those actors choose to support
or oppose, may turn on the manner in which policy-making elites fashion
the complex instruments of modern governance. In policy arenas of great
significance to average Americans, the strategic use of the policy-making
process and the design of programs themselves confer significant political
resources on those most intimately involved in crafting legislation.

These arguments about the role of information in policy making, and the
prospects for manipulation, apply to varying degrees in any modern democratic polity. As Dahl recognized, we have long since passed some invisible
threshold where a highly developed division of political labor is imperative
and renders the vast majority of us relatively passive, and where the complex
tasks of societal management place overwhelming pressures on our limited
cognitive capacities. In both these respects, government has been "big" for a
long time. Nonetheless, it is important to note two respects in which the
massive expansion of government activity in the past half-century has considerably increased the magnitude of the problem.

First, with increasing social complexity and the expansion of government
activity, the problems of cognitive overload and information asymmetries
worsen at an alarming pace. As the number of relevant factors in any system
increases arithmetically, the number of possible *interactions* in the system
increases geometrically. It is precisely this complicated interplay of social
factors—lengthy causal chains, feedback loops, unintended consequences,
interaction effects—which threatens to overwhelm our cognitive capacities.
A comparison of what were arguably the two most ambitious pieces of domestic legislation of the twentieth century—the Social Security Act of 1935
and the Clinton health reform proposal of 1993–94—indicates how much has
changed. By any measure of social complexity—size and detail of the legislation, range of participants involved in formulating the proposals, amount
of research on which participants could draw, number and size of interest
groups seeking to contribute to the debate, extent of media scrutiny—the
difference between the 1930s and 1990s is probably an order of magnitude
or more. In the past half-century, a stream of complexity has become a flood.
The only thing that has not changed very much is the cognitive capacity of
those who must try to make sense of what is going on.

A second implication stems less from government growth per se than from
the fact that this growth seems to have reached some limit. We now confront
the distinctly new problems of government maturation. This development is
relevant because it means a reorientation of political activity toward the difficult task of administering austerity.[30] Politicians increasingly must seek to
avoid blame for unpopular cutbacks rather than striving to obtain credit for
popular new programs. In this new political world, they are drawn to a range
of strategies which allow the exploitation of information asymmetries. Con-
fuse the issue, cover your tracks, leave no fingerprints, blame somebody
else: These are the watchwords of politics in an era of austerity. They are, of

course, all strategies founded on the presumption that the limited supply of information within the electorate creates political opportunities. It is probably not an accident that this new theme of information asymmetries emerged in studies of policy making shortly after the era of austerity began.

At this stage, it is difficult to know how much to make of these arguments about the role of information asymmetries, and the possibilities of manipulation, in policy making. There has been even less effort to draw general conclusions from this literature than in the case of the New Pluralist research discussed earlier. Much of this research into policy making has focused on particular events or programs and is therefore subject to the usual criticisms about generalizability. However, the research has often investigated very important policy issues, which suggests the significance of the phenomenon.

Claims that voters are being led astray are intrinsically difficult to demonstrate and always run the risk of reflecting personal view of politics—one person's example of political manipulation is someone else's sensible decision. What *is* clear from recent research, however, is that political elites spend a great deal of their time trying to structure the signals that are available to voters. In many cases, decisions taken regarding both policy designs and procedures for enacting a policy are simply inexplicable except as efforts to manipulate the flow of information.[31]

Resolving these issues is a formidable task, which I will not attempt here. A useful first step, however, is to return to the arguments of the New Pluralists and ask to what extent their optimism about voters seems well placed, given the concerns that have been raised. Do the claims about heuristics and the aggregative properties of voters provide promising protections against the processes and strategies which those studying public policy have highlighted? This is the issue considered in the last part of this chapter.

MAIN STREET RECONSIDERED

Analysts of policy emphasize the vigorous efforts of political elites to modify the flow of relevant information to voters. Students of mass political behavior, in contrast, stress the relatively efficient coping mechanisms that voters adopt to make sense of a large and complicated social world. What happens when these two conflicting views are put side by side? Unfortunately for those drawn to the clarity of absolutes, the result is likely to be somewhere in the messy middle. One set of arguments is unlikely to completely trump the other. Ideally, though, that messy middle is the promising location for the construction of more sophisticated and convincing claims about the possibilities for democratic politics. These claims, attending to both the cognitive efforts of voters and the manipulative efforts of political elites, would emphasize the particular conditions—such as specific institutional arrangements, or the type of issue at stake—under which voters are most likely to exercise effective political control.

At the very least, however, the new work on policy making suggests some important limitations of the mechanisms stressed in the New Pluralism. I begin by discussing issues about the position of individual voters before turning to the Page/Shapiro argument about aggregation. In both cases, my view is that the recent analyses of policy making strike at a weak point in the new line of thinking about voters, which is the issue of *attention*.[32] As students of cognition and bounded rationality have long recognized, it is limits on attention that represent the real bottleneck in our efforts to make sense of the social world. Voters can pay attention to only a small number of issues at any time, and to only a few facets of the issues that they consider. It is precisely these aspects of attention that attract the manipulative efforts of policy makers. Rather than trying to get voters to change their minds about an issue, they concentrate on getting voters to pay attention to a different issue or to certain aspects of the issue being considered rather than alternative aspects. Inattention allows the exercise of power. As Frank Baumgartner and Bryan Jones put it, echoing Schattschneider, "apathy is the key variable in politics. Some seek to promote it, others to fight it."[33]

The pluralists argue that voters possess good tools, or heuristics, for making sense of the world. But how well do these tools work when elites are attempting to encourage the reception of certain signals while distorting others? The process of "cuing" is critical here, because the standard response to concerns about dissembling by political elites is that political competition eliminates the problem. Policy makers may attempt to deceive, but their competitors stand ready to present alternative arguments, sending the necessary signals to voters.

At best, however, this solution is problematic. If the profile of an issue can be kept low, or the matter rendered so complicated or obscure that voters cannot decipher what the issue is, then "cue givers" may not be in a strong position to help voters out. Political insiders refer to the "Dan Rather test": Can an issue or argument be effectively reduced to a fifteen-second sound byte on the evening news? If not, cues may be difficult to employ. Matters of relevance to voters would seem to need to rise above a certain minimum level of prominence and clarity before the signaling process from other social actors can operate. Many elite strategies are designed precisely to keep issues, or particular aspects of issues, from reaching that minimum level.[34]

In many cases involving complex policies, those attempting to provide alternative information face an almost impossible task. Issues such as the budget or health care reform, for example, are so complicated that clear signals are difficult to send. Consider the recent fight over proposals for a balanced budget: These had such a high profile that it should have offered unusually good opportunities for providing voters with decent information. However, the efforts of Democrats to convey information about the costs associated with Republican proposals quickly gave way to a simple, relentless drumbeat, spearheaded by both congressional Democrats and the Clinton administration, about the threat to Medicare. While eventually effective, the claim of a vast difference between the Medicare proposals of the two parties was arguably highly misleading. In any event, it represented an extraordinary narrowing of focus from a much broader array of important policy issues. The complexity of issues, and the prospect that political elites may actively seek to increase that complexity for strategic reasons, will often limit the utility of cues for mass publics.

Once one considers the possibilities for distorting the flow of information to voters, Iyengar's accessibility and attention heuristics are even less satisfying. Indeed, the fact that voters access information in biased and predictable ways is precisely the kind of result that opens up opportunities for shaping the ways in which voters do or do not respond to decisions in Washington. As Iyengar acknowledges, "people are exquisitely sensitive to contextual cues when they make decisions, formulate judgments, or express opinions. The manner in which a problem of choice is 'framed' is a contextual cue that may profoundly influence decision outcomes."[35] It is these framing parameters that policy makers can try to manipulate, by altering the ways in which decisions are made or by highlighting or obscuring crucial aspects of policy design. And political elites have become quite sophisticated, through their use of focus groups, polls, and the expertise of political psychologists, at finding the frames which most effectively tap into the cognitive biases of citizens. At the very least, the availability of such tools of distortion raises new concerns about the adequacy of individual-level heuristics for sustaining voter autonomy.

Are arguments about aggregation more helpful? At first glance, the Page/Shapiro analysis seems convincing. Through an extremely rich analysis of decades of public opinion research, they do indeed show that, for the most part, electorates retain quite stable preferences on particular issues and that when their preferences *do* shift we can generally identify sensible reasons for the movement. There are, however, three reasons for hesitating before drawing broadly optimistic conclusions about the implications for democratic governance. First, as Bryan Jones has persuasively argued, the Page/Shapiro focus on policy preferences rather than attention is probably misplaced. Voters' broad preferences on particular issues are relatively stable, but what voters pay attention to is incredibly volatile. Mass publics ignore most of the issues most of the time. Furthermore, the process through which issues rise on the agenda seems to be one where public opinion is a following indicator rather than a leading one.[36]

Attention to policy issues does not have the benign characteristics which Page and Shapiro discovered for policy preferences. The public flits from issue to issue, frequently triggered by a single focusing event. The media play a crucial role in this process, which encourages bias both because the media are drawn to that very particular subset of events which "sells" and because they are vulnerable to "priming" by political elites. The volatile shifts in public opinion are at best only loosely related to objective indicators of public problems.[37] The deficit became a massive issue *after* the 1994 election, at a time when the deficit as a percentage of gross domestic product was lower than it had been in a decade and declining.[38] California passed "three strikes and you're out" legislation, with profound policy consequences, following a surge of concern about crime. This shift in the focus of public attention was not driven by indicators of violent crime, which were dropping, but by a media frenzy built largely around a single high-profile case.

Perhaps even more important than the character of issues that attract attention is the character of those that do not. As the literature about policy making emphasizes, much political activity is directed at sustaining a low profile for issues or policies that allow a significant reallocation of resources and power by stealth. These issues are not distinguished by their insignificance.[39] Their common quality is a level of complexity and opacity that does not lend itself to easy slogans or quick clarification on television. These are the issues—or aspects of issues—that make the eyes of many of us glaze over and that as a consequence rarely capture the attention of mass publics.

A second problem with the Page/Shapiro argument, also linked with this issue of attention, concerns the fact that the "policy preferences" they identify are often very loose. The real struggle is often over which aspect of a problem deserves a voter's scarce attention. Take the issue of welfare reform, where the policy debate has shifted dramatically to the right in recent years. Page and Shapiro's polls would have indicated relative stability rather than volatility. Indeed, voters' views on "helping the poor" and "reinforcing the work ethic" are fairly stable. The real political struggle, however, is over which of these linked concerns will be salient at a given time. Those advocating a radical reform of poverty programs have successfully shifted attention from some aspects of policy to others. Again, because the goal of political elites is precisely to modify the focus of attention, evidence of stability or even loose "rationality" in public policy preferences and attitudes may be of limited relevance.

A final problem concerns the implied link between a "rational" public opinion and the goal of civic equality. Even leaving aside the issues already raised, one simply cannot jump from Page and Shapiro's evidence about aggregate opinion to support for the claim that voters share a roughly equal voice in the process.[40] Indeed, the evidence is quite compatible with a world in which politicians respond only to a small minority of voters. Assume, for example, that a relatively small proportion of the electorate—say 5 or 10 percent—has pretty good information about politics, while the rest of the electorate has poor information and is prone to essentially random fluctuations in opinion.[41] In such a situation, public opinion will possess the aggregate properties stressed by Page and Shapiro—stability, movement in response to meaningful external stimuli, and so on. Yet all the "signals" for policy makers will be coming from a small subset of the population. If elections matter, it may nonetheless be that informed subset of the electorate which will be politically relevant and to whom policy makers will be responsive. This might not be a problem if this subset were a random sample of the population. There is, however, good reason to suspect that it would not be and that electoral power would be concentrated in the hands of a "knowledge-rich" minority.

In a way, then, the new focus on information simply resurrects a traditional pluralist dispute in new form: Is knowledge widely diffused, with most actors knowledgeable in the areas of greatest concern to them while ignorant in others, or do knowledge imbalances tend to cumulate? The issue is complex, but data and theory point in the latter direction. Based on a discussion of the literature on cognition, Converse persuasively argues that knowledge inequalities are likely to be cumulative:

> There is ample evidence from both field and experimental settings that it takes past information successfully stored to make larger amounts of incoming information storable. With information as with wealth, "them what has gets," and there is no comforting system of progressive taxation on information to help redress the drift toward glaring inequalities. . . . In short, we are dealing here with a positive-feedback system of a kind where initial inequalities feed upon themselves, and differences best described in orders of magnitude of orders of magnitude are quite conceivable indeed.[42]

Nor can we take solace in the hope that the well informed are just like everyone else. An exhaustive study by Sidney Verba, Kay Lehman Schlozman, and Henry E. Brady of American political participation shows what we would expect: The better-informed are more inclined to participate, and they are systematically unrepresentative of the population as a whole:

> We must recognize a systematic bias in representation through participation. Over and over, our data showed that participatory input is tilted in the direction of the more advantaged groups in society—especially in terms of economic and educational position, but in terms of race and ethnicity as well. The voices of the well-educated and the well-heeled—and therefore, of those with other politically relevant characteristics that are associated with economic and educational privilege—sound more loudly.[43]

Aggregation, therefore, may provide little protection on important matters for those who have the least information about politics.

Forcing the New Pluralism to contend with the arguments of recent research on policy making thus raises fundamental questions, although I recognize that I have done little here to answer them. What the literature on policy making suggests is not only that voters possess limited information but also that much of the "information" they *do* get about politics is in part "constructed" in order to elicit desired responses. Furthermore, the principal target of these elite strategies is the focus of attention, which the public opinion literature has largely ignored and which is much more malleable than voter views about desirable outcomes. This new research thus raises serious concerns about the capacity of voters to protect their interests in an enormously complex world where most political resources, including the critical resource of information, are distributed very unequally.

Difficult questions about the extent and effectiveness of these efforts at manipulation remain. The New Pluralism clearly contains important insights about the conditions that may allow voters to find their way even when the light is very bad. My guess is that more sustained research will not completely undermine the New Pluralist claims, but will instead generate interesting, complicated findings about the restricted conditions under which voters can hope to perform reasonably well. Among the key considerations are likely to be the structure of political institutions, the ways in which information gets disseminated in different societies, and the kinds of issues at stake.[44] However these matters may be resolved, they all point to a crucial and still underexplored aspect of politics in an age of Big Government: the role of information in the continuous efforts of citizens to comprehend, and act in, an extraordinarily complex world.

NOTES

1. Robert A. Dahl, *Who Governs? Democracy and Power in an American City* (New Haven: Yale University Press, 1961), 1.

2. Philip E. Converse, "The Nature of Belief Systems in Mass Publics," in David E. Apter, ed., *Ideology and Discontent* (New York: Free Press, 1964).

3. Paul M. Sniderman, Richard A. Brody, and Philip E. Tetlock, *Reasoning and Choice: Explorations in Political Psychology* (Cambridge: Cambridge University Press, 1991), 3.

4. James G. March and Herbert A. Simon, *Organizations* (New York: Wiley, 1958); Michael Cohen, James March, and Johan Olsen, "A Garbage Can Model of Organizational Choice," *Administrative Science Quarterly* 17 (March 1972): 1–25.

5. Mancur Olson, *The Logic of Collective Action* (Cambridge: Harvard University Press, 1965).

6. Terry M. Moe, *The Organization of Interests: Incentives and the Internal Dynamics of Political Interest Groups* (Chicago: University of Chicago Press, 1980).

7. E. E. Schattschneider, *The Semisovereign People* (New York: Holt, Reinhart, and Winston, 1960), 35. For two recent studies which use complementary methods to document the impact of unequal resources on patterns of political participation, see Steven J. Rosenstone and John Mark Hansen, *Mobilization, Participation, and Democracy in America* (New York: Macmillan, 1993); and Sidney Verba, Kay Lehman Schlozman, and Henry E. Brady, *Voice and Equality: Civic Voluntarism in American Politics* (Cambridge: Harvard University Press, 1995).

8. Charles E. Lindblom, *Politics and Markets* (New York: Basic Books, 1977); Charles E. Lindblom, "The Market as Prison," *Journal of Politics* 44, no. 2 (1982): 324–36. For a largely parallel analysis from a neo-Marxist perspective, see Fred Block, "The Ruling Class Does Not Rule," in Fred Block, *Revising State Theory: Essays on Politics and Postindustrialism* (Philadelphia: Temple University Press, 1987), 51–68.

9. Robert Dahl, *Dilemmas of Pluralist Democracy: Autonomy vs. Control* (New Haven: Yale University Press, 1982).

10. Key works include Sniderman, Brody, and Tetlock, *Reasoning and Choice*; Benjamin I. Page and Robert Y. Shapiro, *The Rational Public: Fifty Years of Trends in Americans' Policy Preferences* (Chicago: University of Chicago Press, 1992); John A. Ferejohn and James H. Kuklinski, eds., *Information and Democratic Processes* (Urbana: University of Illinois Press, 1990); Shanto Iyengar, *Is Anyone Responsible? How Television News Frames Political Issues* (Chicago: University of Chicago Press, 1991); and Samuel L. Popkin, *The Reasoning Voter: Communication and Persuasion in Presidential Campaigns* (Chicago: University of Chicago Press, 1991).

11. Amos Tversky and Daniel Kahneman, "Judgment under Uncertainty: Heuristics and Biases," *Science* 185 (1974): 1124–31.

12. Sniderman, Brody, and Tetlock, *Reasoning and Choice*, 19.

13. See, for example, Edward G. Carmines and James H. Kuklinski, "Incentives, Opportunities, and the Logic of Public Opinion in American Political Representation," in Ferejohn and Kuklinski, *Information and Democratic Processes*, 240–68.

14. Sniderman, Brody, and Tetlock, *Reasoning and Choice*, 24.

15. Shanto Iyengar, "Shortcuts to Political Knowledge: The Role of Selective Attention and Accessibility," in Ferejohn and Kuklinski, *Information and Democratic Processes*, 24.

16. Page and Shapiro, *The Rational Public*, 11.

17. V. O. Key, *The Responsible Electorate: Rationality in Presidential Voting, 1936–1960* (Cambridge: Harvard University Press, 1966).

18. This hyperspecialization, in which the investigation of American politics is broken down into discrete pieces (e.g., Congress, public opinion, or parties) that each attract the full-time attention of armies of investigators, is itself an indication of how complicated the problem of making sense of the political world has become.

19. James A. Stimson, "A Macro Theory of Information Flow," in Ferejohn and Kuklinski, *Information and Democratic Processes*, 365.

20. Iyengar, "Shortcuts to Political Knowledge," 160.

21. Examples include: R. Kent Weaver, "The Politics of Blame Avoidance," *Journal of Public Policy* 6 (1986); R. Kent Weaver, *Automatic Government: The Politics of Indexation* (Washington: Brookings Institution, 1988); R. Douglas Arnold, *The Logic of Congressional Action* (New Haven: Yale University Press, 1990); Frank R. Baumgartner and Bryan D. Jones, *Agendas and Instability in American Politics* (Chicago: University of Chicago Press, 1993); Bryan D. Jones, *Reconceiving Decision-Making in Democratic Politics: Attention, Choice, and Public Policy* (Chicago: University of Chicago Press, 1994); and Paul Pierson, *Dismantling the Welfare State? Reagan, Thatcher, and the Politics of Retrenchment* (Cambridge: Cambridge University Press, 1994).

22. One could analyze these issues in the framework of principal-agent theory, which has recently become a popular tool in rational choice analyses of politics. In principal-agent terms, voters constitute the principals and politicians the agents. The key issue is whether the principals can effectively monitor the activities of their agents, given the presence of massive asymmetries of information. For an introduction, see Terry Moe, "The New Economics of Organization," *American Journal of Political Science* 28 (1984): 739–77.

23. Arnold, *Logic of Congressional Action*. The same basic requirements apply for efforts to reward politicians for positive actions. The processes are not symmetrical, however, both because of the different ways in which voters respond to negative and

160   *Prospects for Democratic Control*

positive events and because politicians will obviously try very hard to make voters aware of positive effects.

24. For an innovative discussion of the cognitive and social processes involved in the construction of causal chains, see Deborah Stone, "Causal Stories and the Formation of Policy Agendas," *Political Science Quarterly* 104, no. 2 (Summer 1989): 281–300.

25. Weaver, *Automatic Government*.

26. See R. Kent Weaver and Burt Rockman, eds., *Do Institutions Matter? Government Capabilities in the United States and Abroad* (Washington: Brookings Institution, 1993).

27. See R. Kent Weaver, "Deficits and Devolution," *Publius* 26, no. 3 (Summer 1996): 45–85.

28. See the discussion of these issues in Paul E. Peterson, *The Price of Federalism* (Washington: Brookings Institution, 1995).

29. Specific features of the new legislation create further incentives for program cutbacks. See Mary Jo Bane, "Welfare as We Might Know It," *American Prospect* 30 (January/February 1997): 47–53.

30. Weaver, "Politics of Blame Avoidance"; Paul Pierson, "The New Politics of the Welfare State," *World Politics* 48, no. 2 (January 1996): 143–79.

31. Admittedly, this does not prove much, since these strategies might be the best available to political elites and still be of only marginal effectiveness. In such a situation, manipulative behavior would be rational, but would represent a limited challenge to citizen control. This objection is similar to Morris Fiorina's argument that politicians rationally devote tremendous energy to constituency services, even though these efforts are only moderately effective. Such a strategy makes sense because while the impact is marginal, it is the one part of the electoral process that individual representatives can best hope to affect. Morris P. Fiorina, *Congress: Keystone of the Washington Establishment* (New Haven: Yale University Press, 1977).

32. For an excellent analysis of this issue, see Jones, *Reconceiving Decision-Making*.

33. Baumgartner and Jones, *Agendas and Instability*, 21.

34. There is some empirical support for the claim that when issues are complicated, voters have a more difficult time. In their "Two Faces of Issue Voting," *American Political Science Review* 74, no. 1 (1980): 78-91, Edward G. Carmines and James A. Stimson found that poorly informed voters were less likely to incorporate "hard" issues into their voting decisions. Page and Shapiro found that policy outcomes were most likely to diverge from public opinion results when polls showed a high percentage of "don't know" answers; Benjamin I. Page and Robert Y. Shapiro, "Effects of Public Opinion on Policy," *American Political Science Review* 77, no. 1 (1983): 175–90.

35. Iyengar, *Is Anyone Responsible?* 11.

36. Jones, *Reconceiving Decision-Making*; John Kingdon, *Agendas, Alternatives, and Public Policies* (Boston: Little, Brown, 1982); Baumgartner and Jones, *Agendas and Instability*.

37. Baumgartner and Jones, *Agendas and Instability*.

38. Given the furor over the deficit, it is worth noting that the United States in 1994 would have met the strict Maastricht standards for joining the European Monetary Union, indicating a level of financial rectitude which only two or three of the European Union's fifteen member states could match.

39. For instance, there is a clear correlation between the complexity and opacity of tax code provisions and the likelihood that the attendant provisions benefit the well-to-do.

40. See Philip E. Converse, "Popular Representation and the Distribution of Information," in Ferejohn and Kuklinski, *Information and Democratic Processes,* 369–88.

41. Much of Sniderman, Brody, and Tetlock's analysis is based on the claim that the electorate is made up of actors operating with widely divergent levels of information.

42. Converse, "Popular Representation," 373–74.

43. Verba, Schlozman, and Brady, *Voice and Equality,* 512.

44. For an innovative effort to explore some of these issues, see Henry Milner, *Social Democracy and Rational Choice* (London: Routledge, 1994).

9

From Social to Legal Norms: A Neglected Cause of Big Government

Richard A. Epstein

THE PREMATURE END TO BIG GOVERNMENT

The topic of Big Government is, it may fairly be said, a big question that has already spawned an enormous amount of controversy, if not acrimony. At times in our recent history, it seems as though the idea of Big Government has been vanquished from our domestic lexicon. Back in 1994 the Republicans rode to power on a social contract that promised to clip the tentacles of Big Government. President Clinton then chimed in with a State of the Union address in which he intoned that "the era of Big Government is over." But this joint revolution proved short-lived, as the Republicans have beaten a ragtag retreat from the ideal of Little Government, while former president Clinton made (in, for example, his 1999 State of the Union address) new promises to every interest group the central talking point of his second administration.

The pressures to expand the use of government power often seem irresistible. It is tempting to increase the size of government by looking in isolation at the benefits induced by any single government program. It is much harder, given the tribulations of political life, to hew to the rigorous discipline that generates prosperity in the first place. Transfer programs do not create wealth. Only production can do that. Production in turn requires a focused government policy that builds a solid infrastructure and fosters strong private property rights and voluntary exchanges. In hard times, the necessity of returning to fundamentals to spur production should be evident. But once prosperity returns it is easy to forget that the discipline that brought prosperity in the first place is needed to keep prosperity alive. The great achievements of one generation will not of their own force last for the long run unless they are continuously replenished. Unfortunately, the rate of depreciation for sound social institutions and practices is so rapid that one generation cannot protect the next generation from its own mistakes. Yet it is easy to forget the fragility of political institutions; too often political leaders relax their guard and indulge in humanistic reforms whose major consequence is to undermine the engine of prosperity that made these reforms thinkable.

The decline of political discipline never takes place because of frontal attack. In the abstract, everyone acknowledges that well-functioning markets can outproduce and outperform comprehensive command-and-control regulation. But the ostensible generality of that position is picked apart by endless ad hoc exceptions. The Democrats (and some Republicans) continue to show strong support for new increases in the minimum wage: After all, in periods of prosperity, the workers at the bottom of the pile are also "entitled to a raise," whether or not the employer wishes to pay it. The Republicans (and some Democrats) find it within their power to bless farm subsidies, as with the continuation of the ethanol program or strict import quotas on cane sugar for the benefit of domestic producers of the more expensive beet sugar. Leaders of both parties are quite happy to override private insurance markets in order to require worker portability of health care insurance in the face of preexisting conditions that cost more to service than the premiums received. It almost seems that once a political party announces that it is in favor of Little Government, it renders itself invulnerable to attack for the new or expanded forms of government intervention it champions. Intellectual consistency in political circles counts for less than the deft articulation of proper public sentiment. But no one should be deceived. Proclamations against Big Government may respond to the yearnings of the majority of the electorate, but these statements do not drive the mid-level choices on economic or social regulation.

This initial dose of cynicism should not, however, lead us to ignore one important shift in the terms of the debate. At one time, Big Government needed no defense. It was thought that the political and constitutional debates of the Franklin Roosevelt era had established the proposition that the well-being of the American public was too important to be left to the vagaries of the market, driven as it was by selfish and shortsighted behavior. Today, fewer people think that private actors have a monopoly on either of these two vices. The gradual reversal of the presumption in favor of Big Government stems from the belated recognition that competitive pressures may provide a needed check against the worst of human impulses, to which government servants are not immune. The evils of private misconduct are checked not by an opposing faction or high-minded regulation but by the simple ability of customers to switch firms when the goods and services that they receive are no longer acceptable. The Internal Revenue Service has never labored under that constraint, so its customer relations take on a rather different coloration from those of a fashionable restaurant or shop. Private monopolies do not behave well, even though they are subject to erosion and decay and, in some instances, government regulation which could easily pull the franchise for inadequate service. Why assume that public monopolies behave any better when they may be propped up indefinitely by the force of law?

ASPIRATION AND POWER:
THE CAUSES OF BIG GOVERNMENT

The case against Big Government, then, rests on an appreciation that the power of self-interest exerts itself equally in both public and private settings. Yet before we use this simple insight to pronounce the death of Big Government, we have to acquire a more complete understanding of the processes that led to its creation. That discussion can take place on two levels, one normative and the other descriptive. I believe that in practice these two levels are more closely intertwined than the formal distinction between them suggests. For these purposes, the solidity of that distinction does not matter. My inquiry straddles the positive/normative frontier to explain why the rise in Big Government has been a constant feature of twentieth-century life.

Some of the obvious causes of the expansion of government should be well known and understood. The two that merit some mention are these: first, the rise in aspirations as to what governments should do; and second, the acceptance of increased powers of government at all levels to work toward those aspirations.

First, a brief word on aspirations. Today we have conquered (or at least think we have conquered) the problem of social order that explained to the traditional social contract theorists the need for government in the first place. No one has come up with a credible system of private contract in a state of nature that is sufficient to ban or control the private use of force. Let 99 percent of the people enter into an agreement not to use force against each other; assume magically that benign institutions to enforce that agreement among its participants are securely in place. No matter, these law-abiding folks, individually or collectively, are at the mercy of the 1 percent of marauders that stay aloof from the collective undertaking. The intransigence of one can disturb the tranquillity of the many. To meet that challenge, it is easy to find a justification for a *small but powerful* government—the ideal to which I still subscribe. Government must restrain the deviant behavior of these isolated individuals so that the rest of us can live in peace. Thereafter, government should strive to leave *us* in peace as well. Its monopoly of force can be justified only if it is constrained.

It is difficult, however, for any society to rest on its laurels, so the tendency emerges to find new tasks for government to perform once the old disputed territory has been brought under its control. If we first had to deal with "physical" coercion, it takes only a small step to say that we next have to deal with "economic" coercion. This form of coercion, while less obvious, is more subtle and more pervasive, and therefore all the more difficult to root out. The transition from one targeted abuse to the other seems small enough indeed, for it involves only the change of a single adjective—"economic" for "physical." The linguistic parallelism between the two expressions, however, should not conceal the vast difference in the nature of these two distinct undertakings.

The preoccupation with economic coercion, however, can often lead us to odd conclusions. Buyers are coerced when they are forced to pay more than they want. Sellers are coerced when they are forced to sell for less than they want to receive. So we need maximum prices for buyers and minimum prices for sellers—but the former could be less than the latter. This leads to a political equilibrium in which customers are supposed to pay less than sellers receive. That gap can only be closed if some third parties overcome the regrettable wedge between buyer and seller. From such considerations, we take the first tentative steps down the path whereby sellers receive government subsidies that the buyers themselves do not pay directly. But we are at a loss to know how to protect the taxpayers who are forced to subsidize these relationships. We reach this impasse because of the false analogy between physical and economic coercion.

In short, it is possible to conceive of exchange relationships without physical coercion. But there is simply too much economic coercion in the world to eliminate all its manifestations simultaneously. Therefore, someone has to decide which forms of economic coercion are good and which are bad. Alas, once we regard the control of economic coercion as a good reason for state action, we have committed ourselves to the potential regulation of the entire competitive economy by government. A flawed analogy can do a lot of harm.

The parallels are easy to extend. One day we conquer explicit forms of government discrimination by race and sex. Thereafter, it is only a short step to say that we have to conquer the de facto and unconscious forms of discrimination of private firms that produce the same baleful effects. The upshot is a government that has it within its power to scrutinize each and every stage of the employment arrangement in order to ferret out discrimination that ought never have existed in the first place. No government, however, can maintain the claim that it is in favor of some idealized pattern of behavior, such as the color-blind principle. Sooner or later it places its own monopoly thumb on the scale and condemns some forms of discrimination as invidious and anoints other forms as justified. At each stage we expand the scope of our enterprise; in so doing, we multiply the size of the government brigades necessary to respond to our enlarged set of civil and social wrongs.

These heightened aspirations lead to changes in power structures. In the United States, the decisive transformation is in federal-state relationships under the Constitution. James Madison may have conceived of a federal government that only had enumerated, limited, and definite powers, but his conception is honored today only in words. There are countless judicial decisions that intone the proposition that unclear federal statutes should be construed narrowly to limit federal encroachment on the power of the states. But these admonitions to the draftsman are at best paper tigers that encourage more specific, unambiguous, and comprehensive assertions of federal power.

This rise of federal power only displaces state power when the two are in conflict. Where the federal government remains silent, however, the power of state governments to regulate both private property and private contract receives an ever-broader construction. The federal government may act like a 900-pound gorilla whenever it pleases: All lesser governments must stay out of its way. But let the federal government retreat to the sidelines, and state governments may increase their regulation of private affairs given the reduced protection for individual rights of property and contract. The modern American practice therefore increases the police power of government at all levels. Where there is a political vacuum, some government will rush in to fill it.

SEPARATING MORALS FROM LAW

I have just recounted two conventional explanations for Big Government: one that goes to a broader set of political ends, and another that goes to the greater political power to achieve them. The cause of Big Government that I focus on in this chapter is not so large as either of these. Yet it is large enough and interesting enough to merit some mention of its own in the larger discourse. The basic point concerns the pattern of interaction between legal rules and social norms.

The thesis that I propose is quite simple: We have lost our sense of direction by the relentless effort to turn all social norms that hold society or its subgroups together into legal norms, that is, norms promulgated and enforced by the state. We have, in essence, anticipated Hillary Clinton's preoccupation with the "global village," by failing to distinguish between the set of informal sanctions imposed by members of a close-knit community and the sanctions used by a powerful police force that are directed to the same ends. The constant theme in Mrs. Clinton's work, and in the work of so many legal writers, is that the persistent gap between social and legal norms is an embarrassment that ought to be overcome, not an important feature of our social life that should be preserved, strengthened, and even cherished. As the class of legal norms expands, the social enforcement of norms is crowded out. Just as we need intermediate voluntary institutions to facilitate interchanges between individuals and the state, so too we need intermediate norms to regulate social behavior. We cannot survive long if we adopt a reductionism that sees only two kinds of behaviors: those that people can choose to do on a whim, and those that are legally required or forbidden. The enforcement of social norms should create a large and diffuse class of implicit norms that place social limits on legally protected choices.

A TWO-TIER SYSTEM

In order to see the magnitude and importance of this social transformation, it is useful to begin with a statement of why and how the original system of two-tier norms developed in our own and other legal systems. The formal ingredients for the system are clear from the outset. Political and moral theorists once were quick to distinguish between legal and moral obligations, between perfect and imperfect obligations. The differences were not regarded as simply terminological but carried with them certain determinate consequences. A legal obligation is one for whose breach the law will supply a remedy, whether by way of damages, specific performance, or injunction. In other words the law will require a defendant to pay money to the plaintiff, to perform specific acts that were promised (e.g., the conveyance of real estate), or to refrain from certain actions that might otherwise be performed (e.g., competing with one's former boss in the same territory). To use the word *legal* in contrast to *moral* did not mean that all legal obligations had no moral base to them. Quite the opposite: Many of the strongest legal prohibitions (keeping promises, not killing other persons) have very strong moral roots. Rather, the basic point here is that the coercive method of enforcement marks these obligations out as legal. The state will interfere in the event of a breach of duty.

Moral obligations also have their origin in the moral sentiments of the community; however, these are enforced not by centralized coercive mechanisms but by a more subtle and diffuse set of social sanctions that depend on the separate actions of private groups and individuals. These could include ostracism and shunning, or expulsion from clubs, or voicing of public or private disapproval of certain kinds of acts. There are not only negative sanctions but also positive ones for actions that are approved of, such as any system of awards or honors for heroic behavior, distinguished service, or exemplary character. It seems quite clear that any society is going to have some mix of these two sets of sanctions. The question is what principles help to establish the sanctions appropriate for the circumstances. Are there any actions for which legal sanctions alone seem to be required and appropriate? More important, are there any situations in which moral and social sanctions should be imposed but legal sanctions should be withheld? The modern position is moving us relentlessly in the direction of using governmental force to counter the deviation from any social norm. The burden of this chapter is to argue that the separation of morals from law often makes sense. Let us now look closely at some of the key cases.

Force

Let us begin with the class of cases in which social sanctions in and of themselves are generally, and rightly, regarded as insufficient. The most obvious case is where one person uses force against another individual. Start with the obvious: People can die from the use of force. Yet the gains from killing them could be sufficiently large that a single individual might think that he is better off by incurring the wrath of a potential victim so long as he is beyond the reach of the law. And he could be emboldened by using the same tactics a second time if social opposition to his position is voiced. What makes the case for using force against force so powerful is that we have a situation in which 99 percent compliance with a social norm offers to those who comply *no* security against the depredations of those who do not comply. The individual who remains outside the moral commands or understandings of the community gains enough from his intransigence that he will continue to act even though his conduct causes losses so large that the social system could not survive their repetition. The wrongful actions of one person, or of a very few persons, are sufficient to destabilize the environment in which hundreds of other persons live. We never want to put people to the choice of having to suffer destruction or imitating their aggressors. The institutionalization of a prohibition against the use of force is the most powerful way to avoid that result. Once the legal norm is firmly established, it takes little imagination to see why religious and social norms will back it up to the hilt. It is far better if the pressure on the legal system can be reduced by discouraging violations in the first instance.

Defamation

The second area in which legal force has usually been imposed deals with the wrongs of defamation. Here we focus on words, and the great temptation is to repeat the old maxim: Sticks and stones may break my bones, but names will never harm me. If there were ever a case where social sanctions seem to apply, then defamation seems to be it. This sanguine view of the world, however, severely underestimates the power that words have when directed toward third parties by those who have no bonds of loyalty or allegiance to the defamed party. That party is not present to defend himself against allegations of treason or treachery, and the charges, if believed, can lead to his death at the hands of someone else, for example, the state. Once again it may not be sufficient to ostracize those who defame from the company of those who do not, assuming that the false statements can be detected without legal intervention. The social sanctions therefore are, and should be, supplemented by a set of legal sanctions. Words can kill, and they have killed, when said falsely.

Contractual Enforcement

The proper scope of legal sanctions is often expanded to cover cases of breach of promise, or at least of contract. Now the discussion is more complex and uncertain, and we have to be careful to distinguish among a number of quite different situations. The first point is one that was long stressed by writers within the classical liberal tradition. The law must enforce contracts in order to promote the security of exchange on which civilized life must rest. The basic argument is quite simple: I promise to deliver goods to you today, and you promise to pay for them tomorrow. If I deliver today and you do not pay tomorrow, then what we conceived initially as an exchange benefiting both sides becomes a "gift" against my will. You both receive the "gift" and retain the money.Thereafter, I may never perform first again unless there is some protected expectation that the money promised will be paid once the promised goods are delivered. A set of social sanctions surely helps to fill this temporal gap, but once again any society runs the terrible risk that exchanges between anonymous parties, so critical to trade, will not take place, or will take place only under very guarded terms that impair the efficiency of the exchange mechanism. It therefore becomes necessary to enforce promises to allow the exchange mechanism to operate over time.

Indeed, by quick extension it becomes clear that oftentimes the best result is to enforce a promised exchange not only after one party has performed but before either has performed. The paying party in the illustration just given may depend critically on the goods to be supplied. If they are not forthcoming, it will do him no good to hold on to the money he has if he is unable to fulfill his own engagements or otherwise obtain the benefit of his bargain. The action to compel delivery of goods, or damages from their nondelivery, is thus an essential part of the overall system. Once again, no set of social sanctions gives adequate protection if the individual promisor decides to breach before performance.

It would, however, be a terrible mistake to assume that the need for coercion in some contractual settings implies a need for coercion in all such settings. The model of the sequential exchange captures an important part of our social universe, but it is only part of the universe. Many ongoing social relationships are designed to survive the unsuspecting changes in taste and fortune that occur over time. The question is how much legal, and how much social, enforcement is involved.

Considering these cases, the key question is not how much protection the law is willing to provide: It will often provide a great deal. Instead the question is how much legal enforcement do the parties to the particular transaction want. Sometimes that question is left unresolved because it is costly to negotiate contracts, and often agreements are left incomplete on some vital term, which requires the courts to step in nimbly to fill in the gaps created by the situation. But it would be a mistake to assume that all lacunae in the legal system are created through a want of foresight and persistence in the creation of legal relations. Rather, as we move from the world of spot transactions to the world of relational contracts, the parties themselves often choose to develop a system that consciously and explicitly contemplates the separation of legal and social sanctions. The legal regime is so structured that it places both parties at risk of sudden rupture and termination. The social sanctions in these circumstances often require some measured response in the empty space that is left by the legal rules. The question is whether the parties will choose to put legal sanctions to one side, and if so, whether we can find any good reason for the legal system to intervene and overturn their judgment. The chain of argument is often somewhat complicated, but the basic outline can be sketched. It is easiest to do so in connection with a single type of transaction which has attracted massive forms of regulation in recent years: the employment contract.

EMPLOYMENT CONTRACTS

The first point to note about employment relations is that workers have protections that are not available to the victims of killings and misrepresentations. They can quit. More precisely, under the simplest employment contract, each side is held hostage to the other, at least with respect to future work for which future wages have not yet been paid. The worker who faces dismissal knows that this course of action carries with it some sting for the employer—the sacrifice of the labor involved—and some benefit to the worker—the release of labor that can be used profitably in some other setting. (And lest this be thought to be an idle rationalization for employer misconduct, note that quits by workers who receive better jobs are a more common occurrence than dismissal, especially dismissal for cause.) The same calculation can be made in the opposite direction: The worker who flees one job forfeits the wages that would otherwise be paid, and opens up a spot for an employer or frees wages that would not be otherwise available. Whatever one thinks about dismissal or quitting, they do not have the dramatic and unfortunate consequences associated with being killed or maimed, precisely because the elimination of one benefit necessarily creates another benefit (even if one of lesser value) in its stead.

The issue concerns the accuracy and cost of the legal system. The legal system starts at a major disadvantage relative to any system of informal enforcement. In law, all decisions must be resolved before a neutral party that has to make findings of fact before issuing any binding decision. That extra step means that persons who know certain truths are in the awkward position of having to prove them to outsiders. This difficulty has been the source of enormous frustration to everyone at one time or another, but there is no way to avoid that problem in organizing a legal response to coercion and defamation. Within the context of an employment relationship, it may well be possible for the parties to agree. It is certainly possible for the law to respect an arrangement whereby each party secures exit rights for itself without having to prove its case before some independent party. The employee who just leaves need not offer any justification for her decisions, and so too with the employer who decides to fire a particular worker.

This system, I will freely confess, is not perfect, but it *is* self-regulating. Those people who know themselves to be well treated will not leave. Those persons who are ill treated have less to gain from the continuation of the relationship and therefore are more willing to go, and make credible threats in that direction. Their freedom becomes worth more to them as the employer piles on the work: The worker's threat to quit thus becomes more credible, on the one hand, and more costly for the employer, on the other. So the system settles into a long-term equilibrium. Some percentage of the relationships rupture; some percentage continue on even terms, and do so because of the ceaseless adjustments that the parties make within the stark legal framework. The simple point is that the legal system is perceived by both sides as less reliable and more expensive than the set of informal social sanctions that can be used in their place. The legal rules thus provide that either side can exit at will, and they leave all lesser adjustments to the parties. Stated otherwise, why spend more money for a system that might prove less reliable?

The recognition of this feature is critical to understanding how relational social systems operate. They presuppose a sharp distinction between the legal rules that set the outer boundaries of its operation and the social norms that influence its day-to-day operation. So long as private parties know that they wish to continue working with each other, neither side will resort to any atom bomb technique. Each will try to make the low-level adjustments and accommodations that are the hallmark of successful adaptive social systems. The reason each is willing to experiment with these adjustments—to meet the other side halfway—is that each side knows it has an exit right if things do not work out. The level of informality and the reliance on conceptions of reasonableness and good faith in personal dealings flourish precisely because a clear legal rule sets the outer boundaries for what people can and should do.

The threat element is not all that is at work. A second element that figures in the equation is reputation. Most critics of open markets believe that reputation offers only a weak constraint against abusive or improper behavior. In practice, the participants in these same markets care a good deal more about their reputation than the outsiders might suspect; losses in reputation are normally thought to be of immense importance. One fancy term for reputation is goodwill, which can be loosely defined as a set of attributes of a given business that increases the likelihood that future customers will return even when they have no legal obligation to do so. Repeat business is the key to success for established firms, which spend millions of dollars to create a consistent level of service and to develop the brand names and trademarks that signal that consistency to consumers who buy from them only in spot transactions.

What are goodwill, brand names, and trademarks but windows to the world of reputation? Unlike an individual's good name, these intangibles can be sold and exchanged between firms like other forms of property and are frequently worth far more than the bricks and mortar that they adorn. Think of the value of the Coca-Cola or McDonald's trade name and ask what catastrophe would befall those firms if they were banned from using their labels or forced to allow others to use them indiscriminately. These embodiments of reputation are protected against theft (that is, use by others) and defamation just as zealously as any physical asset. It is no accident that defamation awards can be large; this is because the damage to reputation

from false statements can be ruinous to credit and to goodwill, solely by reducing the probability of repeat business.

If goodwill and good reputation can be enormous assets to a firm, they
also subject it to powerful constraints that smaller and less conspicuous entities can avoid. The greater the reputational capital within the firm, the more
it has to lose from violating some applicable social norm that governs its relationships to customers or employees. Accordingly, we should expect it to
be easier for an employee to leave an employer in the lurch than it is for an
employer to fire an employee without warning or cause. The reputational
constraint binds the dominant firm, whose questionable conduct would be a
signal to all other employees and customers to reevaluate their relationship
with the business. The level of informal constraint is very high, which is exactly the opposite of what standard theories of exploitation predict when
they claim that size is a reliable proxy for social power.

We can identify powerful reasons that make these social sanctions work.
The single major flaw of modern employer-employee law stems from the judicial and legislative effort to elevate these social norms to legal norms. The
question of termination or major change (demotion, reassignment, and the
like) is thought to require public justification in court from some social point
of view. The system thus presupposes that it is possible to validate judgments to outside parties as they are justified to oneself, one's peers, or one's
workers. The law develops elaborate rules to decide which dismissals are for
cause and which are not. Unfortunately, the huge number of unjust dismissal
cases testify to the inability of any legal system to specify workable adju-
dicative standards on the issue of justifiable dismissal.

The equally frustrating line of cases under the discrimination and labor
laws illustrates the same basic proposition whenever cause (and thus motive) becomes a key element in deciding on the legality of some business decision. The uncertainty about basic facts (did the plaintiff slack off? was the
reduction-in-force necessary? did the new equipment require different personnel? was there friction between the plaintiff and other workers? and so
on) and the legal conclusions that apply to these facts reduces the entire judicial enterprise to determining the reasonableness of the conduct under all
the circumstances of the case. So loose a standard may be fine for a social
norm known to the players, but it is utterly inappropriate to the legal system
which operates with, at best, secondhand knowledge of the customs of the
shop or trade.

There is good evidence that these practices cannot work. In a well-known
Michigan case, *Toussiant v. Blue Cross*, 292 NW2d 880 (Mich. 1980), the
question was whether the protections that were set out in the employer's
handbook were to be incorporated into the basic employment contract. The
purpose of the handbook for the employer was to communicate information
without creating binding legal obligations. That communications exercise
has a great deal of importance because it allows prospective employees to
improve their predictions or estimates of the future state of affairs, just as

predictions of interest rates and market movements can help investors without binding brokerage houses. It also gives some indication that a firm will be reluctant simply to change the rules without explaining why they can no longer be sustained in a new business or regulatory context.

It is important to understand the limits of such handbooks. Their publication falls far short of a guarantee that today's rules are etched in stone for tomorrow. But once courts downgrade these manuals, the employer reaction is typically immediate. The documents in question are all hastily redrafted to remove any suggestion of a legal guarantee. These costs are not trivial, and they leave in the lurch any firm that relies on the older, informal methods of doing business. And the language chosen might not be quite strong enough to displace the judicial presumption in favor of elevating social norms to legal status or to mend an impression created under the prior handbooks.

In response to this friendly reception to the separation of legal and social norms, it will be urged that soft social norms do not have so benign a justification. Rather, their emergence will be attributable to the economic domination that employers have over employees. But the facts do not support that theory. A dominance relationship would never tolerate a rule that allows an employee to quit at will. Under true domination, these workers could be bound for a term (so that they could be enjoined from taking any other job) even though the employer is (on payment of some small sum) entitled to dismiss at will. Yet the bilateral nature of the contract makes perfectly good sense because each side (rich or poor) has to be able to constrain the misbehavior of the other, which can only be done if the two-tier system separating legal from social obligation is respected.

In addition, it is hardly clear why, if dominance were the key, it would only apply to the at-will term of the agreement. We should also see a rapid compression and reduction of wages to reflect the superior power of one side relative to the other. Nor would it be easy to explain why a rule that allows dismissal without cause cuts across all economic strata. Similarly the exploitation story does not account for the fixed severance payments (often based on length of service) commonly paid, often without legal obligation, when an employee is dismissed as part of a reorganization. The simple and the best explanation is that the parties themselves adopt the at-will arrangement, or other contractual term, to improve their joint lot.

LANDLORD–TENANT AND BUYER–SELLER

The distinction between legal and social norms is not confined to the employment context but carries over to many other types of situations as well. Landlord and tenant arrangements are one example. Oftentimes a landlord will create a lease that allows her to terminate the tenant at will, or to charge for certain kinds of repairs. Yet the common practice within the building may be for the landlord to take charge of these routine difficulties in ways that are not required by the contract. It is tempting in these circumstances to argue that the nature of the practice in question should be used to displace the legal obligations that were clearly crafted for the duration of the lease. Doctrines of waiver, modification, estoppel, and novation can easily be introduced to usher in the transformation from one legal order to another. That temptation should be resisted at all costs, however, for the separation of legal from social norms is as important in this social context as it is in others. It is not in the self-interest of any landlord to boot a reliable tenant, thereby incurring the costs of finding a suitable replacement. In addition, landlords are constrained by reputation, especially when they have multiple tenants who can congregate in lobbies and elevators. Their decisions are quickly visible to other tenants, and some conscious and systematic deviation from the terms of the social contract can lead to a mass tenant exodus from the building at the end of the individual leases, especially if other nearby units lay vacant. The landlord who knows this will take pains to use the legal remedies only in cases where she is justified.

The effort to constrain the power to evict at the termination of lease is in effect a disastrous alteration of the balance of power in the ongoing relationship. Requiring landlords to renew troublesome tenants, whether under rent control or with public housing, has third-party ramifications. Few good tenants will want to appear in open court to testify against gangs and thugs who frequent the building. Physical proximity makes the risk of retaliation by force far too great. So the bad tenants stay, and the good ones leave. In this regard, one great weakness of public housing is that the ostensible due-process protections (no person shall be denied life, liberty, or property without due process of law) can easily be read to imply that the Constitution prevents termination by a public landlord unless cause is not only pleaded, but proved. The part-private status of the city as landlord is overlooked in favor of its public role. The consequence is that the good tenants go, and the bad ones remain until the building is no longer inhabitable. It all happens because the state cannot run its own operations with the degree of freedom that can be accorded to private landlords (at least those who are not under rent control or similar renewal obligations).

Contracts for the purchase and sale of goods are not always relational contracts, but they often take place in the context of longer business relationships. To these arrangements, the same basic considerations apply. It is quite consistent to have a very strict set of legal rules that preserve the buyer's right to reject goods that deviate in any way from the description under which they were sold and to have their term routinely waived for a small cash adjustment. Retaining the rejection power is often desired because it nips in the bud the prospect of creeping abuse. Let the buyer be required to accept goods that deviate just a little from those promised, and in short order an errant seller could claim that larger and larger deviations fall within the principle. The strict rule curbs that tendency toward degeneration of the relationship. The buyer can determine just how much of a deviation he will accept and why. The clear rule induces a higher level of performance from the seller and reduces the cost of judicial oversight of commercial transactions.

Rules of this sort are not without their downside. The standard counterexample is when goods are rejected for some trivial defect solely because of a sharp break in the market price, which allows the buyer to get the same goods for less elsewhere. But the merits of all legal rules turn on their comparative strengths over the long haul. Most markets are relatively stable in price, and where they are not, sellers know that they should take extra precautions against the deviations in quality or quantity that could allow a buyer to reject. So the stricter rule leads to the better results, because in practice it will be tempered by the kind of "equity" that others seek to introduce into the situation. We must learn to live with a certain dissonance to keep commercial matters on an even keel.

RESCUE AND CHARITABLE CARE

My last example of this gap between moral and legal obligation comes from yet another growth area in the law: the conversion of charitable obligations into legal obligations. The challenge is to induce a small act of assistance that could yield an enormous benefit. The traditional common law (and civil law) position recognizes a sharp distinction between legal and moral duties in all cases where assistance has to be extended to persons in need. Within the context of tort law, the classic hypothetical is the man who stands on the side of a river and allows a child to drown even though he could rescue the child with little effort and no inconvenience. No one claims that the man was responsible for the predicament in which the child found himself; for all we know, the child's parent could have been negligent in providing care. Under the traditional legal rule, the courts freely concede a moral obligation to rescue the child but are in general reluctant to turn it into a legal obligation. Even with the vast expansion of tort liability in the present century and the barrage of criticism against the no-rescue rule, it remains the dominant legal position today. Why?

No single explanation tells the entire story. Part of the picture is that most rescues are made by people who care not a whit for the legal niceties, but who just want to help someone in need. Before one invokes the power of the state, we should be sure that the problem really exists, and in many cases the rescue hypothetical is just that: a hypothetical with relatively little salience. In addition, we know that when it matters, rescue is a big-time business: Floods, hurricanes, and earthquakes are not perceived to be the fault of the victims, so vast public drives and relief efforts are organized voluntarily or are subsidized with government support. Why would we want to hamper these efforts by imposing legal obligations on potential rescuers that could just induce them to steer clear of the entire effort? Most potential recipients happily would give up a legal right that might blunt the incentive of people to participate in rescue efforts. To the soothing assurance, "Don't worry, the action would only be used in extreme circumstances," the answer comes back: "Why create a new head of liability for extreme and infrequent cases if it may disrupt routine rescue efforts?" It is, of course, necessary to develop a system of rewards for professional rescuers such as salvors. For ordinary individuals, in contrast, there is little evidence that individual rescuers take advantage of their limited legal rights to obtain restitution for their successful rescue efforts. Whatever social institutions control the rescue effort seem to do quite well without the law. So it is that on second sober judgment most of us remain queasy but accepting of this separation of law from morals.

Once the focus has turned to institutional defendants such as hospitals and emergency rooms, the response has been quite different. In the mid-1980s, the United States declared that all private institutions that received Medicare and Medicaid would have to provide emergency care free of charge to all persons in imminent peril and all women in active labor, regardless of their ability to pay. This duty has not been accompanied by a federal willingness to pay the bill for the services so rendered. The costs involved therefore remain a charge on the operating budgets of the institutions that are called upon to administer the care.

This new legal regime stands in evident contradiction to the earlier approach to the subject, which stressed the separation between moral and legal obligations. The prior view was that charitable organizations were private operations, and the nature and the extent of the services that they provided were to be determined by their boards of trustees. Let someone be found half-dead on the doorstep and the organization could leave him there with impunity. Given the huge size of the charitable enterprises, in some cases just that surely has happened. It becomes easy therefore to reason from the anecdote to the rule and to impose the universal duty of service, regardless of the ability to pay.

Yet once again the key issue is whether the anecdote, when true, informs or misleads. I would argue that it does the latter. The key question to ask here is whether the overall performance of emergency and charitable care will be improved by some public imposition of duty of all those who have facilities available for the purpose. The anecdote of the dying man at the doorstep is only one case. Other cases have to be considered as well. It should be evident that charitable institutions do not operate in accordance with the same principles as profit-making ones. It would be odd indeed if charitable hospitals only offered compensated care. So we may assume that the institution is set up to take some cases at a loss, and to help to fund that gap by charitable contributions or from the profits generated by their paying business.

So what happens when the spigot is opened by the government? It is risky to assume that the volume of charitable care that has to be supplied will remain unchanged. Individuals respond to incentives in bad times as well as good. The crush of business imposed on some hospitals and emergency rooms could go beyond their capacity to sustain services in the long run, especially when no financial cap is built into the legal obligation. Faced with these limitations, the charity that cannot handle business through its available facilities may trim the facilities it makes available. Nearly one-third of the major trauma units in the United States have closed their doors in recent years, in part because they could not afford to keep them open. A variable (size of operations) that was once quite exogenous to the question of who receives care and who does not, now becomes endogenous to the system. If the alternative is bankruptcy, then better to close down some facilities, even if it entails inferior services for the charitable cases you want to take. Those locations with the greatest demand will submit to the greatest financial pressures. System-wide, the more stringent the obligation to provide care, the less care is made available.

CONCLUSION

One common rhetorical refrain is that the law should embody our highest moral aspirations. Those standards usually require that individuals act decently and fairly to other individuals and extend them help in their time of need. One can almost say that we have a basic moral code that requires us to show "good cause" whenever our conduct is hurtful to people in a vulnerable position. We simply will not accept the proposition that the failure to save a drowning child when it could be easily done is no different from a choice between strawberry and chocolate ice cream. Our set of social norms is powerful enough to distinguish between these two situations in order to advance the preservation of human life.

Yet this recognition of moral duty coexists only uneasily with the idea of individual liberty: the ability to make choices in one's own life and with one's own talents without having to account for those choices to others. The modern view has been that the moral obligation overrides the claim of individual liberty and thus places on courts and legislatures the task of defining what conduct meets our collective standards of proper behavior and what conduct does not. My view is that this commendable effort to overcome the gap between morals and law is a mistake; the complications that ensue with the translation of moral to legal duties usually destroy the benefits that they seek to create. The classical legal position recognized the separation between law and morals and often defended it, not as a good thing but as a necessary one. That classical position feared that the creation of these new duties could lead to an erosion of the very moral standards to which we all aspire. Make it impossible to fire a worker or to evict a tenant, and good workers will find it hard to get jobs, and decent people will find it hard to rent housing. Demand charitable care for all as a matter of right, and the facilities to supply it will slowly shut down under the strain.

We should resist this commendable impulse toward Big Government and learn to live with the ambiguities that the separation of law and morals necessarily preserves. We should learn to aim low, but to hit our targets. We should concentrate legal sanctions where moral and social sanctions cannot suffice. We should resist the temptation to make all moral claims into legal ones. We should do so not because the moral standards are so weak and diffuse that they fail to command any respect. No, we should do so because these are strong enough to survive and even flourish if they are not converted into legal obligations by an excess of good intentions gone awry.

NOTES

This chapter is a revised version of a talk I gave at Michigan State University on March 14, 1996. I should like to thank Laura K. Clinton, University of Chicago Law School, class of 2000, for her helpful review.

II

The World

10

Notes on Markets, Politics, and "Big Government"

Claus Offe

Neoliberal orthodoxy has targeted the "strong" state and "Big Government" as the main culprits that are to be held responsible for social malaise and economic malperformance. In this chapter, I wish to take issue with that perspective.

First of all, it is not evident what is meant by "big" government. The question of "size" can be measured in two ways: structural and functional. In terms of a structural concept of Big Government, one would have to look at indicators such as the number of intervention points, the size of the state apparatus (in terms of personnel), and the size of the budget. As to the functional measurement, one would look at the number of people being affected by state policies, as well as the intensity of the impact of such intervention. The structural "bigness" and the functional "bigness" of government seem to be orthogonally related, that is, at least potentially, causally unrelated. Governments can still be impotent even if they are big (which explains why many would find their "bigness" so unpopular); they can also be effective in performing their functions even if they are small, provided they can rely upon active and convergent forces within civil society.

Using these two rough categories of measurement, there are two interesting plus/minus combinations. One of them is an inflated state apparatus with little regulatory and governing capacity but with broad "reserved domains"—spheres (military, economic, cultural) in which intervention is prohibited or forestalled, be it *de jure* or *de facto*.

The other is the government of a policy of deregulation, withdrawal, neglect, and inaction (such as the set of policies often associated with Thatcherism) which has—and is intended to have—a major and often devastating impact upon the life chances of great numbers of people. The market is here used as political weapon targeted, for reasons that may be deemed legitimate or illegitimate, against particular categories of people for particular purposes. After all, privatization and marketization are policy interventions, not a return to an allegedly innocent, normal, or "natural" state of "undistorted" social order. It is exactly the function and purpose of neoliberal orthodoxy to conceal this discretionary installation of market forces which are being employed by political authorities for some strategic purpose—a purpose that is by no means self-evidently superior as to its legitimacy or effectiveness.

To be sure, one might well argue that, at a time before economic regulation and social policy redistribution were ever experimented with or even conceived of, the tool kit of public policy was so limited that nobody could even think of policy choices of a more interventionist sort—that, in effect, the market was actually "outside of" and "prior to" policy choices. (However, historians of ideas have mustered strong arguments to the effect that the rule of market-mediated interests was itself the outcome of a powerful moral, political, and ideological campaign of the eighteenth-century bourgeoisie and its intellectual protagonists.)[1]

But in any case, now that these allegedly "innocent" times have passed and the Keynesian welfare state has become an ideological and practical reality, marketization has been turned into an "interventionist" policy as much as any of its alternatives.

As soon as marketization is seen as just one policy instrument among other policy instruments that is being employed as the result of some political choice, the question becomes: What combination of structural and functional parameters of the size or functional scope of government is most rational, beneficial, and desirable?

The answer is: *We don't know!* Or rather, the answer is not one that can be given in the form of a compelling economic or philosophical argument, but only in the course and as the outcome of democratic deliberation. The answer is a matter of "voice," not "proof" or some objective measure of rationality. The relationship and demarcation line between market and politics is itself a matter of politics, and its reconfiguration also a matter of politics.[2] As a consequence, almost any answer to the question of the proper role and size of macro-social organizing principles of the political economy will be controversial and essentially contested.

If the market and its extension is a matter of public policy, the answer to the question of the relative size, scope, and intensity of market versus government (versus community) must correspondingly be a matter of democratic politics. It is this syllogism to which the neoliberal orthodoxy is radically and consistently opposed. Rather than providing arguments about the conduct of deliberation and democratic debate, thereby raising the level of the debate and improving the quality of "voice," the proponents of such orthodoxy silence voice by claiming superior insight into what is called for by the standard of "rationality." Hence the epistemological principle of Thatcherism: "There is no alternative!"—what I call the TINA rule.

The goal of the (anti-) politics of neoliberal orthodoxy is to *disenfranchise* citizens and to preempt potential issues of public debate in the name of truth and scientific insight. It closes the agenda by imposing nondecisions. It uses the market as a prison, as Charles E. Lindblom has argued. Libertarianism creates economic "reserved domains" for investors and employers who are largely situated outside the reach of public control.

If, however, the state is reduced to a contract-enforcing agency subservient to market forces, democracy becomes either pointless or distorted. The distortion I have in mind is the displacement of issues of public debate: Issues of justice, prosperity, and the distribution of life chances (i.e., the core issues of what Seymour Martin Lipset refers to as "the democratic class struggle") are silenced, and what flourishes instead is the politics of morality, religion, identity, and ultimately personalistic populism. Elections turn, under the intellectual and political regime of neoliberal orthodoxy, into shallow though sometimes passionate "moral beauty contests" over issues that have little or nothing to do with the core question of how to organize the political economy.[3] A concomitant phenomenon is the vanishing of the institutional and actual role assigned to intermediary collective actors of all sorts, ranging from trade unions to city councils, from business interest associations to universities. This in turn makes orderly conflict reconciliation more difficult, with the resulting institutional vacuum of interest intermediation quite possibly giving rise to symptoms of rampant social disorganization.

Karl Polanyi's concern in *The Great Transformation* (1944) is to demonstrate that "the institutional arrangements of market societies cause them to be inherently unstable."[4] This is the famous "satanic mill" argument, which derives in turn from the "fictitious commodities" argument and the demonstration that labor, land, and money are commodities that differ from all others in that they do not come into being *as* commodities, that is, as the outcome of an acquisitive production process aimed at the sale of its results for profit.[5] The market cannot *create* "social order" because some of the key ingredients of social order cannot be the result of market interaction. The market is, both genetically and structurally, the creation of nonmarket actors.

On the basis of the satanic mill argument, we can draw the inverse conclusion: If a market economy actually turns out to develop into a sustainable social order, it must be due—to employ an important distinction introduced by Friedrich Hayek—to its quality not of *kosmos* (spontaneous order due to the operation of some invisible hand), but of *taxis* (consciously arranged, instituted, and controlled order).[6] The question then becomes: Who does the *taxis?* How do the social institutions in which the market is "embedded" come into being?

Polanyi's answer to these questions is the state, as the guardian of integration, coherence, and solidarity. But how does the state come to perform that function? There is a strongly functionalist argument in *The Great Transformation*: "Objective reasons of a stringent nature forced the hands of the legislators."[7] Legislators as social actors must be conscious of those objective reasons, however, and they must also be able and willing to comply with what these reasons mandate. The necessary protective devices on which a market society depends for the sake of its integration and sustainability do not become operative automatically. Nor are they self-evident and determinate. No outside observer can tell what measures of what scale and scope must be adopted in order to make a market economy a viable social order. Any practical answer to this question must be willed. And, I submit, the ultimate source of this will is an operational theory of social justice which serves as the source of the citizens' preference formation and political mobilization. The protective institutional devices must be instituted and enacted in accordance with such a theory that guides political action of society upon itself.

Polanyi has shown, in his analysis of Speenhamland and its repeal in 1832–34, that market capitalism is not something that comes into being by the force of evolutionary superiority alone; it rather originates from conscious efforts and strategic interests on the part of the holders of state power to institute it and to create institutional and administrative arrangements that are best suited to it, most importantly the marketization of labor. Capitalism and the commodification of labor as its core prerequisite, in other words, is a political construct.

But so is the protective regulatory framework that eventually came to emerge as a result of the experience that market society, if left to its own, does not result in a stable social order. This is the "powerful countermovement" by which political actors within market society react to its instabilities.[8] If, as Polanyi insists time and again, "the market has been the outcome of a conscious and often violent intervention on the part of government which imposed the market organization on society for non-economic ends,"[9] why should not the same be true for the reverse process in which markets are contained and regulated? Commentators have observed an inconsistency here: While Polanyi is very specific as to the agents that brought about marketization, he lapses into the anonymity of functionalist logic in explaining the reverse process: "Ultimately, what made things happen were the interests of society as a whole."[10] He insists that it was not class interests which gave rise to protective regulation and self-preservation, but that "such measures simply responded to the needs of industrial civilization with which market methods were unable to cope."[11] Again, my question is: Who was it that understood those needs, acted upon them, and eventually succeeded in alleviating them?

The twofold movement that we must recognize in the evolution of modern political economies follows seemingly contradictory trajectories. One is protecting the market from political interference, and the other protecting society, including the market itself, from the corrosive and self-subversive effects of market forces. Contrary to the simplistic reading of Marxism of which Polanyi was utterly critical, this self-correcting tendency that emerged within market society cannot be attributed to class actors alone. But it still must be attributed to specific actors, the means and opportunities available to them, and the ideas that guided them.

Let me briefly turn to a review of the principal actors that played a major role in the creation of the various kinds of protective economic and social policy regimes in Europe as it emerged from the horrors of World War II. After having identified these centers of agency and their shared—or at any rate, partially overlapping—projects of social order, I will turn to the question of whether the order imposed by these social and political forces is likely to be a permanent one—or whether (and if so, for what reasons) we are, as I shall argue, now in the midst of a second Polanyi cycle of disorganization and the still-unanswered need for reorganization.

To make a long story almost intolerably short, the postwar settlement of the problem of social order in West European countries was helped by a number of favorable factors, all of which have now virtually disappeared from the scene. First, the historically unique conditions of sustained economic growth favored the building of social order in that the experience and expectation of a lasting positive-sum game imposed *relative*, not absolute, sacrifices. Second, a consolidated system of nation-states provided the opportunity for building economic and social policy regimes within each country, without much reason to fear adverse transnational repercussions in terms of diminished competitiveness. Third, the fresh memories of the horrors of the war and the Nazi regime, as well as the antitotalitarian consensus that emerged from the Cold War, all helped to solidify the alliance of political forces which, with only minor variations, endorsed patterns of regulatory state intervention and a qualified collectivism involving corporate groups.

Within this set of favorable conditions, there emerged in fact an interclass alliance of liberal, Christian, and socialist normative traditions, embodying respectively the justice intuitions of deserts, needs, and rights. Taken together, these three intuitions make up the model of what in the German terminology is called "social market economy" and which has parallels in most other advanced capitalist economies and their respective "welfare state regimes."[12]

Today we see the atrophy of this alliance due to the disintegration of the normative theories on which society can rely in order to protect itself from the destructive impact of the market. Let me turn to a brief stocktaking of our three regulatory paradigms of a just social order and their respective political proponents. In order to simplify, I employ the conceptual triplets of liberalism–equivalent desert–market, socialism–positive rights–state, and Christian politics–need–communities.

Let me elaborate. Liberalism honors desert as measured by and rewarded through the market. In the original theories of political liberalism, what people deserve includes not only the uninhibited use of property rights and the fruits of such use but also equal and universalistic admission to opportunities and market access, such as schools and health services. In the absence of these universalistic premises (as well as a few others, such as conditions of reasonably full employment), liberty may well somehow "exist" but is rendered worthless and meaningless to all those who lack the preconditions (such as training and jobs) and hence are not in a position to make choices as to their place in society. Today's liberals have largely turned libertarian, shedding off the egalitarian component of "equal liberty"—equal opportunity, entitlement to compensation for "inherited" obstacles to economic participation, and so forth (think of the electoral reaction to the first-wave Clinton domestic policy reforms). Market libertarians have also discarded traditionalist admixtures of social conservatism (think of the fate of the British "one nation Tories" under Margaret Thatcher). Or they have turned from cosmopolitan liberalism to chauvinism (as in Austria), promising the protection of national citizens through the exclusion of those who do not belong to the national community that is to be protected. Ironically, the stronger inclusive and egalitarian liberalism has become as a sophisticated moral and political theory,[13] the more deficient it has become in practice. The emphasis is upon the uninhibited reign of market forces, not upon the preservation of the premise of equal liberty and the protection of society from the market's repercussions.

Socialists originally had a vision of how not only distribution on the basis of positive rights but also production should be organized, both through the use of state power. Apart from some "green" caveats as to how production should not be organized, the theme of production and how to best organize it has virtually vanished from the socialist or social democratic agenda.[14] As socialist distributive projects are today widely seen as being parasitic upon growth and production—and because socialist policies cannot promote them in any distinctive socialist ways—these distributive projects become themselves dubious and easily discredited. And, as inherited corporatist status rights of workers often plainly stand in the way of economic performance, social democrats, exposed to the pressures of fiscal crisis, find themselves in the embarrassing situation of having to tolerate the sacrifice of the former (status and distributive rights) for the latter (competitiveness and performance).

In southern Europe (Spain, Italy, and also France), socialists even seem determined to outcompete market liberals in their emphasis on deregulation. At the least, it is hardly possible to tell a specifically "socialist" concept of industrial organization, modernization, and the promotion of industrial prosperity from any of its competitors. Nor are concepts as to how to intelligently regulate production in ways that guarantee workers' rights at the point of production together with full employment easy to come by in today's open economies. For instance, the very core concept of standard postwar social democratic economic policy making, the concept of "full employment," has been conspicuously absent from social democratic rhetoric and politics in the 1990s. It has been replaced with the more modest and realistic call for "creating more jobs."

Finally, Christian politics in general, and Roman Catholic–inspired politics in particular, is bent upon the protection of needs of individuals and communities, preferably not directly through the state, but in indirect ways that help the community or corporate unit to help itself (through "subsidiarity"). In particular, a kind of protection from the market is envisaged that focuses upon the family and the natural-law entitlements that supposedly are to govern the relations between the sexes, generations, and social classes at the point of production. Many of the doctrines invoked in support of this kind of protection from the market are so grotesquely out of touch with demographic conditions and actual gender and intergenerational relations that they hardly qualify as a plausible rationale for an effective control of the "satanic mill" of the market.

The post–World War II period came to a definitive end in 1989 (if it had not already with the oil price shocks of the mid-1970s). Its end also marked the end of a broad consensus concerning the regulatory regimes underpinning social order and the mode in which disruptive market forces should be contained while at the same time preserving the efficiency-enhancing incentives of markets. While "grand coalitions" reflecting a broad conservative–social democratic consensus on the basics of social order have become rare, the failure of each of the three ideological camps to provide for and implement a coherent concept of order is also manifest. Thatcher's infamous claim that, after all, there is no British "society" (just British individuals and families) actually denies the very object of any effort to establish a "social order"—a denial that is complemented by her refusal to admit the existence of society as a "subject" of the creation of such order, because public policy, according to her (and many of her libertarian followers), is to be guided not by democratic representation and collective choice but by some metasocial TINA logic ("There is no alternative!").

No potentially hegemonic vision of a just social order is at hand, other than that presumably brought about through the unfettered operation of market forces within and between irrevocably "open" economies. This applies to the West as well as to the East. The breakdown of state socialism has rendered obsolete a model of statist authoritarian protection and productivist *dirigisme*, leaving behind in many of the post-Communist societies the craving for a "market economy without an adjective," in the words of Václav Klaus. Many of the post-Communist elites in Eastern Europe follow the belief that problems of social order and social protection can be postponed until after an adjectiveless market economy is firmly installed. In the meantime, they stare in disbelief at the electoral resurgence of the advocates of paternalistic social protectionism that has occurred in many of the former state socialist countries.

To be sure, the great virtue and attraction of market forces and private property consist not in their being the medium of private profit maximization but in their capacity for collective loss-minimization. Markets, that is to say, eliminate in a smooth, continuous, and inconspicuous way all those factors of production that fail to perform according to currently achieved standards of efficiency. The market inflicts damages upon inefficient producers that even the most totalitarian system of governance would not dare to impose. These failing factors are thus forced to adapt and to find alternative and more productive uses.

The power that drives this continuous search is more potent than any political authority or planning agency, be it authoritarian or democratic, can ever possibly be. This is so (provided that a strong law- and contract-enforcing state power is in place) because the market is an anonymous (and hence inexorable) power that we cannot "talk to"; it is not to be irritated by election results or any other kind of "voice." This potency of market forces derives from their anonymity and nonintentionality: If factors of production fail in a particular allocation, nobody can be blamed for having caused this event. Hence, as "no one else" can be blamed for negative market outcomes, the market invites self-attribution of individual failures and activates the individuals' capacity for flexibility, inventiveness, and coping. In this and other, less desirable ways, the market is, first of all, a powerful socializing agent that instills qualities in people ranging from inventiveness to selfishness. It constantly brings to mind the maxim proclaimed by Abraham Lincoln: "If you need a helping hand, look at the lower end of your right arm!" Adaptation, however, does not come automatically, even if all were to mind this maxim. If adaptation is to succeed, it depends on adaptivity-enhancing infrastructure, assistance, and incentives.

In the absence of such adaptivity-enhancing provisions, the market also invites victim-blaming. This is due to the fact that, while anonymous efficiency-increasing pressure is just one side of the market, markets also exhibit three less-desirable features. First, there is the tendency of the market to spread to every aspect of social life, including the capacity of citizens to perform in and adjust to changing market conditions. The market cannot easily be contained, or kept in what we might intuitively assign to it as its "proper place" while respecting the autonomy of the "life world" of culture, socialization (including the formation and preservation of human and "social" capital), and the shape of human biographies. Second, the market, far from being the favorite arrangement of producers, is, wherever feasible, undermined by cartels and monopolies, or distorted by clientelistic favors extracted from the holders of political power. The market engenders no respect, not even for itself. Third, and perhaps most important, what speaks against the market as a generator of social order is its blindness: It fails to register and to translate into price signals both present and future externalities, including the external effects which results in the permanent (rather than transitory) exclusion of people and entire regions. It is these three classes of market deficiencies and market failures that must be addressed in any attempt to integrate market societies and impose upon them a viable social order.

Let me now turn to the question of how we explain the apparent disarticulation of the political camps and forces that have played the role of "governing" the market in the dual interest of preserving it and protecting society from it. A traditional—and highly optimistic—view of the competitive democratic political process (the "political marketplace") has been that it brings to political power those forces that are best capable of contributing to the integration and thus to the long-term sustainability of industrial societies. Electoral competition, in this view, is a mechanism in which the best problem solver wins, and the loser consequently has to learn from the winner and eventually try to outbid him on the next election day. Today, a more realistic picture seems to be that of a downward spiral of fatalistic routine in which each party relies on the fact that its competitor does not have any promising ideas either, which renders unnecessary efforts to develop any of its own. As is well known, the side effects of this spiral are mass political cynicism, low electoral turnout, the decline of stable political support, the denunciation of the "political class" as corrupt and self-serving, and an increasing structural premium on the populist politics of resentment.

I believe that the explanation for the atrophy of not just socialist doctrines of a just social order and policy prescriptions derived from it but also competing doctrines must be looked for on the levels of both the micro-motives and the macro-context of politics and public policy.

Within Western civil societies, centers of political agency—strong collective action based upon recognized similarities of status, interest, culture, and the potential for solidarity—have largely eroded. If anything, communities based on consumption and lifestyle are more likely to arise than those based on similarities within the sphere of production and division of labor.[15] The image that emerges from the vast sociological literature on postmodern social structures (as well as from the communitarian critique of liberal individualism) is that of rapid fluctuations of loyalties, allegiances, and commitments among individuals and diachronically across generations and along the individual's life course. Again, structural disembeddedness and atomization are prevailing features of both West European and post-Communist East European societies. In both, the threat of marginalization through unemployment dominates the scene, and the resulting insecurities and anxieties generate a rational preference for social advancement and social security through individual rather than collectivist means. These feelings and perceptions in turn inculcate a "lifeboat logic" into social life that reckons with the absence or unreliability of communal or state-provided safety nets. The social bases of organized political efforts to protect society from the market are evidently weak and fragmented, and it is by virtue of this sociological context condition that neoliberal economic doctrines are triumphant.

The macro-context of economic, technical, and cultural globalization (as mediated, respectively, by the "three nonverbal *M*'s" of money, mathematics, and music—to which we might add the fourth *M* of migration) discourages any effort to "invest" in or develop commitments toward social order, for such efforts and commitments raise fears of being punished by transnational repercussions. It is increasingly uncertain what the point is up to which a tight domestic regulatory regime is actually helping international competitiveness (e.g., through the reliable protection of social peace and infrastructural advantages) and beyond which such a regime offers opportunities for dumping to *tertii gaudentes* or otherwise becomes vulnerable to exploitation by others.

As borders decreasingly provide a bulwark against the two major undesired events of the outward flow of capital and the inward flow of labor, the resulting sense of loss of sovereignty undermines the tightly confined nation-state on which the social democratic welfare state must be seen, in retrospect, to be parasitic. Moreover, this loss of domestic sovereignty remains largely uncompensated through effective mechanisms of both territorial and functional representation at the level of transnational regimes, such as the emerging European Union. That is to say, even if the centers of political agency had not broken down, the agency and governing capacity of the nation-state to which regulatory political forces would have to address their claims and demands has been rendered increasingly vulnerable and powerless by the factors of "globalization."

What results from both the micro- and macro-contexts that I have briefly sketched is the apparent impotence of state power, as well as that of the political forces and ideas that are willing and capable of using it in the continuous process of creation and fine-tuning of social order. Again, this applies to East and West alike. Yet creative answers to the question of how to mix a mixed economy are not unknown, and they reach far beyond traditional leftist invocations of Big Government.[16] Needless to say, the cures to both these ills are as hard to administer as they are well known. They consist in the cultivation of the associative life of civil society and its legal premises, on the one hand, and the development of democratically accessible and responsive transnational regimes, on the other. In the meantime, it remains a case of misplaced concreteness to ask the time-honored question: "What is to be done?" The real—and logically prior—question: for East and West alike, is: "Is there anybody who can actually do anything?"

NOTES

1. See, e.g., Albert O. Hirschman, *The Passions and the Interests* (Princeton: Princeton University Press, 1977).

2. Cf. Hugh Stetton and Lionel Orchard, *Public Goods, Public Enterprise, Public Choice* (New York: St. Martin's, 1994).

3. Cf. Guillermo O'Donnell's notion of "delegative democracy" in his "Delegative Democracy," *Journal of Democracy* 5, no. 1 (January 1994): 55–69.

4. Michael Hechter, "Karl Polanyi's Social Theory: A Critique," *Politics and Society* 4 (1981): 405.

5. That is to say, human beings as the bearers of labor power are not manufactured but born as children. Land, and the resources it contains, is provided by geological and other processes; these resources are limited and cannot be augmented. Money (as well as taxes, tariffs, and exchange rates) is legislated into being and administered by central banks and other authorities. Some consequences of the fictitiousness of the commodity form for the socioeconomics of labor markets are explored in Claus Offe and Karl Hinrichs, "The Political Economy of the Labor Market," in Claus Offe, *Disorganized Capitalism* (Oxford: Polity Press, 1995), 10–51.

6. Friedrich A. Hayek, *Law, Legislation, and Liberty* (Chicago: University of Chicago Press, 1976), vol. 2, chap. 2.

7. Karl Polanyi, *The Great Transformation* (Boston: Beacon Press, 1971), 148.

8. Fred Block and Margaret R. Somers, "Beyond the Economistic Fallacy: The Holistic Social Science of Karl Polanyi," in Theda Skocpol, ed., *Vision and Method in Historical Sociology* (Cambridge: Cambridge University Press, 1984), 57.

9. Polanyi, *Great Transformation*, 250.

10. Polanyi, *Great Transformation*, 162.

11. Polanyi, *Great Transformation*, 154.

12. The details and diverse configurations of these regimes have been analyzed in Gösta Esping-Anderson, *The Three Worlds of Welfare Capitalism* (Princeton: Princeton University Press, 1990).

13. Cf. John Rawls, *Political Liberalism* (New York: Columbia University Press, 1993).

14. Cf. the apt warning of Rogers and Streeck: "Leaving efficiency to capital and limiting Left intervention to distributive justice not only surrenders the Left's claim for power, but results in less than optimal efficiency and thus hurts society as a whole." Joel Rogers and Wolfgang Streeck, "Productive Solidarities: Economic Strategy and Left Politics," in David Miliband, ed., *Reinventing the Left* (Oxford: Polity Press, 1994), 143.

15. Two workers, one of whom owns a sailboat, have arguably less in common as a shared focus of their associative activities than two owners of a sailboat, one of whom happens to be a worker.

16. See, e.g., Stetton and Orchard, *Public Goods*.

11

The Debate on Big Government: The View from Britain and Western Europe

John Dunn

Whatever may have been true in the United States, it would not be historically accurate to claim that there has been a debate about Big Government in Britain or Western Europe over the last two decades. There has certainly been ample disagreement about the desirable scope and real quality of governmental activities. But to portray this as a single coherent dispute suggests quite the wrong model of what has been occurring: an integrated array of mutually addressed and clearly conflicting social, political, and economic intuitions and causal beliefs, divided irrevocably in the last instance over what is to be done. Except for the stylistic conveniences of portraying it, political contestation is never like that;[1] and to choose to present it as being literally like that is to desert analysis for advocacy and thus espouse (or at least connive at) particular political projects. This, in itself, is not a matter of would-be scientific fastidiousness or *pudeur*, but a matter of the will to understand clearly rather than seek to mold to one's own prior tastes. There are keen psychological attractions to a Manichean image of politics, especially where the warfare between Light and Darkness is not obviously preordained to end in the victory of the latter, and the defense of Light, accordingly, is not impossibly quixotic. But with politics, there is discomfitingly little relation between psychological appeal and analytical or practical cogency.[2]

What *is* true is that in Western Europe over these two decades (as indeed for very long before them) there has been a wide range of political disagreements about a great many issues (causal, ethical, social, aesthetic). Onto this motley range, competing teams of professional politicians, and their professional or amateur coadjutors, have sought, in the quest for tactical or strategic advantage, to impose the simple stylized representation of a clash between mass armies, the endless trench warfare confrontation of the First Great War. Of course, this is a stylized model, too, incompletely applicable to any particular national instance—though more so, for example, to the politics of England than to those of Scotland (let alone Northern Ireland) and more so probably, with a little analytical agility, to the politics of the

United Kingdom treated as a whole than to those of Germany, or even Holland or Italy.

A debate is a discursive entity—an abstract representational device in the first instance, or at least a somewhat etiolated version of any possible human encounter: a tissue of texts. Reasonably alert students of politics, at least since the days of Thomas Hobbes,[3] have recognized that the formal choreography of debate and the counterposed pressure of political forces can in some degree be read off one another: that they must at some ultimate level of understanding, when the signs have been canceled out and all the equations are fully analyzed, be simply equivalent to one another. But to see this far is to see much farther than actually existing political analysts ever can, even if it is often to see no farther than many appear to feel entitled to claim to do. To see the ultimate equivalence of counterposed text and collision of political forces would be to see the politics of a particular epoch or civilization, as though through the eyes of God. Plainly, it would be impolitic to profess to see politics this way oneself (with such finality and decisiveness). But recognition of this hazard is far from invariable, since those confident of the correctness of their own political beliefs are very apt to speak as though they at least were privileged to see it just so.

Historically speaking, the debate on Big Government is an American phrase for an American debate. It may apply to something discursively (and politically) more determinate, and with better boundary maintenance, in the United States than it does in, for example, Britain or Switzerland. (In Switzerland it might still at present be easier to locate a debate on Small Government.)[4] But, of course, many of the imaginative components which have figured prominently in the American debate have been of European provenance, imported in varying bulk largely in the aftermath of World War II and put to work in the lengthy struggle against the heritage of the New Deal and in the eminently hospitable setting of an especially reluctant state model.[5] Wherever its principal ideological counters initially derived from, moreover, the continuing wealth and military power of the United States and, more diffusely, its continuing prominence in the information industries of the world, alongside its residual dynamism as a political, social, and even cultural model, have ensured that what has had real resonance within it will be exported sooner or later, if with varying hermeneutic receptivity, into very large areas of the world. (There would be a case, plainly, above and beyond the demands of politeness, for taking the phrase "Big Government" as an American proprietary formula, a piece of intellectual property right, to be deployed punctiliously in accordance with prior American usage. Any case against doing so will have to rest in the end on the superior analytical utility of construing the phrase in some other distinct manner.)

Big Government is not a phrase of government's friends. It appeals to those who, for one reason or another, or in one respect or another, feel that it would be appreciably better if government were smaller, if there was less of it, if it was weaker, or humbler, or poorer, or altogether less obtrusive. In a landscape in which government is smaller or weaker or humbler or poorer or even simply less obtrusive, it would necessarily be the case that other entities stand taller. Big Government is a comparative or relational concept, deprecating the presence of government in tacit or explicit preference to something else. The political sense of the phrase can only be unpacked reliably by identifying just what else will stand taller and in quite what ways.

Except for those who live for it or off it, there is little intrinsically attractive about government as such. Despite the very considerable semiotic investment in so presenting it over the millennia—the Pyramids, the Arch of Trajan, the Louvre and Versailles, the Imperial Palace in Beijing, the Kremlin—it has never been easy to conceive Big Government as a good in itself. What makes it in the eyes of its advocates and defenders a good in any sense at all is what it defends its subjects against—the other and putatively graver menaces against which it volunteers to protect them. At their most jejune, American critics of Big Government sometimes appear to suggest that there is nothing (or at least nothing domestic to the United States) against which the citizenry of the United States, with their own guns in their own hands, genuinely requires protection:[6] that there is nothing to protect them against but compulsory protection itself. This is not a view likely to occur to most foreign visitors.

The case against Big Government has two main parts. The first (and by far the more politically consequential) is essentially economic. It is that the great bulk of government expenditure is intrinsically wasteful and extrinsically damaging to economic efficiency—that it rests on unjust exaction in the first place and issues in conduct which would very often be damaging in itself, even if it were not made possible only by prior injustice and did not also make most citizens worse off than they otherwise could and would be (in conditions, that is, in which government was smaller). The second is essentially moral. It is that the more governments attempt to do and the larger they are, the less their subjects have occasion to do for themselves, and the less in due course they retain the capacity to do for themselves. Big Government weakens the characters of the subjects whom it professes to help and care for. At the limit, it infantilizes what should be free and adult citizens, replacing autonomy by utter dependence. This resonates with a major preoccupation in the appreciative self-understanding of the genesis of commercial society.[7] If all of these charges could be vindicated, their cumulative impact could scarcely be resisted. But, insofar as they involve causal claims about factual properties of the social, economic, and political world, most of them do not appear to be clearly or straightforwardly valid, so the debate (if that is how you wish to see it) plainly requires a more careful and nuanced treatment.

The causal relation between levels of government expenditure and indices of economic efficiency is intricate and hard to interpret convincingly. It is also a most unsuitable topic for political theorists to dogmatize about. But taking on trust the assessments of International Monetary Fund economists who have been studying the matter,[8] there is a weak connection between the gross domestic product (GDP) proportion of government spending and economic growth, no detectable connection between it and investment, and a relation between it and inflation which is the reverse of that posited by critics of Big Government. Where Small Government countries (at present, among industrial countries, the United States, New Zealand, Australia, Japan, and Switzerland) do surpass their Big Government rivals is in having lower unemployment rates and smaller and less rampant black economies, and in issuing more patents. There is also, however, no detectable evidence that Small Government countries (except when it comes to the size of their prison population) have more discouraging social indicators than Big Government countries—and even there, the effect appears to be due almost entirely to the immensity of the American penal colony.

If the appropriate scale of governmental activity is to be set by the balance between effective protection against evils, on the one hand, and goods forgone to provide such protection, on the other, these findings yield little joy for any distinct ideological interest. Taken along with the news that the gap between government revenues and government expenditure in the great majority of major industrial countries has increased substantially and with little interruption since 1973 (the sole exceptions, for the present, being Belgium, the Netherlands, Ireland, New Zealand, and the United Kingdom), they suggest considerable political confusion and misjudgment—a far from unusual outcome in political history. But the point of having academic political theorists at all (insofar as there is such a point) must be to alleviate such confusion, not to reproduce or aggravate it.

In an uncomplicatedly capitalist economy (unlike one with a high level of basic income) high unemployment rates must be bad from virtually any point of view. In such an economy, working for pay is virtually the only honorable way of securing an income for able-bodied males of appropriate age and tendentially so, increasingly, for able-bodied females. Indeed the effective restriction of the conduits to social honor is now so marked that the categories of able-bodiedness and appropriateness of age have each also been increasingly compressed, or even repudiated, because of their harshly exclusive implications. If it is true that lower levels of taxation are a prerequisite for (or still more if they are a sufficient condition for) appreciably lower levels of unemployment (and especially of relatively protracted unemployment), then this strongly suggests that uncomplicatedly capitalist economies can only work in a reasonably uncruel way if they do so with low levels of taxation. Because a growing gap between tax levels and public expenditure, especially in an economy which is growing relatively slowly (or not growing at all), simply passes a burden of tax or social distress forward in time to future citizens, this is an important result. Social democrats hope to block this result by raising the level of collective provision, in order to diminish the cruelty—one reason why a basic income has such a strong redistributive appeal. But it may well turn out that doing this also simply passes the distress forward through time, and in a way which could scarcely appeal to anyone concerned for distributive justice.

The causalities here are fundamental. Either particular policies have particular predictable consequences or they do not. Policies which have no predictable consequences scarcely recommend themselves. In the case of those which plainly do, everything turns on just what these consequences are. It is still reasonable to regard the market in labor as the key structuring institution of a capitalist economy (not because there are no other powerfully structuring institutions in such an economy, but because no other is as distinctive or as discomfiting to what Adam Smith himself termed the "moral sentiments"). The core project of social democracy was to tame the capitalist labor market—to turn it into a deft and dependable mechanism for redistributive social purpose, without impairing its capacity to further the operating efficiency of the economy as a whole. Large claims have been made at some points for the effectiveness of particular strategies for achieving this result, especially in regard to Sweden. But in retrospect, they do not appear at any point to have been justified. The claim which was in some instances apparently justified is that the mechanisms in place did at that time work quite effectively for the purposes in question. But what enabled them to do so was other features of the societies and economies in question, and of the context in which they operated, not the potency of the mechanism itself. In the very different circumstances of the last decade of the millennium, the supply of well-focused and effective social and economic policies falls appreciably short of the demand.

But even if there were no connection between the scale of government expenditure, the levels of overt and legal employment, and the size of the black economy, the simple inverse tie between lower levels of government expenditure and higher economic growth, if it genuinely holds, would be of the greatest importance. What is not produced cannot be redistributed. What is at present produced in an ecologically destructive and cumulatively undesirable fashion can only be produced in an ecologically more propitious manner in an economy which has the dynamism and flexibility to do more with less.

The residue of social and political hope in Western European countries (from Germany to Spain and Ireland) is that it will prove possible to combine national and European Union–wide productive efficiency sufficient to face intensifying global competition with levels of social protection, created under less arduous conditions but already provenly highly expensive, and to do all this in populations which are all aging, if at rather different speeds. The political demand for these levels remains extremely strong everywhere in Western Europe; and politicians who are conspicuously failing to supply them are viewed with growing animosity by the populace at large. But the failure, in settings where they are attempting to supply it, may just not be theirs. It is one thing for a political party to make it plain that it has no desire (or intention) whatever to provide anything of the kind. (The most ingenuous politician, in Britain or Germany or North America, need not be surprised at the animosity occasioned by such frankness.) To promise to lower taxes has very evident attractions. An open indifference to widespread suffering is less engaging and particularly unlikely to commend itself to those who see themselves as at all likely to *share* in the suffering.

The conception of economic efficiency is none too clear in itself. (Insofar as it can be made conceptually clear, it is apt to prove just as treacherous when it comes to be applied.) But however vague or clumsy it may be, it at least grasps something of overwhelming importance for every modern population.[9] World market price and product competition is the proving ground for modern societies, whether they like this or not, and even if they fail to register that it is indeed so.[10] In the increasingly ferocious competitive struggle of the last few centuries, it is ever more true that the devil will take the hindmost. The struggles seldom, if ever, have a predetermined and clearly legible outcome, not least because the range of interacting structures is so vast and the shifts of comparative advantage often so bewilderingly rapid. What can be done with some accuracy and assurance is to work over the historical record, picking out passages of relatively successful social protection, or relatively successful productive expansion, at different points in the past and isolating the mechanisms which made these successes possible. What cannot be guaranteed is that what worked relatively well there and then in the past will work equally well here and now in the present, or at any given point anywhere in the future. This is a matter of ongoing and necessarily holistic political, economic, and social judgment on the part of political elites. It is an irretrievably hazardous activity, in which it is inherently presumptuous to claim any high degree of comprehension of what one is doing.[11] But it is also a function which every modern society needs to have discharged on its behalf. Judging how effectively competing political elites are in a position to discharge it is both the most depressing and the most exacting component of demotic political judgment in a modern democracy.[12] It is hard to think of a state today in which either demos or political elites are discharging their tasks at all commandingly. But it is easy enough to call to mind instances in which each is performing especially poorly (until extremely recently, Italy came all too readily to mind).

Even if it was relatively weak, a link between lower governmental expenditure and higher economic efficiency would be difficult to resist over time if it reflected a clear causal relation between the two. A country, the politics of which remained durably too confused to choose greater economic efficiency, would suffer acutely in the long run for its incapacity. (Britain for a long time would have been a plausible instance of such a country. Japan has plainly been another over the last seven or eight years. But any country in the future, democratic or autocratic, may well find itself in this predicament. Even if it is often impossible to tell what would be politically or economically well advised today, it is often quite easy to ascertain what must be exceptionally ill advised; and many countries over long periods of time plainly have an abundance of effective political demand for policies which are certain to prove remarkably ill advised.) But even if it is at present true that countries with lower tax burdens are growing faster, it remains difficult to tell how far both of these features are a consequence of other matters and how far the former is the cause of the latter.

What is certainly true of Western European countries at present is that the effective political pressure to monitor this alleged trade-off closely remains very strong. Its doing so is a relatively direct consequence of their degree of democratization (of the extent to which the interests of those who will lose if the tax levels are sharply reduced are still effectively represented within them). But to monitor this trade-off closely, to view it with acute suspicion, is no guarantee of assessing it accurately (any more than a cheery indifference to the fate of those who will lose and a feeble representation of their interests within organized political competition offers any such guarantee either). The difficulty of judging these matters is epistemic, not spiritual. It may be aggravated by politics, but it is in no sense created by politics. The fundamental difficulties raised by these difficulties of judgment are much the same throughout modern democracies, with the challenge of democratically implemented reform on a large scale being formidable in every instance,[13] because this necessarily requires both stability of judgment and constancy of purpose in an incumbent government, and the capacity of such a government to win power in the first place and sustain it over a relatively long period of time.[14]

On a normative view, the balance of taxation should be set at the level that will be collectively the most advantageous, given the goods severally secured and the evils severally averted by this level of public provision, and the private goods forgone as a result of the exaction of the tax itself. (To reject this at all comprehensively is to adopt an indefensibly strong conception of the status of property rights.)[15] But the political determinants of tax levels are seldom or never aptly seen as the deliberative outcome of a collective assessment of what would be most beneficial for the populace as a whole. Tax policy is a peculiarly unpromising setting in which to search for the "general will." The grounds for resistance to high taxation are not elusive. If tax levels depended solely on the direct utility of being taxed, we can be confident that they would be extremely low. Even if taxation is not accurately seen as a zero-sum competitive game, it is certainly often experienced by those compelled to pay it as though that was exactly what it was. Tax donors and tax beneficiaries are not wholly discontinuous categories. But in every society they are a very long way from being identical. (Their nonidentity, in one sense, is precisely the *point* of taxation.)

The politics of tax demand, like the politics of tax supply, are often presented by those who do not like their outcome as an exercise in shamelessness and deliberate mystification. But both, of course, are presented by those who favor the outcome as punctilious responses to the question of how best—most fairly and least wastefully—to fund the provision of enormously important public goods. In the nature of the case, it is extraordinarily hard to see just how far these competing presentations really are valid. Not only are there stark and imaginatively salient divisions of interest (quite different incentive structures for different social and economic groupings) but there are also, as already noted, intricate and remarkably opaque issues of causal judgment. Over and above both of these, furthermore, there are sharp conflicts in values between the bearers of contrasting political sensibilities.

Taxation, familiarly, is the political crux of the central modern conflict over justice in distribution.[16] Those who fully endorse capitalist property relations can accept the normative propriety of taxation only insofar as it serves minimal needs for all and shores up and guarantees the fluent reproduction of these relations. For them, it has a definite and preassigned function within these relations and loses all normative sanction when it goes beyond or deviates from that function. Those who take a more skeptical view of the normative standing of capitalist appropriation, in contrast, do not see particular holdings so derived as rights and hence feel little inhibition in reassigning them in accordance with their own normative tastes.[17]

There are, no doubt, elective affinities (or weak correlations) among egoistic interest, normative conviction, and causal beliefs about economic functioning. But it is not a sign of intellectual indolence or political ingenuousness to see these as three quite distinct sources of political alignment and hence of political conflict. Each of them undoubtedly contributes to the distinctiveness of Western European dispute about the optimal scale and content of government activities and does so very much in its own way. There are politically distinctive traditions of state agency that vary widely across Western Europe, from Sweden or Norway to Portugal, France, or Greece, and that in all instances contrast markedly with those of the United States.[18] There are also professional traditions of policy design and modulation among communities of professional economists, again varying sharply from country to country (if less markedly today than forty years ago).[19] And there are wide variations in the class history of individual countries and in the political organization and ideological contours through which that history has found political expression (and through which, in some measure, it has also been made).[20]

Across all of these sources of political alignment, there is a common tendency for proponents of lower taxation, smaller public sector labor forces, and more restricted deployment of governmental power in economic affairs to see Big Government as economically wasteful and destructive and as disabling or corrupting in its impact on most of those who appear to benefit directly from it. No doubt, too, there is a common tendency for those who favor higher taxation and view the spreading ranks of public servants with some complacency to insist on the prospective or actual efficiency contribution of a wide inventory of public exertions and on the brutalizing consequences of the public custodians of the society's interests choosing to neglect or turn their backs on the poorer and more vulnerable of its members.

One side defends the interests of the welfare state, cost what it may, *à l'outrance*, underlining its political role as the clearest and most convincing way to reconcile the community as a whole to the market in and on which its members must make their lives. The other insists, with rising confidence, that the transfers which fund it are, as they always have been, profoundly illegitimate, that their cost has become increasingly prohibitive, and that their cumulative impact on the autonomy and vigor of the population at large, never a due occasion for applause, is now palpably ever more pernicious.

If it is right to see egoistic interest, normative conviction, and causal beliefs about economic functioning as independent sources of political agency which affect one another unevenly over time,[21] and not as a single structure in which one component reliably dominates over the others in the last instance, there is no obvious and reasonably parsimonious analytical strategy for explaining the contours of the debate over Big Government at any given point in time. (Its best explanation must take the form of an intimate and protracted narrative of political struggle and intellectual disagreement, heavily impacted on one another.)[22] But even this level of disaggregation is insensitive to the contribution to determining these contours that issues from political agency itself. It might be true that tax levels are set solely by the numerical relations between potential tax donors and tax recipients, prescinding from all elements of prior political advantage. But the evidence suggests that this is very far from being the case. What seems at present closer to the truth is that incumbent governments which have accumulated the power to govern effectively for a few years can and do set themselves both to lower public deficits and lower overall tax burdens in the only way in which the two objectives can be combined: by lowering public expenditure. Those that have never contrived to accumulate such power, or find themselves increasingly losing it, make no such attempt (no doubt, in part, because it would almost certainly prove futile). (The cases of Italy and Britain for the present still epitomize this effect.) There appears to be no connection whatever in these cases between the commitment or its absence, and the class structure, normative political tradition, or professional economic judgment of the societies in question.

One way of seeing this is as a crisis in the political self-sufficiency of the nation-state as a political format, to be resolved, if at all, by greatly extending the scale of cooperative and mutually binding political action—by building larger states or quasi states.[23] Here, in effect, a crisis in Big Government is to be addressed by constructing much bigger governments. The crisis is seen as arising from economic globalization: from the huge scale of world currency trading, the intensification of foreign direct and portfolio investment, and the expansion and liberalization of world trade generated by the Uruguay Round of the General Agreement on Tariffs and Trade, the formation of the World Trade Organization, and the pressures to lower tariffs in what was for long the most dynamic sector of the world economy, the Pacific rim.[24] These pressures constrict the range of policy instruments it is prudent for a government to deploy (an effect which goes back a long way in the forging of a world market).[25]

The key question posed by these pressures is less what they do directly to the power of the state in general than what they do indirectly to each state by the impact they have on the relation between that state and its subjects. The modern state was built conceptually and practically on the establishment of very distinctive and exigent claims of state over subject.[26] Its reluctant and always severely limited democratization has blurred the sense of these claims;[27] but it has not (and cannot readily) lead to the state simply relinquishing them. For much of the history of capitalism, there has been some degree of effective segregation between a global market in goods and a more local (eventually a national) market in labor. One purpose in constructing the welfare state was to make the state the custodian of the social consequences and prerequisites of a national market in labor.[28] But the growing liberalization of world trade effectively creates an increasingly global market in labor, with sharp distributive implications for those in wealthier countries whose labor fails to make an internationally competitive contribution at its current price.[29] States (and supra-states) can try to act to mitigate these consequences, at a cost; but they cannot hope to eliminate them.

In this relatively tight triangle of taxation, income, and employment, a large shift has already taken place across Western European countries during the last two decades in the political culture and expectations of the population. This shift is beginning to be reflected in the tax levels exacted, the welfare benefits provided, and the numbers of adults protractedly out of work. The shift, however, has been far more a consequence of directly encountered external force than it has of endogenous change in political taste: a product not of debate, but of reluctant adjustment to economic reality. (In America, no doubt, things have been a bit different.) Where there has been some shift in taste (larger in some countries than in others) has been in the attitude toward state institutions and agencies themselves. A culture of suspicion of public agency has been assiduously cultivated, often under American inspiration, and the suspicion has spread quite markedly. Since suspicion of public agency (like suspicion of private agency) is always in some measure in order,[30] this is an easier process to set in train than it is to channel and keep under control. Career politicians continue to compete for state power, for the right to coerce their fellow citizens by holding public office and making and enforcing laws. But there may over time prove to be less state power to exert, less power in the offices themselves, less effective coercion, less docility of subjects in face of the law. The contrast between Big and Small Government is not analytically compelling here. Cheap government need not mean feeble government. Costly government need not mean potent government. Densely populated government need not mean effective government. Fewer public cadres of higher quality and with greater conviction may prove more effective than more public cadres of lower quality and with understandably less conviction. (Better fewer but better, as V. I. Lenin lapidarily observed.)

For the convinced critic of Big Government, the larger (the costlier, the more heavily populated, the more comprehensively and promiscuously authorized) the government, the more depleted and disempowered the society and economy over which it holds sway. This is an altogether more adventurous hypothesis than that which merely attributes some cost in economic growth to any large increase in the GDP proportion of public expenditure. It is bold to assume that this more adventurous hypothesis does capture a causal relation, or that all the causality within it can run in the same direction. Highly sophisticated economies require sophisticated legal systems and fluent and accurate monitoring of the effectiveness and responsiveness of these systems. Environmental protection and the regulation of natural monopolies of energy, water, or other necessities of life require the exertions of a great many highly skilled and well-protected public servants. Privatization of publicly owned industries and public services may often offer the possibility of major efficiency gains. But ensuring that these gains are secured in practice, and that they are not accompanied by other plainly undesirable and publicly unintended consequences, requires skilled supervision and a residue of highly effective public authority.

The educational, transport, and health needs of a modern population cannot simply disclose and enforce themselves through a system of self-constituting markets. (Show me anywhere where they have succeeded in doing so.) Insofar as markets can operate to meet these needs with any precision and reliability at all, they will do so only where their scope is defined clearly and enforced effectively by public servants well equipped to judge what that scope should best be. Very little of what is required for these relations to go well or badly can be captured merely through the conception of the relative scale of government. There is no doubt as to the importance of these questions, but all too much doubt over what is needed to answer them at all reliably (or, to put the point more politically, over whose answers to them we would be well advised to trust).

In interpreting the political history of public commitment in different countries over these murky causal judgments, it is hard to exaggerate the influence of the distinctive normative traditions of the countries in question: Germany, the United Kingdom, France, the Netherlands, Sweden, and Norway. A picture of how it is impermissible to treat a fellow citizen can be intuitively far clearer and affectively much more potent than any axiom of political economy. This clarity may make it a most undependable guide to public policy; but it need not in any way lessen its political impact. It is important that both the case against Big Government and the case in its favor can be and have been expressed with great force through the idea of how it must be impermissible to treat fellow citizens (or even fellow human beings).

"Individuals have rights, and there are things no person or group may do to them (without violating their rights). So strong and far-reaching are these rights that they raise the question of what, if anything, the state and its officials may do."[31] The first political question here is how to establish what rights they really do have (or if you do not care for a vocabulary of rights or for moral realism, how better to express the more decisive and fundamental claims the members of a society may justly make as demands on one another and not as simple pleas for charity). Once this question has been answered, there follows the question of how these rights (or other more tastefully interpreted mutual claims) can best be secured in practice.

One answer, notoriously, has been by making government total—by giving it comprehensive authority and responsibility, backed by absolute power. However many governors it might take to achieve this in practice, it is hard to see how there can be a bigger government than that. Another answer, equally notoriously, is by eliminating government completely, since the claim to govern is necessarily a violation of right in itself. Even philosophical anarchists or would-be libertarians plainly have difficulty in believing that this settles the issue, since the radical absence of government also plainly militates against the securing of a great many other at least equally convincing candidates for the status of a right.[32]

Partly because of the relative efficacy of the welfare states built in Western Europe in the long postwar boom,[33] and partly because of the subsequent establishment and deepening of what is now the European Union, the conception of what it is to treat a fellow citizen impermissibly is very densely institutionalized in all Western European countries in the form of publicly provided welfare benefits.[34] This does not necessarily reflect less-brutal class histories or wider human sympathies, even over this restricted period, but it is at least the relatively stable and salient outcome of a protracted series of bargaining games between conflicting classes.[35] There is every reason, even in such a potent national economy as that of Germany, to suppose that this level of public provision is now competitively disadvantageous for European producers. But to shrink it at all drastically and rapidly has proved politically impracticable so far virtually everywhere. Even such a domineering and long-lasting political leader as Margaret Thatcher made, in the end, very little dent in it.

If the efficiency costs of these arrangements are as high as many economists now believe, there is little doubt that in the end the levels will have to fall. But what is already clear virtually throughout Western Europe is that this will become practicable when, and only when, this causal conviction has penetrated the political elites deeply enough to convince them that there is (as Thatcher used to say) no alternative and to induce in them sufficient corporate solidarity to nerve them to share the conviction frankly and eloquently with their prospective electors. It is not necessary to be a game theorist or a habitual student of the routine politics of capitalist democracy to appreciate that most of the standard operating procedures of professional politics in such states militate pretty virulently against the formation (let alone the maintenance) of any such degree of corporate solidarity. Even if most career politicians can now discern the advantage of there being an effective coalition of this kind, the willingness to run risks to promote its creation is most unlikely in the near future to match the vividness of the temptation to defect from it as soon as it begins to take shape. (Consider the present intraparty pressures on Britain's chancellor of the exchequer.)

Where movement is much easier, however, is in the judgment of the consequences of different ways of organizing or withholding public provision of welfare benefits. Here, a political process with considerable internal momentum, confidently cumulative and exquisitely politically convenient for those whose purposes it suited, has given way to spreading doubt as to just what purposes most of its constituent practices did and do serve, how cost-effective they ever were, and how much harm (or good) would be done by abandoning or truncating any given one. The construction of the massive central and local welfare bureaucracies of postwar Western Europe was not fueled solely or even principally by social or economic credulity or competitive political advantage, but it was certainly lubricated by relaxed inattention to many of the consequences of building and extending these institutions. Today, the pressures for greater causal skepticism are increasingly pervasive, and the longer-term prospects for improved causal judgment are perhaps somewhat enhanced. (One should not, of course, be too optimistic about the last assessment. The epistemic difficulties of assessing social causality remain as formidable as ever, and greater incentives for resolving them are unlikely to prove sufficient to ensure their resolution, while the prospective political rewards for claiming at any point to be able to resolve them in a politically convenient direction will always remain high.)

In the fields of education, health, employment, and perhaps even technological innovation, the optimal scope and organization of a society's institutions must depend in the end on enormously complex causal judgments, essentially internal to the domains in question. The determination of the role within them that should be played by the institutions of government (coercively, fiscally, organizationally, even ideologically) must rest steadily on these causal judgments, rather than issuing from a robust prior conception of what a state really is, either normatively or practically—what it must do, or should do, or may not even attempt to do, or can be confidently trusted without further inspection to prove able to do. I doubt very much whether there has yet been any clear and reliable progress in causal understanding in these domains, and therefore I doubt even more that one can anticipate much stability or political robustness in the present outcomes of the last two decades of party squabbling over how the contours of these institutions should most appropriately be determined.

Strong claims for the infelicity of governmental presence here must be claims either of its palpable impropriety, of its manifest functional unsuitability for delivering the goods in question, or of its even more evident prospective insolvency in face of a voracity of demand unchecked by any internal limit. Much of the most powerful criticism of excessive governmental scale over the centuries has been very much aimed at its presumption—at the impropriety and arrogance of claims to use coercive authority to determine the content of others' beliefs (and of practices expressing those beliefs) over matters which they deemed of especial importance. The struggle for the right to religious toleration was the privileged site in Western Europe for its elaboration and elucidation.[36] It will always be hard to stop determined rulers from acting on such presumption. But in the course of the last decade the claim to be entitled to decide the content of subjects' beliefs on their behalf has taken a remarkable degree of punishment. It is unlikely ever to be effectively expelled from political life, but its presence today is notably shiftier and less assured across the world as a whole than at any earlier recorded moment in world history. If most governments no longer have the nerve to be openly didactic about issues of major existential commitment, it is reasonable to assume that that fact alone will set some political limit to the resources they can hope to exact and the scale on which they can expect to be allowed to operate.

But the prospect of establishing more determinate, or externally better secured, limits to governmental agency (and hence to governmental scale), either by historically given features of socioeconomic reality or through clear normative restrictions on legitimate interference with individual liberty, is not promising. Liberty of action requires a secure setting for its exercise; and that security, in turn, requires careful and authoritative monitoring of the mutual interference of each actor's practical interpretation of his or her own liberties. Sooner or later, the clarity of the claims must be blurred drastically by the onerous pragmatic requirements for their mutual realization. Even the most offensively petty of state regulations (such as Singapore's prohibition on chewing gum) can be vindicated without complete absurdity as solutions to real collective action problems.[37] It is hard coherently to deny the need for (and hence the entitlement of) the political authority to judge these pragmatic requirements and act upon them.

Powerful, confident, wealthy, active societies can deal with their governments with greater firmness, energy, and dexterity than weak, anxious, poor, passive societies can. But no society can be strong, confident, rich, or active for any length of time independently of how its government has recently been conducting itself.[38] The concept of civil society may serve helpfully as a loose heuristic device for capturing the political (as well as social and economic) efficacy of a particular human community at a given time. But the more analytical and causal weight is placed upon it, the less determinately real it will prove to be, and the more plainly self-deceptive the expectation that one can derive from it political conclusions of any force and precision. The more seductive our image of what civil society really is, the less we can reasonably expect it to prove able to dominate political history on our collective behalf. If governments are to be diminished in scale and compressed in cost, they will have to choose this downsizing firmly for themselves, carry it through themselves, and cleave determinedly to the purpose for the prospective future. It would be extremely surprising in electoral democracies if they either prove steadily inclined to do anything of the kind or find themselves protractedly permitted to do so.

There is just one very large and important respect in which the pretensions of Big Government virtually throughout Western Europe have wilted drastically in the last decade, and done so once and for all. An old and long vivid hope (or specter) has been laid to rest. The presumption that socialism (or, for that matter, Communism) represented a comprehensive, strongly internally related, novel, and plainly superior way of collective life has lost every vestige of plausibility and has done so with bewildering speed. I do not myself believe that we yet understand at all clearly quite why this happened.[39] Those who always regarded socialism with hostile incredulity still find it hard to focus on the question of why so many for so long found it so seductive. Those who have only recently and painfully let go of the hope are in no condition to press the question of why their own prior credulity lasted for so long.[40] The collapse was never likely to mean the disappearance of political corporations previously organized under the aegis of socialism, and the reviving competitive fortunes of such corporations (in Poland, Hungary, and Russia, for example) have naturally elicited a concomitant revival in their political effrontery. But there is nowhere in the world today where a ruling apparatus, or even a serious contender for rule, still evinces any shred of belief in the holistic and comprehensive superiority of socialism to capitalism, or even in very determinate economic contrasts of a desirable kind between the former and the latter.

This is a real turning point in world history. Unless and until the turn is reversed, we can be very confident that it carries deep implications, both practical and imaginative, for the scope of governmental pretensions and opportunities. If we do not yet know exactly why it occurred where and when it did, this is a key lacuna in our understanding of contemporary politics.

NOTES

1. John Dunn, *Political Obligation in Its Historical Context* (Cambridge: Cambridge University Press, 1980), chap. 2.

2. John Dunn, "Hope over Fear: Judith Shklar as Political Educator," in Bernard Yack, ed., *Liberalism without Illusions* (Chicago: University of Chicago Press, 1996), 45–54.

3. Thomas Hobbes, *Behemoth; or, The Long Parliament*, 2d ed., ed. Ferdinand Tönnies (London: Frank Cass, 1966); Quentin Skinner, *Reason and Rhetoric in the Philosophy of Hobbes* (Cambridge: Cambridge University Press, 1996).

4. Yannis Papadopoulos, *Complexité sociale et politiques publiques* (Paris: Montchrestien, 1995).

5. Stephen Skowronek, *Building the New American State* (Cambridge: Cambridge University Press, 1982). Cf. David Calleo, "America's Federal Nation-State: A Crisis of Post-Imperial Viability?" in John Dunn, ed., *Contemporary Crisis of the Nation State?* (Oxford: Blackwell, 1995), 16–33.

6. John Dunn, *Interpreting Political Responsibility* (Princeton: Princeton University Press, 1990), chap. 3; John Dunn, *The History of Political Theory* (Cambridge: Cambridge University Press, 1996), chap. 4.

7. John Dunn, *Rethinking Modern Political Theory* (Cambridge: Cambridge University Press, 1985), chaps. 1 and 3; see especially the judgments of David Hume and Adam Smith quoted on 13 and 32.

8. Vito Tanzi and Ludger Schuknecht, "The Growth of Government and the Reform of the State in Industrial Countries" (International Monetary Fund working paper, Washington, 1996), cited in Hamish Macrae, "Size Does Matter, at Least to the IMF," *Independent on Sunday*, April 21, 1996.

9. Cf. John Dunn, *The Politics of Socialism* (Cambridge: Cambridge University Press, 1984).

10. John Dunn, ed., *The Economic Limits to Modern Politics* (Cambridge: Cambridge University Press, 1990); see especially the extended contribution by Istvan Hont, "Free Trade and the Economic Limits to National Politics: Neo-Machiavellian Political Economy Reconsidered," 41–120.

11. Dunn, *Rethinking Modern Political Theory*, chap. 7.

12. Dunn, *Interpreting Political Responsibility*, 193–215; John Dunn, *Understanding Politics* (London: HarperCollins, 2000).

13. Stephan Haggard and Steven B. Webb, eds., *Voting for Reform: Democracy, Liberalization, and Economic Adjustment* (New York: Oxford University Press and World Bank, 1995).

14. Cf. Albert Hirschman, *The Rhetoric of Reaction* (Cambridge: Harvard University Press, 1991).

15. Dunn, *History of Political Theory*, chap. 7.

16. Dunn, *History of Political Theory*, chap. 7.

17. Jeremy Waldron, *The Right to Private Property* (Oxford: Clarendon Press, 1988).

18. Cf. Skowronek, *Building the New American State*.

19. William J. Barber, *From New Era to New Deal* (Cambridge: Cambridge University Press, 1985); Peter A. Hall, ed., *The Political Power of Economic Ideas* (Princeton: Princeton University Press, 1989); Peter Clarke, *The Keynesian Revolution in the Making* (Oxford: Clarendon Press, 1988); Robert Skidelsky, *John Maynard Keynes: The Economist as Saviour 1920–1937* (London: Macmillan, 1992).

20. Adam Przeworski, *Capitalism and Social Democracy* (Cambridge: Cambridge University Press, 1985).

21. Dunn, *Economic Limits to Modern Politics*; Dunn, *History of Political Theory*; Dunn, *Understanding Politics*.

22. Dunn, *Political Obligation*, chap. 3; Dunn, *Rethinking Modern Political Theory*; Dunn, *History of Political Theory*; Dunn, *Understanding Politics*.

23. Dunn, *Contemporary Crisis*, 3–15.

24. Vincent Cable, "The Diminished Nation-State," *Daedalus* 38 (Spring 1995): 23–53.

25. See especially Hont, "Free Trade and the Economic Limits to National Politics."

26. Quentin Skinner, "The State," in Terence Ball, James Farr, and Russell Hanson, eds., *Political Innovation and Conceptual Change* (Cambridge: Cambridge University Press, 1989), 90–131; James Tully, "Governing Conduct," in Edmund Leites, ed., *Conscience and Casuistry in Early Modern Europe* (Cambridge: Cambridge University Press, 1988), 12–71; Marc Raeff, *The Well-Ordered Policy State* (New Haven: Yale University Press, 1983).

27. John Dunn, ed., *Democracy: The Unfinished Journey* (Oxford: Oxford University Press, 1992); John Dunn, *Stato nazionale e comunità umana: Possibilità di vita, obblighi e confini della società* (Milan: Edizioni Anabasi, 1994); Bernard Manin, *The Principles of Representative Government* (Cambridge: Cambridge University Press, 1997).

28. Gosta Esping-Andersen, *Politics against Markets: The Social Democratic Road to Power* (Princeton: Princeton University Press, 1985).

29. Adrian Wood, *North–South Trade, Employment, and Inequality* (Oxford: Clarendon Press, 1994).

30. Public agents are just as human as private agents. Cf. John Locke: "Allegiance is neither due nor paid to Right or to Government which are abstract notions but only to persons having right or government." John Locke, *Notes on William Sherlock's The Case of Allegiance*, Bodleian Ms Locke c28, f 85r.

31. Robert Nozick, *Anarchy, State, and Utopia* (Oxford: Basil Blackwell, 1974), ix.

32. With regard to philosophical anarchists, see A. John Simmons, *On the Edge of Anarchy* (Princeton: Princeton University Press, 1993); and Robert Paul Wolff, *In Defense of Anarchism*, 2d ed. (New York: Harper & Row, 1976). On the would-be libertarians, see Nozick, *Anarchy, State, and Utopia*.

33. Alan Milward, *The European Rescue of the Nation-State* (London: Routledge, 1992).

34. Compare the very different predicament, as the century draws toward its close, of refugees or would-be immigrants.

35. Przeworski, *Capitalism and Social Democracy*.

36. John Dunn, *History of Political Theory*, chap. 6.

37. John Dunn, "Asian Cultures and Democratic Potential: A Western View," in Ra Jong-Yil, ed., *Democratization and Regional Cooperation in Asia* (Seoul: Kim Dae-Jung Peace Foundation, 1996), 83–111.

38. John Dunn, "The Contemporary Political Significance of John Locke's Conception of Civil Society," *Iyyun* 45 (July 1996): 103–24.

39. For a study of the question focused as parochial intellectual farce, see Sunil Khilnani, *Arguing Revolution* (New Haven: Yale University Press, 1993).

40. Dunn, *Politics of Socialism*; Dunn, *History of Political Theory*, chap. 14. Cf. Alain Bergounioux and Gerard Grunberg, *L'Utopie à l'épreuve: Le Socialisme européen au XXe siècle* (Paris: Éditions du Fallois, 1995).

12

The Leninist Debris; or, Waiting for Perón

Vladimir Tismaneanu

> The clearest fact is that we are living in a time of transition, but whether we are going toward liberty or marching toward despotism, God alone knows precisely.
>
> Alexis de Tocqueville, 1831

Left, Right, Center: All these notions have strange and elusive meanings under post-Communism. Using interpretive Western paradigms would simply create false analogies and would explain little, if anything. Initially, the abuses committed in the name of the Marxist faith in the former Soviet Union and East Central Europe engendered apprehensions about any explicit socialist program. But the nostalgia, soon evident, for the benefits of the socialist welfare state has deepened and is widespread—a reason for the phenomenon of the "Communists' comeback." It has become increasingly obvious that large numbers in all social strata resented communist ideology without detesting the state socialist illusions of security, protection, and stability. Yes, there was scarcity, but there was no unemployment, and there was also a feeling that the future was predictable within an immutable universe.[1]

Post-Communism presents the individual with unique opportunities of affirmation and risks of failure and self-destruction. Freedom means assertion of diversity and individuality, and many people have not easily adjusted themselves to this situation. In the words of Václav Havel:

> The fall of communism destroyed this shroud of sameness, and the world was caught napping by an outburst of the many unanticipated differences concealed beneath it, each of which—after such a long time in the shadows—felt a natural need to draw attention to itself, to emphasize its uniqueness, and its difference from others. This is the reason for the eruption of so many different kinds of old-fashioned patriotism, revivalist messianism, conservatism, and expressions of hatred toward all those who appeared to be betraying their roots or identifying with different ones.[2]

Along with exhilaration and excitement over the regained freedoms, individuals find themselves demoralized, disoriented, lost in the new political and economic chaos, and without defense against what they perceive as threatening, uncontrollable forces. These feelings have led to the idealization not of the Communist forms of coercion, but of the old system's egalitarian claims and paternalistic practices. Thus, the political parties that succeeded Communism have had to come to grips with this schizoid social psychology and have often acted in contradiction to their own ideological claims.[3]

A NEED FOR NEW CONCEPTS

The old mythologies of the Left and the Right require a dramatic overhaul in light of the major changes in these countries. What remains of the leftist pledge to install a classless society? And what is one to make of the astounding transformations of the former Communist potentates (presumably leftists) into robber barons, successful bankers, and free-market enthusiasts? Indeed, is populism to the left or right? What about liberalism? Do democratic socialist ideals still have a future in the former Leninist societies? Or, rather, have these countries entered, together with the West, a postutopian age in which all ideologies are extinct? Will the social hybrid made up of mafiosi and former apparatchiks (what Polish sociologist Jacek Tarkowski once called the *entrepreneurchiks*) that is now running the show in Russia and in so many of the former Communist countries eventually turn into a new, law-abiding bourgeoisie?

The truth is that, even after the demise of Marxism, individuals need to believe in something. They crave ideas and values to justify their options and commitments. Nature abhors a void, and so do the post-Communist societies. Political creeds, liberal or antiliberal, continue to orient them, to generate passion, emotions, and polemics. The public's moods are extremely volatile. The same majorities that one day favored fierce anti-Communist politicians can bring the born-again socialists (post-Leninist parties) back to power the next day.[4] And later, as they become disenchanted with the pace of reforms, they may support other varieties of politics, including the populist demagoguery of ethnocentric prophets.

The appearance of an intellectual proletariat, obsessed with conspiracies and specializing in producing impatient slogans rather than serious economic analyses and alternative programs, is a salient feature of the post-Leninist political cultures. Condemning decadence, moral nihilism, and anarchy, they appeal to the losers in the transition, to all those who resent the new forms of social injustice and see the "aliens" as guilty for all their troubles. An illustration of this logic is embodied in Miroslav Sladek, a former Communist censor converted to far-right politics, who is the leader of the Czech Republican party. Indulging in outrageous racism, he appealed to his supporters to rally against gypsies, whom he described as "inferior," "animals," and simply "subhuman." Before the country's breakup in December 1992 (the so-called velvet divorce), Sladek cultivated the dream of "Greater Czechoslovakia" and blamed the West for its failure: "We won't allow another Munich! Havel, Klaus, and Meciar have sold us to the Germans. The West is afraid of united Czechoslovakia. Today we have the best chance ever of becoming the world's fourth superpower after the United States, Russia, and China."[5]

Aberration aside, xenophobic demagoguery found enough support for the Czech Republican party to win nearly 8 percent in the 1996 elections. Is Sladek, an antielitist, anti-Communist, and ethnocentric politician, just an exponent of the traditional Right? Or does he speak for the rise of a new radicalism, mixing traditional chauvinistic themes with lingering Leninist reflexes?

In the same vein, Corneliu Vadim Tudor, the chairman of the Greater Romania party, does not tire of inveighing against corruption and the role of the Jews in the country's presumed bankruptcy. At the same time, each issue of *România Mare*, the party's weekly, extols ad nauseum the memory of the late dictator Nicolae Ceauşescu and publishes panegyrics about pro-Nazi Marshal Ion Antonescu, who was executed as a war criminal in 1946. And, as President Ion Iliescu avoided a true break with the extremists, in 1994 Vadim's and other like-minded nationalist parties became members of the government's coalition. Theirs is obviously a new version of radicalism that combines themes of the Left and the Right in a baroque, often unpredictable alchemy.[6]

On the one hand, these parties declare their commitment to European values. On the other, they do their utmost to denounce any form of criticism of the resurgent authoritarianism and xenophobia as inimical to the national interest. In my view, hostility to liberalism is more than a peripheral phenomenon. To a greater or lesser extent, populist and intolerant trends exist in most post-Communist countries, even if they are less influential in the three "core countries" (Poland, the Czech Republic, and Hungary). Think of the outbursts of *ressentiment* that followed the Polish presidential elections of 1995 and the revival of confrontational, mutually exclusive styles on the part of the competing political actors that could undermine the democratic process itself.[7]

For the foreseeable future, the East European situation (regardless of the hegemonic self-congratulatory narratives) will remain in the ideological age; symbols, myths, rationalized miracles, liturgical (ethnoreligious) nationalisms, and teleological pretense have returned after the short-lived "postmodern" interlude of the revolutions of 1989—and with them, the politics of emotion, irrationality, hostility, anger, and unavowed, unbearable shame. This is indeed the politics of rancorous marginality, "cultural despair" (to use Fritz Stern's term), and convulsive impotence that the nascent democratic (dis)order can barely contain. The fate of Yugoslavia tells much about the infinite capacity of elites in these societies to restore the fallacies and follies of the past to the rank of new national mythologies in the attempt to maintain and expand their hold on power. Thus, the latter-day explosions of hatred are not just a return to a kind of recurrent Balkan malediction, to wild tribalism, but rather the exploitation of ancient fears and vengeful fantasies by cynical elites obsessed with and ready to use any means to foster their supremacy.[8]

Political adventurers like Bosnia's Serbian leader Radovan Karadžič have shown immense ability to use myth as a dangerous weapon.[9] In Karadžič's mind, the Bosnian Serbs were not simply fighting a war for territorial control and expansion; they were engaged in a genuine crusade against Islam, "Europe's last anti-colonialist war." He argues that their struggle was justified by Serbian sacrifices in the past and their refusal once again to be subjected to persecution. This is indeed the ideology of preemptive genocide.[10]

Without necessarily sharing British political historian Robin Blackburn's pessimism about the West's democratic accomplishments and the nefarious role of international financial institutions, I find his diagnosis of the Yugoslav tragedy poignantly instructive. In his view, whereas ancient enmities do of course matter, they are not the only key to the explanation of the resurgent nationalist and radical rage.

Though the latter have played their part, they were lent a potent new virulence, recklessness, and desperation by such modern furies as wrenchingly unequal development, hyperinflation, mass unemployment, austerity programs, media demagogy, militarism, political corruption, ethnic totalitarianism, and that intolerant frenzy of unstable majorities that one could call democratic dementia. Indeed, one of the most ominous aspects of the breakup of Yugoslavia is that its setting is only too modern and that its evolution in the 1980s foreshadowed many of the domestic and international recipes which are being tried out in the 1990s on other post-Communist states.[11]

Or, as the Slovene social philosopher Slavo Žižek argues, the issue is who will be accepted as part of the West and under what circumstances: "What is at stake in contemporary post-socialist states is the struggle for one's own place: who will be admitted—integrated into the developed capitalist order—and who will be excluded."[12]

The Yugoslav disaster is an example of a worst-case scenario for other countries in the region. It shows the extreme limits of a political game inspired by fanatic nationalism, paranoid delusions, apocalyptic fears, and contempt for pluralism. Since "forewarned is forearmed," I believe that it is better to understand such dangers and avoid them, rather than to play the already obsolete, pseudo-Hegelian tune of the "ultimate liberal triumph" in what Ken Jowitt described as "a world increasingly marked by political weakness, disorientation, institutional mimicry, and disintegration."[13]

As British philosopher Karl Popper often said, "the future is entirely open." In his view, marked by a healthy skepticism regarding any historical messianism, "we have as individuals a moral responsibility to shape the future and not regard ourselves as mere flotsam or jetsam in some irresistible current of history."[14]

Indeed, what we deal with is not the strength but the fragility and vulnerability of liberalism in the region: the backwardness, delays, and distortions of modernity, and the rise of majoritarian, neoplebiscitarian parties and movements.[15] These are among the salient threats to fledgling democracies. Fantasies of redemption stimulated by the promises of self-appointed charismatic saviors that offer instant gratification to lonely and uprooted crowds abound in all the post-Communist countries. How else can one explain the electoral successes of aggressive demagogues like Russia's Vladimir Zhirinovsky, Romania's Gheorghe Funar, or Hungary's Jozsef Torgyan?

Zhirinovsky's rise to prominence cannot be separated from the postimperial malaise experienced by so many Russians. Ten years after the upheaval, the former Sovietized world is confused, disconcerted, rudderless, nervous, and exasperated. The old paradigms are exhausted, the new ones still inchoate. It is as if there is a yearning for a new figure of the future, an expectation of a true revolution that would put an end to all the current ordeals and anxieties. The project of modernity, itself linked to the heritage of the Enlightenment, is being challenged by the rise of atavistic discourses of hatred, intolerance, racist exclusiveness, religious fundamentalism, and Third World–style radicalism.

As mayor of the Transylvanian city of Cluj and chairman of the Romanian National Unity party, Funar has consistently banked on chauvinistic, anti-Hungarian sentiments among Romanians.

Torgyan is the leader of the Smallholders party, which has managed to outrun in popularity the government of former Communist Gyula Horn by combining staunch nationalism and an open criticism of the post–World War I Trianon Treaty. Like his peers in Russia, Serbia, or Romania, he resorts to the symbolism of the "Great Fatherland" amputated by mischievous or insensitive foreigners. While other Hungarian parties treat the legacies of the twentieth century as an inescapable reality, Torgyan has raised his voice to criticize the West for its alleged treason. Irresponsible demagogues have the advantage over the realistic politicians because they do not need to worry about the implications of their hateful, often bellicose statements. Ignoring or challenging established taboos, they can stir responsive chords in many disoriented citizens who blame the West for their country's fate. "The Hungarians were protecting the West for centuries against the barbarians, and what did we get for that?" Torgyan said to an American reporter. "When the Hungarians went against the Communists in 1956, the Americans just said our children should go against the tanks with empty hands."[16] Similar sentiments can be heard from Belorussian, Croat, Polish, Romanian, and Serbian experts in national self-aggrandizement.

Critical intellectuals, so involved in subverting the communist pretense of cognitive infallibility, have clearly lost much of their political impact. In general, one notices the *retrenchement* of the universalistic, supranational discourses and the prevailing role of the rhetoric of identity, belonging, and collectivity. The celebration of ancestral roots and traditions as a basis of identity is making an unsettling comeback: Again, this is not the "privilege of the East." Wolf Lepenies, the German sociologist of melancholy, captures these phenomena when he writes:

> The unexpected fall of the communist regimes has been fatal, not only for Western governments but for Western intellectuals as well. . . . The responsibility of both politicians and intellectuals has increased. The task before them is to reflect upon values capable of guiding the world, and to formulate convictions that are livable and instructive for the global market economy. In the face of this challenge the strategies of retreat followed by intellectuals today loom large. . . . Inebriated with the idea of Europe, . . . the West has lived in the illusion of being able to forge supranational policies in a limited space with worldwide repercussions—all the while forgetting that people need local identities and loyalties in order to live and function. . . . We are now experiencing the return of regional loyalties and the rebirth of ethnicity.[17]

The search for new eschatologies is simply more visible in the East, where all social tensions are exacerbated and where the individual senses the tragic breakdown of old identities with more acuity. Cultural legacies are invoked to justify contemporary political choices. In all these countries, political movements have emerged that proclaim their affinities with the interrupted interwar traditions. And these traditions were not predominantly liberal. The region's political culture includes intense anti-Westernism, feudal romanticism, anticapitalism, and even anti-industrialism—all sentiments that preceded Communism. In pre–World War II Romania, Croatia, and Hungary, homegrown fascism resented capitalism and money-related activities as alien, corruptive, and destructive of national identity. These movements were defeated, or silenced, but much of the archaic, antimodern nostalgia they had appealed to remains. The phenomenon is worldwide: The return of neoromantic, anticapitalist mythology is part of the universal uneasiness with the boring, cold, calculated *zweckmässig* rationality of what Max Weber described as the "iron cage." Prophets and demagogues (often the same persons) who implicitly or explicitly denounce the heritage of the Enlightenment do have audiences in the East as well as in the West. The West, however, is better protected; institutions function impersonally, and procedures are deeply embedded in the civic cultures based on social trust.[18] In the post-Communist world, both civil and political societies are only incipient.

In my examination of these post-Communist uncertainties and the psycho-ideological responses to them, I call these anti-Enlightenment fantasies *myths* because they give a vivid image of reality and are rooted in imagination, approximation, and magic thought. They give vent to feelings of exhaustion regarding overblown rhetoric and to a popular sentiment that politicians and parliaments are in the business of cheating. Corruption is seen as a pandemic disease, which makes these societies more like Latin

America (or Southern Europe) than any Anglo-Saxon model of pluralism. At the same time, it is precisely this exhaustion of traditional worldviews, this postmodern syndrome of repudiation of grandiose teleological constructs in favor of minidiscourses, that is conducive to ennui and yearning for alternative visions that would not be fearful of boldness and inventiveness.

For example, although the post-Communist region is a secularized world, the desire for the sacred, New Age mystique, and religious revivalism is contagious. No less attractive are ideas that reject modernity, capitalism, and parliamentarism and exalt force, contempt for minorities, and action for action's sake.[19] Fascism as a phenomenon cannot be simply linked to one personality or the specific economic conditions in Italy, Germany, or Romania in the 1920s and 1930s. Its roots are to be found in the readiness of desperate masses to follow supremely self-confident and unwavering leaders.

To be sure, the cult of the providential savior is still limited to relatively small parties, but one should not forget how fast this fascination with the leader can grow under the conditions of mass anguish. Stern has emphasized the psychological appeals of nationalism and socialism as combined in the Nazi ideology; in times of axiological disarray, the need for belonging becomes paramount, whatever the price paid by the individual in terms of autonomy of the mind, dignity, and freedom.[20] All these phenomena cannot be severed from the more general disaffection with traditional politics in the West as well.

It is important to see why, in achieving the overthrow of Sovietism, many of the countries in Eastern Europe have not achieved liberal democracy or political stability.[21] While arguments can be made that democratic stability cannot happen without massive inflows of Western economic aid, my point is that a lack of capital is not *the* determining factor in the region's future. A nation's wealth is no guarantee of every citizen's liberal-democratic sensibility. More important, in my view, is the debility of social capital; the loss of emotional ties of solidarity between the members of the political community; the weakness, decline, or inertia of civil society; and the overall erosion of any source of authority. In the words of Wiktor Kulerski, a former Solidarity activist, the primary illness of the post-Communist societies is linked to their deeply entrenched attitude of suspicion, in which envy and hatred make individuals blind to the real choices and opportunities: "Not only do we have a skewed view of the world, the world itself is becoming skewed as a result of our manner of perceiving it. We live in a warped world of our own making, a world where we take our dreams and delusions for reality. We see threats where none exists and security where danger lies. We put our trust in swindlers and thieves as we reject and slander individuals of good sense and good will."[22] Kulerski's jeremiad is perhaps overstated, but it would be hard to deny that he highlights real aspects of the post-Communist collective anxieties and aggressiveness.

Discussed below are several complex internal factors that make the fall of Communism in Eastern Europe a disquieting victory indeed. Many other dangers, including external ones, are not discussed here.

THE LENINIST HERITAGE AND
TESTS OF NEW DEMOCRACIES

Of all the authors who acclaimed the breakdown of Communism in Eastern Europe, Ralf Dahrendorf has turned out to have been the most prescient in pointing to the many perils marking the road to an open society, especially in the light of the not-so-solid, that is, quite problematic, democratic traditions in the region.[23] After all, it was Karl Marx who, in his *Critique of the Gotha Program*, so clearly indicated that any new society would carry the marks of its birth for a long period of time. In the case of post-Communist countries, these marks include the habits, mores, visions, and mentalities (*formae mentis*) associated with the sectarian and militaristic faith called Leninism. Amazing as it may seem, the "new man," the *Homo sovieticus* extolled by the Communist propaganda, has become real—not in the Trotskyite utopian sense of the average communist man as more gifted than Aristotle and Goethe, but rather as an individual hostile to risk, to fair competition, and to pluralist values.[24]

Not only did people listen to the official Communist parlance but many internalized it. Collectivistic, panic-ridden, mobilizational rhetoric sounds familiar to them. It is enough to analyze political discourses of people as different as Boris Yeltsin, Ion Iliescu, Vladimir Meciar, Franjo Tudjman, or even Lech Walesa with his calls for a "war at the top," in order to recognize the persistence of a certain self-sufficiency so characteristic of the Leninist logic of monopolistic truth. Needless to say, these people have different philosophies, but they all share an authoritarian political style. As Leninists used to revere the "class viewpoint," these politicians all worship the ethnic nation as the ultimate reservoir of hope and the main source of individual dignity. True, some of them pay lip service to liberal values, but their true commitment is to a vision of politics that subordinates the individual to the interests of the nation-state (as defined by them, of course). Instead of valuing statesmanship and compromise, they play on neurotic sentiments of victimization. National consciousness is thus manipulated to legitimize nationalist practices of discrimination against minorities.[25] That the psychological background of certain populist leaders is often marked by deep traumas is of course an important element. But more important than the fact that both of Slobodan Milosevič's parents committed suicide has been the readiness of so many Serbian officials and intellectuals to endorse his policies.[26]

One sees that democratic institutions have emerged, that democratic elections have been held, and that the affliction of Balkanization so far plagues only the former Yugoslavia and bubbles in some areas of the former Soviet Union such as Abkhazia or Chechnya. Some authors believe that the democratic "habits of the heart" have set solid roots among politicians. In reality, however, democracy remains fragile and unloved. Constitutional pluralism is marred by its very universalistic formalism, by its coolness and lack of magnetizing virtues. It is based on procedures, not emotions. While individuals long for reassuring stories of glory and redemption, for the advent of some providential leader, democratic regimes offer them endless debates on laws and regulations and corrupt politicians.

Such thinking recalls the 1930s; when society was deeply split, and the constitutional foundations were widely questioned by desperate elites and mobilized mobs, the charismatic demagogue did not need any sophisticated demonstrations to arouse fanatical support. In Romania, Corneliu Zelea Codreanu, captain of the Iron Guard, was killed by King Carol's police in 1938, but the fanaticism of the Guard—Guard members chanting, "Let the Captain make a country like the holy sun in the sky"—outlived his death, leading to the horrible pogroms of 1940–41. In Germany, a Nazi slogan put it very clearly: "Our program consists of two words: Adolf Hitler!" Simplicity, ruthlessness, and violence become virtues, as the *novus dux* allures the masses into the new millennium of honor and grandeur. Identifying with him, following him against all odds, they partake in the mystical adventure that European messianic thinkers since Giacchino da Fiore have prophesized as the advent of the charismatic savior "with a scintillating forehead." Did not Hitler proclaim in front of his ecstatic votaries as early as 1924 that he was the "new light," the apostle that had seen the revelation: "It is the miracle of our age that you found me, and that you found me among so many millions of individuals. And the fact that I found you, this is the chance for Germany."[27]

Democracies are not prepared to provide such fantasies of ultimate regeneration. Recently born and still inexperienced, Eastern Europe's democracies have had difficulty adjusting to pressures resulting from collective efforts aimed at reverting, subverting, and obliterating the project of modernity (which I tentatively understand as the substantive construction of politics in an antiabsolutist, individualistic, and contractual way).[28] In many of these countries, reasserted presidentialism, ethnocentrism, dirigism, and etatism are reminiscent of Latin American (Perón-style) experiments in corporatism and authoritarian single-party rule.[29] Corporatism, after all, has a long tradition in the region. During the 1930s, Romanian economist Mihail Manoilescu was among the most influential theorists of revolutionary-nationalist corporatism. Such ideas seem to come back with a vengeance in the discourse of fundamentalist populists of various stripes (extreme Left or Right). Their appeal in the 1990s, like fascism's in the 1930s, is linked to their ability to "combine resentful nationalism with a plausible theory of economic development that emphasized authoritarianism, mass mobilization of the population, and the retention of supposedly traditional, pure, non-Western values."[30]

But this "return of the repressed," real and often disturbing, does not exhaust the picture. Indeed, with all the predicaments and setbacks, the spiritual condition of Europe (and Eastern Europe in particular) is crucial to the attempt at *the reinvention of politics*. As Julia Kristeva so cogently insists:

> The problem of the twentieth century was and remains the rehabilitation of the political. An impossible task? A useless task? Hitler and Stalin perverted the project into a deathly totalitarianism. The collapse of communism in Eastern Europe,

which calls into question, beyond socialism, the very basis of the democratic governments that stemmed from the French Revolution, demands that one re-think that basis so that the twenty-first century will not be the reactional domain of fundamentalism, religious illusions, and ethnic wars.[31]

Kristeva's essay highlights the uncertainties of this political drama, the possible fractures, delusions, and pathologies, and the still untested freedoms and new forms of human solidarity.[32]

The growing political appeals and uses of myths and the omnipresent selective memory (and forgetfulness) have led to the resurrection of historical phantoms (for example, Admiral Miklos Horthy, the Iron Guard's Codreanu, Marshal Antonescu, and Ustasha leader Ante Pavelić). Obsessive self-pity, the absence of empathy, and the inability to mourn with others or to understand their plight is indicative of a general collective self-centeredness that constructs fences around the in-group and elaborate, manufactured, inhibiting images about the "Other." Even when expelled from the Krajina region in Croatia in 1995, Serbs resisted being resettled in Kosovo among the "inferior" Albanians. In turn, Albanians see the coming of Serbian refugees as part of an old plan to alter the ethnic structure of the region (whose population of two million is 90 percent Albanian).[33] Indeed, this exclusive national arrogance is a latter-day expression of what Sigmund Freud called the "narcissism of minor differences."[34]

But, once again, is this phenomenon uniquely East European? Can we not link these explosions of nationalism to the rejection of a civilizational model based on the disenchantment of the world and the longing for collective identities (ethnic or religious)? Are not these new (or not so new) fantasies part of a more widespread need to redefine identity and authority in a post-Leninist and post-utopian world? Are not the March 1994 elections in Italy as disturbing as the fascist revival in the East? One could thus argue that the absence of legitimizing signals from the West and the presumed reconciliation between Western intelligentsia and liberalism, the invention of the "democratic intellectual," diminish the chances for the Eastern neofundamentalists to really enjoy a second life.[35] But this argument seems to have been mooted by the Italian events, with the breakdown of the Center, the paralysis of the Left, and the extraordinary mobilization of the far Right, a Right that impossibly combines "Italy First–ism," xenophobia, regionalism, an anachronistic anti-Marxism, and Silvio Berlusconi's *condottiere*-cum-buffoon histrionics on television. The failure of this coalition did not alter the fact that old-fashioned party politics in Italy is finished. Indeed, the Italian case shows that ideological labels born out of the French Revolution are outworn. Post–Cold War Europeans are simply tired of the traditional parliamentary waltzing. In the meantime, new ideas, which are neither Left nor Right, have emerged that advocate either a new internationalism or a resurrection of community-based loyalties.[36]

In the East, the landscape is utterly puzzling. The achievements cannot be simply dismissed. Since 1989, East Central European societies have evolved from authoritarian, ideologically monistic, extremely centralized, and bureaucratically corrupt regimes toward protodemocratic forms of political and economic organization. To focus exclusively on their difficulties during the transition period is to miss the drama of social and political experimentation in that region. To deny these dangers is myopic and in the long run would be disastrous.[37]

The region has inherited a combination of pre-Communist and Communist forms of authoritarian Manichean thought; even the most adamant anti-Leninists today adhere to the logic of "Whoever is not with us is against us." This is indeed the profound meaning of Adam Michnik's rebuff of "anti-Communism with a Bolshevik face," a symptom he diagnosed among the most vocal proponents of radical decommunization. For generations, these people have been deprived of the chance of dialogue, their ears exposed to the monotonous rhythms of the official propaganda delivering the same trite platitudes again and again. And now, suddenly, they hear so many voices, so many discourses, each one competing with each other, each one disrupting each other. The past seems harmonious, the present chaotic, confusing, and troublesome.

Not without melancholy, one can ask what do Benjamin Constant, John Stuart Mill, and Alexis de Tocqueville have to say to these people of the post-Leninist world? Furthermore, we have to assess the meaning of the great transformations unleashed by the cataclysmic events of 1989. Are the newly awakened societies propitious for pluralism? Or, as G. M. Tamás argues, will the upper hand eventually belong to illiberal, antimodern, ultranationalist demagogues? "When the heady wine of socialist utopia evaporated from the poisoned chalice of Soviet 'federalism,' what was to hold the tribes together?"[38] Indeed, what could keep together all these groups and individuals for whom Sovietism meant a way of life, a form of survival, an escape from responsibility? And how many of those who took to the streets in 1989 do not regret today the relative tranquillity and infinite boredom of state socialism?

Can the revolutionary promises, which at least during the period immediately following 1989 were predominantly civic and "cosmopolitan," be, to use Bruce Ackerman's term, constitutionalized?[39] What are the chances for these countries to build up a *constitutio libertatis*, to rid themselves of their legacies of autarchy, obscurantism, "tribalism," and resentments and safeguard the recently acquired areas of autonomy?[40] Thus formulated, the issue bears upon the future of the region, of Europe, and of international security. Ken Jowitt's warning is apposite:

> Liberal capitalist democracy has aroused a heterogeneous set of opponents: Romantic poets, Persian ayatollahs, the Roman Catholic Church, and fascists. For all the real and massive differences that separate these oppositions, one can detect a shared critique. Liberal capitalist democracy is scorned for an inordinate emphasis on individual materialism, technical achievement, and rationality . . .

[and] for undervaluing the essential collective dimension of human existence [and the] human need for security.[41]

CULTURE OF DISILLUSIONMENT

Intellectual stupor, moral disarray, and yearning for the "magic savior" are symptoms of the post-Communist culture of disillusionment. In the language of political science, it is identified by the Polish philosopher Marcin Krol as a "cognitive mess," by Ken Jowitt as a "new world disorder," and by Martin Jacques as a post–Cold War political and intellectual anarchy linked to the disappearance of the adversarial image. The end of the Soviet Union as the absolute (constitutive) Other has left the West without a clear-cut symbol of the enemy. In the East, a whole institutional universe has fallen apart. The ideological extinction of Leninist formations left behind a cultural chaos in which emerged syncretic constructs that draw from the pre-Communist and Communist authoritarian, often irrational heritage.

The moral identities of individuals have been shattered by the dissolution of all the established values and "icons." There are immense continuity gaps in both social and personal memory; the same arguments that ensured one's career before 1989 played the opposite role after that watershed year. Being well connected with the party bureaucracy and secret police was once a sign of political trustworthiness in these countries, ensuring not only social success but also a relative economic prosperity; after the revolutions, the same background became, at least initially, a liability. Thousands and thousands of teachers in all these countries (except the former East Germany, where most were replaced by Westerners) used to lecture on the universal truth of "scientific socialism"; now they praise the virtues of the market economy. Too many moral zigzags, too many political travesties, have created a sense of deep cynicism among the citizens. There is very little public trust and only a vague recognition of the need for a shared vision of the public good. Assuming responsibility for personal actions, risk taking, and questioning of institutions on the basis of legitimate claims for improvement are still in embryonic stages.[42]

For Czech philosopher and former Charter 77 activist Martin Palouš, the prospects for democratic development depend on the civic awareness of the real stakes involved in the ongoing political struggles: "The most important and most dynamic factor in post-totalitarian politics has to do with the way people in post-communist societies perceive and conceptualize the social reality and political processes they are a part of."[43] The difficulties and ambiguities of the Left–Right polarization in post-Communist regimes are linked to the ambiguity and even obsolescence of the traditional taxonomies. Marxism and Leninism have ceased to be exhilarating ideological projects, and the references to the Left (in its radical version, at least) are opportunistic gestures rather than expressions of genuine commitment. As Michnik once wrote, "the issue is not whether one is left or right of center, but West of center." Liberal values are thus seen by some as Left-oriented simply because they emphasize secularism, tolerance, and individual rights; the different varieties of radicalism, including "civic" or "ethical," clericalism, or even theocratic fundamentalism do not. At the same time, as shown in new radical-authoritarian trends (often disguised as pro-democratic) in Russia, Ukraine, Bulgaria, Romania, Slovakia, and so forth, lingering reflexes and habits inherited from Leninist and pre-Leninist authoritarianisms continue to exist: intolerance, exclusiveness, rejection of any compromise, extreme personalization of the political discourse, and longing for charismatic leadership.

The ideological syncretism of "Stalino-fascism" capitalizes on the delays in the exercise of political justice. In reality, the instant of such an approach was universally missed, even at the level of a genuine historical debate.[44] Demagoguery, hollow rhetoric, and the continuous indulgence in scapegoating, as well as fictitious boundaries between "martyrs" and "criminals," undermine the legitimacy of the existing institutions and allow the rise of ethnocentric crackpots.[45] This repression of a public discussion is bound to fuel discontent and frustrations, thus encouraging demagogues and mafiosi.[46] Instead of lucid analyses of the past, new mythologies are created to explain the current predicament. In the Czech Republic, for instance, the Right has obsessively claimed that the Velvet Revolution was in fact a conspiracy fomented by Freemasons, the CIA, the KGB, and the Mossad. In Poland, it is frequently said that the resurrection of the former Communists indicates that the revolution had been just a smoke screen to ensure their conversion into the new capitalists.

Former *Securitate* colonel Filip Teodorescu was directly involved in the savage repression of the anti-Ceauşescu demonstrators in Timişoara in December 1989. Released from prison after a short term, he published a memoir full of surreal stories about foreign plots to destroy Romania's sovereignty. Another ex-intelligence officer, Pavel Coruţ, specializes in novels that combine Thracian-Dacian mythology, Orthodox symbolism, science-fiction, and the exaltation of *Securitate* officers as the supermen of Romanian-ness who thwart the vicious conspiracies of foreigners, primarily Hungarians who want to dismember the country and take Transylvania back. Coruţ's novels sell hundreds of thousands of copies and, in spite of their lunatic fabrications, many read them literally—another instance of what pop psychology calls "magic thinking" (or reading).

Political corruption, economic frustrations, and cultural despair are the ingredients for the rise of the anomic mass phenomena of panic, belief in miracles, millennial expectations, pseudochiliasms, and sectarian magic. This was demonstrated, for instance, in the case of the "Caritas" pyramid scam in Cluj, Romania. In that city in 1992–93, more than two million Romanians put all their savings into the hands of a self-appointed savior, Ion Stoica, who announced that every single player in the Caritas "mutual aid" society would get back eight times the amount of his or her invested sum. Called the "New

Messiah," he turned out to be a con man in league with local elites, the secret police, and Gheorghe Funar, the notorious nationalist mayor of Cluj.[47] Writer William McPherson reported that booklets that praised Stoica for his presumed patriotic performance were circulated. One of them, signed by an Orthodox priest, elaborated on the salvationist meaning of Caritas: "But how would Clujeans be happy, or Transylvanians, if they had neither food nor money to buy food . . . ? Who made himself happy? Only foreigners in our land! . . . The Caritas phenomenon has come as a divine phenomenon, not only for men, that they should have money and happiness, but as the salvation of the Romanian people."[48] Of significance here is the mass psychosis, the readiness of thousands of Romanians and Hungarians to endow a charlatan with the attributes of a demigod. Social malaise and anomie have fed gullibility and delusional thinking.

NOSTALGIA AND POST-COMMUNIST POSSIBILITIES

There is a growing nostalgia for the old regime and the revival of reactionary rhetoric.[49] But is this restoration truly possible? For such a development to take place, ideological zeal and utopian-eschatological motivation are needed. Mircea Snegur in Moldova, Zhan Videnov in Bulgaria, Algirdas Brazauskas in Lithuania, Ion Iliescu in Romania, Kiro Gligorov in Macedonia, Vladimir Meciar in Slovakia, Milan Kucan in Slovenia, and Slobodan Milosevič in Serbia are all former Communists. But they are not neo-Communists, in the sense of being committed to a certain political and economic vision inspired by the doctrines of Marx and Lenin. They are rather cynical pragmatists, chameleonlike survivors, ready to espouse any creed with lightning speed if it upholds their stay in power.

For a genuine Left to emerge, its proponents need to rethink the reasons for the Communist debacle and assume their intellectual and moral responsibility. In discussing Latin America, Mexican political scientist Jorge Castañeda captures well this post–Cold War dilemma: "The left found itself in a no-win situation. Either it stuck to its guns—which were not really its own, but were foisted on it—and defended the undefendable, a state-run, closed, subsidized economy in a world in which such a notion seemed totally obsolete; or it turned around and supported the opposite, apparently modern, competitive, free-market course. In that case it ended up imitating—or being assimilated by—the right and losing its raison d'être."[50]

In addition, the successor formations to the Leninist parties have to cope with a widespread disaffection toward any explicit socialist rhetoric.[51] The cases of Russia's Communists, headed by Gennady Zyuganov, and the Romanian Socialist Party of Labor, chaired by Ilie Verdeţ (one of Ceauşescu's former prime ministers), are emblematic of the current trend toward the cooperation between radical nationalist forces and those nostalgic for bureaucratic collectivism. The foundation of this trend is the ideological vacuum created by the collapse of state socialism, with populism being the most convenient and frequently the most appealing ersatz ideology. And, as we know, populism is neither left nor right. As Argentine dictator Juan Domingo Perón used to say, "I have two hands, a left and a right. I use each one whenever convenient."[52]

The landscape of loss and uncertainty is fertile ground for paranoid visions of conspiracy and treason, hence the nationalist salvationism as a substitute for what Freud described as the "oceanic sentiment." Exaggerated as they may be, references to "Weimar Russia" capture the psychology of vast numbers of people whose traditional set of collectivistic values has collapsed and who cannot find their way among the often contradictory new ones based on individual action, risk, and intense competition. Similar trends exist in Bulgaria, Poland, and Hungary (for example, populist, anti-Semitic writer Istvan Csurka's Hungarian Life and Justice party).

Furthermore, the distortion of the past is not limited to the Communist period and has produced some truly bizarre effects. The rehabilitation in Romania, for example, of Marshal Antonescu has been accompanied by eulogies of the marshal's legitimate persecutions of the "ungrateful species of cheaters and exploiters." The need for protection, for authority, for "order and rigorous discipline," and the yearning for the "Father" (cruel, brutal, but always present) explain why thousands of Romanians on January 26, 1995, went to lay flowers on Ceaușescu's tomb. As there is yearning in Russia for Stalin's days of certitude, there is increasing nostalgia in Romania for Ceaușescu's days of equality (even if only in misery).

The politics of suspicion, calumny, and paranoia is not a figment of fervid imaginations but an everyday experience in most of Central and Eastern Europe. Social demagoguery and populist exploitation of mass discontent represent one face of the post-Communists' tactics. The 1994 elections in Belarus brought to power Aleksandr Lukashenko, a demagogue ready to promise everything to everybody (is this reminiscent of Peru? of Italy?). A former Communist Party member and state farm manager, Lukashenko in his campaign combined anticorruption with anticapitalism and offered only vague responses to the truly painful problems that his country is confronting. Successfully banking on mass disaffection with the government's ineptitude, Lukashenko declared: "The current privatization scheme will be stopped within days after I become President. We will just take everything back and get everybody working again."[53] Similar statements assured the electoral victories of ex-Communists in Romania, Serbia, and Slovakia (less so in Poland). The political comeback of the "comrades" is to a great extent the result of their ability to blend social populism with ethnic radicalism.

FLUIDITY OF POLITICAL FORMATIONS AND VALUES CRISIS

With a private sector and entrepreneurial class still in the making, political liberalism and the civic culture associated with it are under siege. Politically, the most important sectors to be reformed are the legal and the military ones; as long as property rights are not fully guaranteed, economic reforms cannot really succeed. Strategy is as important as tactics, and the will to reform is as important as the articulation of concrete goals.

But political parties in most of these countries are coalitions of personal and group affinities, rather than collective efforts based on the common awareness of short- and long-term interests—hence fragmentation, divisiveness, political convulsions, and instability.[54] Think of the avatars of the Democratic (Freedom) Union in Poland or of the Alliance of Free Democrats in Hungary; although counting among their leaders some of their countries' brightest minds, neither of these parties managed to establish strong bases outside the major cities. They have remained, in more than one respect, discussion clubs. As they opposed lustration-style decommunization, their enemies could easily brand them as crypto-leftist.

The weakness of the political parties is primarily determined by the *general crisis of values and authority* and the no-less-widespread skepticism regarding a *culture of deliberation*. A "social glue" is needed, but the existing formations have failed to build the consensus needed in order to generate "constitutional patriotism." The strong attacks against opponents of radical decommunization (such as Tadeusz Mazowiecki and Zhelyu Zhelev) as "protectors of the establishment" are an expression of the search for a second revolution, rooted in the need for protection from the changes of the transition and in a neoromantic populism. If it gathers momentum, this trend could jeopardize the still-precarious pluralist institutions. People sense a "betrayal of the politicians" and desire "the new purity." This is the rationale for Csurka's "radical revolutionism" as well as the political resurrection of the former Communist parties (for example, in Lithuania, Romania, and Bulgaria). What is the meaning of the Left–Right dichotomy when the ex-Communists often carry out programs as inimical to their supporters' interests as those of the execrated free marketeers? In the words of a disaffected Polish citizen: "I voted for the communists, but they cheated and lied to us. It's much worse under the former communists than it ever was under the center-right governments."[55] Here is expressed the impotent fury against the state for failing to behave as a patriarchal "good father." Peter Reddaway correctly labeled this yearning for the state as a nostalgia for the protective "nanny."[56]

THE ABSENCE OF A NEW POLITICAL CLASS

Delays in the coalescence of a political class are also linked to the weakness of a democratic elite; political values remain vague, programs tend to overlap, and corruption is rampant. (This situation is particularly dangerous in Russia, where there is a conspicuous absence of political competition between ideologically defined and distinct parties.) The distances between political parties are often minuscule, and only personal vanities can explain why an individual decides to join one particular party instead of another. True, Hungary's FIDESZ (Federation of Young Democrats) distinguished itself by its nonconformist style, remarkable legal expertise, and the decision to keep the age of thirty-five as an upper limit for party membership—but its ideological program was not markedly distinct from the Free Democrats. Yet, instead of attacking the populist Democratic Forum, FIDESZ leaders spent their time disassociating themselves from the Free Democrats rather than allying itself with this party to which it was closest. Consequently, after a brief period of immense popularity, FIDESZ lost momentum and at the 1994 elections suffered a major defeat.

A political class needs a political myth to fully identify with, what Italian sociologist Gaetano Mosca called a political formula. To enjoy credibility, the new elites have to demonstrate that they are different from the old ones. Their legitimacy is linked as much to their professed espousal of democratic values as to their ability to live up to their pledges. This is precisely what is missing in most of these countries; while everybody speaks about constitutionalism and democracy, there is little consensus on the meaning of these terms.

Further, instead of new, clean faces, people notice the perpetuation of the old elites with new masks. In Russia, the case of Aleksandr Yakovlev is emblematic. First an ideologue under Leonid Brezhnev, then ambassador to Canada, he became Gorbachev's chief doctrinaire and a fervent proponent of *perestroika*. Later, he broke with Gorbachev, resigned from the Communist Party in 1990, and joined the Yeltsin camp. Between 1993 and 1995, he served as chairman of government-controlled television. For many Russians, the political survival of people like Yakovlev is an indication that no revolution took place. Similar cases can be documented in other political groups as well, with former ideological apparatchiks converted to the new discourses in favor of free market and pluralism. Some have no masks at all: For several years, Yeltsin's chief personal guard was a former KGB officer whose sole political credential was his personal loyalty to the Russian president.

The most striking illustration of this elite continuity is, in my view, Romania. President Iliescu is a former party ideologue who was demoted by Ceauşescu because of his mild criticism of the dictator's most egregious measures. Never a dissident, Iliescu remains attached to what he liked to call "the noble ideals of socialism." The free market and an open society are notions he has long distrusted and even despised. Especially after 1992, Romania's political class was dominated by individuals who had been directly involved in the old regime's policies. Democratic forces were fragmented and beset by inner conflicts, and the government continued to postpone significant reforms. Nationalist sloganeers became members of the government, while former dissidents found themselves isolated and viciously besmirched. Looking into the situation in countries like Russia, Serbia, Romania, and Slovakia, one is sometimes tempted to recall a sad line in Giuseppe di Lampedusa's novel *The Leopard*: "In order for nothing to change, everything had to change"—at least in appearances, if not in content.

THE SPLIT BETWEEN INDIVIDUALISTIC
AND COMMUNITARIAN VALUES

Because the political space is still extremely volatile, ideological labels conceal at least as much as they reveal. As Adam Michnik and others have consistently stated, the urgent choice and conflict are between personalities, parties, and movements that advocate individualism, diversity of thought, an open society, and risk taking, on the one hand, and those who promise security within a homogenizing (and mythological) nation-state, on the other. Although opinion polls in the whole region indicate strong support for democracy, rights awareness is still low, and so is the degree of tolerance for minorities. Many who claim to favor democracy do indeed support new forms of fundamentalism viscerally inimical to liberal individualism.

In Poland, for instance, this opposition takes the form of a struggle between the proponents of a liberal, secular republic and those who believe that the Catholic Church as a national institution has the right to impose political values. Clericalism is still a marginal trend, but many Poles found disturbing the Church's insistence on religious education in schools and its efforts to issue antiabortion legislation. To be sure, there are enlightened sectors within Polish Catholicism that do not share the vision of an organically united nation under God. But there is also support for strong voices that speak of the role of the Church in terms of a moral crusade for the "reconquest of Poland" by the "true Catholics." In their endeavors to wrench the country from the hands of "leftists," they define Polishness exclusively on the basis of a common religious identity. Their ideology is imbued with the belief that "the Church knows no limits." As Michnik put it with characteristic poignancy:

> The primary challenge confronting democracy in the post-Communist era is religious fundamentalism. The controversy over the place of religion and of the church in a democratic country is the focal point of the debate over the form that democracy is to take in Poland. This question conceals an even broader issue: Will the utopia of totalitarian communism be replaced by a democratic order, a tolerant nation and a pluralist society; or will it be replaced by a new utopia based on religious or ethnic ideologies—the instruments of a new servitude?[57]

TYRANNY OF THE MAJORITY

Political reform in all these post-Communist societies has not gone far enough in creating and safely guarding the countermajoritarian institutions (independent media, market economy, and political parties) needed to diminish the threat of new authoritarian experiments catering to the subliminal but powerful egalitarian-populist sentiments.[58] The main dangers are the formulas linked to etatism, clericalism, religious fundamentalism, ethnocentrism, and militaristic fascism. These themes appear clearly in the discourse of the ethnocratic populism as evinced by Marian Munteanu's "Movement for Romania" and among supporters of Serbia's Slobodan Milosevič and the xenophobic groups and movements generically described as the "Russian party."[59] The key question of democracy's future therefore is linked to the risks for further political fragmentation in the region, with the more developed countries (Poland, Hungary, the Baltic states, and the Czech Republic) developing a culture of impersonal democratic procedures, and the southern tier and most of the successor states of the Soviet Union increasingly beset by what Ken Jowitt refers to as "movements of rage." All these threats create a generally disenchanted political landscape. Dispirited political cultures are plagued by the rise of new collectivisms, the marginalization of the former heroes, and, more recently, by the return of the former Communists (in fact, in Romania and Serbia, they never left). Michnik's term for this general trend is "the velvet restoration," which he sees as inevitable. He assumes that it may help these societies avoid Jacobin-style "second revolutions." He may be right, but at the same time one should not forget the deep causes of the 1989 collapse: The Communist elites had failed miserably in their attempt to create Utopia. Without their ideological legitimation, they were completely lost and eventually had to give up power. They still have nothing to offer in terms of ideological resources, unless they combine nationalism with a sense of communitarian vision.

I propose the concept of "velvet counterrevolution" to indicate the direction of this phenomenon, especially as indicated in the rise of strong anti-intellectual and illiberal trends. Independent thinkers are derided as "leftists," "sentimental dreamers," and "incurable moralists." To be sure, these sentiments had existed under the Communist regimes, and much of their subliminal motivations did indeed communicate with the official ideology. Unlike Ceauşescu's nationalist socialism in Romania, Kadarism in Hungary was not xenophobic, but both included strong egalitarian and collectivistic components, whose resurrection in the post-Communist discourses is not too astonishing. When other ideological devices turned out to be impotent, Communist regimes played on the chord of national pride. They all insisted that, thanks to Leninist policies, their societies had escaped economic underdevelopment.

Although the post-Leninist parties made spectacular comebacks, they have not asked for tribunals and other forms of vengeance. This is obviously an indication that the refusal to organize collective political justice was after all the correct approach. Otherwise, these societies would have been caught in an endless succession of purges. The argument that, had the Communists been excluded from political life *en bloc,* their return would have been impossible, or at least more difficult, does not stand logical scrutiny. In reality, collective punishments generate collective hatreds and deep suspicions about the role of an independent judiciary. When crimes can be identified, they must be examined individually, in full respect of the legal procedures. Offering immediate satisfaction in the form of retroactive justice to radicalized masses can provide only temporary benefits. For example, the argument I heard from those involved in the decision to kill the Ceauşescus was that had he been alive, his fanatic supporters (the "terrorists") would never have given up their resistance to the new regime. In reality, no "terrorist" was ever brought to trial, and the parody of justice inflicted on the dictatorial couple sullied Romania's revolution from its very beginning.

It was not my purpose in this chapter to put forward Cassandra-like apocalyptic scenarios for post-Communist societies. More than one possible future can be reasonably thought through, and the likelihood for the worst-case scenario—Eastern Europe run by neofascist, paranoid dictators engaged in ethnic cleansing and foreign aggressions—is somewhat dubious.[60] Although a tempting exercise in political thought, cataclysmic forecasts are much too hyperbolic and defy evidential demonstration. *Bellum omnium contra omnes*, a state of wild and protracted anarchy, and the loss of the recently acquired civic rights in favor of Stalino-fascist simulations of cohesion and collective will are not in the offing in most of the post-Leninist states. Ralf Dahrendorf's imagination was trembling in 1990, envisioning grotesque militaristic regimes strangling the new democracies and fascist police states replacing the budding democratic governments. So far these predictions have not come true, but the potential for ethnocratic or theocratic experiments still exists because certainly an involvement with ethnocentric, religious fundamentalist, and racist politics has begun.

Again, the most obvious and horrific example of staunch nationalist discourses and ethnocentrism being used by elites interested in nothing but power is the dissolution of Yugoslavia. The exploitation of real or imaginary grief, collective wounds, offended identities, and the exacerbation of sentiments of humiliation, panic, and insecurity are real ammunition for prophets of hatred and envy in all the post-Communist nations. The feelings of betrayal, especially in Russia, and the Third World–ist, populist belief that the West's ambitions are dictated by greed and contempt for the less-modernized nations of the East are motifs used and abused by the neopopulists (Slavophiles, Hungarophiles, Romanophiles, and other ethnocentric demagogues) throughout the region. This type of xenophobic, anti-Western, and antiliberal rhetoric was skillfully used by Andreas Papandreou and his Panhellenic Socialist party (PASOK) in the 1970s. Describing his movement as revolutionary and dynamic, Papandreou often declared his opposition to "optimistic liberal thought."[61]

New homogenizing discourses and spiteful narratives of betrayal and victimization have emerged to offer immediate consolation for sentiments of loss, despondency, and historical helplessness. Zbigniew Brzezinski identified the rise of "metamyths" as a salient feature of our times. These cultural archetypes are adjusted to meet the need for metapolitical answers to the widespread, often excruciatingly burdensome consciousness of crisis, and offer what I call fantasies of salvation.[62] Brzezinski accurately sees these myths as "an irrational but compelling blend of religious impulse to seek salvation, of the nationalist self-identification as being superior to outsiders, and of utopian social doctrines reduced to the level of popular slogans."[63]

Nowhere do Isaiah Berlin's thoughts on the rise of nationalism in what might be called "battered societies" more appropriately apply than in the devastated moral landscapes of post-Bolshevik Russia and post-Titoist Yugoslav states. In these worlds of disarray, moral anarchy, and triumph of the demagogue, there is propitious ground for the most eccentric discourses of resentment. Xenophobic nationalism, combined with neo-Darwinism and Nazi-style racism, are part of the rise of the vindictive, pseudochiliastic mythologies.

I say "pseudochiliastic" because the salvation they promise is one based on elimination, exclusion, and marginalization of the very category of Otherness. It is not the universalistic call for the unity of mankind in the glory of redemption, but rather the achievement of self-esteem by destroying, punishing, castigating, and stigmatizing the different, the nonconformists, the archetypal "foreigner." The purity of the race, allegedly tarnished by aliens, gays, or cosmopolitan vermin, is a theme that emerges in the discourses of new political movements from Zagreb to Bucharest and from Budapest to St. Petersburg. They draw on and elaborate on the Stalinist obsessions with the capitalist world conspiracy, but add to these the myth of the "universal Jew" ominously lurking behind every single political or economic event.

Such nationalist movements and protoparties appeal to the sentiments of frustration, anguish, and isolation and to the general and contagious feelings of abandonment and alienation; that desperation and failure seem to be the hallmark of the post-Communist psychological condition. People look for solid points, for sources of moral inspiration, and what they see instead is corruption, arbitrariness, cynicism, and rapaciousness.

A number of disturbing questions arise that beg for critical and enlightening scrutiny: Whatever happened to the ethical, transnational project of "civil society" and "Central Europe"? Was the celebration of dissent more the result of the Western intelligentsia's narcissistic projection and search for political atonement than expression of homegrown intellectual and moral trends?[64] How can one account for the rise of the communitarian, collectivistic, and egalitarian paradigm that simply (or not so simply) reconverts, refunctionalizes, and reshapes the same values that underlay the defunct Communist project? How can these societies reconcile their predominantly nonliberal political cultures (excluding the Czech Republic, to be sure) with the yearning to belong to Europe? No less significant, especially in the light of Samuel Huntington's somewhat ramshackle hypothesis on probable "clashes of civilizations," is the interpretation of cultural fault lines in Europe.[65] Do the Balkans belong to "the West," or are they irretrievably part of the "rest"?

After the extinct period of "legitimation from the top" (through ideological rituals of simulated participation, mobilization, and regimentation), it seems that, in most of these countries, the nascent process of legal-procedural legitimation is paralleled (or countered) by something that, echoing Eric Hobsbawm's insightful analysis of the new discourses of hatred, could be called "legitimation from the past."[66] The more inchoate and nebulous this past, the more aggressive, feverish, and intolerant the proponents of the neoromantic mythologies. In my view, the redemptive, vindictive, scapegoating, and neo-utopian myths are tending to become prevalent in these societies, forming their ideological bases.[67] Again, I use the term *myth* in the broadest sense, indicating the world of fantasies, illusions, expectations, and yearnings, rooted in anguish, doubt, and uncertainty, and often rationalized as political messianism and other radical discourses. On the one hand, the rise of nationalism as compensation for perceived failure and externally imposed marginality and as a means of flight from the complexities of modernity into the politics of collective salvation is linked to this ambiguous Leninist legacy and to the pre-Leninist, ethnic-oriented cultural forms in the region. On the other hand, the eastern part of Europe is not the only candidate for the embrace of these follies. I think that we deal with a resilient, persistent form of barbarism that, again, is situated in the very heart of modernity.

Nationalism is the absolute exacerbation of difference, its reification, the rejection of the claim to a common humanity, and the proclamation of the ethnonational distinction as the primordial fact of human existence.[68] A maxim dear to the hearts of intellectuals like Hannah Arendt, Walter Benjamin, and Adam Michnik, who rehabilitated the notion of *pariah* and emphasized the nobility of exclusion versus the humiliation of forced inclusion, was written many years ago by Franz Grillparzer: "From humanity, through nationality, to barbarity."

NOTES

To the memory of Ferenc Fehér. An earlier version of this chapter was presented as a paper at a conference organized by the Symposium on Science, Reason, and Modern Democracy at Michigan State University, East Lansing, Michigan, April 21–24, 1994. The author benefited from important comments from G. M. Tamás and Martin Palous.

1. This point was made clear by Miklos Haraszti in his "Paradigm of the Boots," in Vladimir Tismaneanu and Judith Shapiro, eds., *Debates of the Future of Communism* (London: Macmillan, 1991), 45–49.

2. Václav Havel, "The Post-Communist Nightmare," *New York Review of Books,* May 27, 1993, 8.

3. In Hungary, for instance, the government run by the former Communists (in alliance with the Liberal Democrats) initiated in March 1995 a reform of the Kádár welfare system more drastic than anything advocated by the liberal parties.

4. For excellent analyses of the November 1995 Polish presidential elections that led to Lech Walesa's defeat and the victory of the post-Communist politician Aleksander Kwasniewski, see Timothy Garton Ash, "'Neo-Pagan' Poland," *New York Review of Books*, January 11, 1996, 10–14; and Wiktor Osiatynski, "After Walesa," *East European Constitutional Review* 4, no. 4 (Fall 1995): 35–44.

5. Thomas Orr, "The Far Right in the Czech Republic," *Uncaptive Minds* 6, no. 1 (Winter–Spring 1993): 67–72. A similar case is Gheorghe Funar, the mayor of Cluj, Romania, whose anti-Hungarian rhetoric was the vehicle for his lightning political ascent as chairman of the Romanian National Unity party, the political branch of the ultranationalist *Vatra Românescă* (Romanian Hearth) movement.

6. In November 1995, the alliance between Romania's ruling (presidential) party and some of the extremists came to a provisional end as Vadim Tudor's representatives were forced to leave the government. It is still too early to decide whether the acerbic polemics between Vadim and Iliescu's supporters will result in a restructuring of Romania's political alliances. Be that as it may, one cannot simply dismiss the exchange as a "family quarrel."

7. For a most insightful analysis of the implications of these elections, see Aleksander Smolar, "The Poland of Kwasniewski," *Tygadnik Powszechny*, January 7, 1996 (English translation in FBIS–Eastern Europe, February 1, 1996, 48–56).

8. Michael Ignatieff, "The Politics of Self-Destruction," *New York Review of Books*, November 2, 1995, 17–19; and Laura Silber and Allan Little, *The Death of Yugoslavia* (London: Penguin, 1995).

9. For Karadžič's career, see Roger Cohen, "Karadžič's Bosnian War: Myth Becomes Madness," *New York Times*, June 4, 1995. In 1995, the Russian Writers' Union (dominated by nationalists) bestowed on Karadžič the Sholokhov Prize.

10. Many of my points on the Yugoslav catastrophe owe much to my discussions with historian Nicholas J. Miller.

11. Robin Blackburn, "The Break-up of Yugoslavia and the Fate of Bosnia," *New Left Review* (May–June 1993): 100.

12. Slavo Žižek, "Ethnic Danse Macabre," *The Guardian*, August 22, 1992, quoted in Blackburn, "Break-up of Yugoslavia," 101.

13. Ken Jowitt, "Dizzy with Democracy," *Problems of Post-Communism* 43, no. 1 (January–February 1996): 4.

14. "'The Best World We Have Yet Had': A Conversation with Sir Karl Popper," in G. R. Urban, *End of Empire: The Demise of the Soviet Union* (Washington: American University Press, 1993), 208.

15. See Georges Mink's distinctions among "partis consensuelists, tribunitiens et querelleurs," in his "Les partis politiques de l'Europe centrale post-communiste; état des lieux et essai de typologie," *L'Europe centrale et orientale en 1992* (Paris: Documentation française, 1993), 21–23.

16. Jane Perlez, "Hungarians Rally to Cry of Old Party," *New York Times*, July 29, 1995.

17. Wolf Lepenies, "The Future of the Intellectuals," *Partisan Review* 1 (Winter 1994): 117–18. Lepenies has a drastic view of this defeat of the critical intelligentsia after the short-lived moment of an euphoric *état de grâce* when they thought the spirit had come to power in 1989: "The illusion that intellectuals can participate in European politics has faded" (113). But this is still a topic to be debated. Maybe the "revolution of the intellectuals" has failed, but the role of the intellectual in defending the values of spiritual autonomy and protest against the triumph of philistine activity remains as urgent as

ever. Instead of renunciation and melancholy bowing to the status quo, critical intellectuals still have a significant position in their societies. After all, even in France, the role of the critical intelligentsia was to sensitize public opinion to the prevailing lies about the Vichy regime. The same can be said about Germany, where intellectuals have been among the most perceptive critics of the post-1990 arrogance of the former West Germans toward the new German citizens from the old East Germany.

18. Francis Fukuyama, *Trust: The Social Virtues and the Creation of Prosperity* (New York: Free Press, 1995).

19. For the persistence of the Fascist syndrome, see Umberto Eco, "Ur-Fascism," *New York Review of Books,* June 22, 1995, 12–15.

20. Fritz Stern, *Dreams and Delusions: The Drama of German History* (New York: Knopf, 1987).

21. What has emerged, however, is a novel political structure that Lenard Cohen accurately described as "ethnic democracy." See his *Broken Bonds: The Disintegration of Yugoslavia* (Boulder: Westview, 1993).

22. Wiktor Kulerski, "The Post-Totalitarian Syndrome," *Uncaptive Minds* 5, no. 2 (Summer 1992): 111.

23. Ralf Dahrendorf, *Reflections on the Revolution in Europe* (New York: Random House, 1991).

24. For the myth of the "new man," see André Reszler, *Mythes politiques modernes* (Paris: Presses Universitaires de France, 1981), 141–70.

25. Katherine Verdery, "Nationalism and National Sentiment in Post-socialist Romania," *Slavic Review* 53, no. 2 (Summer 1993): 179–203.

26. For interesting glimpses into Milosevič's personal life, including the possible tensions between him and his wife, Belgrade University sociologist Mirjiana Markovič, see Stephen Kinzer, "Serb First Lady Plays Powerful Role," *New York Times,* August 10, 1995.

27. Jean Rouvier, *Les grandes idées politiques de Jean-Jacques Rousseau à nos jours* (Paris: Plon, 1978), 159, quoted in Reszler, *Mythes politiques modernes,* 193.

28. Agnes Heller and Ferenc Fehér, *The Grandeur and Twilight of Radical Universalism* (New Brunswick, N.J.: Transaction Books, 1991); Leszek Kolakowski, *Modernity on Endless Trial* (Chicago: University of Chicago Press, 1990). These philosophers have long since noticed the dissolution of the "redemptive paradigms" and the rise of the alternative, parallel discourses, although they did not anticipate the ongoing rise of the narratives of hatred and revenge.

29. For instance, the Croat president, Franjo Tudjman, can easily dispense with his own party (at the moment critical voices are heard), use his influence on parliament (without support of his own party) to gain approval of all his choices, and still appear as a "supporter of democracy." The same can be said of Romania's Ion Iliescu and Ukraine's Leonid Kuchma. For Latin American disillusionment with leftist radicalism, see Jorge Castañeda, *Utopia Unarmed: The Latin American Left after the Cold War* (New York: Knopf, 1993).

30. Daniel Chirot, *Modern Tyrants: The Power and Prevalence of Evil in Our Age* (New York: Free Press, 1994), 251.

31. Julia Kristeva, *Nations without Nationalism* (New York: Columbia University Press, 1993), 68–69.

32. For the concept of uncertainty, see Valerie Bunce and Maria Csanadi, "Uncertainty in the Transition: Post-Communism in Hungary," *East European Politics and Societies* 7, no. 2 (Spring 1993): 240–75.

33. Llazar Semini, "Albania Warns Serbia on Kosovo," *Washington Post*, August 16, 1995.

34. This point is often made by Michael Ignatieff in his contributions on the Yugoslav disaster, especially in the *New York Review of Books*.

35. Olivier Mongin, *Face au scepticisme: Les mutations du paysage intellectuel ou l'invention de l'intellectuel démocratique* (Paris: Éditions la Découverte, 1994).

36. Anthony Lewis, "The Italy We Want?" *New York Times*, June 26, 1995.

37. For perceptive explorations of these issues, see George Konrád, *The Melancholy of Rebirth: Essays from Post-Communist Central Europe, 1989–1994* (San Diego: Harcourt Brace, 1995).

38. G. M. Tamás, "A Legacy of the Empire," *Wilson Quarterly* (Winter 1994): 79.

39. Bruce Ackerman, *The Future of the Liberal Revolution* (New Haven: Yale University Press, 1992).

40. About tribalism as the barbaric component lying at the core of modernity, see Hannah Arendt's masterpiece, *The Origins of Totalitarianism* (New York: Harcourt Brace, 1951), and Theodor W. Adorno and Max Horkeimer's *The Dialectic of Enlightenment* (New York: Herder and Herder, 1972), which, as Wolf Lepenies has recently emphasized, is not a rejection *de plano* but an invitation to an epistemology of doubt, opposed to the Voltairian exaltation of reason. I insist on this because there is a growing trend to set up a barrier of sorts between a dark, unpredictable, Southeastern Europe, almost inherently irrational, tribal, and violent, and a Central Europe, presumably more able to articulate and internalize the discourse of reason. See Adam Seligman, *The Idea of Civil Society* (New York: Free Press, 1992).

41. Ken Jowitt, "The New World Disorder," *Journal of Democracy* 2, no. 1 (Winter 1991): 16–17; idem, *New World Disorder: The Leninist Extinction* (Berkeley: University of California Press, 1992).

42. See John Rawls's discussion of criteria for assessing civic freedom and the idea of a well-ordered society in his *Political Liberalism* (New York: Columbia University Press, 1993), 30–40.

43. Martin Palouš, "Post-Totalitarian Politics and European Philosophy," *Public Affairs Quarterly* 7, no. 2 (April 1993): 162–63.

44. Arpad Göncz, "Breaking the Vicious Circle," *Common Knowledge* 2, no. 1 (Spring 1993): 1–5. See also "Cette étrange époque post-communiste: Adam Michnik's entretien avec Václav Havel," in Georges Mink and Jean-Charles Szurek, *Cet étrange post-communisme: Rupture et transition en Europe centrale et orientale* (Paris: Presses du CNRS/La Découverte, 1992), 17–48.

45. See Julian Barnes's disquieting novel *The Porcupine* (New York: Knopf, 1992).

46. For the immense power of these new mafiosi that have become a challenge second to none to the establishment of the rule of law in Russia, see K. S. Karol, "Moscou sous la loi des gangs," *Nouvel Observateur* (Paris), March 17–23, 1994, 36–37; and Steven Erlanger, "A Slaying Puts Russian Underworld on Parade," *New York Times*, April 14, 1994.

47. Rumors had it that it was a form of money laundering for the Italian mafia (after 1992, Romania replaced Yugoslavia as a major traffic route for weapons, drugs, and other dirty trades).

48. William McPherson, "Transylvania's S&L: The Pyramid Scheme That Is Eating Romania," *Washington Post*, November 21, 1993; Michael Shafir, "The Caritas Affair: A Transylvanian Eldorado," *RFE/RL Research Report* 2, no. 38 (September 1993): 23–27. For an illuminating exploration of the Caritas affair, see Katherine Verdery,

234   *The Leninist Debris; or, Waiting for Perón*

"Faith, Hope, and Caritas in the Land of Pyramids: Romania, 1990–1994," in her book *What Was Socialism, And What Comes Next?* (Princeton: Princeton University Press, 1996), 168–203.

49. See Albert Hirshman's splendid analysis of the "perversity argument" in his *Rhetoric of Reaction: Perversity, Futility, Jeopardy* (Cambridge: Harvard University Press, 1991).

50. Castañeda, *Utopia Unarmed*, 247.

51. For the former Communists, see Andrew Nagorski's perceptive book *The Birth of Freedom: Shaping Lives and Societies in the New Eastern Europe* (New York: Simon and Schuster, 1993), esp. chap. 2.

52. Personal interviews with Argentine political émigrés, Caracas, Venezuela, June–September 1982.

53. Michael Specter, "Discontent of Belarus Voters Fueled Landslide for Outsider," *New York Times*, December 7, 1994.

54. For the global impact, in terms of norms definition, see James N. Rosenau, *Turbulence in World Politics: A Theory of Change and Continuity* (Princeton: Princeton University Press, 1990).

55. "Poles Hold March over New Budget," *New York Times*, February 10, 1994. This was one of many protests against the austerity budget in February 1994. It turned out to be the largest antigovernment demonstration since the collapse of Communism (about 30,000 people).

56. Peter Reddaway, "Russia on the Brink," *New York Review of Books*, January 28, 1993, 30–35. Reddaway notices a multilayered feeling of moral and spiritual injury related to loss of empire and damaged identity: "Emotional wounds as deep as these tend to breed anger, hatred, self-disgust and aggressiveness. Such emotions can only improve the political prospects for the nationalists and neo-communists, at any rate for a time." Needless to add, in the meantime, Reddaway has become even more pessimistic.

57. Adam Michnik, "The Church and the Martyr's Stake in Poland," *New Perspectives Quarterly* 10, no. 3 (Summer 1993): 32.

58. See Andrew Arato, "Revolution, Restoration, and Legitimization: Ideological Problems of the Transition from State Socialism," in Michael Kennedy, ed., *Envisioning Eastern Europe: Postcommunist Cultural Studies* (Ann Arbor: University of Michigan Press, 1994), 180–246.

59. For the "Movement for Romania" as a reincarnated Iron Guard, see Vladimir Tismaneanu and Dan Pavel, "Romania's Mystical Revolutionaries: The Generation of Angst and Adventure Revisited," *East European Politics and Societies* 8, no. 3 (Fall 1994): 402–38. For the ongoing intellectual fascination with the former Iron Guard doctrinaires, see Vladimir Tismaneanu, "Romania's Mystical Revolutionaries," *Partisan Review* (Fall 1994): 600–609.

60. For such a pessimistic approach, see Jan Urban, "Europe's Darkest Scenario," *Washington Post*, October 11, 1992.

61. For an insightful exploration of Papandreou's anti-Western radicalism, see Robert Kaplan, *Balkan Ghosts: A Journey through History* (New York: St. Martin's, 1993), 260–81. See also the excellent discussion of "Third World populism" as an alternative to traditional Leninism in Dimitri Kirsikis, "Populism, Eurocommunism, and the KKE: The Communist Party of Greece," in Michael Waller and Meindert Fennema, eds., *Communist Parties in Western Europe: Decline or Adaptation?* (New York: Basil Blackwell, 1988), 102–6.

62. See Vladimir Tismaneanu, "Fantasies of Salvation: The Dynamics of National-ism in Post-Communist Societies," in Kennedy, *Envisioning Eastern Europe*, 102–24.

63. Zbigniew Brzezinski, *Out of Control: Global Turmoil at the End of the Twen-tieth Century* (New York: Charles Scribner and Son, 1993), 19.

64. In this respect, see Tony Judt, "Misjudgement of Paris: French Illusions and the Eastern Europe That Never Was," *Times Literary Supplement*, May 15, 1992; G. M. Tamás, "The Legacy of Dissent," *Times Literary Supplement*, May 14, 1993; and my re-joinder: Vladimir Tismaneanu, "NYR, TLS, and the Velvet Counterrevolution," *Com-mon Knowledge* 3, no. 1 (Spring 1994): 131–42. One of the best explorations of the role of *ressentiment* in post-Communist politics is Irena Grudzinska-Gross, "Post-Communist Resentment; or, The Rewriting of Polish History," *East European Politics and Societies* (Spring 1992): 141–51.

65. Samuel Huntington, "The Clash of Civilizations?" *Foreign Affairs* 72, no. 3 (Summer 1993): 22–49.

66. See Giuseppe De Palma, "Legitimation from the Top to Civil Society: Politico-Cultural Change in Eastern Europe," *World Politics* 44, no. 1 (October 1991): 49–80; and Eric Hobsbawm, "The New Threat to History," *New York Review of Books*, De-cember 16, 1993, 62–64.

67. One might say that the real problem (folly?) of Eastern Europe is the desperate search for and manufacture of an ideology instead of an ethics. Ironically, the blatant amorality of the Leninist age was followed by a widespread distrust of ethical values, a flight from individual responsibility, and a repudiation of genuine political commit-ments. Thus, in Poland, it is paradoxically those who are the beneficiaries of the new freedoms (the successful business people) who are politically apathetic. None of these societies has been able to formulate the set of values that would define the ex-istence of a "transcendental good." And how can "civil society" exist in the absence of such a metaphysically grounded status of the individual freedoms? (I owe many of these thoughts to Jay Tolson's critical remarks to a book proposal written while I was a research scholar at the Woodrow Wilson International Center for Scholars in the summer of 1993.)

68. For an excellent discussion of nationalism, see Tzvetan Todorov, *On Human Diversity: Nationalism, Racism, and Exoticism in French Thought* (Cambridge: Har-vard University Press, 1993).

13

Party, Ideology, and the Public World in the Former Soviet Space

Charles H. Fairbanks, Jr.

> By the nature of human infirmity remedies are slower than diseases; and
> as our bodies grow slowly, but decay quickly, so spirits and exertion may
> be more easily depressed than summoned; since there is a sweetness of in-
> activity itself, and the sloth we hate at first we later love.
>
> Tacitus

Had I been writing this chapter about Britain in 1720, my main concern
would have been the Jacobite and Hanoverian parties, the followers of the
deposed Stuart kings and of the new German dynasty. In taking this obvious
course, I would have neglected the rising forces that were, only fifty-six
years later, to culminate in the American Revolution and then the French
Revolution. This historical case is only one of many that can warn us against
an overly narrow view of the contemporary political terrain: If we describe
only formal parties and ideologies in a place so rapidly changing as the former USSR, we could easily miss much more fundamental elements of the political landscape. In these pages I will try to capture both realities. I begin
with the formal situation at the present moment.

There are few real political parties in the former Soviet Union, and those
that exist are weak. There are, in our sense, no widely held ideologies either.
Before justifying this conclusion, I will define my terms and deal with the
necessary qualifications: the "parties" which are not real, and the ideologies
that are held by narrow groups or the opinions that are the traces of ideologies dead, remembered through a senile haze, or descried arriving from far
away. I will deal not only with Russia, but with all the states of the old USSR,
for two reasons. First, it remains a question whether all these states can maintain their unnatural borders and their independence; a new Soviet Union or
some organism altogether new may arise in this part of the earth. Second,
similar processes are at work in all the countries of the former Soviet bloc,
including "Eastern" (now "Central") Europe (to which I will refer in passing),
but at a different speed and in a different equilibrium with opposing forces.

In 1992, Tajikistan and Georgia seemed quite different from Russia, but these weak states pointed to the direction in which Russia, or part of it, is trending.

What are parties and ideologies, anyway, and why do we care about them? We think of a party as a group of people, united by a common vision of the public good, which competes with other such groups having alternative views of the common good to impose its vision on the community. The most important way a party imposes its vision is by laws that cover the entire community. Almost as important is the election of executive officials who carry out the public business along the lines of the party's vision and interest. The term *ideology* has come to be used to mean a vision of the common good that is highly specific, complete, and clear. We were most accustomed to call the visions of the common good held by the now almost-vanished fascist and Communist regimes "ideologies," but the *open* competition of parties with names and platforms, distinctive to modernity, presupposes both that there is a common good and that it is properly the subject of argumentation and eristic "victory" within the community, rather than being a matter of tradition or culture taken for granted by all. In this sense, all post-Enlightenment politics is ideological. The liberal and totalitarian regimes have disagreed not over the compatibility of rational debate with politics, as the ancients would have, but over the extent of life that can properly be changed by the victory of a party and its vision of the common good: the whole or only the "public" part.

A party implements its vision of the common good by winning elections and placing its supporters in governing positions where they serve the public by implementing that vision; the public is willing to be ruled if they are persuaded that a party's vision of the common good is plausible. Officials and citizens, in this formula, are "bourgeois": The former does not resent serving, nor the latter obeying. Officials serve the public, in this admittedly "ideal type," not for any wages commensurate with the magnitude of their responsibilities, but out of "principle" (ideology), a desire to serve, anticipation of future gains, vanity, or ambition. Ambition is the indispensable queen in the grumbling hive of liberalism, which completes the magic transformation by which "every part is full of vice / Yet the whole mass a paradise."[1]

The purpose of these definitions has been to show that modern multiparty democracy, in spite of its long and wide success in many parts of the globe, requires certain concepts, state institutions, and feelings that are not inevitable, which may be gained or lost: a common good, limited public spirit, law as opposed to administrative whim or tradition, ideology in the sense of belief in the potential power of principles over public life, willingness to serve the public and to obey, and political ambition.

POLITICAL PARTIES

As previously stated, there are few political parties in our sense in the former USSR, except for the surviving Communist parties, which now operate largely under different names. These parties take two forms. The first is seen in the republics (Uzbekistan and Turkmenistan) that clearly continue an organized Communist apparatus under a different name. In both these countries, there is a crucial difference in the function of the party. In Soviet times, the party dominated the state; now the relationship is reversed.

The second form is found in places where Communist parties do not rule, or where they have a complicated relationship to the president. Here, the nonruling Communist parties still have some organizational continuity with the Communist Party apparatus (the salaried employees of the party). In most post-Soviet countries there are three types of parties which descend from the Communist Party of the Soviet Union (CPSU). There is usually a large party, with an extensive organizational network in cities and towns, representing a moderate communist orientation. There is usually an Agrarian party, or one with a similar name, which represents the rural networks of the CPSU. Finally, there is usually one or more radical parties that try to conserve the ideological heritage of the CPSU. I will consider these Communist parties in discussing communism as an ideological pole of attraction.

Outside of our definition, there are vast numbers of formal political parties—there were some eight hundred in Russia alone in 1995—but their very number and their lack of continuity, local organization, parliamentary discipline, and local roots prevent most of them from playing the role that political parties play in democratic countries. Most of the parties are essentially the personal followings of a chieftain, as in many Third World countries, or coalitions of such followings thrown together for the purpose of contesting an election. Of the thirteen alliances that qualified to compete in the December 1993 Russian parliamentary elections, for example, seven were formed specifically for the occasion. The others had undergone so many splits and recombinations that their organizational identity was scarcely established. After the radical reformists did poorly in the elections, most people blamed the lack of unity in their camp. But this opinion did not prevent most of the reformist coalitions from splitting again after the elections.

These constant splits are due above all to the personal nature of the parties. Vladimir Zhirinovsky's party calls itself in print "The Liberal Democratic Party of Zhirinovsky," and calls its newspapers *Zhirinovsky's Falcon* and such names. Because the personalities in a party tend to feel that it is serving the interest of a personality rather than a cause, they find it hard to cooperate, in the absence of democratic centralism.

Many of the dominating personalities are sudden, rootless growths like mushrooms, the creations of the unexpected twists and turns of a revolutionary period. Consider the case of Grigory Yavlinsky, the success story of the December 1993 elections among the democrats. Yavlinsky came to public notice as one of the many young free-market economists momentarily picked up by Mikhail Gorbachev in his most fickle phase. He drafted on his kitchen table in the middle of the night a vague and rhetorical concept for rapid marketization and called it the "500-Day Plan." The 500-Day Plan was picked up by an ambitious Harvard professor, Graham Allison, who built it into a Western media sensation reamplified in turn inside the USSR by the controlled media. The 500-Day Plan eventually sank into oblivion, but not before Yavlinsky, who had never held an administrative office, had begun to be mentioned as a future president—all on the basis of a transatlantic publicity stunt. Yavlinsky's mushroom origin does not prevent him from having real talents and real support, but such political figures tend to fade quickly: This has been the fate of politicians as well-known and widely admired, for different reasons, as Anatoly Sobchak, Nikolai Travkin, Gavriil Popov, and Arkady Volsky. Now Viktor Chernomyrdin and Zhirinovsky seem to be fading. Such figures do, however, form a group of professional politicians who are not dependent for their stature on the state apparatus; they give democratic politics in Russia a certain momentum.

The most revealing feature of most Russian parties is their lack of ideological or policy definition; as the feuding personalities quarrel and recombine, one sees the most bizarre bedfellows, who seem able to cross the ideological landscape like nomads.[2] After the Christian Democratic party split, its chief, Viktor Aksyuchits, went to the quasi-Fascist Right, while Father Gleb Yakunin was long Boris Yeltsin's most loyal supporter.

For another example, take the history of the Democratic Party of Russia (DPR). The DPR was probably the most genuine non-Communist political party in the country; its leader, Travkin, controlled the party for years, in spite of constant splits, and it had a real organization modeled on the CPSU. I will use the DPR as a short case study of post-Soviet parties.

During the last year of the USSR's existence (1991), the DPR appeared to be the organized arm of radical anti-Communism; it was the DPR that first began using the Imperial Russian flag when that seemed an act of treason to the existing regime. Since 1991 the DPR has split again and again, entering and exiting coalitions as divergent as "Democratic Russia" and the state enterprise directors' lobby, Civic Union, all the while slowly drifting to the right. In December 1993 the DPR featured at the top of its ticket Travkin; Oleg Bogomolov, a very respectable member of the Yuri Andropov–Gorbachev brain trust; and film director Stanislav Govorukhin, an extreme Russian nationalist and monarchist and the veteran of the "Red-Brown" congresses, in which he proclaimed—together with Stalinist generals such as Albert Makashov and Stalinist street toughs such as Viktor Anpilov—the existence of a conspiracy between Yeltsin and NATO to undermine Russia. These people have nothing in common except their personal ambitions.

During the 1993 campaign, Travkin and Govorukhin made violent attacks on part of the Left, the part of the Democratic Movement that had remained in Yeltsin's camp, as well as the Right. In a television commercial, the DPR called Yegor Gaidar, the head of the government-allied party, Russia's Choice, a thief. In campaign speeches, Travkin assaulted Zhirinovsky, the anti-Semitic and nationalist founder of the Liberal Democratic party, as a Hitler.[3]

The strategy pursued by Travkin after 1991 met with disaster in the election; his campaign tactics halved the support the DPR enjoyed before the campaign began. Prior to the campaign, the DPR had an advantage over other parties, or was tied with another party, among the following groups, according to one poll: people in cities under 100,000 population; skilled workers in cities under 100,000 population; skilled workers in the defense sector; students; people in cities with 100,000 to 1,000,000 inhabitants; and people aged 18–29. This impressive support, given the multiplicity of the parties and coalitions and the DPR's nonparticipation in the government, is a testimony to Travkin's attempts to create local organizations and his willingness to make nationalist appeals. But the outcome of the campaign showed the great difficulties in combining the appeal to anti-Yeltsin and nationalist attitudes with political seriousness. As Matthew Wyman et al. note, "the groups among whom the DPR lost the most votes—students and young people generally, the working class and inhabitants of small and medium-sized cities—are groups among whom the LPDR [Zhirinovsky's party] gained heavily."[4]

Not long after the 1993 elections to the Russian parliament, the Duma, Travkin split from the oppositionist course of the DPR when he was named minister without portfolio and deputy prime minister in Prime Minister Chernomyrdin's government. This act was an astonishing reversal of the political course that Travkin had steered since the beginning of his splits with other leaders of the Democratic Russia coalition in 1991. Travkin had staked his political future on the public discontent with economic "shock therapy," as practiced by Yeltsin and Gaidar, and with the destruction of the USSR. In both respects his instincts seemed tactically correct. But after December 1992, politics had become completely polarized between Yeltsin and a Communist-nationalist parliamentary majority that seemed increasingly against the reforms of 1987–91. In the confrontation and armed clashes of September–October 1993, Yeltsin had won. Travkin's sudden reversal of allegiances looks like self-interested opportunism; it could only be defended by noting that Yeltsin's government had also moved to the right, particularly on the question of the restoration of the USSR.

Travkin did not cut his ties with the DPR, where he had a group of personal supporters who would follow him. But his erratic tactics produced a crisis in the party. Three factions emerged: the Travkin loyalists; the supporters of Sergei Glazyev, who had become the leader of the parliamentary committee on economic reform; and party activists who emphasized not leadership but grass-roots organization—an orphaned element from Travkin's earlier agenda.[5] These factional struggles culminated on October 11, 1994, when most of the deputies in the party's parliamentary group, led by Glazyev, voted no confidence in Travkin as a leader. On October 18 Travkin struck back by forcing a party vote on admitting new members— his supporters—to the parliamentary group. The sequel shows how intransigent the atmosphere of factional struggle tends to be in Russian parties:

Out of 15 deputies present eight gave Travkin their backing, which was recorded in the minutes. Questioning the authenticity of the minutes, opponents of the DPR leader called another, roll-call, vote in which nine deputies voted against expanding the faction without the Congress's consent.[6]

Such struggles did not improve the ability of the DPR to contest the parliamentary election approaching in December 1995. Travkin was forced out, joining the government party "Russia—Our Home." The remaining DPR leaders realized they had little chance of surmounting the 5 percent threshold for parliamentary representation.[7] Glazyev decided to join KRO, the Congress of Russian Communities headed by General Aleksandr Lebed and Yuri Skokov, in return for third place on its proportional-representation ticket. Govorukhin found a place in the Party of Self-Governing Workers headed by the millionaire eye-surgery entrepreneur Svyatoslav Fyodorov, then split again from that party, fielding his own slate in the 1995 parliamentary elections.

The Democratic Party of Russia simply disintegrated. At Russian independence in December 1991 the party had been by far the best organized of the non-Communist parties; it was full of élan and vigor. Michael McFaul, one of the keenest observers of Moscow politics, thinks even now that "had there been elections in the fall of 1991, the DPR would have taken off."[8] The short, sad history of the DPR shows how—and in how many ways—hostile the post-Soviet space is to party-building.

Among the wreckage there remains Travkin, the party's founder and builder, who has now held for several years the position of head of administration of a rural *raion* (comparable to an American county or a French *arrondissement*) near Moscow. Travkin hoped that this position would give him a reputation for the real accomplishment which, he knows, the public found missing in most politicians. But it has not prevented him from sliding into obscurity. Also among the wreckage of the DPR there remain some regional organizations, abandoned by their leaders, which are now joining Russia's Voice, the latest of the democrats' ephemeral umbrella organizations.

Presidential Power

Our account of parties would not be complete unless we noted that the space they operate in is limited by the presidency. In most post-Soviet nations, a president who is very unpopular is still usually able to remain in office. President Yeltsin had poll ratings of less than 10 percent for years; he even had such ratings a few months before the 1996 presidential elections—but he won.

There is a widespread feeling that the Russian president has replaced the general secretary or first secretary of the CPSU and that he will ultimately rule in spite of formalities. In the last Russian presidential election, the Communists seem to have given up at a certain point. Perhaps they believed statements by Yeltsin's staff that they would not be allowed to take office. After both rounds, the KPRF—the Communist Party of the Russian Federation, the biggest successor to the CPSU—claimed, with good reason, electoral fraud. But then they simply dropped the issue.[9] Perhaps one can suspect, in this case, that the Communists saw Yeltsin's regime as supported by loyal security forces as well as public opinion. But there is also some dislike of the alternative to the president; in Russia, where the Communists have been the strongest alternative, this is a factor. Finally, I suspect that fear of the unknown works to keep some unpopular presidents in office. As a young Georgian told me at the end of a long discussion of politics, "basically, I think we're all just afraid."

A combination of these factors, depending on the country, means that electoral outcomes are not usually very uncertain and that the best of these states are therefore only what Larry Diamond calls "electoral democracies," states in which rulers are selected by elections but the other features of democracy are lacking.[10] But the presence of elections is, in my judgment, a real constraint. Everywhere except perhaps in parts of Central Asia, the basis of legitimacy is elections. A ruler who loses an election would need to quit. Precisely for this reason, control of money, the media, and the electoral mechanism is essential to the former Soviet Union's presidents.

Why Post-Communist Parties Are Weak

To seek the causes of the weakness of parties and ideology is a purpose of this chapter, and there is much that will become clear only later. But at this point I would like to list the most obvious, short-term reasons for this state of affairs.

The clearest reason is the public's distaste for the word "party" and the very concept. A local official from Murmansk, in the far north, explained in 1995:

> If you tell someone that you are a member of a party, it is immediately thought that you are, consequently, a careerist. You are considered, at best, simply odd—involving yourself in "rubbish" instead of making money. To run in elections on a party ticket is virtually to lose in advance. Everyone in our oblast Duma is "nonparty," except for P. Sazhinov.[11]

Audible in this attitude is the exhaustion of the hopes put in "reformist" political parties in 1990–92, together with the success of the reformist advice to get rich. But there is something deeper: the long frustration with the CPSU. Although the Communist Party was not a political party in the Western sense, its compulsory rituals of spontaneity—the evening party cell meetings and lectures, the "voluntary" work on the weekends, and so on—bred a distaste for the word "party."

Another, in some ways opposite, reason is surely the traditional Communist style of rule. Communist regimes had nominal collective leadership but usually were dominated by the general secretary (or, in the non-Russian republics, the first secretary). This idiosyncratic feature of Communist systems necessitated hidden maneuvering; it certainly did not encourage identification with a long-term constituency, as democratic parties do. Georgian scholar Ghia Nodia has explained better than anyone else why this Communist style has made all post-Soviet leaders reluctant to join a political party:

> [Georgian President Eduard Shevardnadze] sees parties as just political groupings between which he has to find balance. . . . He could have helped the CUG [Citizens' Union of Georgia, his government party] to become a real party but he has chosen not to. He prefers to show himself above parties, perhaps partly because he is the President but also has the legacy of a communist nomenklatura fighter. . . . Commitment to one group is not within the rules of the game. You have to be flexible.[12]

It is probably because of this tradition, and the widespread distaste for the name and concept of a party, that post-Soviet leaders did not found dominant or hegemonic parties, using the government's powers of patronage and its ability to tap into local patron-client networks to give a party system reality. In other transitions from authoritarian or foreign rule, leaders in Italy, India, and Japan used the Christian Democratic, Congress, and Liberal Democratic parties to develop a real multiparty system. There are many parties formed specifically to support presidents. But, as Nodia explains, post-Soviet leaders have tried both to use them and to keep them at arm's length. As a result, they seem secondary, not serious.

I am compelled to add the widespread—and largely correct—perception that parties are not ideological movements serving social purposes, but vehicles for the ambition of their leaders. Once again our Murmansk official gives perfect expression to a widespread view: "Unfortunately, the disease of chiefism is still alive. The Social Democratic Party of Russia has broken up into three parts in a power struggle, and they are still settling their internal matters, and they have no strength left over for policy as such."[13] The sad history of the splits in the Democratic Party of Russia seems to confirm this estimate of the role of personal ambition.

It is easier for a politician to be self-interested because of the fickleness of the public, which oscillates between ideological extremes more easily than the leaders. In Latvia, for example, the Popular Front achieved independence by annihilating the Communists in the first free elections, but it did not reach the 4 percent minimum threshold for parliamentary representation in the first elections after independence. Some of these reactions are due to the hardships and to a reclaiming of socialist and traditionalist instincts, but one can identify a tendency to repudiate a leader or party as soon as it gains power. In Belarus, former chairman of the Supreme Soviet Stanislav Shushkevich, brought to power on a wave of anti-Communist enthusiasm, saw his popularity plummet in two months; the same has happened to Alexander Lukashenka. In other words, parties have difficulty developing through reliance on a constituency because the public is constantly shifting.

The root of this phenomenon may be a deep feeling that political power has no legitimate authority. If the public feels this, its sympathy will go to the "bastards and usurpers," to political forces that seem to be rebelling against politics or political authority itself. (This is the phenomenon political scientists have begun to call "antipolitics.") But when the politicians who had seemed antipolitical begin to exercise authority, they seem once more like ordinary politicians. The realization floods back over the public: Power is fundamentally corrupt, fraudulent, stolen.[14] And at this point people remember that they do not like to be told what to do, to be directed; the rebellious instincts at work in crime, tax fraud, and draft evasion, now rife in the former USSR, boil to the surface. In other words, as Tacitus writes, legitimate authority, once repudiated, is difficult to put back together.

Politicians tend to confirm these instincts not only because most of them *are* corrupt but also because they resent serving the public. The nightmare in the Soviet economy was the service sector—salespeople in stores, waiters, and so forth—because proletarian revolution and despotism left in their wake a deep, stubborn anger at the very idea of serving someone else. This resentment comes out in politicians when Yeltsin stalks out of the parliamentary session, or when Danilov, an administration head in Belarus, simply refuses to appear in a court case involving him.[15]

The root of the weakness of the party system is the absence of the associations and interest groups in civil society that create constituencies to which politicians would appeal. It is astonishing, for example, that there are many strikes but no party dominated by militant workers. There certainly exist the beginning of political constituencies in cultural/class groups that do vote with some consistency in one direction or another. The April 1993 referendum and the December 1993, December 1995, and June 1996 elections displayed, for example, broadly similar geographical patterns of support for Yeltsin. For years the existence of interest groups or lobbies has seemed a very promising sign of long-term democratic development in Russia and some other republics. One interest group is intimately linked to a single party in several republics: the collective-farm chairmen and agro-industrial managers to the agrarian party. These are not peasant parties, as in some countries of interwar Europe, but parties representing the rural *nomenklatura*.

However, it has come to seem that influential interests can get what they want by direct relationships with individual leaders and parliamentarians, without going through parties. The weakness of the party system does give money enormous power in politics; the most important structural interests are banking, foreign trade (especially the export of oil and gas), and the defense industry. Particular firms and individuals from these groupings are important sources of support for parties and politicians.

In some cases the common interest of "lobbies" has translated into joint positions on policy and partisan struggles. The oil and gas lobby inside and outside the Russian government, for example, has often pressed its interest as a group. The opposite is true of the highly publicized political activity of the big bankers in Russia. They united to get Yeltsin reelected president in 1996, but seemed to split after the Russian economic crisis of 1998 into groups led by Vladimir Potanin (and Anatoly Chubais), on one side, and by Boris Berezovsky, on the other. Prime Minister Evgeny Primakov issued an arrest warrant for Berezovsky, who fled the country. Berezovsky struck back in spring 1999, according to Moscow rumor, by successfully persuading Yeltsin to dismiss Primakov. These events are a picture of clientelistic politics as practiced in the Philippines or Sierra Leone; economic interests did not translate into political forces.

IDEOLOGY

I have shown above that the Russian party system is only weakly defined by ideology. There are, however, three ideological poles of attraction in politics: Western liberal democracy, communism, and nationalism.

Capitalist Democracy

Western liberal democracy is the most intellectually coherent of the three poles of attraction. The activist democratic camp, which does exist in the former Soviet countries, by no means reduplicates the range of democratic politics in the West. Its dominant discourse is "libertarian" in the American sense or Thatcherite: cosmopolitan, emancipated from tradition, individualist, and ambitious in its vision of the potential of politics to liberate the individual. Given the power of inchoate feelings of socialism, envy, imperialism, and Slavophil communitarianism, this tends to isolate the genuine democrats and to polarize politics.

The concepts of democratic elections, the market, and human rights continue to enjoy a real hegemony over political discourse outside of Central Asia. With the exception of small but influential groups of nationalist-fascists and of Communist revanchists, all the popular leaders and all the parties, including the Communist parties, are for democracy and the market in principle, with modifications only for the sake of practicality or in the transitional stage. This hegemony gives the democratic side, with all its problems, an enormous advantage. But it creates a *chasm between the legitimate ideology and political practice.* Most of the parties accept the market and democracy in practice but are working to slow or block further movement in this direction. Because empty, obviously fraudulent extremist appeals (like Zhirinovsky's) are popular in politics, there is also a chasm between legitimate ideology and political rhetoric.

Communism

A second ideological pole is Communism. Genuine belief in Leninist ideology seems to be confined in the Slavic republics to a few small minorities periodically outlawed by the government, such as Anpilov's "Trudovaya Rossiya." These groups have little public support but have shown a power to change history by breaking the taboo against political violence in May–October 1993 and radicalizing the respectable Right.

In Central Asia classical Communism, inextricably merged with local clan politics, remains dominant. Whether Central Asian Communism can long remain viable without a Communist Moscow is highly doubtful. Key Communist habits such as democratic centralism appear to be decomposing rapidly. In Tajikistan the Communists were able to win the civil war only with the help of criminal/warlord militias. Turkmenistan is a special case where the final, Communist utopia, as defined in the 1961 CPSU program, briefly replaced "socialism" with the help of energy profits. Turkmens were given free housing, utilities, and bread. This brief stage proved unsupportable by the Turkmen economy, and all recognizable Communist rhetoric has faded from the Turkmen scene.

The bulk of the Communists are opportunists irritated by the changes since 1987 but with no program to reverse them. They were forced to choose between the party's ideology and the state apparatus, and they chose the state. After the collapse of the USSR, the Communists, in places where there were real elections, split along the fissure between their urban and rural bureaucracies. The former are usually called Communists or socialists, the latter "agrarians." Both are better organized than any other political parties; they have inherited the problem-solving and mutual-protection networks of the old system. The Communist and agrarian parties are quite separate but tend to cooperate.

We need a better definition of this new and powerful political reality, which may be called "subcommunism." All the experiences and habits of these people were shaped by Communism. Both President of Ukraine Leonid Kravchuk and Kazakh President Nursultan Nazarbayev said that their countries need a new ideology which, of course, could not be Marxism-Leninism. But their politics are Communism with some key elements subtracted: ideology and democratic-centralist discipline, as was shown by Kravchuk's difficulties in controlling his Communist Parliament. For these people, any return to the old Soviet system is blocked by the fact that they are rapidly "privatizing"—that is, stealing—the state's resources.

Because the old Communist elite is a large part of the new rich, a large proportion of their children are being raised in un-Communist flamboyant wealth, are acquiring Western contacts and tastes much more rapidly than the average, and are often being educated abroad. Because subcommunism is such a class-based phenomenon, it may be subject to rapid erosion in the next generation. Already the supporters of the Communist and subcommunist parties are older on average than the supporters of the other groups, and their youth organizations are particularly weak. There will remain widespread habits and tastes from the Communist period, such as egalitarianism, belief in consensus, disbelief in political conflict, and helplessness. Ultimately these habits and tastes will probably have to find a new political home, most probably in the nationalist camp. In the meantime there has been a marked tendency for the Communists to return to power in the second free election after the collapse of the old regime. The perceived illegitimacy of all political rule will act to curtail this political resurgence, while the Communists' superior skills will prolong it.

Nationalism

The third group of ideas and feelings that could be labeled as an ideology is nationalism. It is easier to acknowledge the awesome power of nationalism, which shattered the granite colossus of the USSR, than to satisfactorily delineate its varieties and the nature of each. But it is worth beginning to sketch the necessary distinctions.

Elsewhere in the world one might divide political visions into those comfortable with modernity (the ideas and institutions of the Enlightenment) and those who hanker, usually vainly, for something antimodern. Both alternatives are certainly present in the former USSR; in the former category could be put the "reformers" who may try to use or participate in Russian nationalism, led by Yeltsin. In the latter category are the political and literary successors of the nineteenth-century Slavophil current, such as author Aleksandr Solzhenitsyn among the quasi democrats and, among the Russian authoritarians, the nationalists who firmly reject Communism. But everything is complicated by the Soviet regime, which was so "modern" in its politics and economy (or at least in attitudes toward technology, reason, and the future) and so traditional in its society. Those who fill the role of real conservatives in other countries, in the sense of people who distrust change, are those who seek to conserve as much as possible of subcommunism. This fact makes post-Communist politics essentially different from politics in Western Europe or North America.

The order of exposition here is artificial in the sense that the subcommunist ideology, if one calls it that, is not incompatible with the nationalist one. As subcommunism goes on, it increasingly rests for its legitimacy on a form of nationalism; it tends to blend with antimodern and anti-Western views. However, there is an essential distinction between three geographical domains.

In Russia, the Gorbachev, Yeltsin, and Putin governments have been perceived as relatively modern, and the subcommunist and antimodern columns tend more and more to merge. Antinationalist Communism or socialism of the Roy Medvedev type is becoming less and less visible in the political arena.

In the non-Russian independent republics, on the contrary, subcommunism is a force that limits nationalism. The remaining Communist elites are invariably more friendly toward Russia, economic interdependence, and the Commonwealth of Independent States than the non-Communists. Accordingly, a modern, Western-oriented variant of nationalism was only the object of somewhat vague efforts by Yeltsin and his followers, while it is a much more powerful force in areas such as Azerbaijan, Moldova, the Baltic Republics, Ukraine, Georgia, Armenia, and Kyrgyzstan. There is also an antimodern, anti-Russian variant of nationalism that is vaguely democratic, as seen in the Islamic Revival party in Tajikistan and the Union of Georgian Traditionalists in Georgia.

It is crucial to avoid the mistake to which most Western intellectuals are predisposed: thinking that there can be no modern, Western-oriented nationalism. The Georgian thinker Ghia Nodia has cogently argued that under post-Soviet conditions only nationalism can mobilize most communities for a democratic transformation.[16] While nationalism is more dangerous in the Russian case because of its closer connection with Communism and Russian imperialism, it remains true even in Russia that nationalism is an essential element in a serious attempt at transition to democracy. Yeltsin succeeded in dissolving the USSR underneath the feet of Gorbachev and in disrupting the Communist Party's organization because he cleverly saw how to use nationalism to a democratic purpose.[17] Yeltsin's enterprise began to go wrong when, among other things, he allowed his opponents to seize the banner of nationalism, then hurried to imitate them. Of course, this leaves out entirely the dark side of nationalism, to which we will come shortly.

A third set of relations governs nationalism in the autonomous republics within Russia (including Chechnya and the other republics of the North Caucasus, Tatarstan, Bashkortestan, Sakha, and Tyva). With the exception of Chechnya, de facto independent since 1996, and the Kalmyk republic, all of these areas are basically ruled by the old Communist nomenklatura. Because the titular nationality tended to be disproportionately concentrated in the party apparatus (salaried employees of the party) and they find themselves at odds with the Russian government (and sometimes with local Russians) over autonomy or independence, there is a tendency toward divorce between subcommunist politics and the weak nationalism we see in the independent non-Russian republics. In the North Caucasus, however, there are stronger nationalist pressures from the societies and a reaction against the strong nationalism of the Chechens, so that the nomenklatura-ruled governments draw closer to Russia to remain in power.

Religion is a "particularistic" factor that should also be considered in the context of nationalism. The collapse of the Communist regime in the USSR has led to the re-emergence of religion as an open factor in politics. In most of the Muslim areas and to a lesser extent in Russia, some ruling elites have seen religion as a replacement for Marxist-Leninist ideology in the ideological legitimation of politics. As time goes on, traditional religion, which during the collapse of the regime had an anticommunist significance, tends to become a symbol of political conservatism, often in bad faith.

In most traditionally Muslim areas there is a particularly wide gap between rhetoric and reality, because there is wider religious observance and more mass attachment to religion as a symbol of identity, while the upper stratum of the ruling elites is, in spite of its new Muslim label, equally attached to atheism and secularism as a marker of modernity and class identity. Where the regimes remain essentially dictatorial, religion is likely to increasingly become, as it has in Tajikistan, a focus for populist political opposition. This opposition was labeled in Russia and in the West as "fundamentalist," and the armed opposition in Tajikistan was compelled to share some of the fundamentalist identity of its Afghan sponsors. But the "Islamic" side in Tajikistan has really been a coalition of disadvantaged regional groups.

In the Islamic republics of the former Soviet Union there have been organized political movements based on opposition to secularism and modernity—such as those seen in Iran or the Arab world—only in Tajikistan, the Uzbek province of Ferghana, and Chechnya. In Tajikistan the Islamic opposition has been a mixture of views; in the other regions "Salafi" or "Wahhabi" movements are found. The Salafis, who model their Islam on that of Saudi Arabia, are strong in Russian Dagestan, Chechnya, and perhaps in the Ferghana Valley. Iranian government policy, closely aligned with that of Russia, has stayed away from organizing Islamist political movements, except in Azerbaijan.

The power and shape of Islamic movements in the future are likely to be conditioned by cultural and regional variations in attachment to religion. In Central Asia, the traditional nomadic cultures (Kazakhs, Kirghiz, Turkmens, Karakalpaks) were less religious than the settled cultures (Uzbeks, Tajiks, Uigurs) or nomads who had settled close to them. In the Caucasus, the mountain peoples of the northeast (the Chechens and Daghestanis) were traditionally more religious than the Azerbaijanis (ca. 70 percent Shi'is) and the mountain peoples of the northwest Caucasus (Abkhazians, Adygei, Cherkess, Karachai, Balkars, Kabardians, Ossetians). Religion is so weak in this area that the Muslim-Christian division among Abkhazians and Ossetians no longer matters.

Ukraine, a special case, displays the greatest impact of religion on political movements. The Uniate Church (orthodox in ritual but allied to Rome) is closely identified with the cause of Ukrainian nationalism and the parties (democratic and fascist) that express it; in Ukraine the most vital religion is reformist or revolutionary, not conservative.

While religion does play a role in politics, "particularism" in the former USSR essentially reduces to nationalism, and nationalism means ethnonationalism, the nationalism of a "people" inside or outside of state frontiers. There are probably no nations in this region where people with different cultures and languages exist happily inside the same state as they do in Switzerland or Spain. When Russians and others coexist well in Ukraine or Belarus, it is based on their cultural closeness. In Kazakhstan there are enormous latent or merely unreported tensions, as yet damped down by traditional elite habits of accommodation and by the political passivity of the population. Even among the tiny language groups of Daghestan, sometimes confined to a single village, there seem to be stirrings of a desire to affirm their identity. Nationalism is the strongest of the three poles of attraction.

Thus the political world of the former Soviet Union seems as familiar as the evening news, or the nineteenth century. However, it would be very misleading to leave readers with this impression. Nationalism *is* the strongest pole of attraction, but it is a strange kind of nationalism.

Just how strange can be seen by looking at Russia's first war to recover the seceded republic of Chechnya from 1994 to 1996. Beginning in the summer of 1993, there was an increasingly nationalist, "reintegrationist" agenda in Russian foreign policy. By 1994 there seemed to be a consensus that Russia needed to assert herself more, to claim a sphere of influence coextensive with the former USSR minus the Baltic Republics, to protect Russians abroad, and again to protest the dominance of the United States. This consensus was shared by most of the Westernized intellectuals who comprised the strength of the democratic movement in Russia. Chechnya was a test case for Russian nationalism.

How did Russians respond to the beginning of the war? Among the Russian public, apparently increasingly nationalistic, polls indicated 65 to 80 percent opposition to vindicating Russia's territorial integrity. The biggest surprise is what the Russian nationalist parties and politicians did. The Communist Party, although it publicly advocates the restoration of the USSR, vehemently opposed the fighting in Chechnya. Zhirinovsky eventually became one of only three prominent politicians supporting the war, but this was his party's first reaction: "The anti-national government in the Moscow Kremlin conceives the war in Chechnya as an endless war, till the death of the last Chechen."[18] The most prominent Russian ultranationalist thus expressed more solicitude for those who seceded than for the Russian losses. As for the army, the bulwark of nationalism, General Boris Gromov, the deputy minister of defense, and General Lebed, both officers on active service and heroes of the far Right, publicly opposed the policy of the president and defense minister.

Part of the explanation is partisanship: If Yeltsin is doing it, it must be wrong. But partisanship did not prevent the European socialist parties in 1914 from rallying behind the kings and armies they hated. It would appear to be the very definition of nationalism that the attachment to the nation takes precedence over attachments to party, sect, or class.

This anomalous situation is not confined to the war in Chechnya, nor to Russia. With the exception of Zhirinovsky, who never concealed the histrionic half-serious character of his nationalism,[19] nationalist candidates have not done particularly well in Russian elections. While there is considerable concern about seceded territories in Moldova, Georgia, and Azerbaijan, there appears to be little interest in retaking them by force, as there was in France over Alsace-Lorraine between 1871 and 1914. Nationalism made the Russian parliament, in the summer of 1993, proclaim Sevastopol' in Ukraine to be part of Russia, but it never has enforced any effort to rebuild an army capable of taking or holding the Crimea. Many of the Russian provinces, where Westernizing reform of the Yeltsin-Gaidar type is far weaker than in Moscow and St. Petersburg and traditional Russian nationalism seems far stronger, are showing their Russian nationalism by not paying taxes and not obeying the Russian state. In Georgia, President Zviad Gamsakhurdia persecuted the Ossetians and the Abkhazians in the name of Georgian nationalism; when the battle to hold onto Abkhazia, Georgia's richest province, was hanging in the balance, however, Gamsakhurdia apparently made a deal with the Abkhazians and the Russians to undermine the Georgian army in the rear.[20] As G. M. Tamás has put it, "this nationalism is not patriotism."[21]

The appearance of this new kind of nationalism has confused Western opinion thoroughly. The kind of nationalism we are familiar with, the nationalism of the nineteenth century, of fascism, and of the Third World, is intimately associated with the *state*. Nationalism created states. The internationalists, primarily socialists, had as their ultimate goal the withering away of the state. A "German nationalist" was someone who wanted to unite Germans in a common, strong state, not someone who enjoyed being a German in Switzerland, Austria, or Bavaria.

Today nationalism often produces an intense feeling that, for example, Russia or Georgia is being mistreated or threatened, as became very clear during the Kosovo war of 1999. That is, nationalism produces a strong feeling of membership in a community. Acts of ethnic cleansing, which have occurred in Abkhazia, Georgia, South Ossetia, North Ossetia, Azerbaijan, Armenia, and Nagorno-Karabakh, presuppose a community that is exclusive of other communities, feels threatened, and therefore must act against another community. But this strong feeling of community does not transfer to the state. Why?

THE STATE IN POST-COMMUNIST CONDITIONS

To understand the nature of parties and ideologies in the former Soviet space, we clearly must understand the state: its role, form, and function in post-Communist society. The market reforms which Yeltsin and Gaidar undertook beginning in 1992, and Western countries' support of them, rested upon the assumption that with the disappearance of the Communist *regime*, the *states* beneath them would remain intact to carry out the reforms. By 1999, however, it became clear that this expectation was mistaken.

It is now common for political scientists to speak of Russia, and most of the other newly independent states, as "weak states." (Uzbekistan and Turkmenistan, which largely retain their Soviet organization and have added sovereign powers, are not weak states in the same sense, and the following discussion does not apply to them.) The term *weak state* is rather imprecise. The nineteenth-century British and American liberal states were weak in that they had few employees, carried out far fewer functions, and collected and distributed a far smaller part of gross national product (GNP). In contrast, the Russian government at all its levels (local, state, and federal) collects about as large a percentage of revenue as the government collects in the United States.[22] (Some states that are even weaker, such as Georgia, do seem to collect a small part of GNP in revenue.) The government bureaucracy is twice the size it was when the Soviet Union collapsed.[23]

So in what sense are these states weak? I see them as weak in three primary respects. First, the various levels and organs of the government, even within the executive branch, do not operate in a united way; official orders are disregarded. This I would call *disintegration*. Second, the government has given many of its officials private sources of income outside the budget, which I would call *feudalization*. Finally, and as a result, the government does not perform many of the functions that it claims to perform. Its failure to do so exacerbates a crisis of legitimacy that is one of the fundamental causes of all these problems. In April 1992 a newspaper polled more than one hundred Parliamentary deputies about who exercises authority in their provinces; 56 percent replied that "nobody exercises any authority in our region."[24]

Disintegration and Feudalization

Perhaps the most obvious sign of disintegration of government is the secession of smaller territorial units from larger ones: the Union republics from the USSR, Chechnya from Russia, Abkhazia and South Ossetia from Georgia, and so forth. We tend to attribute these events to nationalism, and this played a great role in most of the cases noted. But nationalism is accompanied by a simple desire of the officials who head the small territorial units not to obey outside orders and to exploit any local resources for themselves. The Ajar Republic in Georgia is a good example. It is ethnically Georgian, and the local boss, Aslan Abashidze, has never raised any question of secession from Georgia. He wants simply to do what he wants and to enjoy the profits of vacation hotels, tropical products, and smuggling across the border with Turkey. There seems to be nothing public in Abashidze's motives; he is operating essentially like a small businessman. The Russian garrison on the border, whose main occupation seems to be smuggling,[25] gives Abashidze the protection to defy the central Georgian government; the Moscow government approves this arrangement because it limits Georgian independence from Russia. Similar motives seem to be at work in the greater and greater subdivision of Russian Siberia into independent entities.

The consequence of state disintegration is that lower bureaucracies often disobey higher orders—beginning with Gorbachev's orders during the August 1991 putsch and then the orders of the ministers who rebelled against him. During the disturbances in the North Caucasus leading up to the Chechen war, for example, "the Yaroslavl [Province Council] decided to suspend the Russian MVD [Ministry of Internal Affairs] leadership's instructions to send local military personnel to North Ossetia and Ingushetia."[26]

In many cases the disintegration of the state structure is due to the fact that its parts are supported by private sources of income as well as the state budget. The part of this that is visible is called in several post-Soviet republics "non-budget funds." To take a very recent example, when Sergei Kiriyenko was prime minister of Russia in 1998 he publicly told the Russian Space Agency that it must raise its own funds through commercial activities to continue its present programs; in other words, the prime minister was telling the agency to raise private funds to carry out its public functions.[27] Almost all large bureaucratic units in the former Soviet space possess a source of non-budget funds, ranging from a cafeteria in their headquarters to weapons sales to Iran or China. What we see is only a small part of the private profit from state functions, most of which comes from "corruption." The term *corruption* usually applies to officials who take a cut of transactions, and it is misleading about the gigantic scale by which state officials help their friends to steal state assets, in return for immense bribes.[28]

The creation of non-budget funds, and this kind of corruption, amount to a feudalization of the state. The state, in return for the performance of some state function, for political favors, or for friendship, turns over to one of its officials a state-controlled resource. Because the aftermath of the collapse of Communism is taking place at the end of the twentieth century, we tend to think of it as some sort of modern process. However, it is essentially no different from the process that occurred in the ninth century when the Carolingian emperors, finding themselves unable to defend France against the Vikings, allowed nobles to take the products of peasants' work and the allegiance of knights in the area, in return for protecting the coast. In order to understand what is happening in the former Soviet space, we need to have a much larger range of historical comparison. The result of the disintegration and feudalization of the state is that the state now *claims control over certain social functions but no longer performs them.*

This outcome has rarely been illustrated better than in the following description of Svanetia, the mountainous area of Georgia between Abkhazia, Mingrelia, and Racha, in 1993:

> Without exaggerating in any way . . . there is no longer any government in Svanetia and the Georgian State's jurisdiction . . . in its strictest sense, no longer extends there. There have probably been more murders this year than between 1917–93. No records are being kept and no criminal proceedings have formally been instigated. . . . Representatives of the government have not been in Svanetia for goodness knows how long.[29]

In Georgia generally, the situation has improved since this report, although there are no recent reports from Svanetia. There are, however, places in the post-Soviet world where there has been, for years at a time, no state in the sense we understand the term. In Chechnya the Maskhadov government apparently does not control larger military forces or financial resources than the warlords, does not collect taxes, and has little influence in part of the country's territory.[30] The case of Kosovo is perhaps even more unusual.

Kosovo became familiar to Western audiences during the 1999 war between NATO and Serbia, but even then the strangeness of the situation that existed from 1989 to 1998 was little discussed. It seemed then that the anarchist dream was realized.[31] Kosovo, like Bosnia, was the site of ethnic conflict between the Albanians (90 percent of the population) and the Serbs, guarding their holy shrines. After Slobodan Miloseviĉ took away the autonomy of Kosovo in 1989, a few Serb Titoists still occupied the government offices and, on paper, ruled the province. But the Albanians simply seceded from the state without leaving its territory. They left the parliament, left their official positions, quit their jobs in state-owned industry, and left the state's schools. They did not pay taxes to the provincial government, rent, or utility bills. Instead the Albanian parliamentarians reassembled secretly, elected their own government, and assessed informal taxes on their community.

For nine years the Albanians obeyed their informal government, apparently without coercion; lived by agriculture, smuggling, and remittances from Kosovars in Western Europe; and attended informal schools in houses and mosques. In Chechnya there is still constant violence; in Kosovo, in contrast, until the Dayton agreement which triggered the rise of the Kosovo Liberation Army, the Albanians seemed to be living in a community without a state. It lasted no more than nine years, but it showed that there is, in former Communist countries, some strong tendency to such a formula.

THE FATE OF THE PUBLIC WORLD

It is not adequate just to define the political positions of parties and movements in the former USSR, because the phenomena we have surveyed go beyond trying to replace the present form of politics with another form of politics and even beyond trying to reduce the importance of politics altogether. We see an instinctive shrinking from any organization that is not spontaneous or voluntary, from obedience that is expected or compulsory, from "political obligation," to use an old technical term of political theory. The best possible evidence lies where communities need obligation and obedience the most: to fight wars. I have analyzed post-Communist warfare and armies elsewhere, and I will only give the gist of what I have found.[32]

There have been in the last decade at least eleven ethnic and subethnic wars in the post-Communist world, from Croatia to Tajikistan. But of all the states and peoples involved, only Russia, Armenia, Nagorno-Karabakh, Croatia, and Serbia have had armies in the modern sense. And many of these armies have been shot through with an unwillingness to fight, to obey, and to serve. So rotted by these inclinations was the Russian army that it was routed by some four thousand amateur Chechen fighters loosely brought together by the idea of a Chechen people. Most the wars were fought, and many of the victories won, by informal groups of volunteer fighters linked by personal ties to a chieftain.

Precisely where the public good seems most to call for the formalization of loyalty and commitment, post-Communist man most rejects it. This is a far more extreme version of the weakness of political parties. What is its root cause?

In earlier writings, I proposed as the deepest root a flight from the public world. This captures the essence of it, but I now realize that it is not quite exact. In the nationalism of ethnic cleansing, people act in the name of a public world—their ethnic group—which grips their behavior strongly enough to overcome compassion, friendship, and morality. It seems more exact to say that people are *fleeing from a formalized public world.* They want to act out of inclination, not obligation. They prefer an "ought" that is enormous but vague—what a Serb owes to "the Serbs"—to duties that are limited but defined, such as their obligations to a state. During many decades of the twentieth century, millions of people wanted to be directed and formed—think of the Nazi rallies, of the Communists' willingness to submit to Joseph Stalin, of the young Red Guards in the Chinese Cultural Revolution. The intense aversion to formalized public demands is thus an abrupt turn in history. What is its source?

Perhaps the new phenomenon has its source in the old. The millions who lived under Communism are profoundly weary of being told what to do; of being reproached for not measuring up to standards set from above; of the discipline, order, and planning that were Communist obsessions. Most of all, they are sick of the *state.* The state became in the nineteenth century the embodiment of the public world, and under totalitarianism the state squeezed out everything else that was public. Under Communism many things were forbidden. But there were also many things that were demanded: *aktivnost'* [being active], *partiinost'* [party spirit], vigilance. . . . A list would fill a page. At one point this may have been inspiring, but eventually it became deadening. Living in a Communist regime was like attending a revival meeting seventy years long. At the end of those seventy years there was the feeling of a tremendous *burden.* It is from that burden that people are fleeing.

THE ATTRACTION OF THE VOLUNTARY

Toward *what* are people fleeing, then? For a moment we should think of the military forces and (often indistinguishable from them) the gangs that fight the past and future ethnic wars.

When people agree to fight for something outside themselves, particularly important in establishing that willingness is the *public oath.* In Tajikistan the civil war was fought between warlord followings, which elected their officers. When the "Communist" side had won, the Kulyab militia swore an oath (later broken) to the state.[33] In Belarus the official, pro-Russian army was balanced by the nationalist *Belaruskoe Zgurtavannoe Vayskoytso*, whose members—bemedaled and uniformed officers, students in sweaters, haggard old men—knelt in the center of Minsk and took an oath to defend Belarus. Many of the young men, probably, were among those who are not in the army because they failed to show up for conscription.[34] Elsewhere militias serve the state but take an oath to themselves. Local Cossack units, like those before 1917, joined Russian border guards in Kyrgyzstan, but with a modern touch: Their "oath of fidelity to the Cossacks" can now be sworn not only on the Bible but also on the Koran or at a statute of Buddha.[35]

There is something medieval about such formations. Historian of the medieval period R. W. Southern notes:

> Medieval society was prolific in creating forms of association to which entry was obtained by some form of oath. This connection between freedom and individual acts of acceptance of its responsibilities again emphasizes the rational character of freedom. The serf's unhappy freedom from law was involuntary, but the submission of the knight, the baron, the clerk, the monk, the burgess, to their various codes of law was voluntary. The nobleman was bound by several codes of law— as a Christian, a baron, a knight, a subject of the king; and he could suffer all manner of penalties for a breach of any of these codes of law. Into all these obligations he had entered by an individual contract in the ceremonies of baptism, homage, knighthood and fealty. If he was punished, even by being burnt as a heretic, he could reflect that he was being punished for breach of contract.[36]

We are so used to oaths that we forget we have them, at least in part, because modern republicanism developed out of feudalism. Why did the men of the Middle Ages so insist on them? An oath makes the point that the obligation in question does not follow involuntarily simply from being a citizen; it is an obligation which you freely lay on yourself. An oath is a symbol of being free to enter or not to enter an organization. The nineteenth-century French politician and historian François Guizot expresses very clearly this difference between ancient and medieval society: "Franks, Visigoths, Burgundians, Saxons, Lombards, none of these new peoples lived as the Greeks and Romans had, under the sway of an essentially political idea, the idea of city, state, and fatherland: they were *free men, and not citizens; comrades, not members of one and the same body.*"[37]

By the same historic movement, ancient patriotism and morality were transmuted into honor and chivalry, the behavior toward others that one owes to oneself. These are the reasons our questions about party and ideology are not adequate. How can parties compete, guided by some ideology, for control of the public world if there is no institutionalized public world? How can parties rule if people resent being ruled and politicians resent serving? And why would they serve if there is no political ambition, as opposed to a desire for money and notoriety?

THE FUTURE OF PUBLIC LIFE

In the last part of this chapter, I want to develop two alternative pathways that the former Soviet space might follow in the next few centuries. Projections so far from the present are always wrong as predictions. But they serve to *liberate* us from the present. People living at any time in history invariably project the present situation, and present trends, indefinitely into the future. At the edge of a new millennium, when everyone realizes we are in a time of transition, it is important to remember: History exists; at some point, there will be fundamental changes.

Development toward Strong Democratic States

One pathway for the former USSR states is a prolonged and difficult transition to democracy. This remains a real possibility. The presentation of the existing conditions given above may seem relentlessly pessimistic. But it is probably no more pessimistic than it would have seemed in France in 1799, in Turkey in 1918, or in Japan in 1937. One's estimation of the likelihood of this outcome in specific cases probably depends more on one's general reaction to Francis Fukuyama's thesis about the "end of history" than on the current facts.

There are some favorable factors. Democracy and the market remain in possession of a monopoly over intellectual legitimacy or respectability. And the aversion to discipline, sacrifice, and war which accompanies the flight from the public world constrains any recourse to regimes that are seriously and openly communist or fascist. Military regimes, in our times the most common alternative to democracy, are not very likely. Of the twenty-seven reorganized states and seven unrecognized ministates (Republika Srpska, Herzeg-Bosna, Kosovo until 1999, Transdniester, Abkhazia, South Ossetia, and Chechnya) in the former Soviet bloc, only two (Chechnya and Croatia) had military men as presidents, and in both cases they came to power in genuinely democratic elections. In Chechnya, the "Shura" or Council formed in 1998 as a sort of rival government by the opposition warlords may owe the little strength it has to military power; it is, however, legitimized by Islam. In Georgia, the Shevardnadze government in its earlier years was held up by two warlords, both later purged by Shevardnadze. Given the instability of many of these areas, the weakness of civilian governments, and the importance of military force in their post-Communist history, it is clear that post-Communist man has a remarkable allergy to military rule.

The present authoritarian or "superpresidential" regimes are dominated by leaders who emerged from the upper levels of the CPSU apparatus and who govern with the skills in "corridor intrigue" they learned there. Many of these leaders are now old and in poor health or have faced repeated assassination attempts. It is not clear that successors from another generation would or could maintain the same type of rule. In this respect, the personalization and noninstitutionalization of many post-Soviet regimes cuts in two directions. It limits their democratic development at present, but it also means that the personalized constitutions and system may not endure. An originally authoritarian leader who allows a democratic transition, such as Shevardnadze in Georgia, could succeed present leaders. Or there could be an attempt to rule through a wider consensus—the formula that Primakov pioneered briefly in 1998–99 as prime minister of Russia. Russia is in such a deep hole that it needs a leader like Gustav Stresemann at the time of the Locarno Treaties (1925)—someone who will save what can be saved and abandon what cannot. Such a leader might be compelled to make a clean break with the Communist heritage and the desire for empire and to fasten onto democratic legitimacy as the means of leaving an enduring heritage.

Outside Russia, the Western model attracts more strongly. Its closest competitor is "Asian authoritarianism" in the style of Malaysia, Indonesia, or Singapore, but the East Asian economic crisis of 1998 certainly reduced the prestige of these systems. Meanwhile, the pressure from the West for democracy, however hypocritical or intermittent, works on the new states' desire for foreign aid, international respectability, and membership in organizations such as NATO, the World Trade Organization, and the Council of Europe. Western democracy-building organizations, which are often more serious than governments, penetrate the societies and create nongovernmental organizations (NGOs) modeled on them.

The effect of NGOs can be seen in Georgia and Armenia. In neither place have there been presidential and parliamentary elections that were both vigorously contested and fairly administered. In Georgia, Shevardnadze's margin in the presidential election did not reflect the great discontent with him. In Armenia, international observers questioned the presidential elections of 1995 and 1999; in early 1999 President Levon Ter-Petrosyan was forced out by thinly veiled military pressure. In this environment of apparent authoritarianism, there was a strange, anomalous efflorescence of NGOs in both countries. In Georgia at least, NGOs succeeded during 1997–98 in blocking the proposed Press Law and in removing the minister of communications. The speaker of the parliament, Zurab Zhvania, met with the NGOs to discuss "the causes of the current political crisis and ways to overcome it."[38]

Finally, as time goes on, generational change will bring in both rulers and citizens who are free of Communist political culture. So there are many trends developing toward a version of the democratic state with democratic institutions, political parties, interest groups, and so forth. The question is only whether these relatively weak tendencies may be engulfed by vast tendencies operating in the whole world. It is to this question that I finally turn.

A Long Decline of the State

The other pathway I want to entertain is far more alien to us. I have tried above to expose a side of post-Soviet politics that is altogether outside the normal political map. The possibilities of post-Soviet politics go beyond shifts in support from one party or ideology to another; beyond redefinition of political positions, beyond even the rise of completely new political positions. Powerful forces are at work against politics itself and against any public world. We perceive these forces only dimly, and they are just beginning to work free of the fossilized forms of Communist politics. Without trying to predict the future, it is worth trying to look at another era of history in which the public world almost dwindled away. (This exercise is not to suggest that events would take the same course in parts of the post-Communist world; historical events never occur in the same way twice.) The purpose of this final section of the chapter is only to remind readers of the reality of fundamentally different forms of social organization. The forms we will now encounter in late antiquity and the Middle Ages should be considered only as signposts to new possibilities we are not now ready to see.

After the collapse of the Roman Empire in the West, new forms of social organization arose: new relationships established by voluntary agreement among individuals—what we usually call feudalism—and a universal church. The weakness of the medieval state was the other side of the strength of feudal ties and of the Church. We noted already how there was something medieval about the militias in many of the Soviet successor republics. Perhaps the public world went through something similar to what it suffered under Communism during the Roman centuries.

In any event, this was the opinion of French historian Numa-Denis Fustel de Coulanges and of G. W. F. Hegel. Fustel traces in great detail the Greco-Roman "municipal spirit," that is, the public-spiritedness of the city-state, and its fate in the age of Hellenistic monarchies and the Romans.[39] He shows how the Romans legally annihilated the laws, institutions, and religion of the subject cities, putting them under a governor who was not subject to their law because he was "the living law."

> The Roman Empire presented, for several generations, this singular spectacle: A single city remained intact, preserving its institutions and its laws, while all the rest—that is to say, more than a hundred millions of souls—either had no kind of law, or had such as were not recognized by the ruling city. The world then was not precisely in a state of chaos, but force, arbitrary rule, and convention, in default of laws and principles, alone sustained society. Such was the effect of the Roman conquest on the nations that successively became its prey. Of the city everything went to ruin; religion first, then the government, and finally private law.[40]

The next stage was the one in which the conquered nations very slowly entered the Roman "city," which step by step extended itself legally to fill the vast empire. This stage was concluded as late as the third century A.D., when the emperor Caracalla, for tax-gathering reasons, made everyone in the empire nominal "citizens." By then there was no shred of republican institutions left, so that Romans became equal citizens in a slave city.

The emperor Diocletian turned the empire into an oriental despotism even in form, with seclusion of the ruler (as in the USSR); the compulsory practice of many professions, including local government, as a duty to the state; and the binding of peasants to the land as serfs.[41]

Uniformity of opinion behind the regime was assured by savage persecutions of unauthorized religions—of Jews, of Christians, and then, after Emperor Constantine made Christianity the official cult, of paganism and of philosophy, which was allied with it. From the reign of Constantius, Constantine's successor, the practice of paganism was punishable by death.[42]

These changes made every inhabitant of the empire experience the pressures which from the beginning of the empire had beset the political class. As early as the end of the first century of the Christian era, Tacitus, a senator and consul, had devoted his first historical work to the destruction of freedom, energy, and political ambition by the Roman Empire. In the reign of Domitian, as under Nero, the emperor's envy of political accomplishment was such that "inactivity was wisdom."[43] Because Roman freedom was taken away by the emperor, the patriotic task of Roman expansion becomes, for Tacitus, the expansion of "this old, universal slave-gang," something ugly and monstrous.[44] What Tacitus remembers best of his father-in-law, the Roman general "praised" in the ironic *Agricola*, is his frequent musings about how easily Ireland could be conquered, "so that Roman arms would be everywhere, and liberty disappear as if sunken out of sight."[45]

Some despotisms encourage this flight from politics, from patriotism, and from the public world without clamor, without falsehood. Pseudo-republican regimes, like the Roman principate and the USSR, can be more demanding; they sometimes wind up destroying the public world in the name of the common good. Rome preserved the language of republican virtue and self-sacrifice into the empire. The business of government is invariably discussed in a special, inflated jargon, like the Old Church Slavonic jargon of Soviet exhortation. As Ramsay MacMullen puts it:

> Government in its almost childish view appeals against inflation by excoriating greed; against the impossible costs of the military, by blaming war in the abstract; and against the inadequate trickle of the tax yield, by calling for the taxpayer's zeal and loyalty. "It tries to cover all its acts with moral principles and divine approval," for the crisis is one of people's wickedness that must and can be reformed through the redirection of their desires. In addition to his strident sermonizing, the personal qualities of the emperor are to be offered to his subjects for their instruction.[46]

Just like Lenin, Stalin, Khrushchev, and Brezhnev.

With the arrival of an evident oriental despotism under Diocletian and his successors, historians note no decline but a "sharp upswing of appeals to *utilitas publica.*"[47] Such hypocrisy withers any vestiges of loyalty to the common good; tax payments are now called "the august" and the gold extorted from the empire's desperate subjects by a special, confiscatory tax is minted into coins with the legend "Romans Rejoice!"[48]

Ancient history, I am arguing, was a history, from Alexander to the collapse of the Western Empire, a span of eight hundred years, in which the sense of the public good as it existed in the *polis* was first weakened, then misused, next degraded, and finally travestied into annihilation. What followed was a new world, the world in which the center occupied in antiquity by the political community or state was filled by the Church, on the one hand, and, on the other hand, by the feudal relationship in which two specific individuals freely contract with each other a relationship of hierarchy (vassalage). For more than ten centuries the political community in the form of the nation-state under kingly rule struggled to establish for itself a space between the competing charms of heaven and of the local community.

From State to Church

What was the relationship between the death of the public world and the birth of the Church and of feudalism? In an early, unpublished work Hegel examines the mystery of the disappearance of paganism. The key point, for Hegel, is this:

> Greek and Roman religion was a religion for free people only, and, with the loss of freedom, its significance and strength, its fitness to men's needs, were also bound to perish.
>
> The picture of the state as a product of his own energies disappeared from the citizen's soul. The care and oversight of the whole rested on the soul of one man or a few. . . . Each man's allotted part in the congeries which formed the whole was so inconsiderable in relation to the whole that the individual did not need to realize this relation or to keep it in view. . . . Either everyone worked for himself or else he was compelled to work for some other individual. Freedom to obey self-given laws, to follow self-chosen leaders in peacetime and self-chosen generals in war, to carry out plans in whose formulation one had one's share—all this vanished. All political freedom vanished also; the citizen's right gave him only a right to the security of that property which now filled his entire world.
>
> Without a country of his own, the citizen lived in a polity with which no joy could be associated, and all he felt was its pressure. He had a worship to whose celebration and festivals he could no longer bring a cheerful heart, because cheerfulness had flown away out of his life. . . .
>
> They despised the mundane joys and earthly blessings they had to forgo and found ample compensation in heaven. The idea of the church took the place of a motherland and a free polity, and the difference between these two was that, in the idea of the church, freedom could have no place. . . . Thus the despotism of the Roman emperors had chased the human spirit from the earth and spread a misery which compelled men to seek and expect happiness in heaven; robbed of freedom, their spirit, their eternal and absolute element, was forced to take flight to the deity.[49]

This account is convincing at least as an account of the practical circumstances that encouraged the replacement of paganism by Christianity. But in
one respect important for us now it is quite unfair. When Hegel says that
"freedom could have no place" in the Church, he means freedom in the sense
of Jean-Jacques Rousseau's general will and Immanuel Kant's categorical imperative. As regards ordinary, subjective freedom, the consciousness of the
early Christian must have been just the opposite. By the time of the later empire, no one could even delude himself that there was any freedom at all in
his relationship to the Roman state. But in choosing the new Christian faith, a
Roman did act freely; the persecutions only confirmed the free character of
his act. The attraction of Christianity was in part the attraction of membership
in a community that was not expected or coerced, like membership in the
Roman Empire or the municipalities within it that had lost all autonomy.

To the extent that the flight from public life in the USSR resembles the flight
from public life in the Roman Empire, one form of organization that the former
subjects of the USSR may resort to is religion or something like religion. Something "like religion" might be very distant from our experience; in the United
States the religious instinct, operating in conditions of de-Christianization, has
issued in phenomena as diverse as the temperance movement, health-food
businesses such as Kellogg's (an offshoot of Christian Science), the "self-help"
and "human potential" movements, and perhaps now environmentalism and
"political correctness." But it is not impossible that the transition from Communist rule will end in a transformation of human associations and loyalties as
great as the transition from classical antiquity to the Middle Ages.

The Feudal Transformation

The other response to the decline of public spirit under Roman rule was,
I suspect, the institution of feudalism. Historians have discerned a long series of practical events, from the binding of Roman peasants to the latifun-
dia to the Magyar onslaught, that conditioned the rise of feudalism. But if
one understands the death of public spirit in the ancient world, it seems
significant that, in feudalism, people were not bound by obligations that
they did not, in principle, accept personally by their free oath. This is precisely the attitude that creates militias in the post-Communist world instead
of armies.

We do not have to ask whether the death of the public world will re-
create feudalism; it already exists. Patron-client relationships, such as the
khvosty of leaders once studied by Kremlinologists, were already a central reality of Soviet society and a key operating mechanism of the political system
by the 1920s; they have been reinforced by economic scarcity and the breakdown of public order.[50] We know from the Third World how such social realities are exceptionally tenacious even in the face of rapid modernization. In
the aftermath of failed transitions, the question is not whether feudal relationships of some kind will grow but whether they can largely replace the

state, as they did during the Middle Ages, and what kind of formal rules and culture (such as chivalry, heraldry, or courtly love) will grow up around them.

WHILE THE WEST WAITS

We scarcely think of the possibility that any independent tendency could emerge from the post-Communist world because it is now so much weaker. It is now surrounded in Europe, North America, and East Asia by stronger, more confident areas. So it seems destined to imitate these areas or to relapse into some decayed form of its old patterns. History, however, moves in more complex ways. The Eastern Roman Empire moved in the direction of a weaker state, with feudal structures and a stronger church. But this movement was feebler than it was in the West, where the old structures had been cleared away.

The chance of something new in the post-Communist areas is increased by the fact that the West is not static; we see around us many strange new tendencies without knowing what they hold. Both in the post-Communist zone and in the Western democracies, there have been tendencies toward a loss of the old content of the public world. But in the post-Communist areas, which went through an exaggerated demand for public-spiritedness that was suddenly discredited, these tendencies have suddenly accelerated.

Increasingly, our own moment in the West is named "postmodernity," that is, a time of waiting. But what are we waiting *for?* Already something is beginning to happen to the public world. Arriving from the ex-Soviet bloc once again on American soil in 1998, one would quickly notice that the public world was filled with accusations of scandal about private life: the sexual, financial, and criminal allegations about President Bill Clinton and First Lady Hillary Clinton. The attempt to decide whether a ruler would remain in office not on the grounds of his political principles and actions, but on the grounds of his private morality, had begun with the Left during Watergate, but it was now embraced by the Right as well. In one sense this sort of agenda is very political—it takes partisanship very far—but it erodes the distinction between public and private worlds that are self-sufficient, with special habits and standards for each.

In fact, the distinction between public and private worlds has been breaking down for a long time. One striking sign of this shift is the decline of political oration as a type of discourse that is different from other types and is appreciated as such. In fact the fundamental formula of modern capitalist democracy is the emancipation of self-regarding desires, like the desire to acquire or personal ambition, in order to achieve a better public world. This formula seems inherently fragile or unstable, vulnerable both to excessive concern for the public world (the explicit topic of Bernard Mandeville's *Fable of the Bees*) and to the submergence of the public world in private satisfactions (the worry of Rousseau and Alexis de Tocqueville). In fact, it can hardly be disputed that patriotism and nationalism, the most obvious signs of concern for the public world, have been declining in most Western countries since the time of World War I. We rarely think of the consequences of a further decline.

It is in this context that we need to see contemporary political movements. The Republican Party won a historic victory in the 1994 congressional elections in a campaign against the traditional Republican target of Big Government. The meaning of this term is highly ambiguous, however. Doing away with Big Government could mean having a state of the proper size and a stronger community culture (a view expressed by Newt Gingrich), or it could mean having as small a state as possible and complete individualism. The latter view is close to the post-Communist flight from the public world, without its search for a stateless community.

It is on the left that we encounter an interest in a stateless community, although the distrust in the public world is less explicit than it is with the Republicans. When intellectuals of the Left talk about "community," they do not mean the nation-state; they detest nationalism and demonstrative patriotism. They seem to mean the local or subpolitical community, such as the minority cultures defended by multiculturalists.

G. M. Tamás has noticed that the fading of the public world in dissident thinking, where it was replaced by the concept of civil society, has to be seen in the light of the difficulty of finding a secure place for public spirit within modern liberalism itself.[51] Tamás has gone on to propose that there are some similarities between Western "multiculturalism" and the new nationalism of ethnic cleansing. Both suggest that some sort of primordial ethnicity is the most important thing, but both differ from the old nationalism in rejecting the extension of one culture over another (by conquest or assimilation). In this sense, both draw on the relativist or (using Friedrich Nietzsche's vocabulary) nihilist mood of modern thought, in that there is no idea that can confer superiority on one group or create links between groups that are not "given." Both try to use politics to better the status of groups, but neither proposes a specific political order that is best for man or for this particular group; both are, in this sense, anarchist or antipolitical.[52]

In practical terms these movements tend toward a reversal of the present relationships between the public and private worlds. What is most private—sexuality—is becoming the content of politics ("sexual harassment," "homophobia," "gender"). At the same time the intergroup tensions of civil society—the question of whether ethnic groups and their cultures are "marginalized" or "privileged"—become the focus of literature, of public education, and, as yet incompletely, of politics.

Modernity had consigned religion to the innermost part of the private realm. Now, at the limit of these dawning transformations, the most universal thing—nature or "the environment"—seems to be turning, step by step, into a kind of religion. In the face of the extinction of a species, modern secular man recovers his sense of the forbidden and the numinous. And the recycling of waste (in religious language, the category of the impure or polluted) restores the personal rituals that have vanished from "mainline" religion. The careful sorting of pure and impure substances might strike an anthropologist as resembling the Jewish dietary laws or the sacralization of good manners, order, and cleanliness ("next to Godliness") in nineteenth-century Protestantism. In this sense, feelings that had been made private during the last stage of history are becoming public again in environmentalism.

All of these tendencies have contradictory implications, and their eventual outcome is hidden in the future. These uncertainties are inevitable in a transition between two historical epochs. But whatever tendencies away from the public world there may be either in the former Soviet Union or in the West will be reinforced by some trends that are much less ambiguous. These are the globalization of the economy and the revolution in telecommunications.

The market has always been a way of organizing or coordinating society, like government. But the birth of a truly global market in the past few years is something new; the market is bound to make more decisions that would otherwise be made by states. And people's perception that prosperity does not depend decisively on the nation-state, as in many European countries today, is bound to reduce interest in that part of the public world confined to one's own country. The greater and greater mobility of information and people between states, though it can easily be overstated, presses in the same direction.

Still more destructive of the public world is the revolution in telecommunications and data processing. All telecommunications technologies have ambiguous potentials to privatize or to politicize people because they bring the public world "into the living room." In the case of television, the effect seems to have been more privatizing: Television probably has something to do with the decline of oratory. But the interactive telecommunications technologies, such as telephones or the Internet, have a more explosive effect. They enable individuals to reach other individuals with similar tastes or interests without going through the public world, as we used to do in publishing, broadcasting, or old-fashioned politics. With these technologies, there is no need for capitals or government offices. And it has been asserted that the very nature of large telecommunications networks that must exchange information with each other, such as telephones or personal computers, means that they cannot be efficiently managed through a central authority. Technology itself discourages, by this argument, hierarchy.

In Western countries, the erosive potential of all these cultural and technological forces is limited by the solidity of the existing institutions. In the former Soviet Union, the institutions have been twice shattered, first in creating the all-absorbing Soviet state, then in its disintegration. In a place like Georgia, the state does not control all of its nominal territory, does not defend against foreigners, and only tenuously maintains public order. In order to cope with the erosive forces, what is necessary is to *re-create* the institutions of the modern state, in the face of a deep dislike of all institutions.

The Impact of Relativism

I will end with a discussion about an influence on contemporary history that is elusive but deep. This is *relativism*, the belief that "values" are subjective and cannot be deduced from facts. Nietzsche and Martin Heidegger, who recognized and also spoke for this deep conviction of contemporary man, used the term *nihilism* rather than relativism. I will do so as well. A deeper probing of the meaning of nihilism in Nietzsche and Heidegger uncovers "something decisive for its understanding: nihilism is a *process*, the process of devaluation, whereby the uttermost values become valueless."[53] For Nietzsche, this process goes at least as far back as the origins of Christianity and Buddhism.[54] Heidegger greatly developed this post-Hegelian understanding of nihilism as the unfolding of an inner logic in history.

What does this interpretation of nihilism imply for the public world? First, that all modern political institutions, movements, and "values" issue from nihilism. If we realize the frightful consequences of nihilism as a historical phenomenon, we will lose our respect both for the present public institutions and for the movements that (until 1991) attempted to replace them. According to the section of Nietzsche's *Thus Spake Zarathustra* entitled "On the New Idols," the state claims to be above religion and ethnicity. The state is "the death of peoples," and

> where there is still a people, [the state] hates it as the evil eye and a sin against ethics and rights. . . . Every people speaks its tongue of good and evil [i.e., its "values" or culture]: the neighbor does not understand it. [A people] invents its own speech of ethics and rights. . . . But the state lies in all the tongues of good and evil. . . . Confusion of tongues of good and evil: this sign I give you as the sign of the state.[55]

In other words, the modern state, like the biblical Tower of Babel, claims universality, but it is a false universality. Nietzsche is speaking not of the generic state of contemporary social science, but of the state in a more exact sense: the modern ethnically and religiously neutral state; the state created by the American Revolution, the French Revolution, or Napoleon; or the state created by the Enlightenment reforms of the Emperor Joseph II, Frederick the Great, and Catherine the Great and elaborated in Hegel's *Philosophy of Right*. The title of Nietzsche's aphorism, "On the New Idols," parodies Hegel's assertion that the state is "the march of God on earth."[56] This is the state that severed the connection between itself and the national brand of Christianity, giving the Jews, Protestants, Irish Catholics, or Tartars equal rights.

The modern state is, as the Enlightenment understood it, a *constructed* political community, originating in a social contract whereby all the individuals, acting out of the universal fear of death natural to man and not from any ethnic or religious "values," give up their power to a sovereign, an artificial "Leviathan." Such a constructed political community, unlike the Greek *polis* or the Islamic *umma*, can "naturalize" people from another ethnic group or religion who accept its intellectual formula, without requiring they change their "values." Although we have lost its intellectual underpinning, it is also our state.

Toward these states, which have become the public worlds for modern Western man, Nietzsche expresses uncompromising hostility. Elsewhere he includes in his critique of modern values "liberal institutions"; among the "modern ideas" he derides as false are "freedom, equal rights, humanity, . . . *das Volk* [the People], race, the nation, democracy, tolerance."[57] He altogether prefers the political communities that indissolubly fused the community with an exclusive, intolerant set of values: the tribal community, the ancient polis, the aristocratic republic of Venice, perhaps the medieval Christian kingdom. For Nietzsche himself these forms have been extinguished by the historical process, and we are left without a public space—a condition difficult to understand or construct in the real world. A less sophisticated reader of his analysis of the falseness of the modern state could be excused for drawing the conclusion that the liberal state should return to the ethnically homogeneous state by ethnic cleansing.

At a practical level, the public world, and today the state, claims the energy of "the most gifted spirits," who squander their talents on "low, mediocre, and not at all indispensable goals."[58] This attitude, shared by Nietzsche's fellow nihilists such as Gustave Flaubert and Richard Wagner, developed into the powerful antipolitical current displayed by Fascists such as José Antonio Primo de Rivera and Adolf Hitler.[59]

On Nietzsche's ground, the alternative to passive contempt for the state and politics is an active attempt to change or destroy it. Nietzsche's rhetoric certainly encourages this alternative: "We must be destroyers!"[60] After Nietzsche, the fascists and Nazis attempted to embody nihilism in a kind of revolutionary politics, at least briefly embraced by Heidegger. It is doubtful that Nietzsche himself could have taken this direction, because his analysis of the revolutionary socialist, anarchist, and liberal-nationalist movements of his day is almost as hostile as his analysis of the state. In the section of *Thus Spake Zarathustra* on revolution, "On Great Events," Nietzsche tells the "overthrowers" that the state, "like you, . . . likes to speak with smoke and bellowing—to make itself believe, like you, that it speaks out of the stomach of things."[61] In other words, the revolutionaries, like the state, sense that in trying to go beyond the traditional community they are superficial; to conceal their edgy lack of confidence and spontaneity they make extreme claims and demand unconditional allegiance, adorning the thinness of what they advocate with pretentious language. The state and antistate revolutions are themselves "incomplete forms of nihilism." "Now everything is false through and through, chaotic, weak, or extravagant"; "everything turns into *histrionics*." Nietzsche gives the examples of nationalist politics, socialism, and anarchism.[62] Nevertheless, revolutionary movements are not quite as contemptible. Zarathustra tells the revolutionary "fire hound" of "On Great Events" that there is another fire hound, who produces laughter and gold.

The worship of the modern state and the desire to strengthen the state were characteristic of nationalist movements in nineteenth-century Europe;

the strength of nationalism, but not of state-building, has recently been shown in the post-Communist wars of secession. These nationalist movements were, for Nietzsche, superficial, false, and histrionic because the deeper reality is "the process of Europeans" (or at least the higher men) becoming similar.[63] Since Nietzsche wrote those words about a hundred years ago, the creation of "we good Europeans" has proceeded far further than anyone else could have predicted after the Franco-Prussian War. About nationalism and the state, Nietzsche was a prophet of the future. Yet as Europeans become ever more similar, nationalisms such as those of the Irish, Scots, Welsh, Basques, Flemings, Corsicans, Bretons, Slovaks, and most of the peoples of former Yugoslavia and the former Soviet Union (save the Russians) have also grown stronger. This paradox might be seen as support for Nietzsche's argument about the artificiality or deceptive character of nationalism: Nationalism is somehow a reaction to an awareness that it is not the trend of the age.

Why Nietzsche prefers the leftist and nationalist revolutionaries becomes clear in a passage from *Twilight of the Idols*:

> Liberal institutions cease to be liberal [i.e., freeing] as soon as they are attained: later on, there are no worse and no more thorough injurers of freedom than liberal institutions. Their effects are known well enough: they undermine the will to power; they level mountain and valley, and call that morality; they make men small, cowardly, and hedonistic.[64]

Men become cowardly because, as Nietzsche explains in the preceding aphorism: "We modern men [are] very tender, very easily hurt, and offering as well as receiving consideration a hundred-fold. . . . Hence each helps the other; hence everyone is to a certain extent sick, and everyone is a nurse for the sick."[65] Here Nietzsche was prophetic. He had not seen modern America, in which those who have unusual sexual tastes no longer have the boldness simply to pursue them but go on television seeking the acceptance and validation of their tastes, while elite opinion, no longer intolerant or merely acting as if it did not know these things, rushes to change laws that might make such special types uncomfortable.

In addition, equality and the professionalization of leadership in institutions such as the Civil Service sap the envy that has been one of the sources of republican revolution. William Shakespeare presents both these sources of republicanism in *Julius Caesar*. Brutus seems to be motivated by the good of Rome and Roman tradition, but Cassius is motivated by unwillingness to accept that Caesar is bigger than he is:

> and this man
> Is now become a god, and Cassius is
> A wretched creature, and must bend his body
> If Caesar carelessly but nod on him.

Why man, he doth bestride the narrow world
Like a Colossus, and we petty men
Walk under his huge legs, and peep about
To find ourselves dishonorable graves.[66]

Shakespeare suggests, I believe, that both kinds of republican spirit are necessary for republics. But Nietzsche, for his part, would ask whether republican envy does not presuppose a society in which there is a vast gradient of rank and prestige between men, with the great ambition and the great envy that the distance between men induces. The coming of Hegel and Fukuyama's "universal recognition," Nietzsche would argue, will erode both. We are still able to understand the experience that Cassius expresses. But who among us would say the same thing?

Perhaps men who grow up under liberal institutions value freedom less because they are "free enough": There is no longer any immediate risk of despotism or of alien rule. In Yemen, not many miles north of the capital's international airport, there still live tribes for whom the only alternative is despotic rule. When the government sends someone to collect taxes, they simply shoot him. Our attitude toward things imposed on us against our will is, for better or worse, far less savage. The institution of school busing from middle-class white to poor black schools, or vice versa, is a striking example. Busing was ordered by the courts, and public opinion polls consistently showed it to be opposed by the majority of the public in most cities where it took place. Opposition to busing evoked a few protests and, combined with simple racism, occasioned support for political movements, like the George Wallace campaign in 1968, that made an issue of it openly or covertly. Yet neither through the easy weapon of electoral politics or by other means was it ever reversed on a wide scale until, decades later, elite opinion began to doubt its efficacy. The response of the richer whites in many southern cities was simply to abandon the public schools that their tax money paid for, sending their children to private schools that were almost all white. By so doing they achieved their aims, educational or racist, by private rather than public means; they showed how little they resented having things imposed on them from above, the resentment that is the most fundamental root of republican government. (In fairness, their response may have also been influenced by an awareness of the injustice they, or their ancestors, had inflicted on African Americans.) They showed, perhaps, how little they conceived of republican government as a good in itself rather than an instrumental good and a habit.

This last example illustrates how the widely diffused wealth, and the welfare systems, of modern liberal democracy make men "small, cowardly, and hedonistic," as Nietzsche puts it.[67] Ancient and medieval democracy did not much shift the extremes of rich and poor. Modern liberal democracy has achieved, through the technological mastery of nature and through capitalism, a wide level of comfort; it becomes far easier to solve problems through one's private resources without using politics. If the cities are declining, move to the suburbs. Thus, the comfort that goes with liberal institutions takes us away from the public world.

Nietzsche goes on to say:

> These same institutions produce quite different effects while they are still being fought for; then they really promote freedom in a powerful way. On closer inspection, it is war that produces these effects, the war for liberal institutions, which, as a war, permits illiberal instincts to continue. And war educates for freedom. For what is freedom? That one has the will to assume responsibility for oneself. That one maintains the distance which separates us. That one becomes more indifferent to difficulties, hardships, privation, even to life itself. . . . The free man is a *warrior*.[68]

What these two passages together mean is that liberal institutions are unstable; they owe their prestige to liberal revolutions, wars of national unification (such as the war of 1870 in which Nietzsche served), and foreign wars in which the nation and its liberal principles are at stake. In peaceful times, says Nietzsche, the liberal demand for freedom ebbs slowly away. If we put this together with Nietzsche's preference for leftist or nationalist revolution over the status-quo state and his general preference for the tastes of the Right, we arrive at this: a revolutionary regime of the Right which lives for war. But this is the political formula discovered by fascism. Nietzsche's captious taste would have scorned the Fascist regimes that emerged in practice, but the attempt to extract practical political recommendations from his very theoretical, impractical reflections on politics must point in the direction of fascism or something of the sort. This is, in passing, an additional reason for doubting, in the very moment of its triumph, the indefinite survival of the liberal democratic state.

Nihilism is the deepest tendency of our time; the evidence for this appears far stronger a hundred years after Nietzsche. The greatest nihilist thinkers, Nietzsche and Heidegger, pointed in the direction of fascism or actually supported it. Their later, more timorous followers shared their extreme contempt for liberal democratic regimes; they have tended to support the politics of the extreme Left, often with a nationalist ("Third World") or Fascist coloring. The greatest lesson of the French Revolution and of the collapse of Communism is that long-prevailing habits of thinking have practical, political consequences. As I write these words, nihilist habits of thinking and acting are a century old in the heart of Europe, some sixty years old in Island America. We, in our turn, are waiting quietly for whatever lesson we may be taught.

Is Nietzsche right that revolutions and wars are the golden age of liberal institutions? There is the odd fact that modern liberal democratic regimes somehow re-enact their founding struggles. The existence of political parties creates a kind of permanent "war." If the parties are loyal to the principles of the regime, they interpret the struggle with their opponents as a struggle for liberty itself.[69] The Jeffersonians, Abraham Lincoln, and the New Dealers all understood themselves in this way. Even in the Soviet Union, a regime "liberal" in some of Nietzsche's senses but in no way democratic, the "Second Revolution" of Stalin, the de-Stalinization after him, and then the reforms of Gorbachev repeated a similar pattern. And in the great wars for freedom, the liberal democratic regimes recovered a waning civic spirit, as George Orwell noticed in 1940. To a soured observer of the 1990s it seems that the Cold War might have kept alive the feeling of being free and the desire to express it in politics.

Perhaps the periodic returns to principle of liberal democratic regimes give them a vitality that Nietzsche did not understand, because he lived in an age when no liberal democratic regime had lived much longer than a generation. Nevertheless, it props up Nietzsche's deeper vision of liberalism: Liberalism seems to have an inner discord between the motives that attract men to it and the way of life that it establishes. Is this discord, however, strong enough to imperil the survival of liberal motives by too much success? In the two hundred years of the United States, the oldest liberal republic, this has not yet happened; it is impossible to predict what another two hundred years will bring.

We can discern, on the basis of Nietzsche's reflections, another cleft in the heart of the liberal state: the discord between liberal or freedom-loving sentiments and liberal institutions. The notion of sovereignty requires that the liberal state, in contrast to other political communities, be highly institutionalized (that is, law-bound, bureaucratized, shaped by institutional doctrines such as the separation of powers). Nietzsche observes:

> I already characterized modern democracy, together with its hybrids such as the "German *Reich*," as the form of decline of the state. In order that there may be institutions, there must be a kind of will, instinct, or imperative, which is anti-liberal to the point of malice: the will to tradition, to authority, to responsibility for centuries to come.[70]

In other words, citizens and officials must feel truly bound by what their "founding fathers" set up, even against their own wishes. To take the simplest example, the citizen who rejects something in the current leadership must wait until the next election that is in his country's institutional cycle to do something about it. And there must be the kind of responsibility for future generations that changes in institutions are not made for partisan or emotional or self-interested reasons, but only with a view to their permanent utility. However, Nietzsche observes for his time:

> The whole of the West no longer possesses the instincts out of which institutions grow, out of which a future grows: perhaps nothing antagonizes its "modern spirit" so much. One lives for the day, one lives very fast, one lives very irresponsibly: precisely this is called "freedom." That which makes an institution an institution is despised, hated, repudiated.[71]

The interpretation of the American Constitution is a perfect example. Liberal judges found that their conviction of what was right in certain situations was not in the Constitution according to "strict construction." They therefore interpreted the Constitution to find there what was just and humane—they discovered, for example, the right of privacy in the "penumbra" of an amendment. They "lived irresponsibly" in the sense that they exploited the Constitution, and the judicial powers granted them as a constitutional institution, to achieve what was needed at the moment, never thinking that the courts could fall into the hands of conservative judges who would use the same freedom for opposite ends. In fact conservative judges have been appointed who used their power to decide issues conservatively but still not according to strict construction. While the example is perfect, the obvious discomfort of democratic man with institutions has remained within limits. Many of the great episodes of disregard for institutions—the Nullification Crisis or the *Dred Scott* decision in America, the 1910 struggle over the House of Lords in Britain—are in the past; there is no obvious trend.

In the lands of the former Soviet bloc a very different situation exists. Old institutions keep citizens in the tracks of their tradition; the very modern tameness of which Nietzsche complains limits the desire to change them. In the former Soviet space the old institutions are discredited and ruined. If ever in our lives we are to see a test of modern man's loyalty to new institutions, it will be here. What do we see? The dislike of armies and uniforms, those great symbols of the Enlightenment state, speaks eloquently. (It is not unknown in the West.) When in 1993 Yeltsin dismissed the Russian Duma, its members refused to go. When they impeached him, he in turn refused to go, and the contest was settled with tanks. Throughout the former Soviet Union, few pay their taxes or their utility bills; factories do not pay their debts to suppliers or the workers' salaries. When courts order officials to do something, they frequently refuse. Mayor Yuri Luzhkov of Moscow, for example, has been told by the Russian Constitutional Court that the city's rules requiring a permit to reside there are unconstitutional; he simply refuses to comply, and the Russian president, who represents the executive power, does not care. We have seen in the vast area of globe freed from Communism a vast flowering of modern man's impatience with institutions. Only after much time has passed can we know whether this phenomenon is more a short-term response to Communist pressure or the emergence of something basic to modern man.

All institutions require organization and therefore create hierarchies. But liberal man resents hierarchies. Nietzsche embodies this trait in developed form in his presentation of the possible end point of nihilism, the "last man." He is addressing not the reality of his time but the future—perhaps our present. The last man says: "Who still wants to rule? Who still wants to obey? Both are too burdensome."[72] According to the presentation of the future culmination of nihilism in *Zarathustra*, "one still loves one's neighbor and rubs up against him: for one needs warmth." Nietzsche goes on to say: "No herdsman and one herd! Everyone wants the same, everyone is the same: whoever feels different, goes willingly into a madhouse."[73] Thus there is, in this hypothetical future, a kind of spontaneous community but no rule and no institutions. Without institutions or rule, there is no state; this prediction fits Nietzsche's observations on the ongoing decline of the state.

Such a condition is hard even to imagine. It does exist, according to anthropologists, in hunting and gathering societies; it is the hypothetical past of all of us. What seems impossible to imagine is how one might get to such a place from here, from the existing states and everything that is interwoven with them. Still, some exceedingly curious phenomena in the post–Cold War world point in this direction. There are, as we have seen, the strange cases of Chechnya and Kosovo. In Kosovo, from 1989 until the rise of the Kosovo Liberation Army in 1997, Ibrahim Rugova "ruled" the Albanian population, but without the army and police that are part of the modern state. Those who opposed Rugova yielded to him voluntarily, or through social pressure, without coercion, because he represented the community.

In Chechnya the 1996–99 government of Aslan Maskhadov did not perform most of the functions of a state; the military and financial strength lay with the opposition warlords. Yet he continued to represent the community. He did not settle the question of rule, in the manner of a Western sovereign, by using the National Guard which is supposed to be the state's army. The reason appears to lie in the community's taboo against Chechens killing other Chechens. The National Guard, as the possession of the whole community, seems to be regarded as properly neutral in disputes over the control of the state, over who rules. This community is one that exists only in imagination, and not in institutions. It includes the Chechens of Urus Martan, who were under the armed control of Islamic extremists opposing Maskhadov. To sum up the apparent state of affairs, the community powerfully sways the actions of leaders, but largely without institutions.[74] It approaches to being a community without a state.

Consequences of Belief in Relativism

So far, we have talked about the impact of unconscious nihilism and about the perspective on the liberal state of Nietzsche, the first consciously nihilist thinker. Beginning about 1890, Nietzsche's philosophical perspective became influential, first in Germany, then in other continental European countries, much later in England and the United States, and finally throughout the world. Like most philosophic teachings, nihilism shifted its meaning as it became accepted. As the late Allan Bloom wrote, "we have . . . [a] peculiarly American way of digesting Continental despair. It is nihilism with a happy ending."[75] As we approach the end of this chapter, we need to be aware of these complexities.

The politically committed reader who follows the arguments of Nietzsche or Heidegger is likely to be impatient. If we live under a despotic government, what are we to do about it? If we should share Nietzsche's low opinion of liberal democracy, are we merely helpless? After an oppressive government is toppled, as in Kosovo, how are we to shape new political institutions? There is no clear answer to any of these questions. There is no nihilist political solution. Some nihilists saw such solutions in various forms of fascism, but their charms did not survive experience.

The first answer suggested by these quandaries is surely: At all costs stay away from politics. Politics seduces and corrupts. It is not clear whether there remains a modest place for a nihilist who acts within politics but without being seduced by political ends. The famous Lawrence of Arabia, for example, acted within politics, but apparently without accepting as his own the goals of either the British government or the sharif of Mecca.[76]

In any case, many nihilists will inevitably be driven by political passion, ambition, or circumstances into political action. Is it possible to say anything more about how nihilism will affect their political action? At the beginning it is important to recognize the essential ambiguity of nihilism. The root is the absence of any rational judgment about "values" or ends, so that it is impossible to say what ends politics should pursue. This starting point can branch either into tolerance for all the competing values, an implication that has been more often drawn out in postwar America, or a belief in the need to choose one value and pursue it with fanatical zeal and determination. Nietzsche's own orientation on this question can be inferred from his assertion that "it is a good war that sanctifies any cause."[77]

To be effective in public life, political actors must be driven by passionate commitment to "values": national independence, or tradition, or loyalty to a dynasty, or emancipation from oppression, or other such feelings. As Max Weber, a thoughtful follower of Nietzsche, wrote: "When speaking at a political meeting about democracy, one does not hide one's personal standpoint; indeed, to come out clearly and take a stand is one's damn duty. The words one uses in such a meeting are not means of scientific analysis. . . . They are swords against the enemies."[78] But these "values" are not susceptible to rational argument. As Weber said: "Speaking directly, the ultimately possible attitudes toward life are irreconcilable, and hence their struggle can never be brought to a conclusion. Thus it is necessary to make a decisive choice."[79]

In other words, what goes on in politics is *private* to each person or political group. The public world breaks up into many private worlds: the religious Right, gays, Amnesty International, Islamic fundamentalists, officials who believe in the national interest, xenophobes, and others. Each of these worlds is illuminated and constituted by privately held values: Christian morality, freedom, and so forth. This casts a bright light on the dark corner of ethnic cleansing in our time. Serbs are motivated by Serb national traditions, but these are private "values": There can be no reasoning with Albanians who happen not to share them, no inclusion of them, so the Albanians must be evicted or killed.[80] Ethnic cleansing is consistent relativism as translated in the sphere of political practice.

Each of these private worlds of political conviction is as private as the world of the people you encounter in public parks, talking or shouting to themselves. Our word *idiot* originally meant in Greek a private person, as opposed to a citizen. The relativist in politics is as closed upon himself, as deprived of communication, as a literal idiot.

The privacy of the relativist in politics explains what Nietzsche said is the histrionic character of modern politics.[81] If you know you have trouble being heard or understood, you raise your voice. Politicians become histrionic to convince themselves, over the slowly dawning realization of nihilism, that they can reach followers. And of course it becomes a vicious circle: Histrionic politics creates skepticism, the leaders of political movements shout louder to overcome it, their audience is more "turned off," and the cycle repeats. The direct effects of the difficulty we sense in communicating "values," and the indirect effects through histrionic politics, eventually take their toll. Although Weber admires the man of passionate, irrational conviction, he confesses that "precisely the ultimate and most sublime values have retreated from public life, either into the transcendental realm of mystic life or into the brotherliness of direct and personal human relations."[82] Eventually this retreat will make the public world a desert, a true abode of emptiness.

I only wish to pose the question of whether the East, the former Soviet bloc, may be anticipating the transformation fated to occur in the rest of the earth. We will not know in our lifetimes whether the East is the incomplete form of the West, as we imply in speaking of "transitions to democracy," or the West's obscure destiny. But wherever great works of destruction, creation, and redefinition are under way across a vast area of the world's surface, it is possible that the future is being forged. If it now should happen so, it is of those figures lost in the Eastern twilight, the refugee in headlong flight from her burning village, the teacher in his heatless classroom, the militia chieftain, of whom it will someday be sung:

> He discerns already in the first sign the consummation
> And flies, the bold spirit, like an eagle before
> Thunderstorms, foreboding, before
> His approaching gods.[83]

NOTES

1. Bernard Mandeville, *Die Bienenfabel, oder Private Laster, oeffentliche Vorteile,* ed. Walter Euchner (Munich: Suhrkamp, 1980), 71.

2. See the revealing article by Valery Vyzhutovich, "Druz'ya . . . ," *Izvestia,* October 21, 1993.

3. Daphne Skillen, "Media Coverage in the Elections," in Peter Lentini, ed., *Elections and Political Order in Russia: The Implications of the 1993 Elections to the Federal Assembly* (Budapest: Central European University Press, 1994), 103.

4. Matthew Wyman et al., "Parties and Voters in the Elections," in Lentini, *Elections and Political Order,* 130.

5. Pavel Voschanov, "'Here I Am in the Kremlin!' What Next?" *Komsomolskaya Pravda,* December 8, 1994 (English translation in FBIS-SOV, December 9, 1994).

6. Natalya Arkhangelskaya, "Raskol v rukovodtsve DPR," *Kommersant-Daily,* October 19, 1994.

7. Michael McFaul, *Russia between Elections: What the December 1995 Results Really Mean* (Moscow: Moskovskiy Tsentr Karnegi, 1996), 19.

8. Michael McFaul, interview with the author, Washington, D.C., July 21, 1999.

9. The best book on the KPRF (Communist Party of the Russian Federation)— Joan Barth Urban, *Russia's Communists at the Crossroads* (Boulder, Colo.: Westview, 1997)—discusses the fraud charges, but draws no conclusion from the fact that they were dropped; see 169, 180–81.

10. Larry Diamond, *Developing Democracy* (Baltimore: Johns Hopkins University Press, 1999).

11. Interview with S. N. Popov, *Polyarnaya Pravda* (Murmansk), February 14, 1995 (English translation in FBIS-SOV, March 30, 1995).

12. Interview with Ghia Nodia, *Georgia Profile* (Tbilisi) 2, no. 7: 25.

13. Popov interview.

14. I owe this to Shakespeare, *Henry IV, Part I,* and Ammianus Marcellinus, *Res Gestae,* 22.2, 3–5.

15. The case involving Danilov was described to me by a Belorussian democratic activist in 1996.

16. Ghia Nodia, "Nationalism and Democracy," *Journal of Democracy* 3, no. 4 (October 1992): 3–22. See also Ghia Nodia, "Underestimating Nationalism," in the forthcoming book I am editing on the lessons of the collapse of Communism.

17. For some details, see Charles H. Fairbanks, Jr., "After the Moscow Coup," *Journal of Democracy* 2 (Fall 1991): 3–10.

18. Liberal Democratic Party of Russia, press release, January 1995.

19. See Charles H. Fairbanks, Jr., "The Politics of Resentment," *Journal of Democracy* 5, no. 2 (April 1994): 35–41.

20. "Consequences of Losing Abkhazia . . . ," supplement to *Georgian Chronicle* (Tbilisi), September 1994, 1. Cf. Valery Russu, "Gruzia: boi prodolzhaiutsya, no uzhe obsuzhdaiut, kuda ubezhit Gamsakhurdiya," *Izvestia,* November 4, 1993. Interview with Tengiz Sigua, *Sakartvelos Respublika* (Tbilisi), January 24–27, 1995, in FBIS-SOV, February 15, 1995.

21. G. M. Tamás, Presentation to the Washington Seminar on the Collapse of Communism, Johns Hopkins Foreign Policy Institute, May 25, 1993.

22. See the agreement, from very different positions, of Andrei Illarionov, "The Roots of the Economic Crisis," *Journal of Democracy* 10, no. 2 (April 1999): 76, and Anders Aslund, "The Problem of Fiscal Federalism," *Journal of Democracy* 10, no. 2 (April 1999): 83.

23. Aslund, "Problem of Fiscal Federalism," 85.

24. "Deputies Polled on Local Power," ITAR-TASS dispatch, in FBIS-SOV, April 3, 1992, 46.

25. This was the confidential opinion of some Georgian officials I interviewed in 1998.

26. Mikhail Ovcharov, "Yaroslavl Militiamen Say No to Hot Spots," *Izvestia,* June 30, 1993 (English translation in FBIS-SOV, July 1, 1999, 49).

27. Harvard University, John F. Kennedy School of Government, Strengthening Democratic Institutions Project, *Russia Reform Monitor,* no. 455 (June 5, 1998): 1.

28. The best description of corruption in contemporary Russia that I know is Anatol Lieven, *Chechnya: Tombstone of Russian Power* (New Haven: Yale University Press, 1998), 152–87.

29. "Georgian State Jurisdiction No Longer Extends to Svanetia," *Kavkasioni* (Tbilisi), November 29, 1994 (English translation in FBIS-SOV, December 15, 1994, 70).

30. For a much more complete account of the situation in Chechnya, see "The Weak State and Private Armies," a chapter in a forthcoming book edited by Crawford Young and Mark Beissinger.

31. This section is based primarily on interviews by the author in Kosovo (in Priština, Peć, and Prizren) and in Belgrade, Serbia, during August 1993. For a brief introduction to the Kosovo problem, see Fabian Schmidt, "Kosovo: The Time Bomb That Has Not Gone Off," *RFE/RL Research Report* 2, no. 39 (October 1, 1993); and *Balkan War Report*, nos. 19 and 24.

32. The most concentrated presentation is Charles H. Fairbanks, Jr., "The Postcommunist Wars," *Journal of Democracy* 6, no. 4 (October 1995): 18–34.

33. Sergei Vologodsky and Nikolai Aleksandrov, "Tajikistan Faces Its Bloody Legacy," *We/My*, June 1993; ITAR-TASS dispatch, September 5, 1992; Radio Moscow in English 2100 GMT September 6, 1992; and INTERFAX dispatch, September 6, 1992, all in FBIS-SOV, September 8, 1992, 54–55.

34. *Narodnaya gazeta* (Minsk), September 10, 1992; *Literatura i matsatstva*, September 11, 1992.

35. See *Vecherniy Bishkek*, December 22, 1994, 1.

36. R. W. Southern, *The Making of the Middle Ages* (New Haven: Yale University Press, 1961), 110; cf. 105, 107–8.

37. François P. Guizot, *A Popular History of France from the Earliest Times*, trans. Robert Black (New York: H. A. Bolles & Co., n.d.), 1:288; italics mine.

38. Liz Fuller, "Georgia: On the Edge of the Abyss," *RFE/RL Caucasus Report* 1, no. 20 (July 14, 1998): 1. Some of this information was from an interview I had with Ghia Nodia on September 29, 1998.

39. Numa-Denis Fustel de Coulanges, *The Ancient City* (Garden City, N.Y.: Doubleday, n.d.), 198–205, 219–23, 337–88.

40. Fustel de Coulanges, *Ancient City*, 379–80.

41. See, e.g., M. Rostovtzeff, *Rome*, trans. J. D. Duff (Oxford: Oxford University Press, 1960), 266–90.

42. A. A. Vasiliev, *History of the Byzantine Empire, 324–1453* (Madison: University of Wisconsin Press, 1958), 1, 67.

43. Tacitus, *Agricola*, 6.3. Cf. 5.3, 7.3, 8.1, 11.4, 39.2, and 40.3.

44. Tacitus, *Agricola*, 31.2.

45. Tacitus, *Agricola*, 24.3.

46. Ramsay MacMullen, *Roman Government's Response to Crisis* (New Haven: Yale University Press, 1976), 28–30, 70–72, quoting E. Verney (1913).

47. A. Steinwenter (1939), quoted in MacMullan, *Roman Response to Crisis*, 244 n. 1.

48. MacMullen, *Roman Response to Crisis*, 72, 245 n. 5.

49. "Die Positivitaet der christlichen Religion," in Herman Nohl, ed., *Hegels theologische Jugendschriften* (Frankfurt/Main: Minerva, 1966), 219–31. This interpretation of the collapse of paganism, unpublished until 1907, was in some respects reached independently by Fustel de Coulanges and by Nietzsche.

50. See the works of John Willerton; Charles H. Fairbanks, Jr., "Clientelism and the Roots of Post-Soviet Disorder," in Ronald Suny, ed., *Transcaucasia, Nationalism,*

and Social Change: Essays in the History of Armenia, Azerbaijan, and Georgia, rev. ed. (Ann Arbor: University of Michigan Press, 1996), 341–74; and Charles H. Fairbanks, Jr., *How the Soviet System Worked* [working title] (forthcoming), chap. 2.

51. "The Legacy of Dissent," *Uncaptive Minds* 7, no. 2 (26) (Summer 1994): 30–34.

52. G. M. Tamás, "Old Enemies and New: A Philosophic Postscript to Nationalism," *Studies in East European Thought* 45 (1993): 117; G. M. Tamás, presentation to the Washington Seminar on the Collapse of Communism, SAIS Foreign Policy Institute, Washington, D.C., June 2, 1994.

53. Martin Heidegger, *Nietzsche*, trans. Frank A. Capuzzi (San Francisco: Harper and Row, 1982), 4:14, commenting on the fragment of an aphorism published as no. 1 of Friedrich Nietzsche, *Der Wille zur Macht* [The will to power].

54. Nietzsche, *Der Wille zur Macht*, nos. 4, 55, 114, 152, 154, 247.

55. Friedrich Nietzsche, *Also Sprach Zarathustra* [Thus spake Zarathustra], pt. 1, "Vom neuen Goetzen," in Friedrich Nietzsche, *Werke*, vol. 4, ed. Alfred Baeumler (Leipzig: Alfred Kroener, 1930), 51.

56. G. W. F. Hegel, *Philosophy of Right*, sec. 258A.

57. *Nachgelassene Fragmente, 1887–1889*, vol. 15 of the Kritische Studienausgabe edition, ed. Giorgio Colli and Massimo Montinari (Berlin: Deutscher Taschenbuch Verlag/de Gruyter), fragments 15 [1] and 16 [82].

58. Friedrich Nietzsche, "The Dawn," no. 149, in Friedrich Nietzsche, *The Portable Nietzsche*, ed. and trans. Walter Kaufmann (New York: Viking Press, 1958), 82.

59. See, for example, Primo de Rivera's powerful speech at the founding of the Falange, in Charles F. Delzell, ed., *Mediterranean Fascism, 1919–1945* (New York: Harper and Row, 1970), 260–61; and Joachim C. Fest, *Hitler*, trans. Richard Winston and Clara Winston (New York: Vintage Books, 1975), 379–81, 761–62.

60. See the fragment inserted in Friedrich Nietzsche, *The Will to Power*, trans. Walter Kaufmann (New York: Vintage Books, 1967), no. 417.

61. Nietzsche, *Also Sprach Zarathustra*, pt. 2, "Von grossen Ereignissen," 144.

62. Nietzsche, *Will to Power*, fragments numbered 28, 30, 68 (quotes), 42, 59, 71, 78.

63. *Jenseits von Gut und Boese*, in Nietzsche, *Werke*, no. 242; see also 253, 254.

64. Nietzsche, *Twilight of the Idols*, "Skirmishes of an Untimely Man," no. 38 (p. 541 in Nietzsche, *The Portable Nietzsche*).

65. Nietzsche, *Twilight of the Idols*, "Skirmishes of an Untimely Man," no. 37 (p. 538 in Nietzsche, *The Portable Nietzsche*).

66. William Shakespeare, *Julius Caesar*, act 2, sc. 2, lines 96–97, 133–36.

67. Nietzsche, *Twilight of the Idols*, "Skirmishes of an Untimely Man," no. 38.

68. Nietzsche, *Twilight of the Idols*, "Skirmishes of an Untimely Man," no. 38.

69. This thought flows from Harry V. Jaffa, "The Nature and Origin of the American Party System," *Equality and Liberty: Theory and Practice in American Politics* (New York: Oxford University Press, 1965), 3–41.

70. Nietzsche, *Twilight of the Idols*, "Skirmishes of an Untimely Man," no. 39 (p. 543 in Nietzsche, *The Portable Nietzsche*).

71. Nietzsche, *Twilight of the Idols*, "Skirmishes of an Untimely Man," no. 39.

72. Nietzsche, *Also Sprach Zarathustra*, prologue, no. 5.

73. Nietzsche, *Also Sprach Zarathustra*, prologue, no. 5.

74. For a more detailed account of contemporary Chechnya, with sources, see Charles H. Fairbanks, Jr., "The Weak State and Private Armies in the Former Soviet

Union and in Africa," to be published in Mark Beissinger and Crawford Young, *Beyond State Crisis* [working title] (Washington: Wilson Center Press, forthcoming).

75. Allan Bloom, *The Closing of the American Mind* (New York: Simon and Schuster, 1987), 147.

76. See, to begin with, the poem that serves as a preface for T. E. Lawrence, *The Seven Pillars of Wisdom* (1926).

77. Nietzsche, *Also Sprach Zarathustra*, part 1, "Vom Krieg und Kriegsvolke."

78. Max Weber, "Science as a Vocation," in H. H. Gerth and C. Wright Mills, ed. and trans., *From Max Weber: Essays in Sociology* (New York: Oxford University Press, 1958), 145. I owe the suggestion to examine Weber in connection with the public world to Pierre Manent.

79. Weber, "Science as a Vocation," 152.

80. For a more detailed exposition of this argument, see Charles H. Fairbanks, Jr., "Wars of Hatred and the Hatred of War," *Weekly Standard* 4, no. 29 (April 29, 1999): 22–27.

81. See the notes published in Nietzsche, *Der Wille zur Macht*, nos. 44, 78.

82. Weber, "Science as a Vocation," 155.

83. "Kennt er im ersten Zeichen Vollendetes schon / Und fliegt, der kuhne Geist, wie Adler den / Gewittern, weissagend seined Kommenden Gottern voraus." Friedrich Hoelderlin, "Rousseau" (1799).

14

Ideological Conflicts in Post–Cold War India

Atul Kohli and Pratap B. Mehta

This essay analyzes the emerging ideological landscape in India. Our thesis is that the emerging political terrain in India will remain quite contentious, but that much of this contentiousness will unfold within some broad areas of consensus. The areas of consensus—especially elite consensus—are a unified response to genuine threats to national sovereignty; the desirability of democracy; and the need for economic liberalization as a way of joining and competing within the global economy. Within this broad framework, everyday politics in India will remain noisy, conflictual, and occasionally violent. Conflict will precipitate along several cleavages. In this chapter we will focus mainly on identity and distributional cleavages. The important thing to note about India is that, while some conflicts will indeed take on a national proportion, given the segmented nature of Indian society numerous local conflicts will dominate the political landscape, periodically sapping the governing capacities of the Indian state.

SOME PRELIMINARY ASSERTIONS

Three general assertions will help set the stage for our more specific discussion. First, the end of the Cold War was not a decisive turning point for Indian politics. While Indian politics, as politics elsewhere, is bound to be influenced by such significant global changes, on balance there is at least as much continuity as change in India's domestic politics before and after the demise of the Soviet Union.

Second, the focus of this chapter is on the emerging ideological landscape of India. We analyze ideologies while assuming that the worlds of ideological and political struggles (e.g., over material conditions and/or involving share of state power) mutually reinforce each other. If one had to choose between ideological and political factors—which fortunately we do not—one could do a lot worse than to accept the Weberian claim that, while over the

280

short run ideas can sometimes become a powerful force in their own right, over a longer time frame ideas and ideologies are difficult to sustain without real "interests."

The last of the preliminary comments concerns the two major dimensions of ideological conflict in India, namely, the Right-Left and the national-identity dimensions. First, we interpret the Right-Left dimension of conflict as expressing conflict between the politics of privilege and the politics of social justice. Given India's deep inequalities, therefore, it is hard to imagine a political world in which ideologies expressing the politics of protecting privilege and ideologies demanding social justice will vanish. Ideological struggles of the future may not involve "conservatives" versus "socialists," but the deeper tendencies that Left and Right reflect—namely, protection of privilege and demands for social justice—are bound to infiltrate the idiom of political conflict.

The second dimension of ideological conflict in India concerns questions of national identity. Politics in India, like elsewhere, often involve asking tortuous questions about who "we" are, especially in relation to some more-advanced "Other," and how we can "catch up" to "them." While issues of identity at the national and especially subnational levels are continuously negotiated and renegotiated, a recurring strain at the national level is likely to revolve around the question: Should we emulate the West or seek indigenous solutions? The pro-Western views or the views of those favoring inspiration from indigenous traditions, or some combination thereof, will thus continue to provide alternative visions of nation-building, generating a second major line of ideological cleavage.

The "Left versus Right" and "Western versus indigenous solutions" thus represent two major dimensions of ideological cleavage in India. They commingle in complex ways and help define the broad contours of India's ideological landscape. The matrix shown in table 14.1 helps express a lot of this information economically.

Whereas Mahatma Gandhi dominated India's nationalist movement and Jawaharlal Nehru's socialism was hegemonic in postindependence India, especially between 1950 and the 1970s, the current ideological landscape of India is more contested and has generally moved toward the right.[1] The main national-level struggle involves variants of the Right: Should India move ahead as a "liberal" political economy in the laissez-faire mold of the West or

Table 14.1 India's Ideological Landscape

	Left	*Right*
Pro-West	Nehru and Nehruvian socialism	"economic liberalization"
Indigenous solutions	Gandhi and followers of Gandhi	Hindu nationalism and Hindu nationalist parties (BJP)

is there a unique Hindu path to modernity? While the traditional Left is not a major force at present in India's national politics, the "leftist urge" for social justice is being expressed in India via numerous local and regional struggles. Identity politics of a variety of sorts also proliferate at the subnational levels and interact with the politics of social justice in complicated ways.

After a brief review of historical materials, we will analyze this contemporary ideological landscape by dividing it up into three types of struggles, namely, those over the state's attempts to redefine the project of "modernity," especially the efforts to liberalize India's import substitution economy; those over issues of identity and self-esteem; and those over caste and class issues.

BRIEF HISTORICAL BACKGROUND

India emerged as a sovereign democratic state in 1947 after a protracted but not particularly violent or revolutionary nationalist movement. Gandhi dominated India's nationalist movement, and prior to independence his vision was central among a plethora of competing ideologies regarding the principles an independent India would embody. By the time the Constituent Assembly met in 1947, however, the Gandhian model—especially his critique of modernity and modern technology, on the one hand, and, on the other hand, his preference for nonparty government and for political structures that facilitated decentralized and self-sufficient villages—had been easily brushed aside. Instead, India adopted a Westminster-style parliamentary democracy, ideologically committed to what came to be known as the Nehruvian consensus.

There were several principal elements of the Nehruvian consensus. First, there was the perceived need for a strong, industrialized, but self-reliant economy. This committed India to use the state to create a sizable industrial base and to promote a policy of import substitution. Second, it has widely held that India's backward agrarian structure facilitated the persistence of both oppression and outmoded forms of production, and that it therefore needed to be transformed. Third, the gamut of India's social relations from caste to gender was also deemed by the "modernizers" as "backward," again needing reform. And fourth, there was the belief that the state would be the locus through which the diverse fabric of India would be woven into a consolidated nation. In some senses the ideological history of postindependence India is the history of how these four planks of the Nehruvian consensus have fared—how they have come to be abandoned or contested.[2]

During the 1950s and 1960s, Nehruvian socialism provided a workable legitimacy formula that enabled diverse societal interests in India to cooperate with the regime. The emphasis on national self-sufficiency reflected the widespread anticolonial, nationalist sensibilities that were the bedrock of the relative political coherence of these decades. An inward-looking economic posture that favored protectionism and visualized a sizable role for the state in not only controlling but also subsidizing private profitability was, on balance, welcomed by both an emerging entrepreneurial stratum and by the educated urban classes who sought public-sector jobs. Agrarian elites were of course threatened by promises of land reforms. For better or worse, however, land reforms were never vigorously pursued. The short-term political legacy was benign: Agrarian elites were slowly co-opted into the ruling coalition, and the poor masses, who were not highly mobilized at this early stage, accepted the rhetoric of incorporation and did not pose serious political threats. Finally, a commitment to secularism, as well as the practice of accommodating the demands of regional elites, enabled Nehru and his colleagues to put together a diverse and effective ruling coalition.

The organizational embodiment of Nehruvian socialism was, of course, India's premier political party, the Congress.[3] Never ideologically cohesive or cadre-based, the Congress nevertheless was a highly effective machine that served to reconcile diverse interests. The basic structure of Congress in its heyday (approximately 1940–69) consisted of long patronage chains that stretched from New Delhi, through regional capitals, all the way down to local "big men" in villages. The logic of the system was simple: Locally influential individuals utilized their influence to mobilize electoral support for the Congress; in exchange, when in power—which was nearly always—Congress leaders channeled governmental resources to these local individuals. Several characteristics of the Indian state and society helped this "system" function: Persistence of traditional authority relations enabled the local influential power brokers to sway the political behavior of the poor masses; the growing role of the state in the economy provided substantial resources in the hands of governmental elites to manage a vast patronage network; the highest elites, especially Nehru, were willing to accommodate power challenges from below; and the glue of a nationalist legacy set boundaries on intra-elite power conflicts.

Over time, both the consensus around Nehruvian socialism and the hegemony of the Congress Party weakened. It would take us too far afield to provide a detailed analysis of the underlying dynamics.[4] Suffice it to note that this old "system" was transformed rather profoundly during the second half of the 1960s. Nehru's death in 1964 enabled several long-term trends to emerge to the surface. The legacy of anticolonial nationalism was declining, and intra-elite strife was on the rise. The spread of democratic competition weakened the hold of the traditionally influential individuals and brought numerous new groups into politics. Repeated failure of land reforms made a mockery of socialist commitments. As newly mobilized groups threw their support behind parties other than the Congress, its hegemony was threatened. As the Congress nearly lost power in the late 1960s, a new political arrangement was clearly imminent.

Indira Gandhi stepped into this growing turbulence and helped generate a new populist political system. If the logic of the Nehru era in India was ideologically guided national development, Indira Gandhi's ruling logic was more blatantly that of securing and maintaining power. She adopted a pop-ulist posture (promising alleviation of poverty as her main goal), put the blame for past failures of "socialism" on "vested interests," split the old Con-gress Party, and used her considerable leadership skills to establish a direct rapport with India's masses. As her popularity soared (especially during 1971–75) she adopted a personalistic ruling style, appointing loyal minions to important positions throughout the country. Gandhi's political idiom also became more conflictual, vis-à-vis both internal and external "enemies." A mobilizing ruling style in turn attracted a mobilizing opposition, culminating in the "Emergency" (1975–77), when India's democracy came to the brink and, for a brief period, democratic rights were suspended.

The inability of the smaller parties to work together has always bene-fited the Congress Party. The experience with the Emergency cost the Congress Party dearly in terms of electoral support and propelled a mot-ley group—the Janata party—to power. An ideological mishmash, this group failed to provide coherent government (during 1977–80) and thus paved the way for the return of Indira Gandhi to power in 1980. The In-dira Gandhi that returned to power was a different Indira Gandhi. Whether chastised or not, she slowly sought to distance herself from her own shrill populism and socialism. Instead, the two political trends she initiated—an attempt to liberalize India's economy, and flirtation with communal themes as tools of electoral mobilization—have over the last two decades emerged as dominant themes of Indian politics.

In terms of a chronology, therefore, past ideological patterns in India are best thought of as a period of Nehruvian socialism, followed by a period of Indira Gandhi's populism, leading to the current period, which began around 1980. While a number of governments have come and gone in India since 1980, the twin concerns of economic liberalization, on the one hand, and communal and identity politics, on the other, continue to intensify. This is not surprising insofar as these concerns represent the two possible reac-tions to increasing modernization and globalization: join or resist. By con-trast, the politics of social justice—so prominent during the Nehru and Indira Gandhi periods—has moved off the national agenda; it instead seeks ex-pression through numerous local and regional struggles. It is to a discussion of these contemporary ideological struggles—over the state's attempts to redefine the project of "modernity," over identity, and over distributional issues—that we now turn our attention.

FROM SOCIALISM TO ECONOMIC LIBERALIZATION: IDEOLOGICAL REDEFINITION FROM ABOVE

The 1980s in India was a decade when a variety of ruling and opposition par-ties came around to the view—some enthusiastically, some reluctantly—that the old socialist model of development was exhausted and that a new, more liberal model might well be necessary. While the exact content of this "liberal" model is still being experimented with and debated, it is worth discussing how decisive a shift this has been, how it has come about, and most important, the implications of such a shift for Indian politics.

After returning to power in 1980, as described above, political and economic pressures forced Indira Gandhi to harness her populist ruling style. Her exhortations to alleviate poverty in India had not borne fruit. Continued recourse to failed policies was not likely to be electorally rewarding. Gandhi was also stunned by the desertion of businessmen to opposition parties in the late 1970s, and she increasingly felt the need to tone down her anticorporate populism. On the economic side, India's industrial growth during the 1970s had been disappointing. While this outcome is open to a number of interpretations, it was consistent with the increasingly influential "neoclassical" argument that India's protectionist trade regime and statist controls on domestic production were hampering efficiency and growth.[5] Quietly but surely, therefore, Gandhi softened her radical rhetoric and started experimenting with removal of state controls on the activities of private business.

The problem that Indira Gandhi faced while attempting this economic shift is a problem all subsequent Indian leaders down to the present have faced, namely, its political implications. If populism and related promises to alleviate poverty were to be muted, how were electoral majorities to be won? The question was especially poignant for Gandhi because she helped destroy the old party organization; her main electoral asset was thus her charismatic, populist leadership. Starting in the early 1980s the reintroduction of communal themes in the Congress's political discourse was thus a product of these electoral pressures. If the majority-minority divide was not to be defined along the poor-rich dimension, then in India it could be redefined as a divide involving the Hindu majority on the one side and such religious minorities as Muslims and/or Sikhs on the other side. It is not surprising, therefore, that as the more economically based populism and socialism have fallen into the background, the more communal politics have emerged to the forefront in India. While there is no direct causal link here, it is nevertheless the case that the political vacuum created by abandonment of socialism is now being filled by attempts to liberalize the economy, on the one hand, and the emergence of a variety of identity conflicts, including the rise of the Bharatiya Janata Party (BJP) as India's ruling political party, on the other hand. That, however, is already moving too far ahead in the story.

The halting process of economic liberalization that Indira Gandhi initiated was embraced more wholeheartedly by her son, Rajiv Gandhi. Following the former's assassination by her Sikh bodyguards in 1984—a by-product of the growing communal politics of the period, further discussed below—Rajiv Gandhi became India's prime minister. Whereas Indira Gandhi had sought to accommodate economic liberalization within a muted socialist framework, Rajiv Gandhi altered the idiom of Indian politics by openly castigating the old shibboleths of socialism. As in the case of his mother, this cost him dearly in terms of political support. Following declining popularity, therefore, Rajiv Gandhi abandoned economic liberalization in the second half of his rule (1986–88) and re-embraced some socialist rhetoric and populist programs. Growing electoral pressures also led him to practice communal politics. Among numerous examples that could be cited, prominent were his eventual failure to deliver promised concessions to Sikhs and most important, his allowing Hindus to worship inside the disputed Babari Mosque.

Economic liberalization was pursued more decisively in India during the 1990s. The catalyst for these changes was as much an economic crisis as any further ideological change. A huge foreign debt accumulated during the debt-led growth of the 1980s, and near-exhaustion of foreign-exchange reserves forced Indian decision makers in the early 1990s to look for help from the World Bank and the International Monetary Fund. This help came with conditions attached. As far as one can tell, Congress leaders were willing participants in the policy changes that followed. These included the lowering of tariffs, devaluation of currency, removal of controls on private production, and some rationalization of public spending.

The BJP came to power in 1998, ostensibly on a platform of economic nationalism. In practice, however, the BJP has also more or less accepted the framework of economic liberalization. Both international constraints and domestic opinion have ensured that, for the time being at any rate, economic nationalists within the BJP are marginalized.

At this point, it appears that most political parties in India share the view that the old statist model needs to be liberalized. This ideological consensus is facilitated by the fact that there are very few new and powerful ideas, especially on the left, concerning how to facilitate economic growth. On the right, an "East Asian model" of sorts could offer an alternative to the liberalization paradigm, but so far it has not entered Indian political discourse in any big way. Given India's history, when India looks abroad for models, it looks more to the West than to the East. So while the aura of elite consensus around liberalization is real for now, it is important to note a few qualifications.

First, economic liberalization in India remains quite incomplete. For example, a large public sector remains mostly untouched, organized labor remains protected, numerous subsidies continue, and deficit spending is still high. While for purposes of this chapter we maintain an agnostic attitude toward the desirability of such changes, what is clear is that if liberalization is pushed further and deeper, some of the apparent consensus may come undone. Second, the attitude of Indian business groups toward liberalization is increasingly mixed. Threatened by foreign products and investors, a sizable number have periodically demanded "slower liberalization." And finally, the most important issues concern the impact of liberalization on economic performance. As is to be expected, the first three years of the reform program had negative impact on industrial growth and investment; and while both picked up toward the middle of the 1990s, the impact of these reforms appears to many to be equivocal. The fact that India was spared by the Asian financial crisis of the 1990s has strengthened the case for a "go slow" approach to economic liberalization. Many argue that India was spared from the contagion because of its weak links to global financial markets.

Whatever the longer-term debates over liberalization, some of the implications of this shift from socialism for ideological and political struggles are already evident. First, the Congress's embrace of a new economic strategy left it groping for a political platform that both incorporated this shift and was politically attractive enough to mobilize electoral majorities in India's poor and diverse society. Even as an opposition party, the Congress continues to search for a new electoral formula. While the BJP's economic preferences are still somewhat vague (though not inconsistent with the main thrust of liberalization), its commitment to finding a unique Hindu path to modernity could in the future act as a brake on India's liberalizing and global approach. Finally, to the extent that the state-initiated liberalization agenda succeeds, it will continue to generate two types of reactions: identity-based reactions from those who want to resist "homogenizing rationality" thrust upon them from above; and distributive politics–based reactions from those whom liberalization leaves behind.

IDENTITY POLITICS

Observers of India during the last two decades have been struck by the relative intensification of conflicts involving identity politics: a serious ideological challenge to the inherited constitutional principle of India as a secular state in the form of the rise of the BJP; periodic secessionist movements in Punjab, Kashmir, and the Northeast; and worsening Hindu-Muslim conflict across India. These and other developments seem to testify to this trend.

A detailed analysis of these conflicts is beyond the scope of this chapter. Instead, we will focus on one specific development with a potential for long-term significance: the rise of Hindu nationalism. What does the rise to national prominence of the BJP represent? What ideological shift does it signify?

The rise of Hindu nationalism, it has been commonly argued, represents a growing and deep disquiet with the secular and modernizing principles that the Indian nation-state embodies. At a social level it represents the most serious systematic threat yet to the fragile fabric of Hindu-Muslim relations. At a political level it represents a shift toward the right in Indian politics. And at a cultural level, and perhaps in the long run most seriously, it represents an attempt to transform the character of Hinduism and its relationship to politics. Hindu nationalism has, for the first time, systematically sought to redefine and canonize Hinduism around one *common* set of symbols that cut across its traditional pluralism. In doing so it hopes to solidify the majority Hindus as a voting bloc that will vote consistently on identity issues. And it has brought into the ambit of politics religious issues and leaders that were normally outside its pale.[6]

On the question of secularism, Hindu nationalism embodies two distinct tendencies, one "modern" and the other less distinctly so. At one level, Hindu nationalism reflects a dissatisfaction with the liberal secular state. A liberal secular state cannot, some Hindu nationalists argue, be the locus of a national identity because there is a systematic gulf between the premises on which such a state rests and the values and aspirations of India's majority community, the Hindus. In this view, the secular state has consistently marginalized Hindu values and preferences and refused to recognize their claims as a majority. It has not allowed Hindus to shape their public culture in accordance with their deeper aspirations by, for example, not restoring to them monuments and temples that are both central to their identity and stand as reminders of their past subjugation. This current of Hindu nationalism thus seeks to recast the national political debate by invoking indigenous cultural themes; to provide Hindus with a renewed sense of an identity through mass campaigns, and to assert vigorously that the premise of India's national identity is Hindu.

The second strand of Hindu nationalism, not incompatible with the first, is interested less in the alleged moral vacuity of secularism or even in religion itself. It argues rather that the state has never been really secular, at least not consistently so. The state's self-professed claim to neutrality, according to this angry reaction, was all along a hoax: It amounted to simply granting undue concessions to minorities, principally the Muslims, giving them a special constitutional status that was inconsistent both with the basis of national identity and secularism. The BJP was thus able to mobilize both those who harbor a *specific* grievance, for example, that a disputed mosque has not been restored as a Hindu temple, as well as those who express consternation at what they see as a wider pattern of concessions to Muslims.[7]

Examples of the principal "concessions" that have fueled political fires include the granting (under article 370 of the Indian Constitution) of special status for the Muslim-majority state of Kashmir, which prohibits Indians from other parts of India from owning property in the state; and the continued preservation of Muslim personal law while Hindu personal laws had been "modernized" in the 1950s and 1960s.

It is undoubtedly true that the motives of those who raise these issues are considerably suspect and are fueled by an unmistakable animus against the Muslims. However, all these concessions are sought to be overturned in the name of *completing* the modern principles enshrined in the Indian Constitution. It is with this sense that the BJP is self-professedly raising a rather decisively modern question: Is a deep legal pluralism, which exempts certain groups in a country from being governed by a common legal code, compatible with the project of the modern nation-state? The BJP's answer, like that of most Western liberal democracies, is a decisive no. These issues are important, not only because of the BJP's electoral fortunes, but also because there seems to be widespread support for these issues, especially among India's middle classes. These issues will thus remain a potential locus of mobilization.

The striking development of the last two decades or so has been that both these critiques—namely, that secular politics is morally vacuous and that it has never placed the same demands on Muslims as it has on Hindus—have become fused ideologically and organizationally. What unites the BJP and other Hindu nationalist organizations such as the Vishwa Hindu Parishad (VHP) and Rashtryia Sevak Sangh (RSS) is this common ideological commitment: India needs a strong unitary national identity, and the locus of this identity will be unambiguously Hindu. Hinduism is defined, in this view, in a relatively broad and inclusive sense that transcends regional and caste differences. However, this view does not accommodate the Muslims, despite their long history on Indian soil, for Islam is considered essentially foreign and incompatible with a sincere allegiance to the Indian nation. If nationhood is taken to be an aspiration, then, Muslims are viewed from this standpoint as an obstacle to that aspiration—either by refusing to assimilate or by refusing to modernize.

As far as the BJP's relationship to modernity goes, it is of course far more ambiguous, partly because the various constituents of its ideology are hard to pin down and reconcile. It certainly does not represent, as Mahatma Gandhi did and Gandhians continue to do so, a critique of civil society and the economic institutions of modernity. Unlike other "fundamentalisms," the BJP does not view commerce and capitalism as a threat. Indeed, its support base has traditionally been merchants, traders, and the lower middle class. A long-standing constituent of its policy has been freer trade and industry. Moreover, as mentioned above, once in power, it embraced liberalization in economic policy.

In relation to state institutions, it is again "modernist." Indeed if any political party believes in further strengthening the coercive arm of the Indian state so as to maintain its raison d'être, it is the BJP. It is also worth reiterating that the VHP/RSS/BJP alliance has accepted much of the social critique of traditional Hinduism. For example, they have emphatically rejected traditional caste hierarchy as a basis of social organization. Given the logic of the electoral system, even the ranks of their leaders are increasingly drawn from the "backward" castes, and, as in other parties, they too have embraced affirmative action for them. Unlike most other forms of fundamentalism, their activities have less to do with fostering an orthodox practice than with the creation of an identity. The BJP thus appears comfortable with some of the trappings of modernity, and its message is not inconsistent with the aspirations of a Westernizing middle class poised for worldly success.

A better understanding of what this movement represents, however, would have to treat the three distinct components of this movement separately. The RSS, founded in 1925, is the oldest of the three organizations.[8] It is an extremely well-organized, cadre-based organization with a formal hierarchy and deeply authoritarian political structure that has firm roots in militant Hindu traditions. It draws upon a culture of severe self-discipline and austerity which fuses together ideals of physical strength and a complete dedication of the individual to the goals of the larger collectivity with those of spiritual purity in its vision of national transformation. It has always conceptualized India's identity territorially and culturally, rather than religiously—though this identity would still not accommodate Muslims, because they do not give their allegiance to this identity—and has kept religious ritual and doctrine to a minimum. Its cadres are the organizational mainstay of the BJP electorally and are routinely connected to Hindu-Muslim riots in various parts of India.

The VHP, founded in 1964, differs in three crucial respects from the RSS.[9] First, the VHP unlike the RSS does not keep religious ritual and doctrine to the minimum; indeed the premise of this movement is to create an identity through mass ritual and canonization of icons rather than to be an organized party. Second, in contrast to the RSS, which was always uncomfortable with traditional Hinduism, the VHP, more than the RSS, has sought to unite *all* sections of Hinduism under one umbrella organization and one authoritative religious narrative. The strikingly worrying thing about this development is that the VHP has managed to erode the authority of any other organized Hindu group or leadership that could have provided, from within Hinduism, a counterpoint of resistance to it. In the past there always had been leaders or organizations who could deploy *religious* authority to counter such claims of canonization. Given Hinduism's character, it is a remarkable feat that the VHP managed to get as wide a spectrum of Hindu leadership on the same platform as it did.

Third, the VHP, more than the RSS, is a strong *transnational* movement; it derives a substantial part of its funding and ideological support from overseas Indians, especially in America. The reasons for this are not entirely clear, but perhaps *their* longing for a sense of identity in a foreign culture makes them initiate such innovations back home. These three features have enabled the VHP to be a considerable presence.

The BJP has, for the last decade or so, been caught on the horns of an ideological dilemma. On the one hand, the Indian electorate continues to favor centrist parties. In order to be electorally successful, the BJP has sought to transform itself into a credible moderate party that has eschewed the more controversial aspects of the Hindu nationalist agenda. It has kept demands for a uniform civil code, abolition of special status for Kashmir, and economic nationalism on the back burner and instead emphasized good governance. This moderation enabled it to emerge as the single largest parliamentary party in India. More important, this moderation enabled it to attract allies among India's regional parties. Both the compulsion to broaden its electoral base and the need for allies will continue to exert powerful incentives on the BJP to act as a centrist party. But the BJP's move toward the center has been fraught with difficulties and tensions. The more centrist it becomes, the more it risks diluting its distinctiveness and its core constituency. A debate continues to rage within the party over the extent to which it can move closer to the center. For the time being there appears to be an uneasy compromise between factions. The hard-liners within the party have been sidelined on most issues—especially those concerning economic policy.

On the other hand, allied organizations such as the RSS and VHP continue their dangerous antiminorities stance. During the last two years or so much of the force of this antiminorities policy has come to be directed against Christians. These new developments suggest that the BJP's attempts to become a credible centrist party have not been entirely successful, and it continues to harbor significant antiminorities sentiment.

There are, however, strong compulsions internal to the party which suggest that the BJP's move toward the center will continue to remain vulnerable to its own right wing for various reasons. For one thing, the BJP's organizational structure is now, more than ever, in the hands of hard-liners; recent organizational changes have only strengthened their hand. In addition, the cadre and mass support of allied organizations such as the RSS and VHP are highly mobilized and are not likely to take kindly to a shift toward moderation. The evidence is overwhelming that the cadre-based discipline of this party has eroded considerably; it is very likely that any move toward centrism will be resisted by these mobilized cadres who now have the capacity to force the hand of the leadership on this issue. This view is strengthened by the fact that electoral politics has less appeal to these supporters than it does to the leadership. Our hunch is that the moderate leadership will, within limits, be able to rein in these cadres so long as the BJP continues to have a realistic shot at power. If the BJP begins to lose serious electoral ground, its allied organizations will precipitate a crisis by once again mobilizing antiminorities sentiment.

Finally, we may raise the general and critical question: What explains the rise of Hindu nationalism? The answer is necessarily complex and has several components. At the most general level, one suggests, as we did above, that the organizational and ideological decline of the old Congress system created a political vacuum that opened up the space for these mobilizational activities. Beyond such generalities, however, more specific explanations need to be considered. One explanation sees these movements as an outcome of the competitive political process itself: Political elites simply calculate the rewards and risks of mobilizing support around particular tropes. In this view, certain tropes become politically significant only when political entrepreneurs tie them to possible gains in material resources and power. Political elites thus make decisions based on an electoral calculus about what groups to mobilize and when. This explanation has the obvious advantage of accounting for two things. First, it is best able to account for the timing of the salience of Hindu nationalism in Indian politics and the unevenness of its appeal across states.[10] Second, it suggests that events that crystallize identities, such as communal riots, are not spontaneous phenomena, but are instead politically orchestrated. The fact that politicians think that communal hostilities and violence can be put to use in competitive electoral politics by making one party appear to be the true defender of Hindus or Muslims or Sikhs suggests that the mix of electoral politics and a multicultural society will remain potentially explosive in Indian politics.

Since the intensity of communal hostilities in Indian politics varies over both time and space, one needs to think of a series of proximate causes that have further contributed to the rise of Hindu nationalism. First, in some sense, Hindu nationalism feeds off its "others"—secessionism and regionalism. Paradoxically, all three require one another for their sustenance. Arguably Hindu nationalism has emerged in part due to the anxieties generated by a series of secessionist movements in the early 1980s about another partition of India. Paradoxes abound here: These secessionist movements (in Punjab, Kashmir, and the Northeast) were themselves a response to the increasing centralizing tendencies of the state and, under the Congress, the grudging unwillingness of leaders to abide by the federal spirit of constitutional norms, especially when it came to dealing with states. Second, it bears repeating that the demise of the Congress Party organization in the north left a vacuum which a patient, cadre-based party that had been literally decades in the making was poised to fill. Third, a series of much-publicized incidents in the mid-1980s, such as the Shah Bano case, provided the pretext for a confrontation with the Muslims. Fourth, there was the double game that the Congress was playing in terms of both claiming that the Babari Mosque would be protected and at the same time allowing Hindus to worship within the mosque property. This provided both the political and legal opening for the BJP to take up the mosque issue. And, fifth, the character of the Indian middle class has undergone a considerable transformation over the last ten to twenty years; not only has it grown in size but large sections of it, especially in the Hindu-speaking heartland, feel alienated from the English-speaking, more secular elite in Delhi.

These proximate causes have their roots in the contingent trajectory of Indian politics; while some of them are products of deeper trends, they also represent a combination of political opportunism and historical blunder. The deeper question is: Is the liberal secular state doomed to be subject periodically to this mode of resistance—that is, to periodically generate its own nemesis, nationalism? Is the politics of identity going to remain the only viable, credible, and organized form of resistance to the modern state?

The answers to these questions are far from certain, but three things suggest that a confrontation between the state and ethnic nationalisms is likely to continue. First, there is the fact that India's ruling elite had, to a large degree, appropriated secular nationalism in a manner that minimized disputes over its content. As V. S. Naipul has argued persuasively, recent "awakenings" in India are at least in part attempts to democratically redefine those terms.[11] Such politics runs risks. Nevertheless, if democratic aspirations run deeper, so will the desire that the public culture be reshaped in accordance with these aspirations.

Second, the cause is more psychological. Alexis de Tocqueville argued more than a century ago that democracies are susceptible to what he called "pantheism." In the face of mass society in a period of transformation, individuals feel a loss of agency. Tocqueville hypothesized that this diminution in agency leads to a yearning for a single cause that links the multitude of consequences.[12] Nationalism rather than pantheism may be the modern answer; the quest is not to seek a single cause but create one. Nationalism and nationalist rhetoric can thus be viewed as attempts to reclaim *agency* in the face of globalization and the conquest of seemingly impersonal forces. One of the striking and, to our minds, false myths of nationalist rhetoric is that the restoration of unity, or the endowing of a nation with a singular will, can be a panacea for many ills. This myth feeds on the belief that weakness and loss of agency are themselves *causes* that explain various ills. The resulting *desire* for a unitary agency is not likely to abate in the near future; indeed, with the state constrained more and more by the imperatives of the international economy, this sense of a loss of agency is likely to continue and will seek the "national will" as a surrogate, as a substitute that answers the vicissitudes of history.

Third, the politics of nationalism is at the base a politics of self-esteem, a fact that may partly explain its apocalyptic character. The central question is whether the secular nation-state can successfully accommodate these explosive demands for self-esteem. It is a peculiar fact about modern secular nation-states that they have had to satisfy two demands simultaneously: They have to appear legitimate, and they also have to embody the distinctiveness of the people that inhabit their territories. This sense of distinctiveness may draw upon many sources: political ideas, ethnicity, culture, religion, history. But in most parts of the world there will be an ongoing contest over who defines the terms and content of the distinctiveness.

To conclude this discussion, it appears the anxieties that sustain Hindu nationalism are not likely to abate soon. Hindu nationalism, as we have suggested, feeds both on widespread distrust of the Muslims and on other secessionist movements that sustain anxieties about further partition of India. For various reasons that are beyond the scope of this essay, both tendencies are likely to continue, giving Hindu nationalism a set of fears that it can capitalize on.

The rise of Hindu nationalism has managed to swing the axis of conflict away from the traditional Left–Right conflict. Indian politics is now more openly colored by a "Hindu hue" than it was in the past. Even the Congress, India's old secular party, is now openly committed to building a temple on the site of the Babari Mosque, which was demolished by Hindu nationalists. Whether such a shift in emotive sensibilities is capable of having a more permanent institutional effect or not remains to be seen. That outcome may turn in part on the resolve of parties other than the BJP to defeat such a trend, partly on the BJP's ability to demonstrate a continuing capacity to govern, and in part on the extent of the Congress's ability to make a comeback. It may well turn out that the BJP and the attempt to institutionalize a unitary Hindu nationalism will founder on the shoals of India's social pluralism and its own internal weaknesses, facilitating conditions that may push distributional politics again to the forefront in India.

DISTRIBUTIONAL POLITICS

Old and rigid inequalities of caste linger in contemporary India and mix in complicated ways with emerging new inequalities of wealth and class. Nearly a third of that country's sizable population, moreover, lives in abject poverty. Given this social profile and competitive democracy, it is highly unlikely that distributional issues will vanish from India's politics; there is no "end of history" in sight. Instead of the old rallying cry of socialism, however, distributional pressures in the future will probably be expressed in newer terms. Many of these pressures will emerge at local and regional levels, dotting the political landscape with multiple conflicts, garbed in a variety of idioms of caste, class, feminism, and environmentalism. If and when these movements take on national proportions, they are less likely to demand property and asset redistribution and more likely to press for access to state-controlled resources. Reserved access to public jobs for lower castes, increased public investments into health and education, new forms of taxation, and safety nets for those displaced by deliberate economic restructuring are some examples of future distributional issues.

The rhetoric of social justice has been fairly central to India's political discourse. Mahatma Gandhi pressed for the removal of untouchability within India's caste society, Nehru championed socialism and land reform, and Indira Gandhi made poverty alleviation the central plank of her early mobilization strategy. The gap between this rhetoric and the meager achievements on the ground, however, has also been consistently large and is well known to students of Indian politics such as Francine Frankel and Atul Kohli. What needs to be reiterated is an issue analyzed above—namely, that starting around 1980 India's ruling elite put less and less emphasis on distributional issues. This shift continued during the 1980s so much so that by the 1990s Congress leaders had more or less abandoned their earlier commitment to socialism.

The irony of this rightward shift is that India's lower strata in the 1990s are considerably more mobilized politically than they were in the 1960s and 1970s, the heyday of Indian socialism. It appears that Indian elites mobilized the poor as a political resource, but once mobilized these active poor groups have now become constraints on such redefined elite goals as economic liberalization. Demobilization and/or channeling the energy of the mobilized onto alternate paths (such as Hindu chauvinism) thus seem to be the current political strategy of the elites. Whereas the latter has had some success, demobilization is rather difficult in a democracy. Mobilized lower strata are thus seeking a variety of outlets for their dissatisfactions in contemporary India.

It is difficult in this brief space to provide anything but a hint of the diverse poor people's movements in contemporary India. In north and central India these movements have taken place along caste lines. On the one hand, these movements have genuinely empowered the lower and middle castes and have allowed them to almost completely dismantle the hold of upper castes on politics. On the other hand, in states like Bihar the upper castes have responded with a vengeance to this challenge to their political authority. Violent repression of the lower castes and the increasing and militant assertiveness of the lower castes in response have created conditions resembling a civil war involving the privileged and underprivileged in states like Bihar.

The dissatisfactions of India's lower strata in other states are expressed in more complicated ways. In some states, such as West Bengal, Communist parties have been able to successfully incorporate the political energies of the lower and middle classes. Regional nationalism in some southern states adopts an antielitist, anti-Delhi stand that is often politically popular. The rise of coalition politics during the last two elections has strengthened the political salience of these parties at the center. This has had the effect of making regional parties feel empowered in proportions beyond what the number of seats they have in parliament would suggest. In yet other instances, calls for protecting the rights of tribal groups, preserving the environment on which the livelihood of specific groups depends, and safeguarding the rights of women, readily became rallying points of political movements.

Along with the poor, the middling groups of rural Indian society have become more politically active over the last two decades. These groups—especially the so-called backward castes—are the mainstay of the nationwide reservation movement, which demands that certain shares of government-controlled jobs and educational opportunities be "reserved" for applicants from certain castes. Demands of this sort have generally had a "top-down" quality: Leaders voice them in hopes of gaining votes from among the large membership of the backward castes. Not surprisingly, such campaigns have provoked a backlash from the higher castes. Some of the political turmoil of the 1980s in states such as Gujarat and Bihar can be traced to such caste conflict. The issue took on national significance in 1990 when Prime Minister V. P. Singh announced a major shift in national policy designed to favor the backward castes. Protest riots led by high-caste students broke out all over northern India, seriously weakening the government. In spite of this opposition, all major political parties in India now favor reservations for backward castes. Caste is likely to remain a salient axis of mobilization in Indian politics. But mobilization along caste lines will display a paradoxical character. Its seeming strength in the political arena will, in all likelihood, lead to its diminution as a social phenomenon. The more the lower castes capture power, the faster Indian society will be rid of the egregious ritual aspects of caste.

Another movement among middle-level rural groups has demanded higher prices for agricultural products and lower prices for production inputs such as fertilizer, electricity, and credit. These initiatives appeal to peasants who have prospered under the government's "green revolution" policies and now wish to transform their new riches into political clout. Fueling their activism is the conviction that the state has catered to the urban upper classes while neglecting the farmers.

Examples of demand groups could be further multiplied. The general point, however, is that a variety of distributional conflicts dot the Indian political landscape. These conflicts are also not about to vanish. It is unlikely that these "million mutinies" (to use Naipul's term) can be readily transformed into a unified protest force capable of transforming the Indian political economy. What is more likely is that plurality of conflicts will continue to mirror the segmented nature of the Indian society. This pattern, in turn, will have two long-term consequences. First, it will continue to sap the governing capacities of the Indian state. And second, as long as India's democracy remains vibrant, sustained pressures from below will ensure that distributional issues remain an integral component of the political discourse.

CONCLUSION

India emerged on the global scene as a sovereign nation state in the middle of the twentieth century. The self-consciousness of that arrival, along with a rejuvenated awareness of India as an ancient and unique civilization, has propelled Indians ever since to define and redefine their position in the world. Following independence, there was a fair amount of consensus within India on such issues as national identity. Elements of this nationalist consensus included democracy, a state-directed private enterprise economy, and self-sufficiency as desirable traits for the domestic political economy, and nonalignment as an appropriate foreign-policy stance toward a world divided by the Cold War.

As the twentieth century comes to an end, and as the Cold War fades into the background, the nationalist consensus in India has evaporated, and Indians are again busy contesting and redefining issues of identity. A commitment to preserving the territorial integrity of India and to democracy continues to remain strong in India. India is also firmly a private enterprise economy by now. Beyond these certainties, however, much else is up for grabs. While the ruling elites are committed to liberalizing the state-controlled, inward-looking Indian economy, the gap between this commitment and the reality on the ground is considerable. Oppositional elites, such as the leaders of Hindu groups and the BJP, are busy questioning India's secular state; their mobilizational success simultaneously empowers some of India's Hindus and threatens India's minorities, especially Muslims. Meanwhile, lower and lower-middle strata are by now relatively well mobilized. Their demands are expressed in a variety of settings, lending urgency to distributional issues.

India's ideological landscape is thus likely to remain quite contentious. Issues of both identity and social justice will contribute to ideological and political conflicts. Whether one considers these conflicts to be "fundamental" or as something less (and thus as more manageable) depends, to an extent, on one's prior conceptions about what constitutes fundamental societal struggles. For some observers, especially in the West, the conflict between democracy and capitalism, on the one hand, and Communism, on the other, has been *the* struggle of recent times. Such observers can rest assured because India is now, as it has been for quite some time, firmly on the side of democracy and capitalism. For many other observers, however, including most Indians, the struggle against Communism was never the defining struggle of our times. Since these observers never defined "history" in such a manner, the "end of history" for them is nowhere in sight. Instead, they remain concerned now, as they have been for some time, about issues of poverty, human dignity, religious tolerance, security in daily life, and collective pride and well-being.

NOTES

1. For an influential account of why this happened, see Partha Chaterjee, *Nationalist Thought and the Colonial World* (London: Zed Books, 1986).

2. Standard accounts of the Nehru period include S. Gopal, *Jawaharlal Nehru: A Biography* (New Delhi: Oxford University Press, 1976), vols. 2 and 3; Francine Frankel, *India's Political Economy, 1974–1977* (Princeton: Princeton University Press, 1978).

3. On the workings of the "Congress system," see Rajni Kothari, *Politics in India* (Boston: Little, Brown, 1970); and more recently, James Manor, "Parties and the Party System," in A. Kohli, ed., *India's Democracy: An Analysis of Changing State-Society Relations* (Princeton: Princeton University Press, 1988), 62–99.

4. For details on the unraveling of this system and its consequences, see Atul Kohli, *Democracy and Discontent: India's Crisis of Governability* (New York: Cambridge University Press, 1990).

5. A brief overview of this debate and guide to further literature can be found in Kohli, *Democracy and Discontent*, 305–39.

6. For a lucid short account of these developments, see Peter van der Veer, *Religious Nationalism* (Berkeley: University of California Press, 1994).

7. On the Hindu demand for building a temple on the site of a disputed mosque, see S. Gopal, ed., *Anatomy of a Confrontation: The Ram Janm Bhoomi–Babari Masjid Issue* (Delhi: Viking, 1991).

8. For brief histories and contrasting views of the RSS, see Walter Andersen and Shridhar Damle, *The Brotherhood in Saffron* (Boulder, Colo.: Westview, 1987); and Sumit Sarkar et al., *Khaki Shorts, Saffron Flags* (New Delhi: Orient Longman, 1992).

9. There is little systematic work on the VHP. Van der Veer, *Religious Nationalism*, contains some useful information.

10. On the timing: Most observers would agree that the 1985 election, which the Congress won by playing the nationalist card after its old populist alliance had

broken down, is a watershed in this respect. It can be easily demonstrated that it was after that election that the BJP leadership decided to take up this theme. On the unevenness of its emergence: This explanation does stress that the political class must be willing to give this form of politics an opening; where the political class has a different electoral calculus based on caste or regionalism, politics will take a different hue.

11. See V. S. Naipul, *India: A Million Mutinies Now* (New York: Viking, 1980).

12. Alexis de Tocqueville, *Democracy in America*, trans. P. Bradley (New York: Vintage, 1954), 32.

15

Left and Right with Chinese Characteristics: Issues and Alignments in Deng Xiaoping's China

Andrew J. Nathan and Tianjian Shi

In 1980s, the first decade of Deng Xiaoping's reforms, Chinese society became wealthier and more complex, and state control of ideology weakened. As public attitudes diversified, new ideological alignments took shape. This chapter explores the ideological landscape in the aftermath of the 1989 Tiananmen pro-democracy demonstrations. It uses data from a 1990 national sample survey that interviewed 2,896 adults throughout China (except for Tibet) to provide a statistically accurate picture of mass attitudes. The technical details of the survey are described in the appendix.

Chinese society in 1990 was split along ideological lines into two large, loose groups, each with distinctive sociological characteristics. One group had more liberal attitudes toward public issues, the other was more conservative. In Western terms, both Chinese issue constituencies stood on the left, in the sense that both demanded Big Government and egalitarianism: The liberals wanted government to fight against special privilege and economic inequality, and the conservatives wanted government to take responsibility for citizens' welfare.

The difference between the groups centered on attitudes toward reform and its consequences. Chinese liberals, who were concerned with the effects of reform on the moral state of society and on good government, thought the way out of China's difficulties was to push forward with economic and political reform. Chinese conservatives for their part worried more about the negative impact of reforms on their personal welfare and thought reform should be slowed or reversed.

We explore the extent to which the dynamics that divided the Chinese population resemble the dynamics of ideological polarization in the West. We choose the West as the case for comparison because that area has been the focus of most of the research and theory on mass ideology and its determinants. We find that in China, as in the West, class—as measured by education, income, and occupation—has a strong effect on issue priorities and democratic values. The urban/rural cleavage is also important, although for reasons that differ somewhat from those that operate in the West. In China one finds some influential social divisions that are not found in the West: that between Communist Party members and nonparty members, and that between employees of state and nonstate units. Nonetheless, the ways in which these attributes affect the individual's ideological standpoint can be understood in terms of the same logic that explains the impact of sociological attributes on attitudes in the West.

In short, the Chinese ideological spectrum is distinctive in substance but universal in the dynamics that shape it. In light of the cultural and institutional differences between China and the West, that is, by the logic of a most-different-case comparison, this finding supports theories of mass ideology hitherto grounded chiefly in studies of the United States and Europe.

IDEOLOGICAL POLARIZATION IN THE WEST

Two issues have dominated the ideological space of the West: the role of the state and the conflicting norms of equality and achievement in the distribution of goods. The Left generally favors more government intervention in the economy and more-egalitarian income distribution; the Right typically stands for relative freedom of private enterprise from state intervention and toleration of higher levels of income inequality. But Left and Right have accumulated additional meanings as well. According to Seymour Lipset and Stein Rokkan, the political cleavages embodied in European party systems crystallized the results of four major historical struggles: between center and periphery, church and state, town and country, and owners and workers.[1] Arend Lijphart suggests seven dimensions of ideology: socioeconomic, religious, cultural/ethnic, urban/rural, regime support, foreign policy, and post-materialism.[2]

The concept of the polarity of Left and Right emerged from a synthesis of these different cleavages, taking different form in each country. Each country varies in whether issue preferences and party loyalties are dominated by class alignments, or by religious, regional, ethnic, or other ones, or by distinctive combinations of several.[3] There is no tight relationship among positions on all these issues. Yet people usually think of themselves as liberal or conservative because they lean one way or another on a series of value dilemmas that characterize their nation's political culture. In the postwar era there emerged a new cleavage dimension—called materialism versus post-materialism by Ronald Inglehart—that generated the "new politics" of the environment, women's issues, and the peace movement. Even though older parties and issues tend to be more closely aligned with the Left/Right scale than the parties and issues of the new politics, citizens still think of the new issues roughly in terms of a Left/Right dimension.[4]

Different people may combine these value choices in different patterns.[5] Left/Right self-placement may reflect a mix of abstract thinking about issues and favorable and unfavorable feelings toward groups and issues.[6] Yet, according to John Zaller, "although there are numerous 'value dimensions' between which there is no obvious logical connection, many people nonetheless respond to different value dimensions as if they were organized by a common left–right dimension."[7] Thus, in a "political action" study of four European countries and the United States done in the early 1970s, respondents were able to locate themselves on the Left/Right dimension in numbers ranging from a high of 92 percent of the respondents in Germany to a low of 68 percent of those in the United States.[8]

Ideas of Left and Right remain broad and vague in the minds of most Western citizens. Depending on the country, only 11 percent to 30 percent of the political action respondents were able to say what the terms meant. "A sizable proportion . . . either could not give any meaning of the terms or else completely reversed their meaning."[9] In America, the country where mass attitudes have been most intensively studied, few citizens are able to relate their overall ideological self-identification to their opinions on particular issues.[10] Still, no matter how vaguely comprehended, many citizens use these general categories to help orient their ideas about politics.

Western respondents align along the liberal/conservative dimension chiefly in response to the combined operation of two forces: social position and cognitive sophistication. Members of different social groups have different economic and other interests, which partly determine their positions on the ideological spectrum. Attitudes on the left tend to be preferred by the working class, urban residents, young people, and members of minority ethnic and religious groups, because they are dissatisfied with their share of benefits in society and think they would be better off if the state intervened to redistribute resources. People who are more satisfied (or less dissatisfied) with the status quo tend to take a more conservative stance toward government activism, social change, and redistribution. In Western societies these groups usually include white-collar workers, suburbanites, middle-aged people, and members of dominant ethnic and religious groups.[11]

While cognitive sophistication is affected by many factors, including education, media exposure, political campaigns, and government propaganda efforts, it is usually measured by education.[12] Cognitive sophistication has mixed effects on Left/Right self-placement. Greater knowledge is associated with higher socioeconomic status, which makes people more conservative. But education also increases openness to change and thus helps to move people toward the liberal end of the spectrum. Education may have different effects on people's Left/Right positions on different issues in different countries: In the United States, for example, liberal social values are promoted in schools, and better-educated citizens tend to be more liberal than those who are less educated.[13]

Whatever the ideological direction of its impact, however, greater cognitive capacity allows citizens to approach issues in a more abstract, generalized, and interrelated way.[14] Without necessarily making citizens less self-interested, political knowledge enables them to see how "'round-about' routes . . . will better secure ultimate gratification."[15] As a result, ed-ucated and knowledgeable sections of Western publics are more likely than are less-educated groups to think about political issues in terms of an explicit ideology or broad policy choices as distinct from immediate self-interest. While the ideological position of a less-sophisticated con-stituency tends to be a direct reflection of its social position, that of a more cognitively sophisticated constituency reflects the combined influence of social interest and an abstract conception of the issues.

LEFT AND RIGHT IN COMMUNIST CHINA

Under Mao Zedong, the meaning of the liberal/conservative dimension was de-creed from above. Mao accepted Joseph Stalin's scheme that history moved from primitive communism to feudalism to capitalism to Communism and that whatever pushed things in that direction was "progressive" and hence leftist. Class became a question of one's stance toward historical change rather than a matter of objective economic interest. And class was a label formally assigned to each citizen by the party authorities, rather than a self-chosen identity.[16]

Mao labeled as the Left those who stood on the side of what he consid-ered progress. Those who went too far in advance of history he designated "ultraleft deviationists" or "adventurists." Those who failed to push historical progress at the appropriate speed were "right deviationists," guilty of class compromise. The position Mao occupied at any moment defined the magic place that constituted the authentic Left between the Ultraleft and the Right.[17]

After 1949 Mao moved this point of reference steadily in a radical direc-tion, speeding the pace of change toward an egalitarian, state-dominated so-ciety. In a series of mass campaigns the Chinese Communist Party (CCP) tar-geted as enemies all those defined as occupying positions on the right—landlords, counterrevolutionaries, "bureaucrats," and "sectarians." In the mid-1950s Mao accelerated agricultural collectivization and launched the Great Leap Forward. He accused party colleagues who failed to keep up of "tottering along like a woman with bound feet."[18] An estimated three-quarters of a million people fell victim to charges of rightism. In the 1960s Mao carried out the Great Proletarian Cultural Revolution to make sure the revolution continued uninterrupted.

With Mao so impatient for historical progress, hardly any space remained to the left of him on the spectrum. The rare exceptions were certain allegedly Ultraleft organizations that arose during the Cultural Revolution, such as the Hunan Provincial Proletarian Association (*Shengwulian*), which called for virtual anarchy, and an alleged anti-Mao conspiracy called the "May 16th Group," which supposedly was prepared to challenge Mao's dominance.

China was like a ship whose passengers all rush to port. During the Cul-tural Revolution every organization proclaimed its progressiveness with names like "Red Guards" and "Revolutionary Rebels." Names of streets (e.g., Anti-Revisionism Street), markets (East Wind Market), and individuals ("Defend-the-East" Zhang) crowded the left side of the symbolic space. For a time the Beijing Red Guards even forced cars to drive on the left side of the street and to stop on green and go on red.[19] In effect, the ideological spectrum collapsed, and ideology ceased to be a meaningful concept because all views came cloaked in nearly identical terminology. When Mao's chosen successor, Lin Biao, fell from power, the party announced that Lin, who had always been praised as the leftest of the Left, was really "left in form but right in essence." In the bankrupt terminology of the day, this meant that Lin had pretended to be a good man but was not. Left and Right had become devoid of substance.[20]

A multidimensional ideological landscape reemerged after Mao's death. The official debate over the speed and content of reform continued to orient itself to the presumed direction of the march of history and to speak partly in terms of Left and Right. But Deng Xiaoping's regime was no longer able to monopolize public debate. In addition, two unofficial ideological dimensions emerged, one focusing on mass grievances toward a variety of targets and the other on ideas of democracy. Attitudes to reform, attitudes of grievance, and attitudes toward democracy constituted the three dimensions of ideology in Deng's China.

The ideas of Left and Right were used in the official reform debate more in attack than defense. Each side claimed to be on the left in a good sense and accused the other of being in some sense conservative. Advocates of reform tried to deny critics access to the progressive and socialist side of the rhetorical spectrum by presenting reform as the self-perfecting mechanism of socialism. Deng claimed to be "building socialism with Chinese characteristics" and to be guiding reform with the "four basic principles" of socialism, proletarian dictatorship, Communist Party leadership, and Marxism–Leninism–Mao Zedong Thought. Critics of reform labeled the reformists "bourgeois liberals" and accused them of fomenting "spiritual pollution," which by implication located them on the right.[21] Reform advocates labeled conservative values ultraleft or "left" in quotation marks.[22]

A second ideological dimension was discernible in the unofficial media and in the liberalized official press. We call it the grievance dimension, but it consisted of many elements: a mix of economic grievances, nostalgia for the past, moral condemnation of social and political corruption, opposition to change, traditionalism, and antiforeignism. Deng had allowed the weakening of party control over ideology and the rise of a partial civil society. Newspapers, magazines, and book publishers eluded tight oversight by the propaganda departments.[23] Public opinion polling appeared, providing leaders and to some extent the public itself with information about mass attitudes, even though polls conducted by Chinese organizations fell short of international methodological standards.[24] Unofficial and private channels of communication came into existence—open letters, underground publications, foreign and Hong Kong–based books and magazines that made their way into China, and a vast realm of private conversation and rumor.

Dissatisfaction focused on a seemingly contradictory mix of targets: the ruling clans, the party and state bureaucracies, nouveaux riches entrepreneurs, dissident intellectuals, and foreigners. Despite their suffering under Mao, many Chinese remembered that era as a time when they could leave their front doors and bicycles unlocked, when prices were stable, when everyone had a job, when officials were honest, and when China was not afraid of war with the West. The new phenomena of inflation, economic inequality, corruption, personal insecurity, and cosmopolitanism seemed part of a general decline of values. Ordinary people were liable to complain about the rise of a new Mercedes-riding class of "bureaucratic capitalists" and "compradores" (*maiban*, an old term for Chinese who served as agents for foreign firms). The bustle of downtown construction prompted complaints that officials were "selling out the country like Li Hongzhang," the nineteenth-century negotiator who ceded Chinese territories to Japan. Dissidents and foreigners were perceived as collaborating with, rather than opposing, corrupt bureaucrats and party ideologues, all undermining what was native and true to China.[25] People complained that even *guanxi*—personal connections, the cement of human relations in Chinese society—no longer carried its overtones of friendship and moral obligation but had become instead cynical instruments in a marketized but lawless system.[26] The popular mood was essentially "anti."

The third ideological dimension was shaped by a broad group of pro-democratic intellectuals. They ranged from Wei Jingsheng, the self-taught dissident, to Wang Meng, a CCP member and government-supported writer of fiction and essays who had once served as minister of culture. They included world-class scientists such as Fang Lizhi and Xu Liangying and teachers in provincial party schools, academic philosophers and senior party thinkers, private-venture entrepreneurs and poets. Despite its diversity, this group agreed on a central point: that China had a historic obligation to learn from the tragedies of the past in order to prevent the reemergence of a Maoist-style dictatorship. Their prescriptions varied from immediate democratization (Wei Jingsheng) to an interlude of authoritarianism (the "new authoritarians"), from civil service reform to Western-style democratization, from "rule by law" to human rights. The core issue across this band of debate was "preventing another cultural revolution."[27]

Although Chinese ideas of democracy are shaped by the heritages of Confucius and Karl Marx, they also bear an essential similarity to Western concepts. The parallel is partly due to the direct influence of Western ideas, but more importantly it stems from the universality of the problem of making government accountable.[28] The party tried to deal with the lessons of the past in its resolution on the Mao years: It acknowledged that Mao had made ideological errors but asserted that the party had now corrected them.[29] This failed to satisfy many Chinese intellectuals, however. By the late 1980s the influence of the liberal intellectuals had gone so far on the subject of democracy that some observers argued their ideas enjoyed a hegemony in unofficial discourse.[30] Pro-democratic ideas were also widespread among the general population.[31]

ISSUE PRIORITIES AND AGENDAS

Our survey data enable us to analyze how attitudes toward these three issue dimensions were distributed among the population in 1990. They also help us probe beneath the surface similarity of Chinese ideological issues to liberal/conservative ideas of the West, to see whether the two sets of ideological dimensions reflect the operation of the same social and cognitive forces.[32] We draw our evidence about the reform and grievance dimensions from a question about citizens' concerns with public issues. Another question, on which we report below, included items relevant to the democracy dimension.

The public-issues question read: "Nowadays, our government is facing many problems, and to solve these problems is not easy. For each of the following problems that I mention, please tell me on which problems you think the government has spent too much effort, on which problems it has spent the appropriate effort, and on which problems it has spent not enough effort." The results are displayed in table 15.1.

The question was not designed to uncover issues of public concern that we did not already know about. Rather, it assesses the relative degree of priority the public places on a predetermined list of issues.[33] The first column of the table displays the issues in the order in which the public ranked them as getting "not enough" government effort (this was not the order in which they were listed in the questionnaire).

Not surprisingly, the two top issues—inflation and corruption—were the same concerns that dominated the 1989 Tiananmen demonstrations. The next four items—crime, bureaucratism, inequitable income distribution, and inadequate government investment in education—were also prominent among the complaints of the 1989 demonstrators. The rank of these six items at the top of the table is consistent with our sense that the public felt beleaguered by the collapse of public and official morality and the rise of self-seeking materialism. It turns out therefore that the concerns of the urban, student demonstrators were widespread across the national sample, which included urban and rural residents, young and old, educated and uneducated. Remarkably high percentages of respondents of all kinds said that the government was not doing enough to solve the same problems that had motivated the demonstrators in Beijing.[34]

The table goes on to reveal how much priority the public placed on greater government effort on other issues. From one-quarter to two-fifths of the respondents wanted the government to do more to solve problems

TABLE 15.1 Attitudes toward Government Handling of Issues (Percentage of Responses, N = 2,896)

Issue[a]	Not Enough Attention	Just Right	Too Much Attention	No Interest[b]
Inflation and complaints				
Price control	55.7	19.7	1.9	22.7
Oppose corruption	53.8	17.9	3.0	25.3
Oppose crime	47.1	28.6	3.0	21.4
Oppose bureaucratism	46.8	16.8	1.8	34.6
Economic welfare				
Income distribution	42.5	15.0	1.7	40.8
Education	42.1	35.6	3.8	18.5
Unemployment	37.8	20.6	1.5	40.0
Housing	34.2	29.0	3.0	33.8
Consumer protection	33.6	21.7	1.7	43.1
Environment protection	33.6	30.3	2.6	33.5
Subsidies	27.9	21.7	7.4	43.0
Population control	24.7	50.4	12.8	12.2
Reform				
Antibourgeois liberalization	21.2	25.2	5.2	48.4
Private enterprise	18.2	25.4	9.4	47.1
Economic reform	17.9	28.6	4.1	49.4
Political reform	17.6	26.6	2.8	52.9
Foreign policy				
Taiwan	17.0	32.5	4.0	46.5
Opening	12.6	34.4	5.5	47.4
Defense	9.8	33.4	3.2	53.6
Foreign aid	5.7	20.0	8.1	66.1

Source: China survey (1990).

[a]Issues were: price control; opposing bribery and corruption, and rectifying party work style; opposing crime; opposing bureaucratism; solving the problem of inequitable income distribution; raising the education level; solving the employment problem; solving the housing problem; protecting consumers' rights; protecting the environment; subsidizing the basic necessities; population control and family planning; opposing bourgeois liberalization; encouraging the development of individual or private enterprises; economic system reform; political system reform; reunifying with Taiwan; opening to the outside world; national defense; and foreign aid.

[b]No interest equals don't know plus no answer.

of daily life, including those related to jobs, housing, shoddy goods, environmental pollution, subsidies, and population pressures. These represent a variety of demands that the government was expected to satisfy in the former socialist society. Now that the socialist system was giving way to a market-based system, a substantial portion of the public seemed to deplore the weakening of government effort in these areas of traditional state responsibility.

The next four items relate to reform. Fewer than one-fifth of the respondents indicated a positive attitude toward reform by stating that the government should do more to promote economic and political reform. A slightly larger percentage expressed a negative view of reform through their concern that the government needed to do more to stop "bourgeois liberalization," a term used by critics of reform to refer to its negative ideological and cultural effects.

Finally, foreign policy ranked at the bottom of the public's list of priorities, as it does in most countries. Among foreign policy issues, the heavily propagandized, nationalistic issue of Taiwan stood above the rest.

The public may assign a low priority to an issue for either of two reasons: because it does not have much interest in the issue[35] or because it feels that the government is already handling the issue adequately. The second and fourth columns in table 15.1 help clarify which of these two attitudes applies to each issue. "No interest" is the label we have assigned to the summed percentage of "don't know" and "no answer" responses. Lack of interest generally increases as one moves down the list of issues. It strongly marks the foreign policy domain and also characterizes public attitudes to reform and to certain economic welfare issues such as subsidies and consumer protection. Thus, the fact that the public did not demand more government action in these areas does not represent a vote of confidence in policy. But for issues higher on the list, such as price control, corruption, bureaucratism, and income distribution, dissatisfaction seems to be a better explanation than low interest for the public demand for greater government effort. "Just right" responses, which show the proportion of the public that was satisfied with the government's handling of the issue, are generally less prevalent than both "not enough effort" and "no interest" responses.

"Too much effort" plays a substantial role in the public pattern of response only toward population control. This was the issue on which the fewest respondents felt no interest, the issue on which the largest number of respondents thought the government was already doing enough, and also the issue on which the highest percentage thought the government was doing too much. The pattern suggests that many people were concerned about population pressure and approved the government's strong policy to limit population growth, yet many were unhappy with the impact of population control policies on their own lives.

The main message of the table is that Chinese citizens were dissatisfied or uninterested in the government's handling of most issues. Only in the area of foreign policy was there a satisfied plurality, and its size was small.

The rank ordering of public concern about the issues given in table 15.1 is not a test of how the public perceived the links among them. A factor analysis, which we display in table 15.2, provides such a test. This procedure sorts the issues into groups according to the frequency with which respondents who answer "not enough attention" with respect to a particular set of issues will also answer "not enough" with respect to another given issue. In other words, factor analysis identifies clusters of issues (we label them agendas) that are related to one another in the response patterns of our respondents.[36]

Table 15.2 shows that the issues were associated in the public mind in much the way our analysis of three issue dimensions would lead us to expect.[37] Following the usual standard in interpreting factor analyses, we concentrate on items with loading scores above 0.5. Items that fall below this level are not closely linked to other sets of issues in the public mind. For example, "opening to the world" was of roughly equal (and as table 15.1 suggests, relatively low) concern to everyone, regardless of respondents' patterns of concern with other sets of issues.

Corruption, crime, bureaucratism, and price control cohere in factor 1 to constitute what we can call the Tiananmen Agenda. They represent an inter-

TABLE 15.2   Factor Analysis of Issue Priority

	Tiananmen Agenda	Reform Agenda	Economic Welfare Agenda	Foreign Policy Agenda
Oppose corruption	.78	.02	.00	−.02
Oppose crime	.75	−.05	.07	.02
Oppose bureaucratism	.65	.07	−.09	−.02
Price control	.59	−.05	−.13	−.03
Education	.35	−.01	−.22	.12
Antibourgeois liberalization	.32	.19	.05	.10
Political reform	−.03	.82	.00	.02
Economic reform	−.01	.81	.00	−.03
Private enterprise	.03	.30	−.18	.09
Opening to world	.07	.25	−.07	.21
Unemployment	.02	.04	−.66	.01
Housing	−.06	−.03	−.65	.04
Income distribution	.21	.05	−.50	−.01
Subsidies	.01	−.00	−.49	−.01
Environment	.10	.17	−.36	.07
Consumer protection	.23	.18	−.35	−.01
National defense	.04	−.04	.05	.79
Foreign aid	−.04	.01	.03	.51
Percentage of variance	32.5	8.6	6.6	5.8
Eigenvalue	5.9	1.5	1.2	1.1

Source: China survey (1990).
Note: The factors are derived from a principal axis analysis of "not enough attention" responses to the issue priority question in oblique rotation. Population control and reunifying with Taiwan loaded weakly on factors 1 and 2, respectively, and a slightly clearer factor structure emerged when they were excluded. This is reported here and used in the correlations and regressions that follow.

related set of issues that implies a critical view of regime performance. The second factor identifies a Reform Agenda, which includes economic and political components. People who wanted the government to pay more attention to economic reform also wanted it to pay more attention to political reform, and vice versa. Although the factor loadings of "encouraging private enterprise" and "opening to the world" are too low to justify a strong statement of their relationship to the factor, they also make sense as reform-related issues.

The third factor separates economic and quality-of-life issues as a distinct agenda, which we label the Economic Welfare Agenda.[38] The fourth factor constitutes a Foreign Policy Agenda. As we saw in table 15.1, only a small number of people assigned a high priority to this last set of issues. The factor analysis shows that there was no strong tendency to link foreign policy issues with any of the other three issue agendas.

These findings deepen our understanding of two of our three suggested ideological dimensions. The Tiananmen and Economic Welfare Agendas both reflect elements of what we called "grievance." The Reform Agenda corresponds to our reform dimension. Foreign policy emerges as a separate agenda that is not important enough to generate a major ideological cleavage in the population. All the agendas call for government action, since that was the subject of this question. But the agendas differ in the type of government role they envision. The Tiananmen Agenda calls for government moral leadership as well as a degree of economic intervention to control inflation. The Reform Agenda calls for government leadership to change the system. The Foreign Policy Agenda calls for government attention to foreign policy issues.

The Economic Welfare Agenda alone calls for direct government intervention in the distribution of goods in order to solve the problems that individual citizens confront with jobs, housing, wages, and subsidies. This is the only one of the four agendas that seems on the face of it to resemble the classical Western Left/Right dimension. To say in Deng's China that the government should do more about jobs, housing, and income distribution was to say that it should create more jobs in the tens of thousands of enterprises that it owned, build state-owned housing to rent at subsidized rates, and raise the salaries it paid to tens of millions of officials, teachers, technicians, factory workers, and other state employees. It is in this sense that the Economic Welfare Agenda resembled the agenda of the Western Left. It was also "left" in the Chinese context—or "conservative" according to the label reversal common in postsocialist and reforming socialist countries—in the sense that it ran counter to the reform effort to reduce direct government participation in the economy and to create more autonomous enterprises operating under market conditions.

ISSUE CONSTITUENCIES

Face comparisons of the Left in the West and China take us only partway toward knowing whether they reflect similar or different ideological structures and mechanisms. Deeper insight can be gained by identifying which kinds of citizens are most concerned with which agendas. We cannot expect to find the same constituencies as in the West any more than we find the same issues, since neither China's issue space nor its sociological structure is a copy of the West's. The deeper question is whether the issue constituencies in China reflect patterns of social interest in interaction with cognitive sophistication that are intelligible in terms of the theories that explain ideological alignments in the Western case.

Table 15.3 presents correlations of selected respondent attributes with the tendency of respondents to give high priority to each issue agenda. Some of the attributes we look at are the same as those found in the West, such as sex, education, income, and age. Others, though different from the West, have a sociological logic similar to that of attributes studied elsewhere. For example, being a party member is a measure of elite status. Membership in a state unit is an indicator of economic privilege and high social status. Urban household registration signals the right to live in the cities, where conditions are better and most residents have access to social services not available in the countryside.[39]

For each attribute, the size of the correlation coefficient is a measure of how strongly the attribute influences a respondent's tendency to be concerned with the items that make up each agenda. The stronger the correlation, the more intense the social cleavage around that issue agenda—that is, the more sharply persons who differ along the particular social dimension differ in the priority they assign to the issue agenda.

All the correlations are statistically significant, and several are strong. Education is the most powerful predictor of issue priorities. Type of work unit is the second strongest correlate. Household registration, sex, and the other variables also have moderate effects on the choice of issue concerns.

TABLE 15.3   Correlations between Respondents' Attributes and Issue Agendas
(N = 2,727)

	Tiananmen Agenda	Reform Agenda	Economic Welfare Agenda	Foreign Policy Agenda
Household registration	.17	.20	−.33	.09
Sex	.24	.20	.22	−.16
Age	−.18	−.17	−.17	.15
Education	.38	.37	−.44	.26
Family income	.15	.16	−.21	.12
Party member	.16	.14	−.16	.12
Occupation	.19	.25	−.25	.13
State unit	.21	.23	−.32	.13

Source: China survey (1990).

Notes: All correlations are significant at the .001 level. Household registration: 1 if urban, 0 if rural. Sex: 1 if male, 0 if female. Education: years of formal schooling. Family income: in yuan. Party member: 1 if member of Chinese Communist Party, 0 if not. Occupation: 1 if white-collar, 0 if other. State unit: 1 if respondent reported working at state organization or state-owned enterprise, 0 if working at collective or other kind of enterprises.

However, there is a tendency for many of these factors to reinforce one another. For example, a person with more education is more likely to be young and male and to have more income. A multiple regression analysis, shown in table 15.4, distinguishes how each attribute functions separately. The standardized regression coefficients (betas) measure the relative strength of each variable in affecting respondents' choice of issue agendas. Education is the attribute that most strongly influences the choice of issue agenda, and it does so consistently across all four agendas. This suggests that differences in cognitive sophistication play a major role in determining the ideological alignments of Chinese citizens, even after taking account of the privileged social position of many educated citizens.

The next three most influential variables reflect the importance of social interest. Different variables more strongly affect different agendas. Sex is the second strongest factor affecting adherence to both the Tiananmen and Reform Agendas; men are more concerned with these sets of issues than are women. Household registration and age are the second and third strongest factors influencing adherence to the Economic Welfare Agenda; rural residents and older people place relatively high priority on this agenda.

When the four variables mentioned so far are controlled, the effects of the remaining variables are nearly all statistically significant. Some of them are quite strong, in particular the tendency (1) of party members to be more concerned about all four agendas, (2) of persons in more prestigious occupations to be strongly concerned with the Reform Agenda, and (3) of employees of state units to be concerned with the Economic Welfare Agenda.

The most important feature of tables 15.3 and 15.4 is the sign of the coefficients. A positive sign indicates that those concerned with the given agenda tend to measure one way on that attribute; a negative sign indicates that they measure the other. Thus, a positive sign on household registration indicates urban registration, a negative sign rural; a positive sign on sex indicates male, a negative sign female; a positive sign on age indicates an older group, a negative sign a younger group; and so on. For each variable in both tables (except for age and sex in table 15.3 and the statistically insignificant relationship between foreign policy and household registration in table 15.4),[40] the sign for the Economic Welfare Agenda is the opposite of that for the other three agendas. This means that with respect to the four agendas, the Chinese public divides into two constituencies with opposite characteristics.

One of these constituencies is relatively more urban, male, young, and well educated; it has above-average family incomes, contains more party members than the other constituency, and tends to work in white-collar occupations and to be employed in state units. This group is disproportionately concerned with the Tiananmen Agenda and the Reform Agenda. It wants more government leadership in attacking the problems of corruption, crime, bureaucratism, and inflation, and it favors more attention to economic and political reform. This constituency is critical of government performance, yet supportive of reform. In the Chinese context, it is relatively liberal. (It is also

TABLE 15.4 Multiple Regression Analysis of Respondents' Attributes on Issue Agendas (N = 2,727)

	Tiananmen Agenda		Reform Agenda		Economic Welfare Agenda		Foreign Policy Agenda	
	Coefficient	Beta	Coefficient	Beta	Coefficient	Beta	Coefficient	Beta
Household registration	.07	.03	.12	.06**	-.35	-.18***	-.03	-.01
Sex	.28	.15***	.20	.11***	-.16	-.07***	.15	.09***
Age	-.00	-.06***	-.00	-.08***	.01	.13***	-.00	-.09***
Education	.06	.25***	.05	.20***	-.05	-.24***	.03	.15**
Family income	.00	.03	.00	.04**	-.00	-.03*	.00	.05**
Party member	.21	.07***	.17	.05***	-.18	-.06***	.21	.07***
Occupation	.07	.02	.29	.10***	-.11	-.04**	.07	.26
State unit	.11	.05**	.11	.05**	-.13	-.07***	.07	.03
Constant	-.45		-.41		.60		-.11	
R-squared	.17		.17		.24		.08	

Source: China survey (1990).

Notes: Household registration: 1 if urban, 0 if rural. Sex: 1 if male, 0 if female. Education: years of formal schooling. Family income: in yuan. Party member: 1 if member of Chinese Communist Party, 0 if not. Occupation: 1 if white-collar, 0 if other. State unit: 1 if respondent reported working at state organization or state-owned enterprise, 0 if working at collective or other kind of enterprises.

* Significant at .10 level.
** Significant at .05 level.
*** Significant at .01 level.

interested in the Foreign Policy Agenda, but we know from table 15.1 that interest in the Foreign Policy Agenda is not strong, and table 15.3 shows that this agenda divides the two constituencies more weakly than the other two. We therefore drop it from the rest of the analysis.)

The second constituency has relatively more members with the opposite characteristics: rural, female, older, less educated, with lower incomes, without party membership, and working in nonstate units. This group is most concerned with the Economic Welfare Agenda. It is uneasy about the impact of reform on jobs, housing, incomes, and subsidies, and it does not support accelerated reform. In the Chinese context, it is relatively conservative.

The attributes that divide the two constituencies are partly the same as and partly different from those that divide Left and Right in the West. But more important, the divisions make sense in terms of the same theory that explains ideological alignments in the West.

First, socioeconomic interest explains why the constituency for the Tiananmen and Reform Agendas consists of the relative winners from reform, while backers of the Economic Welfare Agenda are those who have been most vulnerable to the costs of reform.[41] Although inflation, corruption, and the decline of government services have affected everyone (as table 15.1 shows), they hit hardest those of lower social and economic status, who perceive themselves as more in need of the kind of government protection characteristic of the old system and who are less equipped to take advantage of the market economy that is emerging under the reforms.

Reform dissolved the rural commune system and left village residents to fend for themselves in the market, while urban residents continue to have access to social benefits denied rural residents. Women lost some of the protection they had enjoyed under the old system, in which the government supported relative equality of the sexes; they are now openly discriminated against, especially in the growing private and collective enterprise sector. Older people have seen their guarantees of lifetime employment threatened and their pensions eroded; many lack the energy and skills to take advantage of the new opportunities that reform offers.

Persons with lower educational levels lack the training and connections to get ahead in the new order. Those with lower incomes lack the capital to get started in business. Party members have the connections to get ahead, and some can use their positions to benefit from the corruption that reform has generated. Members of state units, with their privileged employment status, have less need to worry about jobs, subsidies, housing, and the like. The fact that those without privileged access to state benefits show greater concern with the Economic Welfare Agenda reflects the fact that reform has subjected them to risk and deprivation. In short, those social groups who have been relative gainers in the reform process are more concerned with the general public agendas of Tiananmen and Reform. Those who have been relative losers because of the reform process have been more concerned with the personal damage they have suffered.

As sometimes happens in the West, cognitive sophistication reinforces the operation of economic interest by making those who are likely to be liberal even more likely to be liberal. While both constituencies are critical of the present state of affairs, the better educated tend to look at the problems generated by reform in a way that goes beyond immediate personal interest and to see them in terms of broad public issues. They are more likely to understand how indirect measures such as further reform can, over the long run, solve such immediate problems as housing, jobs, income distribution, and satisfaction of consumer needs more effectively than can state intervention aimed directly at these issues. The better educated—more advantaged by reform and so more liberal—are also more willing to trade material benefits for ideological values and to trade immediate benefits for long-term benefits.

In short, there were two distinct issue constituencies in the Chinese mass public in 1990. Although they were not replicas of the classic Western Left/Right constituencies, they resembled them in certain ways. To the extent that they differed from Western constituencies, they did so in ways that can be explained by the same logic of interest and cognition that explains ideological alignments in the West.

DEMOCRATIC VALUES

We turn finally to our third ideological dimension, attitudes toward democracy. Does the pattern of cleavage over democratic values fall along the same ideological spectrum just identified or crosscut it? Our data permit us to answer this question by looking at democratic attitudes and also at two related sets of attitudes: social liberalism and procedural liberalism.[42]

Using an agree/disagree format, we posed six statements about attitudes toward democracy.[43] The pattern of responses is displayed in table 15.5. We also asked six questions about attitudes toward women (social liberalism) and two about criminal procedure (procedural liberalism), some of them in agree/disagree format;[44] the pattern of responses to these is shown in tables 15.6 and 15.7.

The responses to this set of questions contain several points of interest. On democracy, the public's responses would be unexpected in the West but make sense in China. Democracy is understood by most Chinese not as a system of competition and participation, but as a term for the good polity—one that is fair, egalitarian, stable, and honest. What legitimizes government is not pluralism and participation but moral rectitude and administrative performance.[45] The majorities who want "more democracy" want government that is more honest and responsive. They would like top city officials to be elected instead of appointed, because current mayors are often viewed as remote and corrupt. But at the same time substantial minorities fear that too much pluralism will give rise to ideological and social disorder. And only a tiny number are willing to dispense with CCP leadership.[46]

TABLE 15.5   Opinions on Democracy (Percentage of Responses, N = 2,896)

Issues	Pro-democracy	Anti-democracy	Don't Know
More democracy will lead to chaos (disagree)	37.7	22.4	39.9
Multiple parties will cause political chaos (disagree)	29.5	35.7	34.7
Different thinking will lead to chaos (disagree)	32.2	43.0	24.8
Heads of cities should be elected (agree)	67.8	21.6	10.6
China needs more democracy now (agree)	54.8	6.0	39.3
China's democracy depends on Communist party's leadership (disagree)	1.7	76.1	22.2

Source: China survey (1990).

TABLE 15.6   Social Attitudes (Percentage of Responses, N = 2,896)

Issues	Liberal	Conservative	Don't Know
Would you allow son to marry a divorced woman? (yes)	46.0	38.5	15.6
Do you mind if supervisor is a woman? (no)	81.2	5.3	13.5
Wife's educational level should be lower than husband's (no)	70.3	17.4	12.3
Wife's income should be lower than husband's (no)	75.0	15.5	9.5
Do you care if you do not have a son? (no)	63.8	27.1	9.1
Should couples be able to divorce? (yes)	55.0	33.8	11.2

Source: China survey (1990).

TABLE 15.7   Attitudes toward Due Process (Percentage of Responses, N = 2,896)

Issues	Pro–Due Process	Ignore Due Process	Don't Know
Punish without legal procedure (agree)	43.2	40.7	16.1
Judge should solicit opinions of local government (agree)	22.6	57.3	20.1

Source: China survey (1990).

Social attitudes show a consensus for liberal values that is surprisingly strong in light of the poor social and economic status of Chinese women.[47] Most people say they are willing to have a female supervisor and to allow their son to marry a divorced woman. Few say that they think a wife's income or education should be lower than her husband's. Since the Chinese population is still largely rural and has relatively low average educational levels, however, we suspect they have expressed politically correct responses rather than deeply rooted beliefs.[48]

By contrast, procedural liberalism is relatively weak. Faced with what they see as a crime wave, Chinese are not immune from the tendency found in mass publics elsewhere to be less liberal when they think about the rights of suspected criminals than when they think about other issues.[49] This fits with Chinese attitudes of intolerance toward proponents of unpopular political attitudes, which we have discussed elsewhere.[50] In short, liberalism in China is no more consistent a belief system than it is in the West.

In order to discover which sections of the public hold democratic and liberal values, we scaled respondents according to the number of democratic or liberal answers they gave for each set of issues and then correlated the strength of pro-democratic attitudes with the same respondent attributes used in table 15.3.[51] The results are displayed in table 15.8.

Table 15.8 displays the same pattern of correlations as the Tiananmen and Reform Agendas in table 15.3. All three kinds of democratic/liberal attitudes are powerfully affected by education. Urbanites, males, and younger people tend to be more liberal on all three dimensions. Income, party membership, occupation, and unemployment in a state unit also contribute. The cleavage patterns on political democracy and social and procedural liberalism are thus isomorphic with those on the reform issue dimension: the same kinds of people tend to array themselves in the same way along both dimensions. A pro-reform, pro-democratic constituency of the relatively privileged finds its complement in a relatively disadvantaged constituency that wants a return to state responsibility for economic welfare and withholds support from democratic values.

The multiple regression presented in table 15.9 shows that all the variables have distinguishable effects but that education is by far the strongest, with sex, age, household registration, and party membership following. As in the

TABLE 15.8   Correlation between Respondents' Attributes and Degree of Democratism

Issues	Political	Social	Procedural
Household registration	.25	.23	.23
Sex	.28	.16	.18
Age	−.28	−.17	−.10
Education	.49	.39	.34
Family income	.21	.15	.17
Party member	.14	.13	.16
Occupation	.25	.19	.21
State unit	.29	.22	.23

Source: China survey (1990).

Notes: All correlations are significant at the .001 level. Household registration: 1 if urban, 0 if rural. Sex: 1 if male, 0 if female. Education: years of formal schooling. Family income: in yuan. Party member: 1 if member of Chinese Communist Party, 0 if not. Occupation: 1 if white-collar, 0 if other. State unit: 1 if respondent reported working at state organization or state-owned enterprise, 0 if working at collective or other kind of enterprises.

TABLE 15.9 Multiple Regression Analysis of Respondents' Attributes and Degree of Democratism (N = 2,727)

	Political		Social		Procedural	
	Coefficient	*Beta*	*Coefficient*	*Beta*	*Coefficient*	*Beta*
Household registration	.31	.09***	.34	.10***	.14	.09***
Sex	.58	.19***	.24	.07***	.14	.10***
Age	−.02	−.15***	−.01	−.05**	.00	−.02
Education	.10	.27***	.11	.29***	.04	.23***
Family income	.00	.05**	.00	.01	.00	.04**
Party member	.19	.04**	.26	.05**	.15	.06***
Occupation	.22	.05**	.09	.01	.09	.04*
State unit	.27	.07***	.09	.02	.07	.04*
Constant	1.41		2.9		.15	
R-squared		.29		.17		.15

Source: China survey (1990).
Notes: Household registration: 1 if urban, 0 if rural. Sex: 1 if male, 0 if female. Education: years of formal schooling. Family income: in yuan. Party member: 1 if member of Chinese Communist Party, 0 if not. Occupation: 1 if white-collar, 0 if other. State unit: 1 if respondent reported working at state organization or state-owned enterprise, 0 if working at collective or other kind of enterprises.
* Significant at .10 level.
** Significant at .05 level.
*** Significant at .01 level.

United States, cognitive sophistication appears to play an even more important role in the choice of democratic/liberal attitudes than it does in the choice of issue agendas, with social interests having correspondingly less influence.[52] Respondents who are better educated, male, younger, more urban, and members of the party tend to be at once more knowledgeable about politics, better trained in official norms, and more tolerant and less authoritarian in their values. Even though most members of this group are relatively privileged under the current political system, they probably expect Chinese-style democracy to open the system to even greater influence by people like themselves.

CONCLUSION: AN EMERGING CLEAVAGE STRUCTURE

Both constituencies we have identified were nostalgic for some aspects of the Maoist past, but the first group longed for the era of honest government and stable prices, the second for the time when government provided jobs, housing, and incomes. Liberals tended to blame the government for corruption and inflation; were eager to see more progress on reform; and held relatively tolerant, pro-democratic political, social, and procedural attitudes. Conservatives were dissatisfied with the shrinking role of government in solving citizens' individual economic and social problems; did not place a high priority on reform; and held relatively non-democratic and nonliberal attitudes.

Socioeconomic interest and cognitive sophistication explain how citizens aligned themselves on the issues that confronted them. The predictor variables do not work exactly as they do in the West. The impact of education on issue priorities and values is so powerful that it should be understood as not just a surrogate variable for class and cognitive sophistication, as in the West, but as additionally marking a status and role gap between the mass of people and the educated minority that the Chinese call "intellectuals." People in this category, conventionally including anyone who went to college, consider themselves collectively responsible for the fate of the nation. Their sense of a special role probably shapes their response to questions about issues facing the nation.

The urban/rural gap is also especially important in China, defining a wider range of differences than it does in the West. Mao's regime created a castelike division between rural and urban residents to make possible the accumulation of capital from the rural sector for industrial development. Rural residents remain radically disadvantaged today. The role of work-unit type and party membership also reflect distinctive Chinese institutional dynamics—the tradition of lifetime employment in state units with cradle-to-grave benefits, and the small size and total political dominance of the CCP. But however distinctive they are, the impact of all the predictor variables can be deciphered with social-interest and cognitive logics that are as valid in China as in the West.

We found no parallel for Lipset and Rokkan's center/periphery cleavage when we coded respondents on a coastal/inland dimension. Since regional identities are important in China, this deserves further research; different coding might produce stronger results. Nor are religious cleavages important in shaping the distribution of political attitudes across the population as a whole. Although religious issues animate political movements in Tibet, Mongolia, and Xinjiang and there are sizable Catholic and Protestant communities at odds with the state, 92 percent of our respondents described themselves as not religious.

The attitudinal and sociological structure of the Chinese mass public today provides the context within which future political change will take place. As in Europe in the eighteenth and nineteenth centuries and Russia and Eastern Europe in the twentieth, so in China in the twenty-first: The social cleavages of the past are likely to shape the political system of the future. The cleavages we have described are statistical tendencies rather than structured groups. As China moves toward more openness, the issue agendas are likely to become contested issues, and the issue constituencies are likely to become interest groups. When and if a multiparty system forms, the constituencies may form party coalitions. With appropriate adjustments, the issue agendas may become their platforms. Deng Xiaoping's reform may thus have bequeathed to China not only a soft transition to the market but also the beginnings of relatively clear, institutionalized, interest-based cleavages that can either shape a post-Deng authoritarian-corporatist structure or undergird a democratic party system if one should emerge.

APPENDIX

This analysis is based on a survey conducted in December 1990, in cooperation with the Social Survey Research Center of People's University of China (SSRC). The sample was designed to be representative of the adult population over eighteen years old residing in family households at the time of the survey, excluding those living in the Tibet Autonomous Region.[53] A stratified multistage area sampling procedure with probabilities proportional to size (PPS) measures was employed to select the sample.

Since the political structure in the rural areas is different from that in urban areas, political culture and behavior in the countryside were expected to be different from those in cities and towns. In order to obtain separate estimates for rural and urban areas, we divided the whole population into two domains: the rural domain and the urban domain. Because only about 20 percent of the population hold urban household registrations, they were oversampled, and rural residents were undersampled. A poststratification weighting technique was used to correct for household registration, age, and sex, while preserving the original sample *N*. This created a valid national sample consistent with the 1990 census 10 percent sample.[54]

The primary sampling units (PSUs) employed were *xian* (counties) for the rural domain and *shi* (cities) for the urban domain. Before selection, counties were stratified by region and geographical characteristics and cities by region and size. The secondary sampling units (SSUs) were *xiang* (townships) in rural areas and *qu* (districts) or *jiedao* (streets) in urban areas. The third stage of selection was villages in the rural domain and *juweihui* (residents' committees) in the urban domain. For both domains, households were used at the fourth stage of sampling.

In the selection of PSUs, national population data for 1986 acquired from the Ministry of Public Security were used as the database to construct the sampling frame.[55] The number of family households for each county or city was taken as the measure of size (MOS) in the PPS selection process.

For the subsequent stages of sampling, population data were obtained from local public security bureaus or governments. At the village and residents' committee levels, lists of *hukou* (household registrations) were obtained from police stations. In places without household registration, lists were obtained by field count.

The project interviewed 3,200 people, and 2,896 questionnaires were collected, which represents a response rate of 90.5 percent.

The survey instrument was constructed in the United States and pretested in Beijing in December 1988. After thorough analysis of the pretest, we revised the questionnaire. College students of sociology and statistics were employed as field interviewers. Before the fieldwork, project members went to China to train the interviewers in field interviewing techniques.

NOTES

This chapter was previously published in *World Politics* 48, no. 4 (July 1996): 522–50, and was reprinted in Andrew J. Nathan, *China's Transition* (New York: Columbia University Press, 1997). © Center of International Studies, Princeton University. Reprinted by permission of the Johns Hopkins University Press.

The authors acknowledge the support of National Science Foundation grant INT-88-14199, a grant from the United Daily News Cultural Foundation, and the assistance of the Opinion Research Center of China, Social and Economic Research Institute of Beijing, under the directors Chen Ziming and Wang Juntao. An earlier version of this chapter was presented at a conference sponsored by the Symposium on Science, Reason, and Modern Democracy at Michigan State University, April 21–24, 1994. We are grateful to conference participants for their comments and to Michael R. Chambers, Margo E. Landman, Dong Li, Kenneth Lieberthal, James D. Seymour, Robert Y. Shapiro, Lawrence R. Sullivan, Kellee S. Tsai, and Lynn T. White III.

1. Seymour Martin Lipset and Stein Rokkan, *Party Systems and Voter Alignments* (New York: Free Press, 1967).

2. Arend Lijphart, "Political Parties: Ideologies and Programs," in David Butler, Howard R. Penniman, and Austin Ranney, eds., *Democracy at the Polls: A Comparative Study of Competitive National Elections* (Washington: American Enterprise Institute, 1981).

3. For example, see Russell J. Dalton, Scott C. Flanagan, and Paul Allen Beck, eds., *Electoral Change in Advanced Industrial Democracies: Realignment or Dealignment?* (Princeton: Princeton University Press, 1984); Arend Lijphart, "Religious vs. Linguistic vs. Class Voting," *American Political Science Review* 73 (June 1979); and Sidney Verba, Norman H. Nie, and Jae-on Kim, *Participation and Political Equality: A Seven Nation Comparison* (New York: Cambridge University Press, 1978).

4. Ronald Inglehart, *Culture Shift in Advanced Industrial Societies* (Princeton: Princeton University Press, 1990), 273–78.

5. Pamela Johnston Conover and Stanley Feldman, "The Origins and Meaning of Liberal/Conservative Self-Identifications," *American Political Science Review* 25 (November 1981); and Stanley Feldman and John Zaller, "The Political Culture of Ambivalence: Ideological Responses to the Welfare State," *American Journal of Political Science* 36 (February 1992).

6. Shawn Rosenberg, "The Structure of Political Thinking," *American Journal of Political Science* 32 (August 1988); and Paul M. Sniderman et al., *Reasoning and Choice: Explorations in Political Psychology* (Cambridge: Cambridge University Press, 1991).

7. John R. Zaller, *The Nature and Origins of Mass Opinion* (Cambridge: Cambridge University Press, 1992), 26.

8. Hans D. Klingermann, "Measuring Ideological Conceptualizations," in Samuel H. Barnes et al., *Political Action: Mass Participation in Five Western Democracies* (Beverly Hills, Calif.: Sage, 1979), 229.

9. Klingermann, "Measuring Ideological Conceptualizations," 230.

10. Philip E. Converse, "The Nature of Belief Systems in Mass Publics," in David E. Apter, ed., *Ideology and Discontent* (New York: Free Press, 1964). But see Christopher H. Achen, "Mass Political Attitudes and the Survey Response," *American Political Science Review* 69 (December 1975); and Inglehart, *Culture Shift*, chap. 3.

11. Robert Axelrod, "Where the Votes Come From: An Analysis of Electoral Coalitions, 1952–1968," *American Political Science Review* 66 (March 1972); Douglas A. Hibbs, Jr., "Political Parties and Macroeconomic Policy," *American Political Science Review* 71 (December 1977); Seymour Martin Lipset, *Political Man: The Social Bases of Politics*, rev. ed. (Baltimore: Johns Hopkins University Press, 1981), 230–300; and Herbert McCloskey and Alida Brill, *Dimensions of Tolerance: What Americans Believe about Civil Liberties* (New York: Russell Sage Foundation, 1983), 370–414.

12. Cognitive sophistication is also referred to as cognitive mobilization, cognitive ability, cognitive competence, and political sophistication, among other terms. Philip E. Converse, "Public Opinion and Voting Behavior," in Fred I. Greenstein and Nelson W. Polsby, eds., *Handbook of Political Science*, vol. 4 (Reading, Mass.: Addison-Wesley, 1975); Ronald Inglehart, "Cognitive Mobilization and European Identity," *Comparative Politics* 3 (October 1970); Robert C. Luskin, "Measuring Political Sophistication," *American Journal of Political Science* 31 (November 1987); Norman H. Nie, Sidney Verba, and John R. Petrocik, *The Changing American Voter*, rev. ed. (Cambridge: Harvard University Press, 1979), 148–55; and Sniderman et al., *Reasoning and Choice*.

13. Benjamin I. Page and Robert Y. Shapiro, *The Rational Public: Fifty Years of Trends in Americans' Policy Preferences* (Chicago: University of Chicago Press, 1992), 315.

14. Angus Campbell et al., *The American Voter* (1960; reprint, New York: John Wiley, 1980), chaps. 9–10; Daniel Lerner, *The Passing of Traditional Society: Modernizing the Middle East* (New York: Free Press, 1958); Rosenberg, "The Structure of Political Thinking"; Sniderman et al., *Reasoning and Choice*; and James A. Stimson, "Belief Systems: Constraint, Complexity, and the 1972 Election," *American Journal of Political Science* 19 (August 1975).

15. Campbell et al., *The American Voter*, 204.

16. Richard Curt Kraus, *Class Conflict in Chinese Socialism* (New York: Columbia University Press, 1981).

17. See, for example, Mao Zedong, "Resolution on Certain Questions in the History of Our Party," in *Selected Works of Mao Tse-tung*, vol. 3 (Peking: Foreign Languages Press, 1965).

18. *Selected Works of Mao Tse-tung*, vol. 4 (Peking: Foreign Languages Press, 1977), 184.

19. Yan Jiaqi and Gao Gao, *Wenhua dageming shinianshi* (History of the ten-year Cultural Revolution), rev. ed. (Taipei: Yuanliu chuban shiye gufen youxian gongsi, 1990), 1:90–108.

20. Yan and Gao, *Wenhua dageming shinianshi*, 646–48. Cf. William A. Joseph, *The Critique of Ultra-Leftism in China, 1958–1981* (Stanford: Stanford University Press, 1984).

21. Ruan Ming, *Deng Xiaoping diguo* (The empire of Deng Xiaoping) (Taipei: Shibao wenhua chuban shiye youxian gongsi, 1992).

22. As seen in the book title of Lü Wen's *Zhongguo "zuo" huo* (China's "left" disasters) (Beijing: Chaohua chubanshe, 1993).

23. Perry Link, *Evening Chats in Beijing: Probing China's Predicament* (New York: W. W. Norton, 1992); Ching-chang Hsiao and Mei-rong Yang, "'Don't Force Us to Lie': The Case of the *World Economic Herald*," in Chin-Chuan Lee, ed., *Voices of China: The Interplay of Politics and Journalism* (New York: Guilford Press, 1990); and Judy Polumbaum, "The Tribulations of China's Journalists after a Decade of Reform," in Lee, *Voices of China.*

24. Dong Li, "Public Opinion Polls and Political Attitudes in China, 1979–1989" (Ph.D. diss., Columbia University, 1993), chap. 3.

25. Cf. Li, "Public Opinion Polls", chap. 4.

26. Marlowe Hood, "Reflections on Civil Society, 'Black Society,' and Corruption in Contemporary China" (Paper presented at the annual meeting of the Association for Asian Studies, Boston, March 25–27, 1994); Mayfair Mei-hui Yang, *Gifts, Favors, and Banquets: The Art of Social Relationships in China* (Ithaca, N.Y.: Cornell University Press, 1994).

27. X. L. Ding, *The Decline of Communism in China: Legitimacy Crisis, 1977–1989* (Cambridge: Cambridge University Press, 1994); Merle Goldman, *Sowing the Seeds of Democracy in China: Political Reform in the Deng Xiaoping Era* (Cambridge: Harvard University Press, 1994); and Link, *Evening Chats in Beijing.*

28. Andrew J. Nathan, *Chinese Democracy* (New York: Knopf, 1985).

29. "On Questions of Party History: Resolution on Certain Questions in the History of Our Party since the Founding of the People's Republic of China," *Beijing Review* 24, no. 27 (July 6, 1981): 10–39.

30. Baogang He, "Three Models of Democracy: Intellectual and Moral Foundations of Liberal Democracy and Preconditions for Its Establishment in Contemporary China" (Ph.D. diss., Australian National University, 1993), 3, 257.

31. Li, "Public Opinion Polls," chap. 6.

32. Because of our expectation that Left/Right concepts would not be meaningful to respondents, our 1990 survey did not include a measure of Left/Right self-placement. Our 1993 surveys in mainland China, Taiwan, and Hong Kong included not only the issue priority battery reported here, but also a Chinese-traditionalism battery; a Left/Right placement battery for self, CCP, father, and Kuomintang; and a number of other relevant questions (speed of reform and of social change, liberalism, civil liberties, democracy). We plan to use these questions to compare the dimensionality of Chinese political issues across the three Chinese political systems.

33. As with similar questions commonly used in surveys in the West (e.g., Nie, Verba, and Petrocik, *The Changing American Voter,* Page and Shapiro, *The Rational Public*), we asked about issues we knew were on the public's mind. A technique used by researchers at National Taiwan University is to derive the issues they ask about from the platforms of candidates in election campaigns; see, e.g., Fu Hu, "The Electoral Mechanism and Political Change in Taiwan," in Steve Tsang, ed., *In the Shadow of China: Political Developments in Taiwan since 1949* (London: Hurst, 1993), 154–59. This reduces the risk that issues will be arbitrarily left off the list. Because of the lack of competitive elections in China, that option was not available to us. It should also be noted that this item was not designed to be used as we use it here, to test hypotheses about ideological dimensions. Nonetheless, it proved usable in this way.

34. Besides Beijing, there were demonstrations in at least thirty other cities, but few are known to have occurred outside cities.

35. Low expressed interest, in turn, may reflect an issue's lack of perceived salience to the respondent or the respondent's lack of information about the issue, or both. The difference between these two causes is not germane to the analysis here. Alternatively, one might hypothesize that "don't know" answers are given when an issue is politically too sensitive or dangerous to talk about honestly. In another article, however, one of us has demonstrated that this is not the case. "Don't know" responses are correlated with measures of respondents' cognitive deficiency rather than with measures of their political vulnerability. Tianjian Shi, "Survey Research in China," in Michael X. Delli Carpini, Leoni Huddy, and Robert Y. Shapiro, eds., *Research in Micropolitics*, vol. 5, *New Directions in Political Psychology* (Greenwich, Conn.: JAI Press, 1996).

36. Factor analysis is best used to confirm the existence of dimensions that were theorized in advance. Otherwise, the risk is that almost any factor structure can be given a forced interpretation. As noted earlier, we did not have a theory of issue dimensions in mind when we constructed the list of issue items. But since the individual items have the kinds of face relationships that are described in the text, we feel justified in proceeding to factor analysis. The validity of the factor analysis gains further credibility when the factor results prove to be meaningful with respect to other variables in the study, as in table 15.3.

37. There is no reason to expect all the items to cluster tightly around a given number of factors, since the list of items presented to respondents was not drawn up to test a theory of issue dimensions.

38. The weak loading of "environment" and "consumer rights" on this factor may support Inglehart's suggestion that materialist and postmaterialist issues are distinct in the public mind. But a separate factor analysis of these six items alone produced loadings on only one factor, not two. Six items may be too few to reveal the materialist/postmaterialist cleavage.

39. Type of household registration is not a measure of actual place of residence. However, those registered in the cities tend to live in cities, while those registered in rural areas either live in rural areas or are in the cities temporarily, without access to the privileges accorded urban residents. Sulamith Heins Potter and Jack M. Potter, *China's Peasants: The Anthropology of a Revolution* (Cambridge: Cambridge University Press, 1990), chap. 15.

40. And except for the statistically insignificant relationship between foreign policy and household registration in table 15.4, table 15.4 is a better guide than table 15.3 to the impact of age and sex on selection of agendas because it shows their effects when other variables are controlled.

41. For similar arguments about the former USSR, see Ada W. Finifter and Ellen Mickiewicz, "Redefining the Political System of the USSR: Mass Support for Political Change," *American Political Science Review* 86 (December 1992); and Arthur H. Miller, Vicki L. Hesli, and William M. Reisinger, "Reassessing Mass Support for Political and Economic Change in the Former USSR," in *American Political Science Review* 88 (June 1994).

42. These sets of questions touch on what Flanagan calls the "authoritarian-liberal" dimension. Our questions are not the same as his because we designed the questionnaire to collect information on public attitudes to certain specific issues of concern to us. Our 1993 questionnaire includes a "traditionalism" battery that incorporates some of Flanagan's items and others analogous to his. Scott Flanagan, "Value Change in Industrial Societies," *American Political Science Review* 81 (December 1987).

43. The statements were:

If there are too many political parties in a country, it will lead to political chaos.
If people's ideas are not united, there will be chaos in society.
Broadening the scope of democracy in our country now would affect stability.
It is now very necessary to broaden the scope of democracy in our country.
The realization of democracy in our country depends upon the leadership of the party.
Some people believe heads of cities (counties) should be elected by the people, others believe they should be appointed by the higher authorities. What do you think?

44. The questions were:

Do you care if you do not have a son?
A couple has been married many years, but their feelings all along were incompatible, and the wife has fallen in love with another man. Some people think that under this type of situation, it should be permitted for the couple to divorce; some people think it should not be permitted for them to divorce. What is your opinion?
If your unmarried son wanted to marry a divorced woman, would you approve?
If your immediate supervisor were a woman, would you feel annoyed?
The educational level of a wife should not be higher than her husband's.
The salary of a wife should not be more than her husband's.
Ruthless criminals should be punished immediately, without having to follow complicated legal procedures.
When trying a major case, the judge should solicit the opinions of the local government.

45. Nathan, *Chinese Democracy;* this interpretation gains support from the fact that the same constituency supports pro-democratic attitudes and the Tiananmen Agenda, as we are about to show.

46. We acknowledge the possibility that respondents were afraid to withhold agreement from this proposition, since CCP leadership is one of Deng Xiaoping's "four basic principles," which every Chinese citizen is supposed to support. This analysis should not be taken to imply that Chinese political culture is inhospitable to democratization; cf. Andrew J. Nathan and Tianjian Shi, "Cultural Requisites for Democracy in China: Findings from a Survey," *Daedalus* 122 (Spring 1993); and Andrew J. Nathan, "Is Chinese Culture Distinctive?" *Journal of Asian Studies* 52 (November 1993).

47. For example, Elisabeth J. Croll, *Changing Identities of Chinese Women: Rhetoric, Experience, and Self-Perception in the Twentieth Century* (Hong Kong: Hong Kong University Press, 1995); Xiaoxian Gao, "China's Modernization and Changes in the Social Status of Rural Women," trans. S. Katherine Campbell, in Christina K. Gilmartin et al., eds., *Engendering China: Women, Culture, and the State* (Cambridge: Harvard University Press, 1994); and Margery Wolf, *Revolution Postponed: Women in Contemporary China* (Stanford: Stanford University Press, 1985).

48. We asked more questions about gender attitudes in our 1993 survey, which will enable us to test this hypothesis.

49. McCloskey and Brill, *Dimensions of Tolerance,* chap. 4; James W. Prothro and Charles M. Grigg, "Fundamental Principles of Democracy: Bases of Agreement and Disagreement," *Journal of Politics* 22 (May 1960).

50. Nathan and Shi, "Cultural Requisites."

51. Factor analysis confirmed that the three sets of questions concern three different issue-areas, each of which emerged as a distinct factor. Thus, scaling is an appropriate technique here. The democracy and social liberalism scales ran from 1 to 6, and procedural liberalism from 1 to 2.

52. McCloskey and Brill, *Dimensions of Tolerance*; and Page and Shapiro, *The Rational Public*.

53. We decided to exclude Tibet from this study for a number of reasons. Transportation there is difficult since there is no railroad and the highway system is not well developed. Many Tibetans do not speak Chinese. And it is difficult to find qualified interviewers to work there.

54. State Council, Population Census Office, *Zhongguo 1990 nian renkou pucha 10% chouyang ziliao* (Ten percent sample data of China's 1990 census), electronic data edition, ed. Guojia tongjiju renkou tongjisi (Beijing: State Statistical Bureau Office of Population Statistics, 1990).

55. Ministry of Public Security of the PRC, ed., *Quanguo fenxianshi renkou tongji ziliao, 1986* (Population statistics by city and county of the People's Republic of China, 1986) (Beijing: Ditu chubanshe, 1987).

16

Regime Shift: Japanese Politics in a Changing World Economy

T. J. Pempel

For the past several years, Japan has been in the midst of a fundamental regime shift. At least three essentials of the old regime have been undergoing sweeping changes.

First, on the political level, the thirty-eight years of dominance by the Liberal Democratic Party (LDP) ended with the party's internal fragmentation, its loss of a parliamentary majority and executive control, and the introduction of a new electoral system for the Lower House of the Diet. In July 1993 the handsome, youthful descendant of a well-established samurai family, Hosokawa Morihiro of the Japan New Party, cobbled together an ideologically disparate, seven-party coalition that made him Japan's first non-LDP prime minister since that party's formation in 1955. Soon thereafter, the Social Democratic Party of Japan (SDPJ; previously the Japan Socialist Party, JSP), long the LDP's *bête noire*, ended nearly fifty years in the political wilderness as its leader Murayama Tomiichi became prime minister in coalition with the LDP and another small conservative party, Sakigake. After taking power, however, the SDPJ also wound up squandering whatever ideological cohesion it once had by reversing its hitherto sacrosanct policy positions on article IX of the constitution, defense, the U.S.-Japan Security Treaty, and the dispatch of Japanese troops abroad. Largely as a consequence, the party was the heaviest loser in the 1996 elections, and the party's few remaining parliamentarians fell to quarreling with one another.

The mid-1990s were years of rampant party realignment. Kaleidoscopic groupings and regroupings led cynics to suggest that Japanese politicians and political groupings were like passengers standing on a platform waiting just long enough for the next train to come in, when they would jump on board and move on for another station or two. Individual parties and governmental coalitions flashed into view and disappeared with the unpredictability of fireflies. Between 1993 and 1996 alone eleven different political parties shared power, and four individuals held the office of prime minister. Although the LDP reentered government in alliance with Murayama and then became the sole party of government following the 1996 elections, the party no longer exerted the sweeping dominance that it once enjoyed.[1]

Electoral politics and the Japanese party system have been in the midst of a massive overhaul that undercut roughly twenty-five years of previous stability.

Second, on the economic front, Japan's seemingly endless string of achievements from the early 1950s until the end of the 1980s came to a crushing halt with the puncturing of the economic bubble, the simultaneous collapse of both stock and land prices,[2] ten years of almost zero growth from 1991 to 2000, an international downgrading of Japanese bonds, the collapse of a number of substantial financial institutions, and a host of other economic reversals. These represented a dramatic turnaround from the unrelenting successes that had previously marked the national economy.

Third, in international relations, the once-close fraternal relationship with the United States, solidified by common Cold War opposition to Communism, the USSR, and China, became marked by something akin to sibling rivalry: The security-bonded allies discovered they were economic rivals as well. This competition was manifested in a series of trade and market disputes throughout the 1980s and early 1990s that were wrenchingly deviant from the general cordiality that had characterized relations from the 1950s into at least the early 1970s. And in the wake of the Gulf War, U.S.–Japanese differences on security also came to a head, eventually leading to Japan's redefinition of the roles that its Self-Defense Forces could play in international military actions. By the latter years of the 1990s, Japanese conservatives were actively discussing Japan's security and foreign options in ways unheard of a decade earlier. Many had also become worried about long-term dependability of ties to the United States and were expressing worry about the possibility that Japan would be "bypassed" and that China would replace Japan as America's major ally in Asia.[3]

Such shifts have generated a widespread outpouring of analyses. Specific details are plentiful; so are questions about the extent to which the Japanese political economy is, or is not, undergoing "meaningful" changes. Nor is there any shortage of predictions about the alleged inevitability of one or more broad directions in which Japan will be forced to move. Recent events in Japan are providing a Rorschach test onto which all manner of analysts, reformers, and future planners can project their theories, proposals, and fondest hopes.

This chapter presents a different perspective. In it, I argue that the Japanese political economy is indeed undergoing a fundamental, deep, and structural set of transformations. These are occurring at what might be thought of as a middle level of politics and economics, one far deeper than the ever-recurring shifts in personalities and party strengths but far less comprehensive than the kinds of totalistic shifts involved in, say, a transition from authoritarianism to parliamentary democracy or from a centrally planned economy to market-based capitalism. Such shifts are taking place at the "regime" level.[4]

Specifically, I argue that recent political and economic events in Japan reflect much deeper restructuring along the three critical dimensions that constitute a domestic regime: (1) the character of the socioeconomic coalition that rules the country (and by implication, the socioeconomic forces that are its major opponents); (2) the political and economic institutions through which power is acquired and exercised; and (3) the public policy profile that gives broad political direction to the nation. Each has its own analytic autonomy, yet simultaneously all three interact with one another in reinforcing and overlapping ways. In combination, they constitute Japan's political-economic "regime."

These changes, sharpened and crystallized though they have been by recent recombinations in the party system, the economy, and Japan's bilateral relationships, in fact have far deeper roots and structural causes. The shifts currently taking place in the Japanese regime are the result, I argue, first of alterations in the international political economy and the difficulties Japan's prevailing regime had in dealing with them, and second of endogenous changes within Japan's own demographic profile that eroded many of the power arrangements of the old system and that weakened the glue holding the old regime together. This dynamic combination of exogenous and endogenous changes has been the causal core of the restructuring currently taking place within Japan. The consequence is almost certain to be the creation of a new regime that will be based on revised socioeconomic coalitional arrangements, modified political institutions, and uncharted directions for public policy.

The chapter is organized into three main sections. The first outlines the past regime of one-party dominance in Japan. The second examines the changes that undermined that earlier regime. The last section then explores the new institutional, socioeconomic, and policy cleavages emerging as a prelude to the introduction of some new regime, along with the ways in which future conflicts are likely to revolve around these differences. Before proceeding, however, I highlight what this chapter does not attempt to do, lest readers mistake its intent or its claims.

THREE CAVEATS

It is important to make clear from the outset what I do *not* claim in this chapter. At least three potentially mistaken impressions should be avoided. First, I in no way suggest that Japan at some relatively near point in the future will bear no resemblance to Japan as we have known it. Stated in such an extreme way, of course, the point should be self-evident. Political, economic, and social institutions rarely vanish completely despite significant or radical adjustments; cultural predispositions do not shift overnight; personal, group, and institutional power relations are rarely so completely reversed as to leave the once-powerful completely impotent and the once-impotent at the heights of power.

Yet, too often discussions of Japan are reduced to the dichotomous question: Is Japan changing or not? At almost any time period, the simple answer to this question must be *both*. Continuity and change are not dichotomous alternatives; rather, they exist on a continuum. Change is less a matter of yes or no and more a matter of How much? and Along what dimensions? Thus, while I stress the changes occurring in Japan and underline their importance, I intend in no way to deny the probability that numerous important aspects of the Japanese political economy will remain. In speaking of a "regime shift," I seek to identify the central dimensions along which change is occurring and is likely to continue—not to suggest either that resistance will not take place or that all other aspects of Japan's political economy will be comprehensively swept along in the wake of these changes.

Second, this chapter contends that the political economy based on conservative political dominance, a particular version of high economic growth, and a certain bipolar security policy has ended. But I do not argue that a political party called the LDP cannot retain electoral or parliamentary control. Nor do I mean to imply that the Japanese economy has become permanently incapacitated or will never again achieve high and enviable levels of growth and international competitiveness. Nor, in pointing to shifts in the U.S.–Japan relationship, is there any implication of a "coming war with Japan" or any such cataclysmic breakdown in ties between the two countries.[5]

What the chapter does contend, however, is that if a party called the LDP manages to hold political control for another ten or twenty years or more, it will be a very different LDP from that which dominated Japanese politics from 1955 to 1993. Most fundamentally, its socioeconomic base will be different; it will be functioning through altered institutions; and it will be a party pursuing different public policy targets. Moreover, *if* (not *when*) the Japanese economy is revitalized, it will also be a substantially different economy—one lacking, among other things, the hothouse qualities that kept Japan's home market almost completely insulated from foreign competition. Nor will it be an economy in which the major engines of national growth are devoid of substantial overseas investments and operations. Rather, it will be a market with far fewer internationally noncompetitive sectors and firms and one in which economic decisions will be far less insulatable from world market conditions. And finally, while the United States and Japan are likely to remain reasonably close economically and militarily, that relationship is almost certain not to revert to its past levels of unilateral paternalism and protectionism.

Third and finally, in this chapter I make no claims that any specific outcome or mix of outcomes is historically inevitable or morally desirable, strong as my personal opinions concerning various of these points may be. Current assessments of Japan are rife with such predictions, alleging, for example, the "inevitability" of a two-party political system, an end to money politics, greater bureaucratic deregulation, enhanced democratization, more power by elected officials over bureaucrats (or the reverse), liberalization of markets, a more activist role for the Japanese military, closer ties to Asia, and so forth. While I believe that many of these predictions are patently silly and lack any historical or comparative sensitivity, this chapter presents no specific position on any of them. I argue that the old regime has ended; I do not provide a sharp outline of the regime that will eventually take its place. Japan, I argue, is in the midst of a regime shift, but that shift is still in progress. Likely as many specific outcomes may appear in light of the pressures and changes discussed here, ultimately whether most of them occur will be highly contingent on a complex mixture of historical contingencies and human choices. The goal of this chapter is to identify the major forces that are pressing for changes in Japan, not to predict the specific ways in which those changes will play out over time. To the extent that human choices will shape these outcomes, it is safe to assume that some of these choices will be wise and others will be foolish, but none are inevitable.

JAPAN'S CONSERVATIVE REGIME

Past conservative dominance and the contemporary changes taking place in Japan are best understood at what I am calling the *regime* level. As noted above, a regime functions above the day-to-day hubbub of micro-level politics. It is more than the government of the day. But it is also far less, in substance or in longevity, than a complete constitutional order or a political community. A regime involves a sustained fusion among three things: political institutions, particular segments of the socioeconomic order, and a specific mixture of public policies. Within democracies, the character of this fusion—that is, the nature of a regime—is mediated in important ways by elections and the political party system. A stable regime is characterized by a regularized pattern of political and economic interactions that are synergistic in character: All three traits of a regime feed into and reinforce one another. In this sense, "regime" equates with a particular social order and with what E. E. Schattschneider would call a prevailing "mobilization of bias."[6] The character of the conservative regime that dominated Japan for most of the postwar period, and the one that is rapidly being dismantled, can be sketched quite briefly.

For most of the postwar period, Japanese *institutional* arrangements reflected the legacies of late industrialization: particularly concentrated financial and industrial structures and a centralized and powerful national bureaucracy.[7] These traits remained predominant despite the many undeniable changes that took place in various of Japan's prewar structures and the enhanced power of the electoral system and party politics during and after World War II.[8]

Equally critical to the conservative regime was the existence of the LDP as a single electoral vehicle for conservative supporters—both voters and interest associations. The uninterrupted, long-term, single-party rule by the LDP and its predecessors meant conservative control of all the prime ministerships and all but a handful of cabinet posts from 1948 until 1993, the longest period of uninterrupted conservative rule among the industrialized democracies.[9] Long-term conservative dominance of the executive and legislative branches also meant that Japan's conservatively oriented politicians, pressure groups, government officials, and voters had every incentive to work out their differences *within* the confines of that party, rather than looking for choices presented to them by any potential alternative.

Also institutionally critical to the conservative regime was Japan's unusual electoral system. As has been well chronicled, elections for Japan's Lower House were carried out under a comparatively unusual, multimember, single-ballot system. The system had at least three critical consequences. First, the system made it necessary for any party that wished to gain a parliamentary majority, generally only the LDP, to elect more than one candidate per district. This minimized the importance of the party label as a device in generating voter support. It also reduced party control over individual parliamentarians and enhanced the importance of strong personal support bases, that is, the constituency-based and personal-electoral machines known as *kōenkai*.[10] These, in turn, were groups that had diverse memberships with typically diverse economic interests.

Second, the system made it possible to win a seat with as little as 15 to 20 percent of a district's total vote, enhancing the viability of candidates from small niche parties that appealed to narrow constituencies but had little chance of winning more than 10 percent or so of the national vote. This in turn contributed to the ongoing fragmentation of opposition to pro-governmental candidates.

Third, intraparty competition also made it possible for voters to cast their ballots "against" a particular conservative candidate without that vote being registered as a vote against the conservative party as a whole. In numerous instances, a defeated conservative seen as too old, too corrupt, or too linked to the present government would be replaced by a younger, "cleaner," "more dynamic" individual who was also a member of the LDP.[11] Quite typically, 10–15 percent of the successful LDP candidates were such "new faces," but roughly the same number of conservative parliamentarians would be returned to office. In short, the electoral system meant that voter protest could be contained within the party's existing structures; voter dissatisfaction under such a system did not necessarily translate into LDP defeat, the way it would under a single-member district system or strict proportional representation. Systemically, it was relatively easy to vote against individual conservatives but difficult to translate such opposition into a vote against conservatism (or the LDP) as a whole.

Economically, the most striking institutional trait of the regime was its cohesiveness. Individual manufacturing, financial, and distribution firms were linked to one another through webs of vertical and horizontal *keiretsu* ties that linked together multiple corporations, their subcontractors, and their distributors. These were bolstered by a variety of sectoral cartels, extensive cross-holding of stock shares, numerous trade associations, powerful national business organizations, and a host of other similarly unifying institutions. Such ties by no means eliminated the differences of interest found between small and large firms, exporters and importers, manufacturers and financial institutions, specialized producers and producers of commodities, or the differences among various economic sectors or specific companies. Yet, such institutional linkages went a long way toward mitigating such divisions. They also pressed for the resolution of such differences at levels below that of the national political agenda.

Moving to the second element of any regime, the socioeconomic coalition undergirding conservative rule was by no means restricted to the narrow triad of big business, bureaucracy, and the LDP, important as these were to conservative rule. Rather, the dominance of Japan's postwar conservatives rested on an alliance that also included the numerically far more significant constituencies of small business and agriculture so critical to the electoral success of the LDP. Japan's conservative socioeconomic coalition represented an unusual combination in comparative terms, although Italy's Christian Democrats and to a lesser extent the French Gaulists were broadly similar. Rather systematically excluded from this dominant coalition was organized labor.[12] Such power as organized labor eventually garnered was restricted largely to the factory, rather than to the political, level and was tied to the widespread nature of Japan's enterprise union structure.[13]

Finally, turning to the third component of the conservative regime, the policy directions taken by the conservative coalition were relatively consistent on several key dimensions that produced a phenomenon that might be labeled "embedded mercantilism." A succession of postwar Japanese governments focused on stimulating high economic growth in a nationalist effort to "catch up" to the more advanced economies of the world. These governments also eschewed any substantial social welfare role for the state. Meanwhile, security and defense policies tied Japan to the U.S. security system, allowed U.S. troops to maintain bases on Japanese soil, relied on the U.S. nuclear shield, and kept the size and expenditure for Japan's indigenous military forces quite small.[14] From the 1950s into the middle of the 1980s, Japan thus emerged consistently as the Organization for Economic Cooperation and Development (OECD) country with the most rapidly growing economy, the smallest and least expensive government, and one of the lowest levels of military spending as a percentage of gross national product.

Of particular importance to Japan's conservative regime, in terms of both holding its socioeconomic coalition intact and advancing national economic competitiveness, was the conservatives' long-standing ability to insulate large segments of the domestic economy from foreign competition while at the same time enjoying an electoral politics that insulated economic policies from Japanese voters. As I have argued elsewhere, the Japanese government bureaucracy served as the doorman determining a great deal of what came into, and what went out of, Japan.[15] Japan bought few foreign-made consumer or manufacturing goods; instead, its foreign purchases were heavily concentrated in raw materials and other inputs to Japanese manufacturing, giving Japan one of the most skewed import–export balances in the industrial world.[16] Similarly, Japan's capital market was long buffered from external capital markets, allowing currency policies that maintained an undervalued yen, which in turn enhanced export competitiveness, as well as monetary policies that gave strong control over capital to the Ministry of Finance through the Bank of Japan and the large city banks. Meanwhile foreign direct investment in Japan was simultaneously impeded by the Foreign Exchange and Control Law. Despite various liberalizations, as late as the 1980s Japan was a country almost devoid of significant foreign direct investment.[17]

Keeping at bay competition from the outside world's often more competitive products and more capital-rich, technologically and managerially sophisticated firms meant that products produced by indigenously owned firms came to dominate Japan's expanding home market. Eventually, these products and the broader industrial structure gained sufficient strength to compete effectively in markets overseas, and later, as Japan's markets were opened, most continued to profit despite foreign competition at home.

The system also meant, however, that Japan's individual consumers bore the high costs of such insulation. As Richard Samuels has argued, Japan's economy was one in which the consumer existed for the benefit of the manufacturer, rather than the other way around.[18] Oligopoly and cartelization meant higher price levels that responded only sluggishly to market pressures; household saving rates were high to compensate for, among other things, the underdeveloped set of social benefits, but the interest rates paid on these savings were oligopolistically set and typically generated negative rates of real return to savers.

The party system offered little opportunity for national economic policies to be the subject of electoral contestation or voter protest. As noted, the electoral system worked against "either/or" decisions among parties. Furthermore, the major opposition party, the JSP, rarely presented viable economic alternatives to conservative policies; rather, its arguments and voter appeals were made largely on issues of security, defense, the constitution, and foreign relations, particularly ties with the United States. In this sense, too, Japan's mercantilism was deeply embedded, since the electoral system provided no serious alternatives to the economic policies of the conservative regime.

In fairness, citizens had considerable reason not to bemoan the electoral limitations. With growth at rates double those of the OECD countries as a group, most Japanese citizens could typically anticipate continued improvements in their personal economic circumstances. And with unemployment exceptionally low and the overall equality of income levels in Japan exceptionally egalitarian, Japan lacked a substantial body of citizens who could claim they had been demonstrably hurt by the overall conservative policy profile.

The regime was thus heavily buffered from domestic voter pressures as well as from economic pressures from foreign competition. Hence, Japanese government and business leaders could pursue macroeconomic policies with their eyes fixed primarily on domestic political and economic issues.[19] This meant policies that *domestically* were most likely to help them retain their electoral and political dominance. So long as these generated high growth, they functioned to keep the domestic coalition intact and to help the dominant party retain its grip on office.

REGIME UNDER CHALLENGE

From the 1970s into the early 1990s, the smoothly functioning regime described above confronted a host of challenges. First were challenges from the international arena, such as those represented by the two international oil shocks, Richard Nixon's reversal on China policy, the breakdown in Bretton Woods, foreign governmental pressures for a liberalization of trade and investment conditions within Japan, and the continuous escalation in the value of the Japanese currency. Second, there were challenges primarily endogenous to Japan. Certain of these, including the rather rapid appearance of the antipollution and student protest movements in the late 1960s, various media revelations of political corruption among key politicians, and radical economic shifts such as those caused by sudden inflation or changing land prices, were largely external to the regime itself. Other endogenous challenges came from the changing character of the Japanese population. Many of these exacerbated tensions *within* the regime. Some of these challenges were sharp, severe, and largely unpredictable; others were slower to appear, more gradual in their impact, but often, as a consequence, subject to reasonable anticipation. Both, however, provided serious challenges to established pillars of the old regime.

From the end of the Allied postwar occupation until the early 1970s, international influences on Japan had been preponderantly benign and supportive of Japan's conservative regime and its embedded mercantilism. Particularly critical was the broad support Japan received from the United States, which treated Japan as a critical Cold War ally with a vanquished economy deserving of special assistance in both economics and security. The international environment became drastically less hospitable by the early 1970s. From then on, external conditions posed serious threats to Japan's conservative regime.

To understand Japan's current regime shift, two of these external conditions were especially momentous. First, a mixture of challenges was posed to the autonomy of Japanese monetary and currency policies. Second, foreign trade partners—the United States in particular—began hammering for changes in a variety of Japanese institutions and policies on the grounds that these tilted the international economic playing field unfairly in Japan's favor.

The challenges to Japanese monetary and currency policies began in the early 1970s and returned regularly in later years. As a result, the Japanese government lost much of its ability to determine the value of the Japanese currency. The yen underwent four cycles of major appreciation: with the collapse of the fixed exchange rates under Bretton Woods in 1971–73, in the late 1970s, in the mid-1980s, and in the early 1990s. It climbed from ¥360 to ¥290 to the dollar between 1971 and 1974, from ¥290 at the beginning of 1977 to ¥170 by October 1978, to ¥110–120 as a result of the G-5 Plaza Accord of September 1985,[20] and to just below ¥80 to the dollar in 1995. This sequence of escalations made the yen by far the industrial world's most appreciated currency over the period from the Bretton Woods breakdown in 1971 into the early 1990s.[21]

On trade and investment, pressures from the United States initially focused on Japanese reductions of tariff barriers, import quotas, and various nontariff barriers. A series of General Agreement on Tariffs and Trade rounds led over time to a rapid reduction in Japan's formal restrictions. When such reductions failed to reduce the bilateral U.S.-Japan trade deficits, U.S. pressures became increasingly sector-specific.[22] For some sectors, most notably steel, machine tools, televisions, automobiles, and later computer chips, the United States demanded so-called voluntary export restraints by Japan.[23] Later, driven by a variety of domestic interests, American policy eventually moved less toward blocking or restricting Japanese exports to the United States and more toward opening the Japanese market. These steps included the MOSS (market-oriented, sector-specific) talks, endorsed at a bilateral summit meeting in January 1985;[24] the so-called Structural Impediments Initiative that commenced in 1989; explicit efforts at "managed trade as a second-best alternative," such as were embodied in the bilateral Semiconductor Trade Agreement set to run from 1986 to 1991;[25] and the Framework Talks, the all-time peak of bilateral acrimony where talks actually collapsed in February 1994.

The U.S. government also mobilized U.S. trade law and other weapons to exert pressure on behalf of specific U.S. companies or regions, including cellular phones for Motorola; supercomputers for Cray; tobacco, auto, and medical technology efforts for entire sectors; the Florida citrus industry;[26] Washington apple growers; and New York wine merchants, among others. In short, the United States, and to a lesser extent European governments, mounted steady pressures for Japan's conservatives to make substantial changes across a wide swath of the entire political and economic regime.[27]

Interlaced with these external pressures were a variety of internal challenges to regime continuity. Among the most important were a series of demographic changes that rose primarily from the very successes of earlier Japanese economic policies. These put pressure on both the socioeconomic coalitional arrangements and the public policy profile of the conservative regime. Four were especially important: (1) the reduction in the proportion of the population dependent on farming from about 50 percent at the end of

World War II to just less than 6 percent by 1994; (2) the vast extension in expected life spans (between 1950 and 1995 male life expectancy rose by twenty-seven years), accompanied by a zeroing of the population growth and a consequent flattening out of the population pyramid; (3) a tightening of the labor supply due to both declining birth rates and the shrinkage in the flow of former rural residents moving to the cities; and (4) overall urbanization and an increase in living standards, which combined to turn the bulk of Japan's citizen's into what Murakami Yasusuke has called "Japan's new middle mass."[28]

With varying undulations, this combination of pressures and changes induced a host of adjustments in Japan's conservative regime over a period of twenty-odd years. For the most part, the adjustments involved shifts in policy aimed at coping with new international and domestic conditions in ways that would continue economic prosperity and asset appreciation without undercutting the institutional and socioeconomic base of Japan's conservatism. At the same time, many were aimed at reducing the electoral vulnerability of the LDP. And to a large extent, many of these adjustments served effectively to reinforce the positive cycle of high economic growth and continued conservative governance.

Thus, Japanese manufacturing underwent a successful transformation from its high dependence on increasingly expensive imported oil to alternative energy sources with only temporary inflation and almost no serious slowdowns or job losses, unlike the economic crises that prevailed throughout most of the industrialized world.

Over twenty years of fiscal austerity gave way to deficit financing during a large part of the 1970s. Japan's deficit dependency ratio had been just over 4 percent in 1970, but rose rapidly to the 11–16 percent range for 1971–74, and finally up to nearly 40 percent in 1979.[29] Part of this deficit program was linked to the introduction of a series of social welfare programs and environmental improvements during the 1970s. These in turn had beneficial effects on the LDP's popularity while at the same time dealing with the problem of Japan's graying population. With the "administrative reform" program, fiscal austerity was once again reintroduced in the mid- to late 1980s, as was an overall containment of the escalating entitlement costs of new retirement and medical programs, another adjustment with many positive economic benefits. In these and many other ways, responses to certain external and internal pressures had the effect of continuing and/or enhancing Japan's overall economic competitiveness.

At the political and electoral level, the conservatives also showed considerable adeptness. For example, the labor movement, which contained roughly one-half of the work force in the 1950s and pressed a variety of radical challenges to conservative rule, was by the late 1980s virtually halved in its penetration rate and reorganized into a single peak federation with a largely nonpolitical, nongovernmental economic agenda.[30] Also pacified were the country's student movements and its antipollution citizen groups.

Electorally, despite the numerical shrinkage of several key blocs of party supporters such as farmers and owners of small businesses, the party began to attract support from other, once less-supportive groups. Thus, as labor became pacified, the electoral orientations of blue-collar workers began to shift as well, with significant proportions voting for the LDP.[31] Moreover, by the 1990 elections, the LDP was also drawing substantially more of its votes from urban constituencies than it had in the early 1970s.[32] Importantly, however, policy changes designed to attract new supporters and to broaden the socioeconomic support base of the conservative regime did not force the LDP to drop any of its long-standing support groups. Rather, the party enticed and incorporated new groups while protecting the interests of longtime supporters. The party became a "catch-all" party. As a result, by the 1990s, the party was drawing substantial strength from socioeconomic groups that had not been core components of its originally successful quest for office in the 1950s.

The result was that, although the conservative party confronted several close elections during the thirty-eight years of its reign until the loss of Upper House control in 1989, elections per se posed little serious challenge to the regime.[33] Having beaten off the more sustained challenges from the Left during the 1950s and early 1960s, the LDP faced only fragmented electoral opposition in the subsequent two decades.

At the same time, not all of the adjustments redounded to the benefit of the conservatives. Many in fact exacerbated internal tensions within the conservative regime, most particularly among its different socioeconomic supporters, but also in the policy and institutional arenas.

For example, overall economic success and the lack of major party opposition to the LDP did not automatically mean that the Japanese population was becoming increasingly loyal to the party. Rather, more and more voters began to identify themselves as independents and as nonparty voters.[34] As early as 1974, such "nonparty" identifiers came to outnumber supporters of the LDP. This growth in nonpartisanship was especially noteworthy among those in their twenties and thirties, women, and longtime city dwellers.[35] In many elections, LDP candidates were able to garner support from this bloc, but its loyalties were typically quite fickle.

Throughout even its best moments, the conservative regime was beset by the usual miscellany of internal conflicts of interest—divisions over spoils, turf, personal power, policy content, or cold, hard cash, to mention only the most obvious. Nevertheless, when it was working at its best, the regime's constituent elements interacted with relatively low levels of internal friction, particularly when these were compared to the tensions between the regime and its opponents.

High national growth rates and LDP control over the Diet and the cabinet were obviously critical ingredients in ensuring such smoothness. High growth had long prevented otherwise internally conflictual economic and political interests from fracturing surface-level conservative cooperation. Continually expanding assets greatly facilitated congeniality between technologically sophisticated and relatively backward industries, importers and exporters, finance and manufacturing, urban and rural interests, and otherwise fractious bureaucrats, business leaders, and politicians. Continued economic growth diverted attention from foreign policy or security concerns. Conflicts that might have become zero-sum under less expansive economic conditions were more readily reconciled through side payments, compensation, and trade-offs to particular interest groups, voting blocs, or geographical regions. As Ikuo Kume has suggested, the rough edges within the regime were sanded down by economic resources that allowed conservatives to follow a "politics with no losers."[36]

Yet, high growth and LDP electoral dominance masked the fact that large segments of the Japanese economy were in fact insulated from the pressures that would have ensured substantial modernization, and these remained very noncompetitive by international standards. No substantial institutional changes were made to ensure economy-wide changes that would build in long-term national competitiveness across different economic sectors. Also masked was the fact that the challenges and adjustments noted above were generating and exacerbating a host of previously latent divisions among LDP supporters. Only toward the end of the 1980s did this mixture of economic and political tensions within the conservative regime come to the fore, as national economic growth slowed from its hyperkinetic 10–11 percent rate (1952–71) to more modest 5–6 percent growth (1971–89), and then to zero-to-very-low growth (1990–2000), as the LDP's hold on office became less automatic and as foreign policy disputes wedged themselves onto the national agenda.

As the currency's value appreciated, as fiscal policies shifted, as demographic changes occurred, as the Americans targeted various sectors of the Japanese economy, as LDP politicians began to draw their support from different constituencies, and, most important, as the economy slowed, the continuation of once relatively easy intraregime adjustments became increasingly problematic. Erstwhile allies discovered that their respective approaches to the new challenges were incompatible; solutions favorable to one group could very well undermine the powers and privileges of another. The selection of particular policies became ever more nettlesome for conservative officials.

Whereas the outer boundaries of the conservatives' socioeconomic coalition had been expanded by simple addition of new groups during the 1970s and into the early 1980s, by the end of that decade, many public policies and institutional arrangements began to necessitate harder choices among potential supporters. Japan's conservative regime found itself attempting to accommodate ever more demanding and strange bedfellows in an ever-shrinking futon.

REGIME SHIFT

Since the last years of the 1980s, Japan has been undergoing a fundamental shift along all three of the dimensions that constitute a regime. In brief, the public policies and institutions of the past have proven incapable of providing the kinds of benefits—political and economic—that they once did. Simultaneously, a number of once highly integrative economic and political institutions have been unraveling, leaving important components of the past regime far less well connected to one another and much freer to form and enter new allegiances. And finally, the socioeconomic arrangements so critical to the coherence of the prior regime have become splintered. Potential winners and losers are more quickly differentiated as new policy alternatives are proposed and as institutions are rearranged. In short, the conservative regime has become far more fragmented by internal political differences that are shattering its previous façade of minimal internal differences, eliminating its coherent front, and preventing it from marching forward in some collectively shared direction.

One of the most important challenges to existing economic policies and to internal conservative cohesion came in the form of the rapidly rising yen. *Endaka*, as it was known, made it economically suicidal for many Japanese firms not to invest abroad. Continuing to manufacture at home became comparatively more costly in yen terms. In effect, the rest of the world's land prices, labor rates, and corporate valuations had been slashed by one-half or more. Business leaders regularly asked themselves: How can we best take advantage?

Foreign direct investment by Japanese firms in the mid-1960s had been minuscule, as noted above. Yet in 1980, as a result of combined external and internal pressures, Japanese financial markets had been substantially liberalized, particularly with the 1980 revision of the Foreign Exchange and Control Law. Combined with the rising yen and a vast improvement in the facility with which international capital movements could be transacted, this revision allowed, among other things, much freer movement of capital from Japan. By 1996 cumulative Japanese investment abroad totaled nearly $500 billion, making Japan the world's second-largest overseas investor.

In the late 1970s, Japanese investors accounted for 6 percent of direct investment outflows from the major industrial nations, 2 percent of equities outflows, 15 percent of bond outflows, and 12 percent of short-term bank outflows. By the late 1980s, these figures had swollen to 20 percent of international foreign direct investment, 25 percent of equities, 55 percent of bonds, and 50 percent of short-term bank loans.[37] Individual Japanese firms were also largely freed to engage in foreign direct investments abroad. By the middle of the 1990s, Japan had become the world market's major supplier of capital.[38]

Simultaneously, there was an overall decline in the role of main-bank financing for corporations, which in turn had important effects on the cohesion of the keiretsu. During the 1960s, Japanese firms had raised the bulk of their needed capital through borrowing, primarily from the so-called main banks. The debt-to-equity ratio for Japanese firms was as high as 80 percent during the 1960s. By the early 1990s, this had fallen dramatically to

25 percent.[39] This too reduced the internal cohesion among the keiretsu while at the same time allowing individual firms, whether keiretsu members or not, far greater autonomy in their overall business strategies. Individual Japanese companies and financial institutions were, in the mid-1990s, free to issue bonds abroad in whatever was the most suitable currency and then swap the proceeds into yen. Their dependence on financing from home-based banks diminished sharply.

By the 1990s large numbers of Japanese manufacturing firms were basing their activities less on production in, and export from, Japan and far more on truly international production and global investment strategies. The simple export orientation of Japanese economic policies diminished considerably. From 1990 to the first quarter of 1996, Japanese exports grew by only 4 percent, the lowest rate in one twelve-country OECD survey. (During this period, eight countries had export growth of 25 percent or more.) Conversely, Japanese imports grew by 41 percent, the third largest figure in the survey.[40] Even more symbolically, in 1995, Japan manufactured more overseas (¥41.2 trillion) than it exported from the home islands (¥39.6 trillion).[41]

This increase in overseas activities, along with revisions in the Foreign Exchange and Control Act, also liberated many Japanese companies from previous governmental controls. Once subject to heavy oversight from the Ministries of Finance and International Trade and Industry designed to ensure conformity to various governmental industrial plans, overseas firms became freer to pursue their desired business strategies unconcerned about the cudgel of government capital controls. Technology transfer agreements leaped across national boundaries with nary a governmental signature. The capability of firms to raise capital through the domestic equity markets, overseas warrants, international currency swaps, and the like left them much freer to pursue strategies determined primarily by internal, company-specific needs rather than by external government directives or national industrial policy proscriptions.

Many Japanese firms, including many subcontractors, added to their multinational character by forging strategic alliances with foreign-owned firms.[42] Among the Japanese firms that forged partnerships with foreign firms were Toyota and Nissan in auto manufacture; Fujitsu, NEC, Hitachi, and Toshiba in electronics; Nippon Telegraph and Telephone (NTT) and International Telegram and Telephone (KDD) in telecommunications; Softbank and TV Asahi in software and commercial television; and Mitsubishi Heavy Industries, Kawasaki Heavy Industries, and Ishikawajima Harima Industries in a variety of military production technologies. Indeed, Canon went so far as to adopt as its corporate vision for the 1990s the slogan "Symbiosis with Global Partners."[43] The very "nationality" of many Japanese firms became more confused, both in terms of ownership and more importantly in terms of the place and nationality of the workforce. This too undermined previously embedded mercantilist orientations on the part of at least some Japanese companies, softened their ties to the keiretsu, and reduced the leverage of the Japanese government over much of their economic behavior.

Even though such internationalization was taking place in many segments of Japanese business, it was by no means universal. Other firms in traditional industries such as cement and construction, deeply enmeshed in domestic public works projects and tied to the patronage of Japanese politicians, were either unable or uneager to invest abroad. Similarly, while certain subcontractors of Japan's larger manufacturers did follow the major corporations' lead in setting up overseas operations, many more, particularly the smallest, remained in Japan, typically losing significant market share. The resulting "hollowing out" of Japan led to more enhanced demands for protection from foreign competition. And to ensure political support for such protection, increasing sums of money were transferred to the pockets of conservative politicians.

Finally, many of the most protected industries, including those within important service sectors such as insurance, brokerage houses, and even many commercial banks, remained unprodded by the need to compete internationally and essentially locked into the highly regulated and cartelized domestic market, a factor that contributed heavily to the financial crisis of the 1990s.[44]

As divisions were showing up within conservative ranks among big businesses, so too the retention of conservative loyalty among farmers and small business owners had also become problematic by the late 1980s. The ability of the LDP to retain its hold on the disparate support of such groups had long rested on continually high economic growth, the relative insulation of the Japanese market from outside investment and imports, and a series of specific side-payments in the form of farm subsidies, import quotas on key agricultural goods, low- or no-interest loans, and an "anti-big-store law" that effectively gave chambers of commerce veto power over the siting of large department stores or distribution outlets. The influence of virtually all of these was reduced during the late 1980s and into the early 1990s; budgetary support for agriculture and small business in particular declined substantially as a percentage of the total budget.[45]

Many voices within the conservative camp had long echoed the calls from the United States and other foreign countries for a greater liberalization or deregulation of many of Japan's least competitive sectors. These voices were typically from Japan's most internationally competitive firms, eager to prevent retaliatory international protectionism from being mobilized against Japan's cameras, autos, VCRs, and semiconductors. They also were now reflecting their own enhanced international competitiveness and the diversity of their own supplies and markets.

In short, by the late 1980s and early 1990s, the international situation was no longer so uniformly positive for the Japanese conservative regime. Nor was economic growth so automatically guaranteed. As a consequence, the Japanese conservative regime once held together through positive-sum politics began to confront a zero-sum situation: Not all economic supporters of the conservative regime continued to view their interests in compatible ways. And those who were losers on one issue could no longer count on quick and relatively painless compensation from an ever-expanding public treasury on another.

Increasingly, actions designed to benefit one segment of the LDP's socioeconomic support groups often meant the loss of benefits by another. An upwardly biased yen plus economic liberalization drove a wedge between the close collaboration among agriculture, small business, and big business, as well as between specific sectors of big business, all of whom in the past had been so centrally a part of conservative electoral and policy hegemony.

It is within this context that the Japanese bubble gains perspective. At least two elements are critical. First, as the yen continued to rise in power, particularly after the Plaza Accord, the Ministry of Finance, fearing the effects on Japanese exports, "ordered the Bank of Japan to open the monetary floodgates while the ministry injected massive amounts of fresh spending into the economy via fiscal packages and the expanded investment of postal savings funds."[46] Predictably, as the prime interest rate was lowered to a postwar low of 2.5 percent, asset markets in both stocks and land jetted upward.

Second, and equally important, was the severing of the links between major manufacturing firms and the main banks and financial institutions noted above. Cut off from their normal sources of income (corporate borrowers), Japanese financial institutions began to lend to less-solid borrowers—smaller subsidiaries, less fiscally sound firms, land speculators, and organized crime. And in the course of these activities and the subsequent bursting of the bubble economy, it became increasingly clear that while the Japanese economy had a number of exceptionally competitive firms in areas such as automobiles, electronics, cameras, machine tools, and precision instruments, Japan's financial institutions—its banks, brokerages, and insurance companies—were among the most protected and least internationally competitive institutions in the country.

A certain measure of privatization and deregulation had undoubtedly taken place in several sectors during the 1980s and early 1990s. Moreover, once-nationalized industries such as the Japanese National Railways, NTT, KDD, and the Tobacco and Salt Monopoly were privatized. Other industries such as the airlines, the finance sector, and various pension systems had undergone varying degrees of deregulation.[47] Despite all these changes, however, the Japanese market remained largely closed to foreign direct investment. As late as 1994, inward foreign direct investment was roughly $3,400 per capita in the United Kingdom, $2,200 in France, $1,700 in the United States, and $1,500 in Germany, but only $135 in Japan. Japan's economy was between one-tenth and one-twenty-fifth as penetrated by foreign capital and firms as the other major OECD countries.[48]

Certainly, banking and many other sectors remained highly regulated, cartelized, and internationally noncompetitive. The fact that the Japanese financial sector had amassed a tremendous number of bad loans was but the most tangible manifestation of this lack of true competitiveness. Problem loans in November 1995 totaled ¥37.4 trillion, of which ¥18.3 trillion was deemed unrecoverable. This meant that an average of 6 percent of the loans outstanding by private-sector banks were bad.[49] The Ministry of Finance sought to cover up the extent of the financial problem, only to find that the good faith and credit of all Japanese banks fell heir to international criticism of the attempted cover-up: In June 1995, Moody's, the international rating service, downgraded the creditworthiness of Japanese banks to an average rating of "D" (uncertain), and international money markets began to impose a 0.6 percent premium (known as the Japan Premium) on the cost of short-term funds for Japanese banks.[50]

Ultimately, the Bank of Japan dropped the national discount rate to absurdly low levels (0.5 percent at some stages), in effect providing a mechanism by which Japanese savers would receive negative returns on their money while the failing banking sector could recoup some of its losses through low-cost international arbitrage. Similarly, the government attempted a series of unsuccessful stimulation measures through the public works budget, with large sums for bridges, ports, and new lines on the bullet train system. But the results were dismal.

Japan's conservatives, by the middle of the 1990s, had shown that they were incapable of re-creating the spectacular economic policies and performances that their predecessors had overseen up until only a few years earlier. The fanatical wave of self-confidence witnessed in Japan in the late 1980s proved to be like the euphoria of Icarus soaring toward the sun—just before his wax wings melted.

Once the bubble economy burst, the capacity to reward inefficient sectors out of the public treasury was drastically reduced or made politically problematic, allowing economic tensions to reverberate into the political arena. Most tangibly, the long-ruling Liberal Democratic party split in July 1993 and its thirty-eight-year control of government gave way to a series of coalitions and party reorganizations. In addition, a new electoral system for the Lower House of the Diet was introduced that injected further uncertainty and division into the ranks of conservative parliamentarians.

The party split over two immediate and related issues: political corruption and the call for a new electoral system. But these in turn were linked to several deeper issues, most notably the introduction of a consumption tax in 1989 and the LDP defeat in the Upper House election of that year; in turn, these were tied to the changing character of the Japanese voting population and the long-term stagnation in the national economy.

One of the little-noticed effects of Japan's bubble economy was that it began to divide Japanese citizens along economic lines in ways that the previous regime had been able to avoid. The rapid growth, based as it was on escalating land and stock prices, no longer benefited "all citizens equally" as had been generally true of earlier high growth. Rather, those with land or stocks got rapidly richer; those without quickly fell behind. Japan's Gini index, a measure of income inequality, showed increasing disparities of income. Those left behind by the bubble became resentful of the high growth that excluded them. And then when the bubble burst, political resentment rose among those members of the nouveau riche whose wealth had dropped most sharply.

The consumption tax was something the Ministry of Finance had been eager to institute for a decade or more. Of particular concern was the ministry's desire to put into place a system that would ensure long-term fiscal stability and allow it to avoid the issuance of deficit-covering bonds such as had occurred in the 1970s and early 1980s. Such bonds would lead to higher long-term interest rates, lower profitability for financial institutions, and increased costs to firms borrowing to expand and develop, as well as an overall reduction in Japan's external surpluses.

The consumption tax, despite the fact that it meant an actual reduction in the total tax burden of many urban salaried workers, was wildly unpopular. Farmers and owners of small businesses were almost certain to see their tax bills increase. Many consumers were irate at paying such a visible tax on virtually every purchase they made, regardless of whether their ultimate annual tax bill would rise or fall.

The 1989 Upper House election took place in the midst of widespread voter frustration with the consumption tax, agricultural liberalization, the opening of the market to larger distribution outlets, and a variety of money and sex scandals associated with prime ministers Takeshita Noboru and Uno Sōsuke. The results were devastating for the LDP, which was denied a majority of seats for the first time since the party's formation in 1955.[51]

Corruption scandals were hardly new to Japan or to the LDP, but the so-called Recruit scandal of 1988–89, which forced Prime Minister Takeshita to resign, made it unmistakable that a massive amount of money had come to suffuse electoral politics and that it did so in part as a means of bypassing the normal processes of bureaucratic regulation of the private sector. Similarly, in the subsequent Sagawa Kyūbin case, longtime political godfather and LDP deputy prime minister Kanemaru Shin was arrested on March 27, 1993, in conjunction with a payoff of ¥500 million from an up-and-coming trucking company hoping for special treatment from transportation regulators. The Kanemaru scandal made particularly good television coverage when some $50 million in gold bullion was discovered in the raid by public prosecutors of his office. The two scandals led to massive media and public criticism of "money politics" and "politics as usual" in response to revelations of the deep and systematic levels of corruption.[52]

Keidanren, Japan's major business federation, increasingly frustrated with the closed economy and the LDP's protectionism to begin with, also began to demand electoral reforms. It underlined its call by refusing to provide campaign funds for LDP factions. The media were also aggressive in their demand for structural overhauls to clean out the Augean stables of Japanese electoral politics.

Further complicating the political situation was the 1991 Gulf War and U.S. demands for a more active role by Japan in peacekeeping operations. Japanese conservatives were racked by internal debates about the possible dispatch of troops in ways that had not divided the party since the late 1950s and early 1960s. Following a wrenching domestic debate, Japan in 1991 passed legislation (the United Nations Peacekeeping Operations Coopera-tion Bill) that allowed its troops to be used, under very constrained condi-tions, in UN-sponsored, noncombat peacekeeping activities abroad. As a re-sult, Japanese minesweepers moved into the sea lanes within the Persian Gulf after the fighting between the United States and Iraq had ended. More-over, Japanese military personnel were sent to participate in UN peacekeep-ing operations in Cambodia and subsequently in several other locations. Under all previous interpretations of article IX of the constitution, such ac-tions would have been clear constitutional violations. None would have been politically possible in the middle of the 1960s. The Gulf War catalyzed within the conservative camp, and the country more broadly, wide-ranging debate about the entire spectrum of Japanese defense and security, issues that had for the most part been smothered under the consensus around high economic growth, low military expenditures, and a broadly "pro-American" foreign policy that had prevailed since at least the Ikeda administration (1960–64).

Consequently, conservative political cohesion gave way to various divi-sions over several specific issues. A number of politicians, starting with Hosokawa Morihiro who eventually formed the Japan New Party, began to demand internal reforms within the LDP. Specific concerns over eliminating corruption became linked internally to the introduction of a new electoral system. And these in turn were linked to divisions over security. Ironically, Ozawa Ichirō, himself a close ally of Kanemaru and a major recipient of monies from Sagawa, jumped on the "reform" bandwagon and called for what many conservative politicians had long hoped for: a replacement of Japan's multimember electoral system with some version of a single-member district system and Japan's movement on security issues toward the status of a "more normal" country. When LDP prime minister Miyazawa Kiichi failed to deliver on electoral "reform," Ozawa and his followers, along with several other groups of LDP dissidents, left the party, paving the way for the anti-LDP coalition that ended the LDP's long-standing parliamentary hegemony.[53]

What had become clear to many individual LDP politicians was that loyalty to the party no longer provided a vehicle guaranteed to enhance one's per-sonal career. The party's loss in 1989 showed its vulnerability. The wave of anti-LDP sentiment associated with the corruption scandals made it clear that association with the party had serious downside risks. And many conserva-tives were genuinely divided on matters of security and foreign policy. In par-ticular, many younger urban conservatives determined that it made little sense to plan their political careers around a lifetime of membership in a party that seemed committed to economic policies hostile to the nation's urban dwellers and detrimental to long-term economic growth. To many conservative parlia-mentarians, leaving the party suddenly offered the possibility of presenting themselves as more attractive, principled, and electable alternatives.

As party politics fragmented, so did the once-close ties between cabinet and bureaucracy. Long tradition had kept promotions and retirements within the Japanese civil service more or less insulated from direct political interference (although this noninterference had a strongly pro-LDP guarantee). But on December 16, 1993, a member of Ozawa's New Frontier Party, Kumagai Hiroshi, took over as minister of international trade and industry and, as one of his first acts, forced the retirement of a prime candidate for the highest nonpolitical position in the ministry, Naitō Masahisa. Clearly, this was an explicitly partisan effort by the new, non-LDP government to shatter one of the key institutional arrangements of the previous conservative regime, that is, a "nonpartisan" treatment of all bureaucratic promotions.

Simultaneously, the bureaucracy was shaken by revelations that various top-level bureaucrats had been active participants in the various bribery scandals tainting the world of elected officials. Most significantly, at the end of 1996 the administrative vice minister of the Ministry of Health and Welfare (MHW), Okamitsu Nobuharu, resigned following allegations that he had been given membership in a golf club worth ¥16 million, along with other expensive favors, by the owner of a company operating a string of old-age homes that had been seeking MHW subsidies of ¥9 billion. Okamitsu emerged as just the tip of a very corrupt bureaucratic iceberg, as seven additional officials came under investigation. Okamitsu, who ironically had been appointed to the ministry's top job in order to clean up his agency's HIV mess, was subsequently arrested in early December, the highest-level bureaucrat ever to be arrested in the postwar years.

In short, along a host of dimensions, the conservative regime that had so successfully managed Japan's economy and so effectively contested elections seemed a hollow shell of its former self. The economy seemed stuck in low. Certain individual firms prospered, but far more were hunkering down behind protectionist barriers. And in the face of it all, the political world seemed incapable of generating policies that would shift to a higher gear, primarily because it was divided about whether to support the interests of the more internationalized segments of the economy and society, or of those who had long benefited from protection and regulation. Yet given the inability any longer to control currency and monetary movements, important tools once critical to the government were no longer at its disposal.

CONCLUSION: JAPAN'S POLITICAL ECONOMY AT THE TURN OF THE CENTURY

Beyond the fragmentation of the LDP, the decline of the socialists, and the continual grouping and regrouping of various politicians into new parties and party fragments, Japanese political reorganization had its most tangible institutional manifestation in the introduction of a new electoral system for the Lower House of the Diet. Under the new system, 300 of Japan's 500

Lower House members are chosen from single-member districts. The rest are chosen through proportional representation contests in eleven geographically determined, and individually calculated, districts. Such a system surely will bring about many changes in the party system and in the biases of elected officials.

Most clearly, however, the system will do little to aid any single party in bridging the widening economic gaps among Japan's different constituencies, the way the old system helped the LDP to keep most economic sectors somewhat content. Under the new system, the size of single-member districts is considerably smaller than the previous multimember districts. Consequently, the localist bias in Japanese electoral politics will be enhanced, thereby encouraging representatives to take an even more "local" perspective on economic policies. The kōenkai of individual parliamentarians is likely to gain, rather than lose, in importance.

In this new political climate, it is highly improbable that a candidate running in rural Oita or Shimane would campaign *against* agricultural subsidies, rural electrification projects, or special subsidies to equalize nationwide living standards, regardless of what the candidate's party stood for officially. Similarly, it is hard to imagine two candidates in the Azabu area of Tokyo or the Umeda district of Osaka taking competing positions on such issues as the need for lower consumer prices even if that means more foreign imports, making an argument for higher consumption taxes as a way to benefit Japan's dwindling number of orange growers, or calling for an increase in nuclear waste disposal sites or garbage dumps within urban and suburban areas. In short, the new system is heavily biased against the articulation of clear economic policies by a single political party and is likely to minimize policy choices within specific electoral districts. The result is almost sure to be that Japan will continue to reflect the widespread dictum that "all politics is local politics." And with local economic interests so increasingly diverse from one another, any single political party will find it extremely difficult to agree among its members on any clear and bold strategies for national direction.

In particular, with the electoral system biased toward local economics and pork-barrel politics, it is very unlikely that any government will soon be able to generate national policies conducive to the high levels of economic growth that prevailed from the 1950s to the end of the 1980s and that in turn made broad political consensus so easy to maintain. Thus Japanese economic and security policies are likely to be far more electorally divisive in the future than they were in the past.

One possible counter to this would come from the parliamentary seats chosen by proportional representation (PR). Competition for these seats will give most larger parties an incentive to articulate broader, rather than narrower, policies calculated to appeal across local districts (although even the PR seats are not chosen nationwide, but in the eleven regional districts). At the same time, the PR segment of the new system is sure to enhance the continued viability of small niche parties—as has been true of the Free Democrats in Germany, and as was perhaps reflected in the relative success of the Japanese Communist Party in the 1996 election. And such parties by definition appeal to narrow and selective constituencies.

Consequently, no new Japanese government will easily paper over the fundamental tensions and the increasingly divergent interests of Japan's various socioeconomic groups. It will be exceptionally difficult for any single political party to generate policies and institutions that will bridge the wide gaps that now separate those groups in Japan that are prepared for and will benefit from an increasingly internationalized and less-regulated domestic economy from those that are desirous of continuing past protections and regulations from which they benefit. As the currency moves slightly up or down and as the international economy continues to penetrate Japan, those tensions become ever more clear-cut.

Nor is it likely that some particular economic policy, such as that which prevailed under embedded mercantilism, could provide the kind of broad and sweepingly general benefits that would mobilize most segments of the economy behind it. Similarly, any changes from Japan's security policies are likely to be highly controversial—but so is a continuation of past policies. Instead, real divisions requiring real political choices are increasingly being revealed.

For the moment, political parties only vaguely hint at offering such choices. Members of the current LDP are substantially more rural, protectionist, and nationalist than those of the Democratic Party. Several of the smaller parties are preponderantly younger and more urban. But party platforms among all strands of conservatism are broadly consensual and totally devoid of specifics. None articulates a set of proposals that is clearly "internationalist and open" or conversely "protectionist and closed." Instead, all favor "deregulation," "internationalization," and "compensation for those negatively affected." Most also call for "more time" to "reach consensus."

In this sense, the system is ripe for the emergence of political entrepreneurs able to mobilize voters around their increasingly divergent interests. Yet there is also no guarantee that the tensions that now divide Japan will readily be translated into competing political platforms offered by different political parties. Creative political entrepreneurs are surely a possibility, but they are by no means guaranteed. Equally plausible, at least until the pain of inaction becomes unbearable, is a continuation of a politics of vagueness and personalism that avoids the articulation of separate and clear economic or security choices by the major parties. And, offered few appealing choices, voters certainly have the option of staying home as they did in the 1996 election. But in such a situation, it is also unlikely that any elected government will have the capability of taking the kinds of bold measures needed to regenerate the national economy. Nor are new and substantially different security and foreign policies likely to be forthcoming.

In short, Japan is facing a choice between a regime that continues to blur the important underlying economic and security tensions reflective of real divisions of interest among Japanese citizens, and one that offers such choices but runs the risk of creating a country with far sharper demarcations between winners and losers. What seems unmistakable is that the once-invulnerable conservative regime can no longer operate with the fluidity or internal cohesion it once enjoyed. Rather, Japan is in the midst of an unmistakable regime shift.

What will actually come to replace the ancien régime is, as of the late 1990s, unclear. The process of socioeconomic recombination is still under way; so is the process of party system realignment and electoral recalibration. Certain new institutions have been created, and more might well appear, but the implications of such changes are still murky. And no public policy profile with anything like the clarity of "embedded mercantilism" and high economic growth has yet come into view.

Japan, in many ways, is like the Communist regimes in the former Soviet Union and Eastern Europe. It is clear that the old regime has been displaced. Transition is under way, but precisely how that transition will play out is less clear-cut.

The LDP may retain some measure of electoral success; but it will be a very different LDP from its 1955 namesake in terms both of support and policy direction. Major portions of the Japanese economy may continue to be exceptionally competitive within world markets; indeed corporate profits and market shares of many major Japanese manufacturers were up substantially as the worst of the post-bubble economic debris came to be cleared up. Yet, the former links between finance and manufacturing, small and large firms, and exporters and importers have been broken. So have many of the old keiretsu ties. Japan's economy is unlikely ever again to be labeled "Japan, Inc." The Japanese bureaucracy will almost certainly retain powers that in comparative terms are quite substantial, but it is unlikely that either agencies or civil servants will command the same levels of control over business or society as a whole, let alone the same levels of social support, as they did in the 1960s. Japan will almost certainly continue to maintain close strategic, military, and economic ties with the United States, but it is unlikely to enjoy the same levels of unmitigated support from the United States that it received during the height of the Cold War; nor is it likely that Japanese elites will themselves be anxious for such a return. What is clear, however, is that like Humpty Dumpty, the old regimes, in Japan or in the former Communist countries, cannot be put back together again.

NOTES

1. On Japanese conservative dominance in comparative perspective, see T. J. Pempel, ed., *Uncommon Democracies: The One-Party Dominant Regimes* (Ithaca, N.Y.: Cornell University Press, 1990). In Japanese, see "Ittō yūisei no hōkai," *Leviathan*, special issue, 1994.

2. On the collapse, see Noguchi Yukio, *Baburu no keizaigaku* (Tokyo: Nihon Keizai Shinbunsha, 1992), 25.

3. E.g., Terashima Jitsuro, "Nichi bei chū toraianguru kuraishisu o dō seigyo suru ka?" *Chūōkōronsha*, August 1996.

4. My analysis of the concept of *regime* is found in "Restructuring Social Coalitions: State, Society, and Regime," in Rolf Torstendahl, ed., *State Theory and State History* (London: Sage, 1992), 118–48; and is elaborated in my book *Regime Shift* (Ithaca, N.Y.: Cornell University Press, 1998).

5. George Friedman and Meredith Lebard, *The Coming War with Japan* (New York: St. Martin's, 1991).

6. E. E. Schattschneider, *The Semisovereign People* (New York: Holt, Reinhart, and Winston, 1960).

7. Alexander Gerschenkron, *Economic Backwardness in Historical Perspective* (Cambridge: Harvard University Press, 1962).

8. T. J. Pempel, "The Tar Baby Target: 'Reform' of the Japanese Bureaucracy," in Robert E. Ward and Sakamoto Yoshikazu, eds., *Democratizing Japan: The Allied Occupation* (Honolulu: University of Hawaii Press, 1987), 157–87.

9. The literature on the LDP and this point is extensive. See, inter alia, Masumi Junnosuke, *Nihon seijishi yon* (Tokyo: Tokyo Daigaku Shuppankai, 1988). More recently and journalistically, see Kitaoka Shinichi, *Jimintō: Seikentō no sanjūhachinen* (Tokyo: Yomiuri Shinbunsha, 1995).

10. See, e.g., Gerald L. Curtis, *Election Campaigning, Japanese-Style* (New York: Columbia University Press, 1971); Kobayashi Yoshiaki, *Gendai Nihon no senkyō* (Tokyo: Tokyo Daigaku Shuppankai, 1991).

11. Such a candidate, if he were not running with the official endorsement of the party, would compete as an "independent," joining the LDP after an electoral success at the expense of an endorsed candidate.

12. T. J. Pempel and Keiichi Tsunekawa, "Corporatism without Labor? The Japanese Anomaly," in Philippe C. Schmitter and Gerhard Lehmbruch, ed., *Trends toward Corporatist Intermediation* (Beverly Hills, Calif.: Sage, 1979), 231–70.

13. Here I find myself in general agreement on specifics with, but widely different on interpretation from, Ikuo Kume, *Disparaged Success: Labor Politics in Postwar Japan* (Ithaca, N.Y.: Cornell University Press, 1997).

14. This basic foreign policy orientation has been treated by Kenneth Pyle and others as the "Yoshida Line," named after Prime Minister Yoshida Shigeru. See Pyle's *The Japanese Question* (Washington: American Enterprise Institute, 1992), esp. chap. 3.

15. T. J. Pempel, "Japanese Foreign Economic Policy: The Domestic Bases for International Behavior," in Peter J. Katzenstein, ed., *Between Power and Plenty: Foreign Economic Policies of Advanced Industrial States* (Madison: University of Wisconsin Press, 1978), 157. See also Mabuchi Masaru, *Ōkurasho tōsei no seijikeizaigaku* (Tokyo: Chūōkōronsha, 1994), esp. 323–27.

16. See Kokuseisha, ed., *Nihon Kokusei zue* (Tokyo: Kokuseisha, annual) for specific figures. While most of the major industrial countries had imports made up of approximately 50–65 percent manufactured goods, Japan in the mid-1970s had only 30 percent. No other country came close to Japan's 95 percent manufacturing exports.

17. As late as 1986 only 1 percent of Japan's assets was owned by foreign-controlled firms, and just 0.4 percent of its workers were employed by them, a dramatic contrast to the other industrialized democracies. See DeAnne Julius, *Global Companies and Public Policy* (New York: Royal Institute of International Affairs/Council on

Foreign Relations Press, 1990), as noted in *The Economist,* June 23, 1990; see p. 67 of *The Economist* for the comparative figures.

18. Richard J. Samuels, "Consuming for Production: National Security, the Domestic Economy, and Nuclear Fuel Procurement in Japan," *International Organization* 43, no. 4 (Autumn 1989): 625–46.

19. This provided a somewhat skewed balance in the two-level games all countries must play between domestic and international politics. Robert D. Putnam, "Diplomacy and Domestic Politics: The Logic of Two-Level Games," *International Organization* 42, no. 3 (Summer 1988): 427–60.

20. Edward J. Lincoln, *Japan: Facing Economic Maturity* (Washington: Brookings Institution, 1988), 252–65.

21. See also C. Fred Bergsten and Marcus Noland, *Reconcilable Differences? United States–Japan Economic Conflict* (Washington: Institute for International Economics, 1993), 15, 233.

22. I. M. Destler, Hideo Sata, and Haruhiro Fukui, *The Textile Wrangle* (Washington: Brookings Institution, 1979).

23. European countries followed the U.S. lead on voluntary export agreements, with France being particularly successful in gaining Japanese consent to restrict exports in color televisions, TV tubes, cars, light commercial vehicles, forklift trucks, motorcycles, quartz watches, and audio devices. David Yoffie, "Protecting World Markets," in Thomas K. McCraw, ed., *America versus Japan* (Boston: Harvard Business School Press, 1986), 66.

24. Four industries were chosen for market-opening measures: forest products, medical equipment and pharmaceuticals, electronic products, and telecommunications equipment and services. On the negotiations and their outcome, see Edward J. Lincoln, *Japan's Unequal Trade* (Washington: Brookings Institution, 1990), 148–51.

25. The phrase is from Laura D'Andrea Tyson, *Who's Bashing Whom? Trade Conflict in High-Technology Industries* (Washington: Institute for International Economics, 1992), 133–36, in reference to the perceived successes of the U.S.–Japan agreement on semiconductors which provided a de facto 20-percent market share to U.S. companies.

26. Kusano Atsushi, *Nichi-Bei: Massatsu no kōzō* (Tokyo: PHP Kenkyūjō, 1984).

27. Watanabe Akio, *Sengo Nihon no taigai seisaku* (Tokyo: Yuhikaku, 1985), 258.

28. Murakami Yasusuke, *Shinchūkan taishū no jidai* (Tokyo: Chūōkōronsha, 1984).

29. Kozo Yamamura, "The Cost of Rapid Growth and Capitalist Democracy in Japan," in Leon Lindberg and Charles Meier, eds., *The Politics of Inflation and Economic Stagnation* (Washington: Brookings Institution, 1985), 497–98.

30. Ikuo Kume, "Changing Relations among the Government, Labor, and Business in Japan after the Oil Crisis," *International Organization* 42, no. 4 (Autumn 1988): 659–87; Shinkawa Toshimitsu, "Senkyūhyaku nanajūgonen shuntōto keisai kiki kanri," in Ōtake Hideo, ed., *Nihon seij no shoten* (Tokyo: Sanichi Shobo, 1984); Tsuinaka Yutaka, "Rōdōkai no saihen to hachijūrokunen taisei no imi," *Leviathan* 1 (1987): 47–72. On the public-sector unions, see also Ōtake Hideo, "Jiyūshugiteki kaikaku no naka no kooporachiizumu" *Leviathan,* special issue, 1992, 122–40.

31. Satō Seizaburo and Matsuzaki Tetsuhisa, *Jimintō-seiken* (Tokyo: Chūōkōronsha, 1986); Miyake Ichiro, ed., *Seitō shiji no bunseki* (Tokyo: Sokobunsha, 1985).

32. Kobayashi, *Gendai Nihon no senkyō,* chap. 5.

33. This point would by no means be universally accepted among students of Japan. Journalists have long predicted the demise of the LDP in particular elections;

the party's secretary general is constantly expressing fears about whatever electoral campaign is in the offing; there was a steady decline in the proportion of the total vote won by the LDP over most of the 1960s and 1970s; and the loss of the Upper House in 1989 would also suggest that the LDP has hardly enjoyed electoral invulnerability.

34. Miyake Ichiro, *Nihon no seij to senkyō* (Tokyo: Tokyo Daigaku Shuppankai, 1995); Miyake, *Tōhyō kōdō* (Tokyo: Tokyo Daigaku Shuppankai, 1989); Kobayashi, *Gendai Nihon no senkyō*; Gerald Curtis, *The Japanese Way of Politics* (New York: Columbia University Press, 1988), chaps. 1 and 6.

35. Muramatsu Michio, Itō Toshimitsu, and Tsujinaka Yūtaka, *Nihon no seiji* (Tokyo: Yūhikaku, 1992), 126; Kobayashi, *Gendai Nihon no senkyō*, 52–59.

36. Ikuo Kume, "Party Politics and Industrial Policy: A Case of Japan." (Paper presented to an International Conference on Government-Industry Relations, May 20–22, 1992, in Exeter, England).

37. Jeffrey A. Frieden, "Domestic Politics and Regional Cooperation: The United States, Japan, and Pacific Money and Finance," in Jeffrey A. Frankel and Miles Kahler, eds., *Regionalism and Rivalry: Japan and the United States in Pacific Asia* (Chicago: University of Chicago Press, 1993), 434.

38. Japan was the world's largest creditor nation in 1996 with 16.7 percent of its gross domestic product, or $742 billion, in net foreign assets. *The Economist*, November 9, 1996, 123.

39. John Y. Campbell and Yasushi Hamao, "Changing Patterns of Corporate Financing and the Main Bank System in Japan," in Masahiko Aoki and Hugh T. Patrick, eds., *The Japanese Main Bank System: Its Relevance for Developing and Transforming Economies* (Oxford: Clarendon Press, 1994), 331–33.

40. *The Economist*, November 23, 1996, 11.

41. *Far Eastern Economic Review*, July 4, 1996, 45.

42. On the general subject, see Michael E. Porter, "Towards a Dynamic Theory of Strategy," *Strategic Management Journal* 12 (1991): 95–117. On such alliances by Japanese electronic companies, see Fred Burton and Freddy Saelens, "International Alliances as a Strategic Tool of Japanese Electronic Companies," in Nigel Campbell and Fred Burton, eds., *Japanese Multinationals: Strategies and Management in the Global Kaisha* (London: Routledge, 1994), 58–70.

43. As cited in Yoshiya Teramoto et al., "Global Strategy in the Japanese Semiconductor Industry," in Campbell and Burton, *Japanese Multinationals*, 82.

44. Noguchi, *Baburu no keizaigaku*; David Asher, "Economic Myths Explained: What Became of the Japanese Miracle?" *Orbis* (Spring 1996): 1–21.

45. *Kuni no Yosan* (Tokyo: Ōkurasho, various years).

46. Asher, "Economic Myths Explained," 2.

47. Ōtake Hideo, *Jiyūshugiteki kaikaku no jidai* (Tokyo: Chūōkōronsha, 1994), 78–161. At the same time, as Steven Vogel argues, in many instances the processes involved "more rules"; *Freer Markets, More Rules* (Ithaca, N.Y.: Cornell University Press, 1996).

48. My calculations from data in Keizai Koho Center, *Japan, 1996* (Tokyo: Keizai Koho Center, 1996).

49. Asher, "Economic Myths Explained," 10.

50. Asher, "Economic Myths Explained," 11.

51. More accurately, the LDP won only 49.3 percent of the seats in the 1979 Lower House election but nevertheless put together a governing majority that included conservative independents. And from December 1983 until July 1986, the LDP ruled in coalition with a tiny conservative fragment, the New Liberal Club.

52. Chalmers Johnson, *Japan, Who Governs? The Rise of the Development State* (New York: Norton, 1995), 224.

53. On the process of the LDP split, see Ōtake Hideo, "Jimintō wakate kaikakuha to Ozawa guruupu: 'Seiji kaikaku' o mezashita futasu no seiji seryoku," *Leviathan* 17 (1995): 7–29.

Index

About the Contributors

SEYLA BENHABIB is professor of government at Harvard University. Her most recent books are *Situating the Self: Gender, Community, and Postmodernism in Contemporary Ethics* (1992) and *The Reluctant Modernism of Hannah Arendt* (1996).

ALAN BRINKLEY is Allan Nevins professor of history at Columbia University. His books include *The End of Reform: New Deal Liberalism in Recession and War* (1995) and *Liberalism and Its Discontents* (1998).

JAMES W. CEASER is professor of government at the University of Virginia. He is the author of *Liberal Democracy and Political Science* (1990) and *Reconstructing America: The Symbol of America in Modern Thought* (1997).

JOHN DUNN is professor of political theory at the University of Cambridge and a fellow in King's College. His books include *The History of Political Theory and Other Essays* (1995) and *The Cunning of Unreason: Making Sense of Politics* (2000).

RICHARD A. EPSTEIN is James Parker Hall distinguished service professor at the University of Chicago Law School. His most recent books are *Mortal Peril: Our Inalienable Right to Health Care?* (1997) and *Principles for a Free Society: Reconciling Individual Liberty with the Common Good* (1998).

CHARLES H. FAIRBANKS, JR., is research professor at Johns Hopkins University's School of Advanced International Studies, where he directs the Central Asian Institute and the Foreign Policy Institute. He has written widely on Russia and the other states of the former Soviet Union.

TODD GITLIN is professor of culture, journalism, and sociology at New York University. His most recent books are *The Twilight of Common Dreams: Why America Is Wracked by Culture Wars* (1995) and *Sacrifice: A Novel* (1999).

ATUL KOHLI is professor of politics and international affairs in the Woodrow Wilson School at Princeton University. He is the author of *The State and Poverty in India: The Politics of Reform* (1987) and *Democracy and Discontent: India's Growing Crisis of Governability* (1991).

HARVEY C. MANSFIELD is William R. Kenan professor of government at Harvard University. His most recent books are *Machiavelli's Virtue* (1996) and a new translation of Tocqueville's *Democracy in America* (with Delba Winthrop) (2000).

PRATAP B. MEHTA is associate professor of government and social studies at Harvard University. He has published articles on Indian history and politics and on moral and political philosophy.

ARTHUR M. MELZER is professor of political science at Michigan State University. He is the author of *The Natural Goodness of Man: On the System of Rousseau's Thought* (1990). He is a director of the Symposium on Science, Reason, and Modern Democracy and an editor of its first four volumes of essays, the most recent of which is *Democracy and the Arts* (1999).

ANDREW J. NATHAN is professor of political science at Columbia University. His most recent books are *China's Transition* (1997) and *The Great Wall and the Empty Fortress: China's Search for Security*, with Robert S. Ross (1998).

CLAUS OFFE is professor of political sociology and social policy at Humboldt–University zu Berlin and Theodor Heuss professor of political science and sociology at the New School University, New York. His books include *Modernity and the State* (1996) and *Varieties of Transition: The Eastern European and East German Experience* (1997).

T. J. PEMPEL is Boeing professor of international studies in the Jackson School of International Studies at the University of Washington. His most recent book is *Regime Shift: Comparative Dynamics of the Japanese Political Economy* (1998).

PAUL PIERSON is professor of government at Harvard University. He is the author of *Dismantling the Welfare State? Reagan, Thatcher, and the Politics of Retrenchment* (1994).

TIANJIAN SHI is assistant professor of political science at Duke University. He is the author of *Political Participation in Beijing* (1997).

VLADIMIR TISMANEANU is professor of government and politics at the University of Maryland, College Park. His most recent books are *Reinventing Politics: Eastern Europe from Stalin to Havel* (1992) and *Fantasies of Salvation: Democracy, Nationalism, and Myth in Post-Communist Europe* (1998).

JERRY WEINBERGER is professor of political science at Michigan State University. His books include *Science, Faith, and Politics: Francis Bacon and the Utopian Roots of the Modern Age* (1985) and *Francis Bacon's History of the Reign of King Henry the Seventh: A New Edition and Interpretation* (1996). He is a director of the Symposium on Science, Reason, and Modern Democracy and an editor of its first four volumes of essays.

DELBA WINTHROP is lecturer in extension and administrator of the program on constitutional government at Harvard University. She has published articles on Aristotle, Solzhenitsyn, and Tocqueville, and translated (with Harvey C. Mansfield) Tocqueville's *Democracy in America* (2000).

ALAN WOLFE is professor of political science and director of the Center for Religion and American Public Life at Boston College. His most recent books are *Marginalized in the Middle* (1996) and *One Nation after All* (1998).

M. RICHARD ZINMAN is professor of political theory in James Madison College at Michigan State University. He is executive director of the Symposium on Science, Reason, and Modern Democracy and an editor of its first four volumes of essays.

MICHAEL ZUCKERT is Nancy Reeves Drew professor of government at the University of Notre Dame. He is the author of *Natural Rights and the New Republicanism* (1994) and *The Natural Rights Republic* (1996).